The Abe Legacy

The Abe Legacy

How Japan Has Been Shaped by Abe Shinzō

Edited by
James D. J. Brown; Guibourg Delamotte and
Robert Dujarric

LEXINGTON BOOKS
Lanham • Boulder • New York • London

3 Quotes from Mindy Kotler The author quotes Mindy Kotler with her permission.
Published by Lexington Books
An imprint of The Rowman & Littlefield Publishing Group, Inc.
4501 Forbes Boulevard, Suite 200, Lanham, Maryland 20706
www.rowman.com

6 Tinworth Street, London SE11 5AL, United Kingdom

Copyright © 2021 The Rowman & Littlefield Publishing Group, Inc.

All rights reserved. No part of this book may be reproduced in any form or by any electronic or mechanical means, including information storage and retrieval systems, without written permission from the publisher, except by a reviewer who may quote passages in a review.

British Library Cataloguing in Publication Information Available

Library of Congress Cataloging-in-Publication Data

Names: Brown, James D. J., editor. | Delamotte, Guibourg, editor. | Dujarric, Robert, 1961- editor.
Title: The Abe legacy : how Japan has been shaped by Abe Shinzō/ edited by James D. J. Brown, Guibourg Delamotte and Robert Dujarric.
Description: Lanham, Maryland : Lexington Books, 2021. | Includes bibliographical references and index. | Summary: "This study of Japanese prime minister Abe Shinzō (2012-2020) answers three questions: How could Abe Shinzō remain in power for nearly a decade? What was the policy mix devised to keep voters happy yet try to promote structural reforms and growth? What is his legacy as chief executive now that he has gone?"—Provided by publisher.
Identifiers: LCCN 2021034361 (print) | LCCN 2021034362 (ebook) | ISBN 9781793643308 (cloth) | ISBN 9781793643322 (paperback) | ISBN 9781793643315 (ebook)
Subjects: LCSH: Abe, Shinzō, 1954- | Japan—Politics and government—21st century.
Classification: LCC DS891.5.A23 A74 2021 (print) | LCC DS891.5.A23 (ebook) | DDC 951.06—dc23
LC record available at https://lccn.loc.gov/2021034361
LC ebook record available at https://lccn.loc.gov/2021034362

Contents

Acknowledgments — vii

Introduction: Eight Years in Power: Assessing Prime Minister Abe's Legacy — ix
James D. J. Brown, Guibourg Delamotte, and Robert Dujarric

1. Transformation of Domestic Politics: Abe's Durable Legacy? — 1
   Nonaka Naoto

2. Abe Shinzō's Economic Legacy — 19
   R. Taggart Murphy

3. Pandemic Downsizes PM Abe Shinzō — 41
   Jeff Kingston

4. Gender Policies and Conservative Values — 63
   Murakami Hiromi

5. Prime Minister Abe's Security Policy: A Broader Spectrum — 87
   Guibourg Delamotte

6. Japanese Military Diplomacy: Abe's Security Legacy? — 107
   Alessio Patalano

7. Japan–U.S. Relations — 127
   Tosh Minohara

8. Japan's Diplomacy toward China under the Abe Shinzō Administration — 149
   Soeya Yoshihide

9   Recriminations and Deepened Distrust: Assessing PM Abe's
    Legacy of Mismanaging Japan–ROK Relations   169
    David H. Satterwhite, PhD and Laney Bahan

10 Abe Shinzō and the Securitization of Japan–North Korea
    Relations   191
    Benoît Hardy-Chartrand

11 Testing a Theory to Destruction: Abe's Legacy and Relations
    with Russia   209
    James D. J. Brown

12 Japan's Foreign Policy toward the Middle East and
    Africa under Abe   229
    Kakizaki Masaki

13 Japan's Global Image   251
    Nancy Snow

14 Japan and the World under Abe Shinzō's Premiership:
    Trying to Become a Rules Maker   271
    Robert Dujarric

Index   289

About the Contributors   299

Acknowledgments

As editors of this book, we would first like to thank our fellow authors who kindly agreed to contribute to this volume, making it possible for us to provide readers with excellent diverse perspectives on Abe Shizo's years as premier. We would also like to thank our editors Alison Keefner, Carter Moran, and Joseph Parry at Rowman and Littlefield for their splendid work and dedication to this project. We also owe a special debt to Laney Bahan for her first-rate editing skills.

We would also like to acknowledge the support we have received from our respective institutions (Institut National des Langues et Civilisations Orientales for Guibourg Delamotte and Temple University, Japan Campus, for James Brown and Robert Dujarric), which allowed us to devote time and energy to this project and especially to George Miller and Mariko Nagai who authorized funding the editing and indexing work.

James Brown

Guibourg Delamotte

Robert Dujarric

Introduction

Eight Years in Power: Assessing Prime Minister Abe's Legacy

James D. J. Brown, Guibourg Delamotte, and Robert Dujarric

"I will be a fire, burning with all the political strength I can muster . . . If I am unable to make Japan a great country and a robust country this time around and pass it on to the next generation, then there is no meaning to the life I have lived thus far."[1] This is the bold message that Prime Minister Abe Shinzō delivered shortly after returning to the prime minister's office following the Liberal Democratic Party's (LDP's) victory in the Japanese general election of December 2012. His enthusiasm was understandable, for his had been a remarkable comeback.

When Abe first became prime minister in September 2006, his future looked extremely bright. At 52, he was Japan's youngest post-war prime minister. Coming from a famous political dynasty, he surely had hopes of emulating the historic premierships of his grandfather, Kishi Nobusuke (1957–1960), and great uncle, Satō Eisaku (1964–1972).

Yet, just one year later, weakened by corruption scandals in his cabinet, as well as his own delicate health, Abe was forced to resign. Less than three years later, the LDP itself was dumped from power, a development that was almost unprecedented in Japan's post-war history.

After Abe limped from the stage in September 2007, most political commentators wrote him off as just another of Japan's short-lived and largely forgettable leaders. Abe himself must certainly have feared that he had blown his opportunity. His return in 2012 must therefore have felt like a second life, and it soon became clear that he was determined to make the most of his political resurrection. Indeed, in one of his first major speeches after returning to the prime minister's office, Abe boldly declared: "I am back, and so shall Japan be."[2]

It was always going to be difficult for Abe to live up to such hyperbole, yet even his staunchest critics must admit that his second stint in power was more successful than the first. Most notably, after a period of six prime ministers in as many years, Abe managed to remain in office for seven years and eight months. Indeed, by the time he announced his resignation on August 28, 2020, Abe had become the longest-serving prime minister in Japanese history. Moreover, from his party's perspective, Abe had acquired a magic touch, leading the LDP to victories in the elections for the House of Representatives in 2012, 2014, and 2017, and for the House of Councilors in 2013, 2016, and 2019. On this basis alone, Abe's leadership since he returned to power in 2012 merits close analysis.

In taking on the task of assessing Abe's premiership, this edited volume is oriented around three simple questions. The first is: How was Abe Shinzō able to remain in power for the best part of a decade when so many of his predecessors were forced from office after only a short period? Was Abe simply lucky during his second stint in office or was his longevity due to some combination of structural factors and personal skills? This is undoubtedly an important question, not least because the answer will provide guidance as to whether Abe's long tenure is likely to be repeated or whether the revolving door of prime ministerial appointments will soon resume spinning.

However, while stability in leadership is desirable, there is little value in power without purpose. Indeed, as Abe said himself in his resignation speech, "In politics, the most important thing is to deliver results."[3] The second question addressed in this book is therefore: What changes did Abe make and were they for the benefit of Japan? This entails an assessment of his policy successes and failures within domestic politics and economics, on the international stage—to which he devoted particular attention—and in the realm of crisis management.

Lastly, all national leaders, and especially long-lasting ones, wish to leave a political legacy. Within Abe's own family, Prime Minister Kishi secured the revision of the U.S.–Japan Security Treaty in 1960, while Prime Minister Satō achieved agreement with Washington in 1971 on the reversion of Okinawa to Japan's sovereign control. What, by contrast, will Abe be remembered for? The third question is therefore: What is Abe's political legacy now that he has left office?

Following this short introduction, there are fourteen further chapters that seek to provide an answer to the three questions above. In chapter 1, Nonaka Naoto focuses on domestic politics, offering a critique of the techniques used by Abe to blunt parliamentary opposition and thereby maximize his time in office. Chapter 2 by Taggart Murphy then addresses Abe's economic legacy, including a discussion of the successes and failings of the economic policy to which the prime minister lent his name.

The subject of chapter 3 is the coronavirus pandemic that dominated the last eight months of Abe's premiership. Jeff Kingston assesses how well Abe can be judged to have dealt with this historic crisis.

Gender was also an important topic throughout Abe's leadership, with the prime minister promising to create a "society where women shine." In chapter 4, Murakami Hiromi evaluates what progress was made in this direction.

Next follow two chapters on security. In the first—chapter 5—Guibourg Delamotte provides a broad overview of the substantial changes that the government introduced in the area of security, not least the reinterpretation of the constitution to permit exercise of the right to collective self-defense. Chapter 6 by Alessio Patalano focuses more narrowly on Abe's use of Japan's self-defense forces as a tool of diplomacy.

After tackling the issue of security, the next six chapters concentrate on foreign policy. This was a field in which Abe—in contrast to many of his domestically focused predecessors—was especially active. In chapter 7, Tosh Minohara discusses Japan–U.S. relations, including Abe's management of personal relations with the very different characters of President Barack Obama and President Donald Trump. In chapter 8, Soeya Yoshihide focuses on bilateral relations with China and Abe's struggle to develop a normal relationship with an increasingly assertive Beijing. Relations with the Republic of Korea were no easier, and, in chapter 9, Laney Bahan and David Satterwhite argue that ideological factors in Abe's outlook were a key factor in aggravating relations with Seoul. Chapter 10 by Benoit Hardy-Chartrand then turns to the subject of North Korea and Abe's approach to solving the abductees, missile, and nuclear issues. Meanwhile, in chapter 11, James Brown examines Abe's unusually active efforts to resolve the long-standing territorial dispute between Japan and Russia. Lastly when it comes to diplomacy, in chapter 12 Kakizaki Masaki explains the nature of Japan's foreign policy under Abe toward the Middle East and Africa.

In the final section of the book, there are two chapters that seek to take a broader perspective on Abe's international importance. In the first of these—chapter 13—Nancy Snow touches on the subject of soft power and examines Abe's impact on Japan's global image. Finally, in chapter 14, Robert Dujarric draws conclusions about the extent to which Abe was successful in making Japan a rules maker in international politics, including through his promotion of a vision of a "Free and Open Indo-Pacific."

Readers will find a diversity of views expressed in these chapters. Some see Abe as a leader who successfully restored Japan to a position of prominence in international politics and delivered much-needed stability at the head of Japan's body politic. Others regard him as a prime minister who was weighed down by nationalist ideology and squandered years in which much needed economic and social reforms could have been introduced.

As noted above, following his return to the premiership, Abe defined success as passing on to the next generation a Japan that is both great and robust. As editors, we leave it to readers to assess whether Prime Minister Abe Shinzō was successful in this endeavor.

NOTES

1. Prime Minister of Japan and his Cabinet, "Economic Policy Speech by H.E. Mr. Shinzo Abe, Prime Minister of Japan, June 19, 2013," https://japan.kantei.go.jp/96_abe/statement/201306/19guildhall_e.html.
2. Ministry of Foreign Affairs of Japan, "Japan is Back By Shinzo Abe, Prime Minister of Japan, 22 February 2013 at CSIS," https://www.mofa.go.jp/announce/pm/abe/us_20130222en.html.
3. Prime Minister of Japan and his Cabinet, "Press Conference by the Prime Minister, August 28 2020," https://japan.kantei.go.jp/98_abe/statement/202008/_00004.html.

REFERENCES

Ministry of Foreign Affairs of Japan. "Japan is Back by Shinzo Abe, Prime Minister of Japan, 22 February 2013 at CSIS." https://www.mofa.go.jp/announce/pm/abe/us_20130222en.html.
Prime Minister of Japan and his Cabinet. "Economic Policy Speech by H.E. Mr. Shinzo Abe, Prime Minister of Japan, June 19, 2013." https://japan.kantei.go.jp/96_abe/statement/201306/19guildhall_e.html.
Prime Minister of Japan and his Cabinet. "Press Conference by the Prime Minister, August 28 2020." https://japan.kantei.go.jp/98_abe/statement/202008/_00004.html.

Chapter 1

Transformation of Domestic Politics
Abe's Durable Legacy?
Nonaka Naoto

INTRODUCTION

The cabinet organized by Prime Minister Abe Shinzō was the longest-running in the history of the constitutional government of Japan. This was in stark contrast with the six previous cabinets, each of which was forced to step down after a year or so. What has the Abe cabinet, or rather Prime Minister Abe, done to deserve such an enduring administration? Has this longevity fundamentally changed Japanese politics? This chapter will explain what the Abe administration has done, under what conditions and circumstances, and what it has changed in Japanese politics.

PRIME MINISTER ABE'S ACHIEVEMENTS

Long-Term Government and the Concentration of Power in the "Kantei" (Prime Minister's Office)

Prime Minister Abe's first achievement was his maintenance of a long-term government. Abe, after Yoshida Shigeru, is the only prime minister in postwar Japan to have set up two cabinets. In addition, since the formation of the second government in December 2012, the cabinet's approval ratings remained relatively stable in the polls. To be sure, when the Act on the Protection of Specially Designated Secrets was passed in December 2014, as well as in September 2015 when the so-called Peace and Security Law was forcefully passed and during Abe's many scandals, his approval rating did fall briefly. Over time, however, cabinet support always recovered, and support for the Abe administration remained robust.[1]

The first reason why a long-term government was possible is likely due to the fact that the previous DPJ government (from September 2009 to December 2012) had fallen far short of expectations. Second, Liberal Democratic Party (LDP) lawmakers also held a strong sense of failure after a devastating defeat in the 2009 general election, which made it significantly easier for Abe to steer his party.[2] Third, the strong nationalistic moves of South Korea and China in particular provided a tailwind for Abe's own right-wing, nationalist ideology. In other words, the political currents and international conditions worked in Abe's favor.

Furthermore, the reforms of political institutions undertaken in the 1990s—most notably the introduction of a single member district (SMD)-based electoral system instead of the previous medium-sized constituency electoral system—as well as changes in the rules for regulating political funding had a major impact. A second series of reforms were aimed at the executive branch and focused on strengthening concentration of power and resources on the prime minister and the chief cabinet secretary.[3] As a result, the small core group in the prime minister's office surrounding the prime minister and his chief cabinet secretary, including the deputy cabinet secretaries for political and administrative affairs, secretaries, and special advisors, has come to constitute a centralized control body. We can call this the *Kantei*. Although *Kantei* literally means the prime minister's office, its contextual political meaning is rather the small core group organized around the prime minister and his chief cabinet secretary.[4] As the following arguments show, the *Kantei* has become the driving vehicle of the Abe government's political leadership.

As this chapter deals with Prime Minister Abe's domestic politics and political methods, I will not comment on the foreign policies themselves. Suffice it here to say that, one, apart from the promotion of some economic partnership agreements, such as the TPP Eleven, its substantive achievements are few. Two, little was achieved in terms of negotiations with Russia on the return of the Northern Territories, nor with North Korea on the return of abductees, or the nuclear and missile issues. Overall, Abe has achieved very few diplomatic successes to live up to his reputation as "the Abe of diplomacy."

ABE ADMINISTRATION'S DOMESTIC POLICY

Abenomics

The so-called "Abenomics" plan to end deflation that Prime Minister Abe announced on his return to power in December 2012 was perhaps one of Abe's most prominent policies, and it attracted considerable global attention. At the time of Abe's reappointment as prime minister, there was almost a national consensus that Japan's economy had been experiencing deflation, since the 1990s, and that it needed to break free from it and revitalize the economy. Abenomics, which proposes a "three-pronged strategy," was supposed to combine three pillars: bold monetary easing, flexible fiscal policy, and structural reform measures.

The prospect of a massive monetary easing policy had a huge impact on the stock market before the Abe administration even stepped foot in office, as the LDP was certain to return to power. When Bank of Japan Governor Kuroda was appointed and clearly steered in a direction that closely reflected Abe's thinking, a major shift to a weaker yen and higher stock prices took place. At least temporarily, the sense of deflation receded and the economy gained strength.

However, Abenomics was not highly praised in subsequent years. Bank of Japan Governor Kuroda announced that the Bank of Japan's massive monetary easing program would begin with a target period of about two years. However, the achievement of a targeted inflation rate, set at around 2 percent, was postponed many times and, in the end, did not materialize at all. At the same time, the damage to the financial system, including the pressure put on the profit structure of financial institutions, has become too great to ignore. Temporary economic expansionary measures may have been necessary to overcome deflation. However, the problem is that few of the structural economic reforms that were expected to be painful ended up being adopted. In other words, Abenomics was merely a big-budget, temporary stimulus package. Moreover, the government is now stuck in an unprecedented negative interest rate policy of ultra-easy monetary policy.

"Slogan politics" and Backward Social Principle

On the domestic policy front, the Abe administration launched many attractive slogans such as "regional revitalization," "100 million member-active society," and "a society where women shine." The government also set forth such policy goals as "zero waiting lists for children," "work style reform," "1.8 desired fertility rate," and "equal pay for equal work," among others.

Rather than implementing the slogans, the reality was that the government simply continued to come up with new ones. It was mostly a transitory dispersal of funds that did little to solve the fundamental problems. Although the Abe administration constantly emphasized the implementation of the "plan-do-check-act" cycle and numerical targets, very little was actually done.

It is also hard to remove the impression that Abe's government was backward-looking in terms of social policy. For example, the conservative response came to the fore on issues such as same-sex marriage and separate surnames for couples. It also failed to establish a policy explicitly condemning and regulating hate speech from right-wing activists. Immigrants were treated as a temporary labor supply to make up for the declining labor force within the country. Policy emphasized the importance of domestic social stability over the idea of an open society with increased international human exchanges. Of course, this conservative approach was not without reason, and ignoring the realities of Japanese society could have also caused disturbances.[5] Taken as a whole, though, Abe's social philosophy was clearly not progressive, instead taking on a nationalistic tone with strong conservative aspects.

PRIME MINISTER ABE'S POLITICAL METHODS

Fixed Personnel Assignments with Personal Connections

One standout feature of Abe's personnel practices is found in his management of cabinet and ministerial appointments, particularly in the *Kantei* and key ministerial posts. Conventions once powerful in the "1955 regime" (the organization of power from 1955 when the LDP first won, until 1993) were weakened if not completely abandoned, with factional influence, and seniority-based criteria having been reduced considerably. However, the more central positions inside the *Kantei* continued to be filled with personal confidants, foremost Suga Yoshihide, who served as chief cabinet secretary consistently from December 2012 (and became prime minister in September 2020). Two deputy chief cabinet secretaries, Katō Katsunobu and Seko Hiroshige, and aides and advisors, such as Imai Takaya and Izumi Hiroto, were also notable figures. The top-down initiatives from the *Kantei* were largely supported by these combined executive positions.

The Abe government gave weight to stability by keeping certain individuals in key cabinet positions, such as the finance and foreign ministers, as well as key positions in the governing LDP, such as secretary general of the party. Finance Minister Asō Tarō in particular was not replaced once from December 2012. Secretary general of the LDP Nikai Toshihiro also held his position consistently from August 2016. When compared to previous administrations, the stability seen in Abe's is remarkable.

The tendency to lock down key positions is also related to the use of new top-down ministerial committees, the most notable of which are the Council on Economic and Fiscal Policy, and Japan's version of the National Security Council (NSC). The latter, in particular, was established at the end of 2013 under the Abe administration and was indicative of the prime minister's proactive stance on national security matters. Under the 1955 regime, not only had the cabinet meetings been extremely tokenistic, but the structure of the committee of ministers (cabinet committee) in Japan did not play much of its intended role. By keeping key ministers in place, these new types of ministerial committees have come into use as tools for top-down policy-making under the Abe administration.

"Political" Appointments that Defy Convention

Another feature of Abe's personnel approach was the unprecedented "political appointments," such as the head of the Cabinet Legislation Bureau. Although cabinet law does give the cabinet (or the prime minister) the power to make such appointments, it didn't always exercise it in practice. The prime minister had a certain amount of influence, but decisions tended to be made after a careful internal process involving major stakeholders. This was customary practice. Under the 1955 system, the appointment of administrative vice-ministers and other executives in ministries and agencies tended to follow the same type of personnel management practice. With this in mind, the head of the Cabinet Legislation Bureau had traditionally been filled with the promotion of an acting director. However, Abe decided to appoint Komatsu Ichirō, a foreign ministry senior bureaucrat who had never worked at the Legislative Bureau, to enable him to change the interpretation of the constitution, particularly on the right of collective self-defense. Komatsu's appointment was the decision of Prime Minister Abe, who strongly desired to change the interpretation of the constitution and, in his steps toward doing so, completely disregarded convention. In other words, the Abe cabinet tried to make appointments in response to political necessity, "politicizing" the appointment process, without consideration for conventional practice or precedent.

Policy Council System Directly Controlled by the Prime Minister and Chief Cabinet Secretary

Policy-making under the 1955 regime saw bureaucracy playing a major role, where the ruling LDP's Policy Research Council[6] and the "tribal" politicians had significant influence over each policy area (politicians said to belong to a "tribe" devote their energies to influencing policy in an area—e.g. agriculture—relevant to a category of their constituents, in exchange for votes and funds). The core functionality of the system included the official council system controlled by bureaucrats and the ruling party's prior-consultation mechanism. In addition, the close cooperation between "tribal" politicians and bureaucrats, which formed a bottom-up policy process, was a strong constraint on the leadership of the prime minister.

In order to break down their power, the Abe administration greatly strengthened a new type of policy council, controlled directly by the prime minister

(PM), chief cabinet secretary (CCS), and the cabinet secretariat. Though Abe was not the first PM to create such policy councils, which he headed directly, his administration greatly expanded their use and came to epitomize the concentration and the personalization of power.[7] In action, either the PM or the CCS would establish a series of policy councils under their direct control and political will, top-down decision-making being strengthened in and through these councils. As a result, the LDP's tribal politicians were downgraded to mere *ex-post facto* follow-up bodies and the prior-consultation mechanism lost most of its substance.

The bureaucracy, who had used official councils as fronts to protect its organizational interests, also saw a decisive decline in its influence. In the post-1955 era, most senior bureaucratic appointments were controlled by the bureaucrats themselves, through regular rotation and bottom-up internal selection. Under the Abe administration's top-down approach, these traditional personnel practices have been almost completely dismantled in favor of the new policy council system. The members of these new councils have been freely selected according to the wishes of the PM or CCS. For the bureaucrats, having a role in a policy council has come to be seen as an important step to take in view of a promotion. It has been said that the *Kantei* replaced the organizational centripetal force of the bureaucracy and that there is now a phenomenon of *sontaku* (忖度, strong anticipatory reaction akin to self-censorship) toward the PM and CCS in individual bureaucrats' behavior.

PRIME MINISTER ABE'S RELATIONS WITH THE DIET

The "Liar" Answer

There have been numerous criticisms that Prime Minister Abe disrespected the Diet. During questioning in the Budget Committee, he responded to an opposition lawmaker's questions by calling him a "liar" (House of Representatives Budget Committee, Feb. 17, 2020). He also fielded unusual interventions, using phrases such as "meaningless questions" when facing opponents who were critical of him over a scandal (House of Representatives Budget Committee, Feb. 12, 2020). Such an attitude is quite unusual in Japan's parliament and drew considerable criticism.

Japan's parliamentary system was built on the assumption that there would be a near complete absence of alternation in power,[8] a fact little known to Westerners though the particularities of Japan's parliament are deeply connected to it. As a result, parliament has been dominated by the opposition party as the main player in checking the government, and it is the opposition lawmakers who take the lead in Q&A sessions. This Q&A session is usually considered as a kind of interpellation, allowing very limited discretion in answering on the part of the government. Most of the Diet deliberations are a repetition of this Q&A interpellation. This was due to the fact that opposition parties had a large influence in the Diet, even though the ruling LDP almost always held a majority of the seats. Paradoxically, the relationship between the ruling and opposition parties was institutionalized in a way that increased the opposition's influence in the Diet in relative terms when in a system of single-party dominance.[9] The whole picture can be understood as follows: supported by the bureaucracy, the government and the ruling LDP determine most of the government's policies and budgets, but they must obtain parliamentary approval before those policies can be finalized and implemented. Reflecting not only on the experience of the post-war period but also historical legacies of pre-war Japan, parliamentary mechanisms give a rather disproportionately strong influence, if not veto power, to the opposition parties. Prime Minister Abe's disregard for the Diet therefore bears important significance in the context of post-war Japanese politics, as his lack of respect impacts the opposition parties' subsequent response to LDP proposals. Although from the standpoint of comparative parliamentary theory it may not always be clear what this level of unconventional intervention implies, it was nonetheless a critical event in a Japanese context.[10]

Denial of Article 53 of the Constitution

In another light, Abe's disregard for the Diet can be viewed more structurally as follows.

Although Abe maintained a parliamentary majority since 2012, he never attempted to have the internal rules and institutional workings of the Diet altered, because the meaning of convention and institutionalization are particularly important in the Diet. Nevertheless, Prime Minister Abe did not cooperate with precedents and conventions. He (officially his cabinet) consistently declined to reply to the opposition's June 2017 request to convene a special session of the Diet under Article 53 of the constitution without providing a clear explanation. Article 53 of the constitution says that the cabinet may determine to convoke extraordinary sessions of the Diet. When a quarter or more of the total members of either house so demand, the cabinet must convene such a session. The Abe government eventually convened for this special session on September 28 but dissolved the house almost immediately. This was an outrageous act—virtually a violation of the constitution— as he had disregarded Article 53, which is the most important power granted to a minority (in this case, a quarter of the members of either House of the Diet) in the body that represents the people. Prime Minister Abe (his cabinet) acted with similar disrespect on three separate occasions.

Abuse of Surprise Dissolution under Article 7

Prime Minister Abe's disregard for the Diet was also exhibited in this dissolution of the House of Representatives. His approach to dissolving the house was, essentially, a "surprise dissolution." This dissolution of September 2017, which even the ruling LDP leadership (other than Abe himself) had not anticipated at all, was most typical. The primary target of the surprise was indeed the opposition, but it was not the only target. Due to it being a surprise, there was no time to write "manifestos" to inform the public on policy proposals. Not only the opposition parties but also the ruling party was completely unprepared for a general election. In addition, Abe attempted to silence policy debate by treating the North Korean problem as a national crisis.

By nature, general elections in Japan are extremely short-spanned. There are only twelve days from the time the election is announced to the time of the vote, and the total number of days counting from the date of dissolution is usually only a little over twenty days. (The December 2014 election took 23 days from dissolution to the polls and the October 2017 election, 25 days.) Combined with Japan's strict regulations on campaigning, it is clear that this very short election period, which makes it virtually impossible to conduct in-depth debates, is an added constraint on political parties. The goal for Prime Minister Abe was, in full knowledge of these conditions, to intentionally bring about elections on a very short notice, forcing them to take place without due preparation. In such a situation, the people are compelled to vote without explanations to guide their choices, which reveals Abe's lack of respect for the people's act of voting.

So, what is the reason for this abuse of the power of dissolution? It is fair to say that for a "weak" prime minister in the 1955 regime, the power of dissolution was almost the only tool that could be used to steer the liberal democrats in a factional coalition system. But for prime ministers in recent years, with great power and resources in their hands, there should no longer be a need for an Article 7-type dissolution of power. The negative aspects of extreme arbitrary dissolution were exemplified here by Prime Minister Abe.

ABE ADMINISTRATION FROM THE PERSPECTIVE OF CORE EXECUTIVE THEORY

In order to make the discussion so far easier to understand from a comparative perspective, I draw on the framework of core executive theory. I will examine the following points in order to clarify later the difference between the Abe administration and a typical administration under the 1955 regime.

The 1955 Regime from the Perspective of Core Executive Theory

According to core executive theory, the 1955 regime can be summarized as follows.

1. Restrictions on the prime minister's substantive powers and authority,
2. Relationship between the government and the ruling party: denial of top-down leadership, factional strife, and prior-consulting system to involve the ruling party in policy-making,
3. Basic nature of the relationship between politicians and bureaucrats: autonomy of the bureaucracy, with its associated constraints on the political leadership,
4. Top structure of the relationship between political leaders and senior bureaucrats (state of the cabinet meetings): extreme loss of substantive roles and paralysis through the institutionalization of a mutual veto system between ministries,
5. Relationship between the ruling and opposition parties in parliament: negotiated parliamentary management with strong opposition influence and significant constraints on the prime minister and government.

These characteristics may be rephrased as follows.

1. Indirect leadership—a weak and passive prime minister.

With the exception of the power to dissolve the House of Representatives, the prime minister could not exercise most of his powers alone, and important policy decisions always had to be made through cabinet meetings. For example, the prime minister could not make a policy speech in the Diet on his own, instead having first to obtain a decision from the cabinet. In addition, the authority to make appointments to senior official positions in each ministry rested with the minister in charge, and the prime minister could not go past that minister to make appointments. As has already been pointed out, the prime minister still does not have the right to request a cabinet meeting for an agenda item. In other words, he was a typically weak or passive prime minister.

2. Government-ruling party relations based on the ruling party's quasi veto power.

In terms of the relationship between the government or the prime minister and the ruling party, the latter's power was quite significant. Before a bill or budget could be submitted to parliament, it had to be approved through a prior-consultation process within the ruling party. This method is not seen in other countries with a parliamentary cabinet system. The reason for this is that the parliamentary system and its solidly entrenched internal conventions severely constrain the status and authority of the government, and the ruling party (not the government) is responsible for negotiating with the opposition in the Diet.[11] Furthermore, the mid-sized constituency electoral system resulted in factional rivalry rather than party-wide leadership within the LDP, so the position of the government and the prime minister remained weak on this front as well.

3. A system of vested interests formed by the collusion of the ruling party and the bureaucracy.

Another feature of the core executive structure during the 1955 regime was close cooperation between ruling-party politicians and the bureaucracy. The bureaucracy maintained organizational autonomy, but as for policy-making, the system rested on collusion between tribal politicians and mid-level bureaucrats in each ministry. This was the backbone of the iron triangle, a divisive, profit-mediated system for vested interests, and of course a serious impediment to top political leadership from the prime minister and the *Kantei*.

4. Skeletonized cabinet and its penetration from below.

Cabinet meetings were formalized to the extreme. Despite being held about twice a week, which was rather frequent, the duration of the meetings was very short, namely because conclusions to be decided at cabinet meetings were prepared in advance in the form of a "cabinet meeting document," and ministers who attended the meetings simply signed off on them without any hesitation. There was no debate between politicians at the meetings themselves. Cabinet decisions required unanimity; this was deemed necessary because of Article 66 of the constitution, which provides for the collective responsibilities of the Cabinet to the Diet. As a result, it was believed that even debate among different ministerial views in cabinet meetings could be considered as cabinet disagreement, and therefore was ruled out. However, these ideas and practices are quite extreme interpretations in terms of comparative political reality and theory. It meant, in effect, that ministries could veto each other. And the careful consensus-building process to contain the vetoes was based around a bottom-up *ringi* (稟議, inclusive and bottom-up style decision-making) system within the government, with the council of administrative vice-ministers (the most senior bureaucrats) at the top. In other words, bureaucratic rules and procedures dominated the entire coordination process.

5. Diet as the main arena for opposition.

As already pointed out in the previous section, the most important feature of the Diet is that it is basically run by negotiation between the ruling party and the opposition parties. As a result, even when the ruling party has the majority of seats, careful negotiations are inevitable, especially in terms of scheduling, where the opposition parties have considerable influence. In addition to this, the prime minister and his government have no power to control the process in parliament. Taken as a whole, the opposition party's influence in the parliament is significant and is a major constraint on the leadership of the prime minister and the government.[12]

The Core Executive in the "1955 Regime"

The system of government of the 1955 regime can be described as one in which power was, in sum, divided among several players and operated through coordination between them. Within this framework, the bureaucracy became an important player in linking the government bureaucracy with interests represented in political parties, especially the LDP. On this base, politicians of the ruling party exerted their influence, making the most of this close cooperation with the bureaucrats and interest groups. This structure placed strong constraints on top leadership from the prime minister and the *Kantei*. Unless the prime minister had strong political power within the LDP, like PM Tanaka Kakuei at one point in time, it was quite difficult for them to exercise leadership. The right to dissolve the LDP can essentially be seen as the only weapon in the prime minister's arsenal in this overall picture.

PM's Long Hours in Parliament

In Japan's parliament, the prime minister is (still now) often required to attend committee questioning, and figures from 2001 to 2012 show that the PM attended an average of 174 hours per year in the House of Representatives alone, of which thirty-six hours were spent in the plenary session, ninety-five hours in the budget committee, and forty-three hours in other committees. Attendance of the PM at committees is required for the examination of important bills, the so-called "Important Broad Bills," as well as in the budget committee. It is largely considered as an agreed convention in Japan's Diet. Moreover, the same amount of time is required for the house of councilors. The necessity of dedicating such long hours in the Diet have had a significant impact on the prime minister's working conditions and have been a major constraint on his ability to travel abroad. When the Diet is in session, ministers' trips to foreign countries need to be approved by it, and opposition parties have considerable say on the decision based on conventions.

Two Political System Reforms and the Transition to *Kantei* Leadership

Two political reforms took place from the 1990s which led to dramatic changes in the situation of Japan's core executive.

First, the introduction of a single-member constituency electoral system weakened the power of factions and increased the centripetal force of the prime minister, who also holds the LDP presidency. Having experienced the 2005 general election forced on them by then Prime Minister Koizumi, and then the 2009 crushing defeat against the Democratic Party of Japan, the LDP's internal factions lost their power. Conversely, the power of the prime minister has grown greatly, and they can now control with wide discretion the appointments of ministers and other key posts of the government. To a large extent, the structural conditions of a weak prime minister have been removed.

Second, an internal reform of the executive branch strengthened it. There were several aspects to this reform, but the element bearing most influence on this chapter's argument was the consolidation of the authority of the PM and the CCS to nominate most of the senior bureaucracy's personnel. At the same time, the personnel rules themselves were changed to allow more flexibility in the exercise of political discretion. In the end, the nomination powers of the PM and their team suddenly became extremely broad. The PM and CCS now control virtually every senior bureaucrat appointment, and can appoint as they see fit.

Using these enormous personnel powers as leverage, the *Kantei* established new policy councils. Now bureaucrats must perform well within this system for further promotion, and these changes have wrought a dramatic transformation to the ministry-based personnel system. Bureaucratic loyalty became directed toward the *Kantei*, leading to a reaction so intense that it was known as "anticipated reaction" (忖度) toward the will of the *Kantei*. The centripetal force of the prime minister has increased dramatically.

To be sure, the cabinet's management style changed little with Prime Minister Abe, but beneath the unchanging surface, the substance of the bureaucracy-led intra-governmental coordination mechanism has changed to the point where it has nearly been dismantled. Several scandals involving Abe can be seen as the result of the decisive breakdown of the traditional order and conventions of policy coordination and decision-making between the prime minister's office, the cabinet secretariat, and senior bureaucrats in various ministries, replaced by arbitrary operations led by the PM and other core staff of the *Kantei*. Obedience to the wishes of the *Kantei* became unavoidable for all bureaucrats. In an environment where new mechanisms and rules were not yet in place, the policies desired by the *Kantei* came to be produced from within the new policy councils in a top-down fashion. The succession of scandals was largely a result of the somewhat heavy-handed use of political power, unrestricted by rules or conventions.[13]

On the other hand, the structure of the PM's relations with the opposition parties in the Diet has hardly changed. This is because little progress has been made on parliamentary reform. In fact, it should be said that Prime Minister Abe has actually put a damper on momentum for parliamentary reform. It is highly likely that he did not have a sufficient understanding of the nature of the Diet as a democratic institution, and it is only with this understanding of the structure of the 1955 system and the role of the opposition parties in the Diet that reform can be considered. Prime Minister Abe, in all likelihood, did not have such a vision.

CONCLUSION: WHAT IS THE LEGACY OF PRIME MINISTER ABE?

The Abe administration was arguably a long-term regime by the standards of Japanese politics. Abe's primary success, therefore, is the long period of time in power itself. However, the duration of power does not automatically translate into political results. What has Prime Minister Abe achieved? And what will remain as his legacy in the long run?

One of the reasons for Prime Minister Abe's success at maintaining a long-term government was his emphasis on expansionary economic and monetary policy that helped him to achieve economic stability. While there will be long-term costs, of course, these policies were effective in maintaining his popularity and power. It is more likely that this type of economic expansionist policy will be used in coming years in Japan than the structural reform policy championed by Koizumi. This is what Taniguchi Masaki, political scientist of Tokyo University, calls "valence politics."[14]

In reality, Abe's valence politics were a set-up for a short-term fix made of a succession of new slogans. This *ad hoc* approach, without serious policy implementation, was also deeply connected to his disregard for public accountability, most apparent in the "surprise dissolution" of September 2017. Ultimately, that "surprise dissolution" constituted an abuse of the constitution's Article 7, making an already extremely short electoral competition even shorter. Such an approach is not the high road to democracy. Perhaps similar dissolution games will continue in the short run, but in the long run, they will be seen as the epitome of an idea that should be rejected.

As for the administration's internal management approach, it became characterized by the fixation of key posts around the *Kantei*, the expansion of political personnel powers, and the expansion of the policy council system to promote top-down policy-making. These approaches will probably be followed by future administrations. For the most part, they displayed skillful use of previously reformed institutional structures rather than fundamental changes on Abe's part. The 1955 regime, which was characterized by the division of power and bottom-up negotiation and coordination, had undergone a major transformation following two reforms of political institutions, as well as through Koizumi administration's structural reform approach and the change of government to the DPJ. By the time Prime Minister Abe formed his second cabinet, the concentration of authority and resources in the hands of the prime minister and the *Kantei* had made significant progress. These methods of governing are likely to be followed by the leaders who will come after him.

In terms of domestic social policy, his response was rather backward-looking. This is not surprising, given Abe's right-wing ideology and view of history. Whether or not Japanese society as a whole has taken a decisive rightward turn is unclear, but given Japan's post-war history, a swing back to center-left thinking and policies is to be expected. However, conversely, the political discourse became increasingly divisive rather than consensual, as reflected in such wide-spread derogatory catch phrases as "nightmarish DPJ government" (悪夢のような民主党政権). The phenomenon may be related to rapidly growing social networks, but its direction is not set in stone. It can be argued that ideas and political methods, which had the potential to divide society, expanded during the Abe administration. This is yet again a negative legacy that requires correction.

With respect to the Diet, Prime Minister Abe's attitude can be described as rather recalcitrant. His continued rejection of requests from the opposition parties to convene the Diet in accordance with Article 53 of the constitution, and his dissolution of the Diet, which could be described as an extreme abuse of Article 7 of the constitution, illustrate his willingness to set aside the principle of democratic accountability to the Diet and the Japanese people. It raises the question of whether or not Prime Minister Abe understood in the first place what kind of parliamentary structure had been established under the long-lived one-party dominant regime of the LDP. Prime Minister Abe, who professes to admire his grandfather, former Prime Minister Kishi, may have been able to envision the 1960 Diet, but did he understand the kind of politics and negotiations that the ruling and opposition parties undertook over the long period of time that followed? In truth, the Abe administration has left almost nothing behind that will have any kind of long-term impact on the Diet. I would venture to say that, during his mandate, the clock was turned back by decades, and that he failed to understand the meanings of various efforts for parliamentary reform over the last two decades or so, especially in the latter half of the DPJ era.

The world of the twenty-first century has become much more fluid, and society operates much more quickly than in the previous century. In light of this swift new world, the need for political leadership has also become much greater. There is no doubt that the Abe administration has tried to respond to that to some extent. To this end, it used the fruits of political reform to introduce a top-down approach to government management, and a significant part of it will be followed in the future.

However, after the dismantling of the structure of the 1955 regime, which had clear operating rules, it is difficult to say that new principles and mechanisms were conceived to replace it. Abe's new approach was, in the end, fragmented and unbalanced. This is because the norms and procedures of political responsibility were completely disregarded while the authority of leaders was being strengthened. What will remain of his style of government after him is unclear. Likewise, many ideological policies (such as conservative reform proposals on the education system), which only caused further confusion, may not remain. The fact that the constitutional reforms set out from the beginning of his administration have ultimately made little progress seems to indicate that Prime Minister Abe has exhibited no real leadership due to his overall lack of both vision and historical understanding.

NOTES

1. See, for example, the public opinion poll conducted by the Jiji Tsūshinsha.
2. See Takeshi Sasaki and Nijū-Isseiki Rincho, eds., *Heisei Demokurashī* [Heisei Democracy], Tōkyō: Kodan-sha, 2013; and Masato Shimizu, *Heisei Demokurashī-shi* [History of Heisei Democracy], Tōkyō: Chikuma Shobō, 2018.
3. Regarding the personnel system of the government, Akiko Izumo, *Kōmuin Seido Kaikaku to Seiji Shudō* [Reform of the Public Administration and Political Leadership], Hiratsuka, Kanagawa: Tokai University Press, 2014 is a useful comprehensive study.
4. How the *Kantei* compares to its counterparts elsewhere in the world, such as the White House, Elysee Palace, or 10 Downing Street, would be an interesting theme to consider. Although I will touch briefly on this point later, detailed and systematic research is a future agenda. See, for example, Naoto Nonaka, "'LDP System' and Japan's Post War Politics: Has the Post War Japan had a Parliamentary Cabinet Government", Paper presented at the Annual Conference of the PSA, Manchester, April 14–16, 2014; Naoto Nonaka, "*Sengo Nihon Seiji wa Majoritarian gata ka?*" [Is

the Post-war Japan's Politics Majoritarian?], in *Japan Association of Comparative Politics*, ed., Comparative Political Studies on Core Executives, Kyōto: Mineruba Shobō, 2016; and Kensuke Takayasu, *Shushō no Kenryoku* [Power of the PM], Tōkyō: Sōbun-sha, 2009.

5. In contrast the Japanese government has made relatively serious efforts to improve its labor policies, including the employment environment.

6. As for the LDP's Policy Affairs Research Council, see: Seizaburō Sato and Tetsuhisa Matsuzaki, *Jimintō Seiken* [LDP Government], Tōkyō: Chuō Kōron-sha, 1986; Nonaka, *Jiminto Seiji no Owari* [The End of LDP Politics], Tōkyō: Chikuma-shobo, 2008; Michio Muramatsu, *Seikan Sukuramu Gata Rīdāshippu no Hōkai* [Collapse of Combined Leadership Style Involving Bureaucrats and Politicians], Tōkyō: Toyo Keizai Shimpo-sha, 2010; and Ellis Krauss and Robert Pekkanen, *The Rise and Fall of Japan's LDP: Political Party Organizations as Historical Institutions*, Ithaca and London: Cornell Univ. Press, 2011.

7. See, for example, Naoto Nonaka and Haruka Aoki, *Seisaku Kaigi to Tōron Naki Kokkai* [Policy Councils and the Debateless Diet], Tōkyō: Asahi Shimbun Shuppan, 2016.

8. Regarding the basic nature and its peculiarities of the Diet, see Takeshi Sasaki, *Hikaku Giinnaikakusei Ron* [Comparative Study on Parliamentary Cabinet System], Tōkyō: Iwanami Shoten, 2019; and Nonaka, "Is the Post-war Japan's Politics Majoritarian?"

9. Sasaki, *Hikaku Giinnaikakusei Ron* [Comparative Study on Parliamentary Cabinet System].

10. However, some political commentators, mostly from right-wing media, argue that the attitude of the opposition, which spends so much time pursuing the prime minister and the government over scandals, is the more pressing problem.

11. As for the PM's power within the framework of parliament, Nonaka, "'LDP System'" offers a comparative assessment with Britain, France and Germany. In short, Japan's PM is by far the weakest one, having almost none of the powers British and French counterparts have.

12. It is also important to understand that the basic nature of the Diet from the 1955 regime has not been changed, as opposed to most other features of that period.

13. Famous scandals under Abe included Moritomo Gakuen, Kake Gakuen, and "Sakura wo miru kai," among others.

14. Masaki Taniguchi, *Gendai Nihon no Daihyōsei Minshushugi* [Representative Democracy in Contemporary Japan], Tōkyō: Univ. of Tōkyō Press, 2020.

REFERENCES

Izumo, Akiko. *Kōmuin Seido Kaikaku to Seiji Shudō* [Reform of the Public Administration and Political Leadership], Hiratsuka, Kanagawa: Tokai University Press, 2014.

Krauss, Ellis and Robert Pekkanen. *The Rise and Fall of Japan's LDP: Political Party Organizations as Historical Institutions*. Ithaca and London: Cornell Univ. Press, 2011.

Muramatsu, Michio. *Seikan Sukuramu Gata Rīdāshippu no Hōkai* [Collapse of Combined Leadership Style Involving Bureaucrats and Politicians], Tōkyō: Toyo Keizai Shimpo-sha, 2010.

Nonaka, Naoto. *Jiminto Seiji no Owari* [The End of LDP Politics], Tōkyō: Chikuma-shobo, 2008.

Nonaka, Naoto. "'LDP System' and Japan's Post War Politics: Has the Post War Japan had a Parliamentary Cabinet Government," Paper presented at the Annual Conference of the PSA, Manchester, April 14–16, 2014.

Nonaka, Naoto. "*Sengo Nihon Seiji wa Majoritarian gata ka?*" [Is the Post-war Japan's Politics Majoritarian?], in *Japan Association of Comparative Politics*, ed., Comparative Political Studies on Core Executives, Kyōto: Mineruba Shobō, 2016.

Nonaka, Naoto, and Haruka Aoki. *Seisaku Kaigi to Tōron Naki Kokkai* [Policy Councils and the Debateless Diet], Tōkyō: Asahi Shimbun Shuppan, 2016.

Sasaki, Takeshi, ed. *Hikaku Giinnaikakusei Ron* [Comparative Study on Parliamentary Cabinet System], Tōkyō: Iwanami Shoten, 2019.

Sasaki, Takeshi and Nijū-Isseiki Rincho eds. *Heisei Demokurashī* [Heisei Democracy], Tōkyō: Kodan-sha, 2013.

Satō, Seizaburō and Tetsuhisa Matsuzaki. *Jimintō Seiken* [LDP Government], Tōkyō: Chuō Kōron-sha, 1986.

Shimizu, Masato. *Heisei Demokurashī-shi*, [History of Heisei Democracy], Tōkyō: Chikuma Shobō, 2018.

Takayasu, Kensuke. *Shushō no Kenryoku* [Power of the PM], Tōkyō: Sōbun-sha, 2009.

Taniguchi, Masaki. *Gendai Nihon no Daihyosei Minshushugi* [Representative Democracy in Contemporary Japan], Tōkyō: Univ. of Tōkyō Press, 2020.

Tsushinsha, Jiji. *Yōron Chōsa* [Public Opinion Poll] Periodical.

Chapter 2

Abe Shinzō's Economic Legacy

R. Taggart Murphy

Any assessment of Abe Shinzō's economic legacy has to start by acknowledging that Japan's economic well-being was never his primary policy objective. Of course, he was happy when GDP, employment rates, corporate profits, trade numbers, and the stock market ticked upward, but they were never what got him out of bed in the morning. The evidence, if any is needed, can be found in his first—and unsuccessful—twelve-month term as prime minister back in 2006–2007. He had convinced himself that the economic recovery under his predecessor (and sponsor), Koizumi Junichiro, had been sufficient that he could embark on what really mattered to him: removing constitutional restraints on military action, restoring patriotism ("beautiful Japan" was his motto for this), and generally advancing the decades-long goal of Japan's conservative elite to dismantle much of the postwar settlement. That postwar settlement with its "un-Japanese" notions of individual rights and democratic accountability of the governing to the governed had been necessary both to end the American occupation, and to reduce the appeal of an organized left that had threatened to seize the levers of power after the Americans departed. However, a half century later, both the global left and a credible domestic left opposition had crumbled. To many on the Japanese right, it seemed accordingly that the time had finally come openly to resurrect the "family state" ideology of the prewar years, implement a proactive foreign policy complete with the jettisoning of the postwar constitution, and rewrite history to cast the events of the 1930s and early 1940s as a justifiable response to intolerable external pressures—all with the aim of fostering the return of a proud and assertive nationalism.

Abe was the logical figure to carry out this agenda. The offspring of one of Japan's most prominent political dynasties—son of Abe Shintaro, whose own universally expected ascension to the *Kantei* (prime minister's office) had been thwarted by collateral damage from the scandals of the late 1980s and his early death, grandnephew of Sato Eisaku, prime minister from 1964–1972, and grandson of Kishi Nobusuke, the architect of the postwar Japanese political order—Abe had few rivals when it came to the all-important *jinmyaku* (personal network) that is the *sine qua non* of political power in Japan. The Kishi connection was particularly critical. Being the economic czar of colonial Manchuria and minister of munitions in the wartime cabinet of Tojo Hideki, Kishi had been the key figure in the re-emergence of Tokyo's prewar elite following the so-called "reverse course" of the late 1940s that saw the release of thousands of suspected "war criminals" from prison to retake positions of power from the leftists who were being systemically purged. Kishi had gone on, with CIA funds, to forge the merger in 1955 of existing conservative parties to create the Liberal Democratic Party (LDP) thereby forestalling an election which would probably have been won by the hard-left Japan Socialist Party.[1] On becoming prime minster himself, Kishi put the relationship with Washington on a stable, semi-permanent footing by ramming the revised U.S.–Japan Security Treaty through the Diet in 1960. The storm of opposition he provoked forced his resignation (over a million people took to the streets of Tokyo in protest), but he nonetheless continued to exercise power behind the scenes well into the 1980s. Among other things, he acted as his grandson's most important early tutor, plugging the boy into his unrivaled *jinmyaku* and instructing him on the long game of dismantling the postwar settlement and the final restoration of what the Japanese right sees as the full sovereignty the country has lacked since 1945.

Thus, not only did Abe have all the "correct" views on issues that matter the most to the Japanese right, he had all the important connections necessary for an ascent to the *Kantei*. And while his views might be hard right, he could be relied upon not to frighten voters with unnecessary saber-rattling—in contrast, for example, to Tokyo's crackpot governor of the time, Ishihara Shintaro.

To be sure, before the right could openly plant its flag on the hills of Kasumigaseki (the Tokyo district where most government offices are located), the economic wreckage left behind by the collapse of the so-called bubble economy of the late 1980s had to be dealt with—but Koizumi seemed to have done just that. Bank balance sheets had been repaired, growth had been restored, and corporate profits had largely recovered. Meanwhile, Koizumi had made several official visits to the controversial Yasukuni Shrine with its enshrinement of indicted war criminals and museum glorifying the events of the 1930s, while burnishing at the same time Tokyo's all-important ties with Washington. All this appeared to enhance Koizumi's popularity with the voters —the economy was humming and his assertive stances vis-a-vis Beijing together with the warm relationship he obviously enjoyed with the

George W. Bush White House reassured many that Japan could finally stand up to its hectoring neighbors without risking its national security. Koizumi was re-elected to a third term—the first time since 1986 that a sitting prime minister had managed that. Taking a leaf from Koizumi's book, Abe whipped up nationalist sentiment over the *ratchi mondai* (North Korean abduction of a number of Japanese citizens a generation earlier), and Koizumi rewarded him by effectively designating Abe as his heir apparent.

So when Abe took over the *Kantei* in September 2006, it seemed the time had come to do what Koizumi had only hinted at: full implementation of the long-held agenda of the Japanese right.

THE KOIZUMI INHERITANCE

Except that it hadn't. Abe did not really understand what had brought about the reputed economic successes of the Koizumi years. Two factors explained the revived economy and neither had much to do with anything Koizumi had or hadn't done.

The first of these was the explosive growth of the Chinese economy that itself was partly facilitated by the stimulative deficit spending of the George W. Bush White House. The new administration had started out with a large tax cut and followed that up with additional spending to finance the wars in Afghanistan and Iraq. The tearing back open of the deficits in America's government accounts—closed in the late 1990s for the one and only time since the mid-1960s—inevitably translated through the logic of accounting into a widening American current account deficit (the broadest measure of the trade deficit, including trade in both goods and services as well as short-term financial flows). Chinese exports poured into the United States while the capital goods needed to equip China's factories running flat out to produce those exports came mostly from Japan (and Germany). Together, China and Japan's incremental purchases of U.S. government securities—that's mostly what they did with the dollars they earned from the exports—financed almost all of Washington's extra spending on its Middle East wars. But the surge of orders from China allowed Japanese manufacturers—particularly makers of capital goods—to finally emerge from the balance sheet recession of the 1990s.[2]

The second factor explaining Japan's seemingly robust economic health in September 2006 lay in the simple passage of time, time that had allowed for the convalescence and rehabilitation of the heretofore ruined banking system.[3] The financial authorities had, a decade earlier, succeeded in preventing its complete collapse—most depositors had been induced to keep their money in the banks even though the collective liabilities of the banking system far exceeded the market value of its assets after the deflation of the late-1980s asset bubble. But the subsequent years of stop-and-start deficit spending by the Japanese government had shrunk the liabilities of the banking system as a percentage of GDP to the point where the system had begun to stabilize without deliberate intervention. The shotgun mergers of the 1990s had also played an important role as healthier banks were forced to absorb their ailing brethren rather than see the latter openly default.

Little of this had anything to do with specific measures taken by Koizumi's *Kantei*. In fact, a premature attempt in 2003 by Koizumi's neo-liberal economics minister Takenaka Heizo to reduce deficit spending had precipitated such a sharply negative turn in Japan's overall macroeconomic numbers that it was quickly abandoned.

Meanwhile, Koizumi's best-known achievement in the economic arena—the "privatization" of the Japan Post Office—was far less than met the eye, at least when it came to the effects on the wider economy. In addition to delivering the mail, the post office acted as what was essentially the world's largest bank. Most of the money it collected went directly into the so-called "second budget"—off balance sheet financing of pork-barrel spending in rural areas. Since most of that spending built projects whose cash flows were insufficient even to cover operating expenses, much less retire debt—roads to nowhere, large museums/halls (*kaikan*) visited by few, airports practically in sight of each other—the post office came dangerously close to a giant Ponzi scheme. Even more to the point, the post office served as the financial power base of the populist wing of the LDP whose roots go back to the political insurrection of Tanaka Kakuei in the early 1970s. Until Koizumi, every single prime minister from Ohira Masayoshi of the late 1970s on owed his position either to the *Tanaka Gundan* (the "Tanaka Army", the name the media gave to the political machine that Tanaka had built) or to one of the successor factions that emerged after its break-up in the late 1980s. Koizumi had styled himself a maverick, but in fact, he represented a return to political power of the mandarin elite that had held the *Kantei* from Kishi's creation of the postwar Japanese political order until the Tanaka insurrection.

Crippling the post office thus accomplished three things: it permanently reduced the power base of the populist wing of the LDP, it held the potential for redirecting infrastructural spending away from white elephants to projects that could actually strengthen Japan's economic sinews, and it formed a necessary step—both economically and politically—for directing spending away from rural districts in structural demographic and economic decline toward the great urban areas that were still growing. It did nothing in the short-term to alleviate Japan's principal economic problem: anemic domestic demand. In fact, it made things worse. Meanwhile, the rehabilitation of Japan's banking system and the repair of corporate balance sheets was not doing much to put money in people's pockets. Orders from China were all well and good, but corporations were increasingly loathe to offer the "permanent" positions (*seisha-in*) that most Japanese had come to identify as essential to economic security. Instead, companies sought as much as possible to fill what demand there was by hiring temporary workers, many of them women, by discreetly relying on a growing, if unacknowledged, immigrant work force (disguised often as "trainees"), and by relocating factories abroad—principally to China.

THE FAILURE OF ABE'S FIRST TERM AND THE LDP LOSS OF POWER

Abe seems not to have understood any of this. Assuming that Japan's economic problems had been repaired, he began taking steps to implement the whole rightist agenda complete with amending the constitution to get rid of the notorious Article 9 that prohibited Japan from maintaining war-making potential and re-instilling "patriotic education" in the schools. Meanwhile, the Health and Welfare Ministry managed to lose tens of millions of pension records. At a time when most voters were worried about how they could pay for their retirement and whether or not their kids could ever land decent jobs, their prime minister was prattling on about "beautiful Japan." The quality press turned on Abe, labeling him an *obotchan* (clueless rich kid) who "couldn't read the air" (*kuuki yomenai*). Just a few days past the first anniversary of his ascension to the *Kantei*, he resigned, pleading poor health. Observers started to write his political obituary.

Abe's resignation did not end the threat to Japan's governing elite; it was just the opening act. As the country stumbled through the short administrations of two more hapless LDP prime ministers, the lowering economic clouds from the collapse of the derivatives-fueled American housing bubble coalesced into the worst world-wide economic storm since the 1930s, bankrupting the American financial system and pulling most of its European counterparts down with it. Japanese finance escaped the worst of the damage, but that was not true of the wider economy. With the entire world descending into recession, demand for Japanese exports—both the direct exports of consumer goods (cars/motorcycles) and the capital exports to equip the Chinese manufacturing plants—plummeted.

There was no hiding these realities from the Japanese electorate. The postwar institutions of economic security—most importantly, corporate pledges to provide for the lifelong well-being of male heads of household (so-called "lifetime employment") and an informal commitment by both large establishment corporations and the financial system (quietly underscored by the official bureaucracy) not to foreclose on weaker and smaller companies—were already under stress for reasons mentioned above, and it seemed to most that they could not survive the maelstrom unleashed by what the Japanese called the "Lehmann shock" (the collapse of the American investment bank Lehman Brothers in September 2008).

What's more, a new and credible political force had appeared on the scene: the Democratic Party of Japan (DPJ). A coalition of fragments of the old Japan Socialist Party, the former "centrist" Democratic Socialist Party, and disaffected refugees from the LDP, its mastermind was Ozawa Ichiro, the most formidable of Tanaka Kakuei's disciples. A brilliant political tactician, Ozawa stitched together a nationwide network of candidacies modeled on the old *Tanaka gundan* while articulating a political platform based on two widely popular planks: the replacement of the existing and obviously imperiled institutions of economic security—institutions that were a matter of practice rather than law such as "lifetime employment" and the extension of financial lifelines to companies in trouble—with an explicit government commitment to a universal safety net on the Scandinavian model, together with a re-definition of the U.S.–Japan security relationship.

The story has been told elsewhere of what happened.[4] In August, 2009, the LDP lost—and lost badly—a nationwide election for the first and only time since Kishi had conjured the postwar Japanese political order into being in 1955. (Control of the Diet in 1993 had briefly slipped out of LDP hands thanks to a walkout by Ozawa and his followers, but no election had been involved.) The DPJ's victory represented not just the defeat of the LDP but an existential threat to the entire Japanese governing setup. The LDP's traditional role in that setup had been to provide political cover for a bureaucracy that actually determined most policy while mollifying various interest groups—farmers, the construction sector—that had the capacity to create politically significant disorder.

Japan's governing elite had been unable to prevent the DPJ's electoral triumph, even when it wheeled out its most formidable weapon: "investigations" launched by the public prosecutor and trumpeted in the mainstream media. In this particular case, the public prosecutor zeroed in on some spurious charges against Ozawa, charges that would be quietly dropped once the objective of forcing his resignation as party leader had been achieved. (The investigations were not fruitless; although they failed to stop the DPJ's electoral steamroller, by ensuring that Ozawa could not become prime minister they ultimately helped cripple the DPJ by depriving it of its most politically savvy leader.) It took more than three years, but the traditional elite finally managed to destroy the DPJ and claw its way back into power.

Their most perceptive members had, however, been badly scared. Among other things, they realized that they had to create at least the appearance of taking seriously the economic interests of ordinary Japanese people.

It was against this background that Abe managed to recapture the leadership of the LDP and lead it to victory in the December 2012 elections. He had brought into his inner circle Iijima Isao, whose mastery of political theater had invited comparison during the Koizumi years with Karl Rove. Akin to Rove's positioning of George W. Bush as a "compassionate conservative," Iijima had played a crucial role in draping Koizumi in the cloak of a "maverick reformer" despite an actual policy agenda of neo-liberalism, austerity, and the stopping-up of pipelines that had watered much of the country with government money. Now, with Abe, Iijima performed something of the same trick: convincing the electorate that Abe's primary concern lay with economic reform and prosperity, not with revising the constitution or imbuing Japanese youth with a bristling nationalism.

THE SUBORDINATION OF ECONOMICS TO POLITICS

It is worth pausing for a moment to consider why a platform of economic reform and prosperity amounted to a kind of ruse. Wouldn't any political leader want this? Don't ideological differences amount to disputes over means rather than ends? Don't they all have widespread prosperity as the ultimate measure of policy success?

No, they don't. The Japanese elites have never seen widespread economic prosperity as an end-in-itself. Japan's late nineteenth-century forced-march industrialization was not implemented to make Japan prosperous but to make Japan strong enough to fend off the threat of colonization and, once that was accomplished, to muscle Japan's entry into the exclusive club of Great Powers. In the immediate postwar years, to be sure, economic reconstruction was the only plausible course for Japan; the realities of the time precluded any more imperialist land grabs. Thus, the restoration of national pride came to involve British kids with Sony Walkmans in their backpacks while Yamaha motorcycles and Toyota cars jammed the streets of Bangkok and Los Angeles rather than Rising Sun banners flapping over Singapore and Manila. Whatever criteria might be used to measure national greatness at one point or another, however, putting lots of money into the pockets of ordinary people was never one of them. Rather, the unspoken goal of economic policy has, since the Meiji period, always been to provide Japan with sufficient leverage to force the rest of the world into dealing with Tokyo as much as possible on Tokyo's terms. That leverage might take different forms at different times—a fearsomely equipped military, a dominant global market position in key upstream industrial components, a vast hoard of claims on the American banking system—but it has always been about securing as much freedom of action for Japan's power elite as circumstances would permit.

Assessing Abe's economic legacy requires at least a two-track approach: the standard criteria of per capita GDP growth, unemployment, corporate profits and all that but also evaluating his economic achievements by what clearly matters to him: making Japan great again, to choose a phrase deliberately; strengthening the economic framework to the point where progress on reviving nationalism and jettisoning the postwar shackles can again become credible goals. To go a step further, there is a third track that we must also consider, something that Abe probably couldn't admit to himself: the preservation of the privileges and prerogatives of Japan's ruling elite.[5] Japan's elites do not differ from elites anywhere in confusing their own continued control of the levers of power with the general well-being of the countries they rule, but that confusion must not extend to outside analysts of policy and consequences.

THE THREE ARROWS: #1, STRUCTURAL REFORM

Guided by Iijima, Abe duly called for the launching of "three arrows" of what the media would come to label Abenomics: structural reform, fiscal stimulus, and monetary easing. Campaign slogans as much as serious policy initiatives (and with an aura of wish fulfillment rather than commitment to the nuts and bolts of serious policy-making—thus the "Abenomics" rubric), they nonetheless provide useful criteria for assessing Abe's legacy.

Let's start with structural reform since it is the arena over which Abe—or any prime minster—has the least influence.[6] The problems of Japanese business are both overstated and understated. It was the understated problems, of course, that Abe promised to tackle. Everyone in Japan now knows that with the huge exception of motor vehicles—cars, trucks, motorcycles—Japanese companies have mostly lost the global cachet in consumer products they enjoyed a generation ago.

The blame is said to rest on a variety of factors—companies like Sony and Nissan paralyzed by factionalism; the stultifying ritualism of Japanese business life: the *"ringi"* system (documents that have to be approved with personal stamps from a whole raft of middle and upper managers before a decision can be implemented), the endless meetings that include all the informal sessions held before the formal so no surprise emerges in the latter, the reliance on paper trails for even the smallest decision; the supposed failure to diversify and/or globalize by incorporating the voices of the marginalized—women, foreigners—into corporate decision-making; the rigid career track that begins with recruiting from name universities followed by the rotation from functional area to functional area every three to four years to pick up a shallow mix of general management skills.

Much of this finger-pointing can be summarized as a kind of "Galapagos phenomenon"— the rubric coined by the Japanese press some twenty years ago when Japan lost control of an emerging mobile phone business that seemed about to drop into its lap. Japanese makers were so concerned with meeting the demanding specifications of the domestic market that they missed wider developments that permitted first Nokia and then Apple and Samsung to seize global leadership in this business.

The term is applicable beyond this sector, however, and it points to why the now well-understood problems of Japanese business are understated: because they can't easily be fixed, certainly not by exhortations emanating from a nationalist *Kantei*. Really "fixing" these problems would turn Japanese organizations into something else. Sure, one can manage some tinkering around the edges, and Abe encouraged that with pleas to hire more women, increase base pay, and boost the number of full-time positions on offer. Some companies even responded. But to go beyond that to fundamental "reform" of Japanese business—cutting short those endless meetings and meticulously documented paper trails for each decision, for example, or forcing companies to ration the resources devoted to customer service by using bottom line criteria such as return on investment (ROI)—put at risk precisely those qualities where Japanese companies enjoy such an obvious comparative advantage: an unparalleled reputation for quality and reliability; a unanimity of purpose and resolve that ensures that once a decision has been made, everyone knows what to do without it being spelled out.

But if deep structural "reform" of Japanese companies can't happen without a cultural revolution that would turn them into something other than Japanese companies, maybe the need for "reform" is overstated—or perhaps it makes the mistake of looking at the problems of the Japanese economy through the wrong end of the proverbial telescope. Yes, Japanese companies have lost the dominant global market shares they enjoyed a generation ago in a whole raft of consumer products, but they still maintain what amounts to an unassailable position in many key upstream components—and where the components are not Japanese, they are likely to be made with Japanese capital equipment. Pull apart complex machines today—MacBook Airs; Boeing 787s, GM cars—to find where the value-added is, and more often than not, it is provided by Japanese companies.[7] According to the late Stefan Lippert, some 250 Japanese companies qualify for the "hidden champion" label—the designation originally coined by Hermann Simon in his study of German business for companies enjoying pre-eminent global market shares in businesses where the purchasing decision is made on the basis of quality and reliability rather than price. Ulrike Schaede in her new book calls this an "aggregate niche strategy" noting that "Japanese companies now anchor global supply chains by dominating world markets in a large number of critical input components and materials, meaning global manufacturing has become dependent on Japanese inputs."[8]

These companies continue to provide Japan with the economic and financial leverage that has been the unstated goal of economic policy in Japan for the last 150 years. Indeed, one can argue that far from a disaster, the economic history of the past generation brought on a salutary retreat of Japanese business into its core competencies, to use business-school jargon. Japan's initial postwar business success—the so-called "Japanese Miracle"—was a function of a unique coalition of factors that are unlikely to return: a large and seemingly infinite American market to which Japan had privileged access, a fixed and undervalued currency, and American business rivals that had grown complacent in the immediate postwar decades. (Indeed, the disappearance of U.S.–Japan trade friction—the occasional spat over autos excepted—testifies to the degree that the U.S. and Japanese economies are now highly complementary, with the United States providing a range of commodities from foodstuffs to minerals together with the marketing, design, and software for complex manufacturing/service hybrids—e.g., iPhones—while the Japanese supply precision components, capital equipment, and state-of-the art materials.) Meanwhile, relentless competitive pressure from countries, such as South Korea and China, that had studied and absorbed the lessons from the "Japanese Miracle" forced Japanese withdrawal from a wide range of consumer products and commodity-like components in which Japan's cost advantage had been permanently destroyed.

But the retreat of Japanese business into those areas where ability to deliver quality and reliability create unbeatable competitive advantage do not necessarily condemn Japan to decline. Most of the problems of the Japanese economy do not lie on the "supply" side and cannot be fixed by "structural" reforms. Free trade agreements, women's empowerment, family-friendly work environments—these may be worthy goals and Abe's efforts to promote them, even if partly rhetorical, must be acknowledged in any assessment of his legacy. However, even if these goals had all been met, they would not have solved Japan's core economic challenge: anemic demand.

The real policy challenge for the Japanese government lies in ensuring that the still-formidable competitive strengths of Japanese business translate into widely spread and rising living standards—in cold macroeconomic terms, in promoting productive domestic investment both by entrepreneurs and by established companies that for the time being lie like sleeping dragons on vast hoards of idle cash. The economic analyst Jesper Koll has pointed out that corporate cash balances in Japan rose to over 120 percent of GDP in 2017 from 20 percent in 2007; comparable figures for the United States are, respectively, 15 and 35 percent; in Germany the number actually fell slightly from the 20 percent it had been in 2007. Koll noted that by the end of 2019, corporate holdings of cash and short-term securities totaled some $6.5 trillion.[9]

The challenges of promoting domestic investment lie in putting more money in people's pockets so they spend more, in convincing entrepreneurs to borrow money, banks to lend it, and established businesses to take some funds from their vast cash pools and put them to work. That can only happen when they all collectively sense that markets are growing rather than declining. It is a demand problem, not a supply problem. Thus, any comprehensive assessment of Abe's economic legacy must turn to the remaining two "arrows": the fiscal and the monetary.

THE THREE ARROWS: #2, FISCAL "STIMULUS"

Alas, "stimulus" goes in quotes because in aggregate, there turned out to be so little of it during the Abe years (until the advent of the COVID-19 pandemic), despite the "second arrow" advertising that accompanied an initial stimulus package in 2013 of some ¥10.3 trillion ($116 billion). That package held out the quasi-Keynesian promise of pulling Japan out of its deflationary trap, and indeed it seemed like a lot of money at the time, but as the years unfolded, the reality was continued austerity. Government borrowing actually fell between 2014 and 2018 from ¥21.6 trillion to ¥10.2 trillion. While government spending rose by ¥6.7 trillion yen between 2014 and 2019, taxes and social security levies (net of social benefits) rose by ¥8.2 trillion yen.[10]

This is not stimulus. Whatever macroeconomic benefits might have stemmed from the 2013 "stimulus" package, the 2014 hike in the consumption tax from 5 percent to 8 percent wiped them out. Indeed, the tightening has been labeled the "most brutal" since the 1996–1997 hike that helped tip a roster of financial institutions into bankruptcy and brought the Japanese banking system the closest it has come to actual meltdown in the postwar period. That didn't happen in 2014, but the tax increase did precipitate a sharp drop in GDP of 1.63 percent as most informed opinion expected it would. As if this wasn't enough, Abe then proceeded to preside over a further hike in the tax in October 2019 with utterly predictable results[11]—the economy promptly went into a tailspin with such key indicators as retail sales dropping like the proverbial stones. Apologists for Abe's policies have blamed the COVID-19 pandemic for the downward spiral, but the evidence was already stark before the pandemic hit—among other things, annualized GDP growth dropped by 7.2 percent in the fourth quarter before anyone had heard of COVID-19.

Why? What for? I have published elsewhere an analysis of how and why Japan's highly trained and brilliant authorities repeatedly commit this kind of egregious policy error: imposing austerity on an economy whose principal long-term challenge is anemic demand.[12] For our purposes here, it is may be sufficient to note:

1. *That Abe had less control over the bureaucracy than is widely understood.* Abe may have been the most politically powerful prime minister in decades, but that power did not extend to overruling the Ministry of Finance (MOF) on matters it deems the highest priority. The MOF has spearheaded a drive that goes back to the late 1970s to turn a value-added tax into the government's principal source of revenue. In pursuit of this goal, the MOF has repeatedly driven the economy into recession and undermined the careers of a number of prime ministers—including that of Abe's immediate predecessor, Noda Yoshihiko, the last of the three DPJ prime ministers. The DPJ had ridden to power partly on the promise of repealing—or at least not raising—this widely hated tax, but Kan Naoto, the second of the three, had already muttered about dropping this campaign promise—the result? A disastrous drop in electoral support that helped precipitate his resignation. When Noda reversed the promise entirely and pushed authorization for a hike through the Diet by cutting a deal with the LDP, a disgusted electorate abandoned the DPJ in droves. Abe thus paradoxically owed his second tenure in the *Kantei* to public opposition to the tax, but no clearer demonstration exists of the MOF's ability to overrule prime ministers and voters than the way it helped destroy the DPJ over this tax—and Abe must know this. However, there is more involved.
2. *The MOF specifically and Japan's entrenched elites in general—including, of course, Abe—do not see anemic domestic demand as Japan's principal economic challenge.* The tax champions maintain it as the only route out of a worsening fiscal dilemma that began with Tanaka's infrastructure spending in the 1970s, continued with the measures to compensate Japanese industry for the loss of an undervalued currency with the Plaza Accord agreement of 1985, and culminated in the deficits needed to prevent Japan from tipping into depression after the collapse of the resultant asset bubble. Tax proponents like to scare themselves—and the public—with nightmare scenarios of fiscal train wreck if revenues are not raised (absurd comparisons with Greece and Italy are particularly popular—comparisons that ignore the fact that Japan finances its government debt from its own citizens in a currency it controls.) What they refuse to see is that there is only one sure way of paying down government debt: growing nominal GDP so that outstanding debt shrinks as a percentage of GDP—and that tax revenues rise as a consequence. Saddling an economy with a regressive tax on its weakest sector—consumption—brings on precisely the reverse. This has been widely understood since the 1930s

when Keynes first articulated the underlying macroeconomic dynamics. But Japan's entrenched elites cannot or will not see it.[13]
3. *That they cannot, despite their obvious intelligence and cumulative experience, form a good example of the old saw that a man whose salary depends on not understanding something can be guaranteed not to understand it.* Japan's economic policy makers are marinated in supply-side thinking about economic policy that goes back to Tokugawa-period obsession with rice yields and was then underscored by the forced industrialization of the Meiji period and on, into postwar reconstruction. Over the last generation, however, that understandable concern with equipping Japanese industry with the sinews that would enable it to compete on global markets has slowly segued into a half-conscious concern with preserving privilege and existing power relations. Real stimulus that would aim at putting lots of money in the pockets of ordinary people and encouraging them to spend freely would undermine the power and privileges of Japan's established organizations—companies, bureaucracies—and the shrinking percentage of an aging population covered by the protocols of so-called "lifetime employment."

At least, or rather until the coming of the COVID-19 pandemic, Abe's fiscal legacy amounted to the shoring up of the status quo. The consumption tax hikes fell most heavily on people without economic security and on smaller companies that lack the global assets of their larger brethren.

Meanwhile, the continued fixation on Japan's fiscal position in isolation ignored an even more troubling fiscal legacy of the Abe years: continued stagnation in fixed capital formation. In a December 14, 2017 exchange with Martin Wolf in the pages of the *Financial Times,* Alexander Kinmont wrote that "In the presence of technical progress, the key to the evolution of the real wage rate is the volume of capital accumulation that is going on. In Japan, it has not been going on at all." In a recent presentation, Kinmont noted that the situation has not improved—and that was before COVID-19 set in. Yes, on the surface, Japan's fiscal position appears troubling—gross accumulated public debt is some 240 percent of GDP, the highest among its developed country peers, although this frequently cited number ignores the reality that Japan services this debt from its own people in a currency it controls. But Abe's fiscal legacy has not only worsened Japan's fiscal dilemma—without growth, inflation, or both, no solution to that dilemma—it even has supply-side implications. The ongoing stagnation in fixed capital formation could conceivably threaten Japan's heretofore formidable advantage in capital equipment and upstream components and materials.

For all the emptiness of the first arrow and the failure of the second, the third arrow did end up mattering, albeit not quite in the way it was advertised.

THE THREE ARROWS: #3, EASY MONEY

On assuming control of the *Kantei* for the second time late in 2012, Abe needed quick and tangible evidence that things were getting better. The LDP was facing an Upper House election in the summer of 2013 that would serve as a verdict on his performance to date, so he turned to the lever favored by governments everywhere seeking a sugar high to revive a stagnant economy: easy money. Abe forced the resignation of the sitting governor of the Bank of Japan (BOJ), Shirakawa Masaaki, and installed someone who would do what Abe wanted: open the monetary spigots all the way. By tradition, the governorship of the BOJ alternates between career BOJ men and senior MOF officials, and it was the MOF's turn. However, rather than acceding to the MOF's usual practice of sending someone from the Budget Bureau—historically the most powerful bureau in the most powerful of the ministries—Abe instead nominated a former vice minister from the international side, Kuroda Haruhiko.

On becoming BOJ governor, Kuroda promptly set about doing something that had long been advocated by prominent foreign economists (most notably, Paul Krugman) but resisted by the BOJ: set an inflation target and flood the economy with money until the target was reached. Impending inflation would surely cause companies and households to open their pocketbooks, buying what they needed today rather than waiting until tomorrow when prices were higher. Meanwhile, as inflation kicked in, at least nominal GDP would rise, thereby reducing Japan's cumulative fiscal debt as a percentage of GDP.

Some saw danger. In particular, they feared that investors in Japanese government bonds (JGB's) would demand higher interest rates in compensation for the damage that inflation would do to JGB valuations. Higher interest rates could not be squared with any resolution of Japan's fiscal dilemma. Richard Koo, for example, long known as an advocate for sustained deficit spending until self-sustaining economic growth has been achieved, feared that Kuroda's policies risked "the beginning of the end for the Japanese economy" since they "altered the market structure of the past two decades" that had allowed Japan to finance large government deficits.[14]

He need not have worried. Japan's government deficits continued to be easily financeable. Interest rates did not rise—but neither did inflation. It turned out that the BOJ's long-standing opposition to inflation targets was not just a matter of professional squeamishness—aren't central bankers supposed to be "sound money" advocates?—but rooted in real fears that no matter how much money was pumped into the economy, it wouldn't be enough to kick-start inflation.[15]

Indeed, Kuroda's easy money had no discernible effect on consumer prices, interest rates, or JGB's, but it was starkly visible in the foreign exchange and stock markets. The value of the yen dropped dramatically while the stock market took off. In the process, Abe got the boost he needed.

On the eve of the election that put Abe in power, the yen was scraping postwar highs—it took only 76 yen to buy one American dollar. The super strong currency may have been of enormous—and unanticipated—benefit to Japan in the wake of the 2011 earthquake-cum-tsunami that saw the country confronted with huge bills for imported energy (Japan's nuclear plants, all taken off-line in the wake of the disaster, had been supplying about one-third of the country's total energy requirements.), but it had become a crippling burden to large, established companies that depended for their profitability on exports made in Japan.

These companies were among Japan's largest employers; their executives and "salaryman" employees the core of Abe's political base. When the yen started promptly weakening as the BOJ opened the monetary spigots early in 2013 (by 2015, it would take 125 yen to buy a dollar), these firms saw their export profits recover, forming a perfect rationale to park the extra credit being created into the stock market. People may not have had that much more money to spend, but the rising stock market brought an aura of good feeling in its wake, a sense that—finally—Japan was turning an economic corner.

Abe used that sense to secure his hold on power with an LDP victory in the 2013 Upper House election, giving him the political space to do what he really wanted to do. (It was in the wake of that election that Abe stacked NHK, the state-owned television network, with rightist partisans and rammed the Official Secrets Act through the Diet, giving the government power to prosecute any and all whistleblowers.) Kuroda's easy money also gave Abe the political space to do what the MOF really wanted him to do: raise the consumption tax. While the hike, as noted above, promptly sent the economy into reverse, the continued easy money almost surely limited the damage. The yen started to strengthen again after 2015, but it has never since reached the crippling levels (crippling at least to establishment exporters) it had before Kuroda had taken charge at the BOJ. Indeed, by 2017, the yen had settled into something of a sweet spot—sufficiently weak to allow establishment exporters to continue to do business without wrenching purges of the thick layers of well-paid, paper-pushing "lifetime" employment jobs at head offices, but not so weak as to provoke retaliation from Japan's trading partners. (There had been some ominous rumbles from Washington and elsewhere when the yen soared in 2013.)

THE COVID-19 PANDEMIC AND ABE'S ECONOMIC LEGACY

I wrote above that assessing Abe's economic legacy requires a two- or even three-track approach: the usual economic criteria of GDP growth, corporate profitability, employment, and so forth; the criteria of what really seems to matter to him and his rightist allies: "making Japan great again;" and the criteria that power holders everywhere are loathe to acknowledge: their continued hold on the levers of decision-making.

On the eve of the pandemic, the best that could be said for Abe's economic legacy is that only by the third criteria—the re-enforcement of existing elite power—could it be called an unqualified success. Economic policy, most particularly easy money with the concomitant weakening of the yen and asset market inflation (real estate values as well as equities rose during the Abe years), helped create sufficient well-being that the continued stagnation in household income and the bifurcation of the labor force between those with secure, stable employment and the rest did not become a political problem.[16] The sluggish numbers for fixed domestic capital formation did not augur well for Japan's long-term economic future, but in the meantime, Japan's industrial plant remained sufficiently formidable to secure adequate living standards for all without requiring any politically significant disruption to existing power relations—whether threatening the continued control of the bureaucracy over taxes and government spending or the ability of established corporations to stymie the emergence of genuine markets in labor or corporate control. (There had been a lot of talk about the final arrival in Japan of empowered investors able to unseat complacent managements with the threat of hostile takeovers and thereby put to better use some of the vast, idle cash holdings sitting on the balance sheets of established corporations, but it remained talk.)

Abe seems to have expected that he could use the Tokyo Olympics scheduled for the summer of 2020 as a counter lever to the depressing effects of the consumption tax hikes that had been the MOF's price for acceding both to Abe's second ascension to the *Kantei* and for allowing him to stay there for the longest term in Japanese history. Surely, the Olympics would serve something of the same function that its 1964 predecessor had, stimulating the economy with infrastructure spending and floods of tourist revenues, all the while promoting surges of national good feeling, and with it, the "animal spirits" that Keynes had identified as the *sine qua non* of a booming economy. (Like most of the rest of the Japanese elite, Abe had never paid much attention to Keynes, much less absorbed his thinking, but on the importance of "animal spirits" at least he could agree.) Meanwhile, Abe had spearheaded a hugely successful drive to promote inbound tourism, in the process reversing what had long been a drain on Japan's external accounts. With hordes of Chinese and other Asians thronging the streets of Kyoto, the hot springs of Beppu, and the ski resorts of Hokkaido, Japan seemed on its way to becoming a kind of Italy of Asia, as least as far as tourism was concerned.

But then, of course, COVID-19 arrived. The Olympics had to be postponed until the summer of 2021—without spectators. Inbound tourism disappeared. Abe's dithering response to the pandemic—it appeared he was desperate to avoid postponing the Olympics—particularly in contrast to that of Tokyo's governor Koike Yuriko, proved a fatal blow to his heretofore Teflon-like reputation. It certainly removed any hope that the Olympics could compensate for the depressing effects of the tax hikes.

However, stepping back from the immediate aftermath, the Japanese economy doesn't seem to have done too badly, particularly in comparative perspective. As natural disasters always do, the pandemic turned a cold and unforgiving light on political and economic arrangements. In this case, precisely because it was a pandemic, those arrangements were judged and measured not only for what they revealed about specific sets of responses—to Chernobyl, Katrina, the 2011 earthquake-cum-tsunami—but in comparison with what was going on elsewhere. It was impossible for the Japanese public not to notice, for example, that whatever might be said about their own country's success in managing the pandemic, that of their heretofore model and supposed guarantor of their security, the United States, revealed a country edging toward political collapse, unable to carry out even the most basic functions of government: protecting people and property.

In that light, Japan managed to look pretty good. GDP shrank by 2.2 percent in the first quarter of 2020, but the number was due mostly to the effects of the consumption tax hike. Purchasing managers index (PMI) provided a better guide to the immediate effects of the pandemic, dropping sharply from March–May, but then beginning to climb again in June and July.[17] Household spending plummeted by 16.2 percent in May from the previous May, but the June year-to-year drop was only 1.2 percent. Second-quarter GDP numbers were admittedly terrible—an annualized drop of 27.8 percent—but not as awful as comparable numbers for Britain and the United States. With a stimulus package worth some 40 percent of GDP yet to be factored in, a solid case could be made that the economic nadir had been reached. Unemployment rose, but not to politically dangerous levels—there were no riots; companies kept "lifetime" employees on the payroll, and the loss of part-time work in entertainment sectors was partly compensated by an increased demand for delivery personnel. The government sent money to every household in Japan, saving some from destitution, all easily financeable. Japan seemed to have earned at least a B or B+ in coping with the short-term economic effects.

Abe couldn't claim credit for much of this other, perhaps, than in his efforts to preserve a status quo that turned out to function relatively well when tested by the pandemic, and in fostering a monetary regime that permitted rapid response to its immediate economic impact. The postponing and possible cancellation of the Olympics may have contributed to the ill-health that brought on his resignation and certainly ensured that he didn't leave office in a cloud of glory—but that's hardly his fault.

The pandemic contains some silver linings. It has helped tighten the labor market. While much of Japanese business clamors for an easing of the restrictions imposed on immigrant labor (much of this labor in the form of "trainees" from abroad), resistance to this pressure may well force business to offer higher wages and more economic security—measures that would in turn put more money in peoples' pockets and give them an incentive to spend it. The pandemic may have helped an ongoing overhaul of infrastructure spending away from white elephants and toward spending with real economic and social benefits, what Andrew de Wit in an article discussing Japan's COVID-19 countermeasures has labeled an "accelerating diffusion of all-hazard, disaster-resilient, policy integration."[18] (Abe can legitimately claim some credit for this.) The early weeks of the pandemic revealed how dependent Japan had become on supply chains based in China; business is responding by healthy diversification—both to other countries and by repatriating some facilities, which could help stimulate domestic demand. A sense is developing that a policy mix of a weak yen and shifting production to China has run its course; Jesper Koll goes so far as to write that "Japan has got what it takes to emerge a winner from the global 2020 great lockdown recession."[19]

Time will tell. The pandemic does show signs of taking its place next to the arrival of Commodore Perry, defeat in war, the collapse of the Bretton Woods system together with the quadrupling of energy prices, and the deflation of the "bubble economy" as one of those singular events in modern Japanese history that forced Japan's power holders to do what they had to do to save their country. Abe's reputation may benefit in retrospect from having been Japan's titular head of government at this time.

Despite his success in passing the Official Secrets Act, Abe failed to realize the hopes of his most fervent rightist supporters or the fears of his detractors. There was no confrontation with China or North Korea, Yasukuni remained unvisited until after the resignation had been announced, and plans for "patriotic" education were stalled in the wake of the Moritomo Gakuen scandal, a private rightist academy with ties to Abe and his wife. Meanwhile, progress toward addressing Japan's deepest-rooted economic problems—anemic domestic demand and fixed capital formation, a financial bureaucracy that is still too powerful and too obsessed with austerity, and a fearful, risk-averse established business elite that instinctively reacts to preserve privilege—was all too slow under Abe. However, there was some progress, perhaps accelerated by the pandemic, and that may be the best economic legacy that he or any prime minister could hope for.

NOTES

1. The covert aid systematically channeled to the LDP by the CIA in the 1950s and 1960s had been long suspected but was finally revealed in an article by *The New York Times* titled "CIA Spent Millions to Support the Japanese Right in the '50's and '60's" in 1994.

2. As Masahiro Kawai and Shinji Takagi noted, writing of structural changes in the Japanese economy in the first decade of the twenty-first century, "Vector autoregression analysis confirms that, as a result of these structural changes, Japanese output became much more responsive to output shocks in the advanced markets of the United States and Western Europe. The structural changes had two components. First, over 90% of Japan's exports consisted of highly income-elastic industrial supplies, capital goods, and consumer durables. Though emerging Asia is Japan's largest export market, its imports from Japan largely consist of intermediate goods used in the production of final goods destined for the US and Western Europe." See "Why was Japan Hit so Hard by the Global Financial Crisis?" ADBI Working Paper Series, No. 153, Asian Development Bank Institute, October 2009. Also, the term "balance sheet recession" coined by the economist Richard Koo refers to conditions in the wake of the collapse of a large-scale asset bubble such as that Japan experienced early in the 1990s. Koo's work represented a significant revision/modification of the Keynesian concept of a liquidity trap, specifically fingering the deterioration in corporate balance sheets as the proximate cause of the structural recession-cum-depression that follows the collapse of an asset bubble. See Richard Koo, *Balance Sheet Recession*, Wiley, 2003; and *The Holy Grail of Macroeconomics*, Wiley, 2009.

3. A comparison could be made to the decade-long rehabilitation of America's money-center banks after the so-called Latin debt crisis of the early 1980s had rendered most of them technically bankrupt. By keeping up the pretense that the loans made to countries such as Brazil and Argentina would ever be repaid—the face value of the loans exceeded the capital of virtually all the major banks—the banks avoided open declarations of bankruptcy.

4. See, among other things, chapter 10 from R. Taggart Murphy, *Japan and the Shackles of the Past*, Oxford, 2014.

5. See my discussion in R. Taggart Murphy, "Privilege Preserved," *The New Left Review*, Vol. 121 (January–February 2020). https://newleftreview.org/issues/ii121/articles/r-taggart-murphy-privilege-preserved.

6. This lack of influence was tacitly conceded by former MOF official Kashiwagi Shigeo in a 2018 article for the *Nikkei Asian Review* titled "The Government Alone Can't Save Japan's Economy," which he finishes by writing "Isn't it time to start asking whether the private sector is serious about structural reform and whether all citizens are ready to embrace reform for themselves?" Kashiwagi has, among other things, served as the Japan's executive director at the IMF.

7. According to Xing Yuqing, "about 45% of the value added of the iPhone X originated from Japan, Korean, and other economies" with Chinese firms claiming an additional 25% (Yuqing Xing, "How the iPhone Widens the US Trade Deficit with China: The Case of the iPhone X," National Graduate Institute for Policy Studies,

Tokyo, October 2019). Furthermore, Julie Johnsson, Andrea Rothman, and Chris Cooper wrote for *Bloomberg,* "Japanese companies designed and supplied 35 percent of the structure of the 787" in "ANA $16.6 Billion Shopping Spree Boosts 787 Dreamliner," March 28, 2014.

8. Ulrike Schaede, *The Business Reinvention of Japan: How to Make Sense of the New Japan and Why It Matters*, Stanford Business Books, 2020.

9. Jesper Koll, "Don't Bet Against Post-Pandemic Japan," *The Japan Times*, June 11, 2020.

10. I am grateful to the analyst Alexander Kinmont for these observations.

11. The predictions of economic damage from the tax hike were not limited to foreigners, such as Paul Krugman. See, for example, Shimazu, "安倍首相のレガシー、デフレ下で消費増税」となる日" [Prime Minister Abe's Legacy: "Raising the Consumption Tax during Deflation"], Reuters, November 11, 2019. Shimazu also contributed the opening chapter to a 2017 book on Abenomics in which he warned of the "悲惨な結果" (dire consequences) of raising the tax. See Chapter One of ザ (討論 [The Debate], edited by the 週刊エコノミスト編集部【編著】 [Weekly Economist Editorial Department], Mainichi Shinbunsha, 2017.

12. Murphy, "Privilege Preserved."

13. The economist Wakatabe Masazumi has written on why Keynesian ideas had so little resonance in Japan's elite circles. Wakatabe contends that at least the earlier generation of elite policy makers were trained by Marxian professors who saw Keynes as something of a reactionary figure attempting to prolong unnaturally capitalism's life. See Masazumi Wakatabe, "Structural Reform in Japan: An Intellectual History," *Industrial Policy of Japan,* edited by Komira Ryutaro, Okuno Masahiro, and Suzumurai Kotaro. San Diego: Academic Press, 1988. The Japanese original was published in 1984 by Toyo Keizai Shimposha. Wakatabe is currently a deputy governor of the Bank of Japan.

14. Quoted in Ambrose Evans-Pritchard, "The Bank of Japan Must Crush All Resistance," *The Telegraph*, May 24, 2013.

15. The reasons lie not simply in the excess capacity that has plagued much of the economy since the collapse of the late 1980s bubble, but also in the peculiar ways in which Japanese financial institutions create credit. See R. Taggart Murphy, "Rethinking Japan's Deflation Trap: On the Failure to Reach Kuroda Haruhiko's 2% Inflation Target," *The Asia-Pacific Journal: Japan Focus*, Vol. 14, Issue 3, No. 4, February 1, 2016. https://apjjf.org/2016/03/Murphy.html.

16. See Andrew Gordon's detailed discussion of the bifurcation of the labor force and rise of "non-regular employment" in "New and Enduring Dual Structures of Employment in Japan: The Rise of Non-Regular Labor, 1980s–2010s," *Social Science Japan Journal*, Vol. 20, No. 1 (2017).

17. See Trading Economics, "Japan Manufacturing PMI," https://tradingeconomics.com/japan/manufacturing-pmi.

18. Andrew de Wit, "Japan's Integration of All-Hazard Resilience and Covid-19 Countermeasures," *The Asia Pacific Journal: Japan Focus,* Vol. 14, Issue 3, No. 2, May 25, 2020. https://apjjf.org/2020/11/DeWit.html.

19. Koll, "Don't Bet Against Post-Pandemic Japan."

REFERENCES

de Wit, Andrew. "Japan's Integration of All-Hazard Resilience and Covid-19 Countermeasures." *The Asia Pacific Journal: Japan Focus,* Vol. 14, Issue 3, No. 2, May 25, 2020. https://apjjf.org/2020/11/DeWit.html.

Evans-Pritchard, Ambrose. "The Bank of Japan Must Crush All Resistance." *The Telegraph,* May 24, 2013.

Gordon, Andrew. "New and Enduring Dual Structures of Employment in Japan: The Rise of Non-Regular Labor, 1980s -2010s." *Social Science Japan Journal,* Vol. 20, No. 1 (2017).

Johnsson, Julie, Andrea Rothman, and Chris Cooper. "ANA $16.6 Billion Shopping Spree Boosts 787 Dreamliner." *Bloomberg,* March 28, 2014.

Kashiwagi, Shigeo. "The Government Alone Can't Save Japan's Economy." *Nikkei Asian Review,* January 18, 2018.

Kawai, Masahiro and Shinji Takagi. "Why was Japan Hit so Hard by the Global Financial Crisis?" ADBI Working Paper Series, No. 153, Asian Development Bank Institute, October 2009.

Koll, Jesper. "Don't Bet Against Post-Pandemic Japan." *The Japan Times,* June 11, 2020.

Koo, Richard. *Balance Sheet Recession.* Wiley, 2003.

Koo, Richard. *The Holy Grail of Macroeconomics.* Wiley, 2009.

Murphy, R. Taggart. *Japan and the Shackles of the Past.* Oxford, 2014.

Murphy, R. Taggart. "Privilege Preserved." *The New Left Review,* Vol. 121 (January–February 2020). https://newleftreview.org/issues/ii121/articles/r-taggart-murphy-privilege-preserved.

Murphy, R. Taggart. "Rethinking Japan's Deflation Trap: On the Failure to Reach Kuroda Haruhiko's 2% Inflation Target." *The Asia-Pacific Journal: Japan Focus,* Vol. 14, Issue 3, No. 4, February 1, 2016. https://apjjf.org/2016/03/Murphy.html.

Schaede, Ulrike. *The Business Reinvention of Japan: How to Make Sense of the New Japan and Why It Matters.* Stanford Business Books, 2020.

Shimazu, Hiroki. "安倍首相のレガシー、「デフレ下で消費増税」となる日" [Prime Minister Abe's Legacy: "Raising the Consumption Tax during Deflation"]. Reuters, November 11, 2019.

Shimazu, Hiroki. Chapter One in ザ (討論 [The Debate]. Edited by the 週刊エコノミスト編集部【編著】 [Weekly Economist Editorial Department]. Mainichi Shinbunsha, 2017.

Wakatabe, Masazumi. "Structural Reform in Japan: An Intellectual History." In *Industrial Policy of Japan,* edited by Komira Ryutaro, Okuno Masahiro, and Suzumurai Kotaro. San Diego: Academic Press, 1988.

Trading Economics. "Japan Manufacturing PMI." https://tradingeconomics.com/japan/manufacturing-pmi.

Weiner, Tim. "CIA Spent Millions to Support the Japanese Right in the '50's and '60's." *The New York Times,* October 9, 1994. https://www.nytimes.com/1994/10/09/world/cia-spent-millions-to-support-japanese-right-in-50-s-and-60-s.html.

Xing, Yuqing. "How the iPhone Widens the US Trade Deficit with China: The Case of the iPhone X." National Graduate Institute for Policy Studies, Tokyo, October 2019.

Chapter 3

Pandemic Downsizes PM Abe Shinzō

Jeff Kingston

The COVID-19 outbreak diminished the domestic political stature of Prime Minister Abe Shinzō, by exposing his flawed leadership qualities, and cast a cloud over the legacy of Japan's longest serving premier. Abe's sudden resignation on August 28, 2020 due to ill health was collateral damage of the coronavirus outbreak that scuttled his Olympic dream, erased all of the GDP growth recorded during his tenure and derailed his plans for constitutional revision. Although Japan fared relatively well, the public was unforgiving of Abe's weak leadership in managing the COVID-19 outbreak in Japan.

NO CREDIT FOR LOW MORTALITY

Japan suffered some 1,650 deaths as of mid-October 2020 from the pandemic, a relatively low death toll, but Abe did not benefit politically because very few people credit him for this outcome. Typically, various other factors are invoked to help explain Japan's low mortality. Early on, perhaps not trusting the government to take the lead, the public adopted sensible precautions and stuck with the program, wearing masks to impede transmission, staying home, and observing social distancing. Moreover, levels of personal hygiene are high in Japan, with relatively few people having the habit of handshaking, hugging, or kissing. Some also argue that the Japanese language itself is a barrier to transmission because the way it is spoken supposedly doesn't project droplets. This linguistic explanation, however, overlooks the high death toll a century ago during the Spanish flu, when over 400,000 Japanese died. And then there is Deputy PM Asō Tarō's suggestion that Japan's low mortality rate is due to the inherent superiority of the Japanese people (*mindo*), an assertion that drew widespread ridicule from his compatriots.[1]

In every domestic public opinion poll, a significant majority criticized Abe's handling of the outbreak and this collective disappointment gained momentum from April 2020. An international poll conducted in twenty-three countries and regions in April ranked Japan's pandemic response dead last with a support rate of just 5 percent for Japan's political leaders.[2] A subsequent poll of domestic opinion in Japan, the United States, United Kingdom, Sweden, and Germany revealed that the Japanese public expressed the lowest public trust in their government's pandemic response.[3] Abe's woes continued to mount during the second wave of the outbreak after the national emergency was lifted in late May and the central government promoted an easing of constraints in an effort to boost the economy. A June Mainichi poll found that 36 percent supported Abe while 56 percent did not, with 26 percent positively evaluating his response to the novel coronavirus outbreak and 51 percent critical of his crisis management.[4] By July, only 17 percent thought highly of Abe's pandemic response while 60 percent did not.[5] On August 11, 2020, NHK reported that in its latest public opinion poll Abe's support rate fell to 34 percent, the lowest since he returned to power in 2012, while his negative rating rose to 47 percent.

DITHERING ABE

Why has the public judged Abe so harshly? Back in early February, when the Diamond Princess cruise ship was transformed into a coronavirus incubator due to botched quarantine procedures, Japan experienced a wake-up call.[6] Setting the tone for subsequent developments, Abe did not provide any crisis leadership and failed to establish a "control tower" as bureaucratic silos impeded a coordinated response.[7] He was also slammed on social media for being missing in action and shirking responsibility, as he kept a low profile during the crisis.[8]

The image of a decisive and competent leader nurtured since Abe returned to power in 2012 evaporated as his aptitude for crisis management came under withering scrutiny. The lessons learned from the Fukushima nuclear disaster were ignored, and Abe's crisis leadership has been judged wanting in comparison with former prime minister Kan Naoto (2010–2011), who Abe disparaged for his handling of the 2011 natural and nuclear disasters.[9]

Abe faced intense criticism over his abrupt decision on February 28 to close schools.[10] His announcement appeared to be an effort to show he was on top of the situation, but it emerged that he did so without consulting health experts or his education minister, making it look more like a PR stunt than a thoughtful public health initiative.[11] Abe's blithe disregard for the consequences of this improvised policy reinforced public perceptions that he is out of touch with common concerns. Parents had only seventy-two hours to sort out child care, generating a backlash reported widely in the media. It turned out that the "solution" to Abe's childcare problem involved many women taking leave from work or quitting their jobs. The increases in women's employment during Abe's tenure have been concentrated in nonregular jobs where pay, benefits, job security, and career growth are much less than for employees with regular, full-time jobs, so this policy served to further debunk any claims about the success of Abe's "womenomics" initiative.[12]

The Abe government also came under fire for limiting COVID-19 testing and downplaying the crisis in a desperate but abortive effort to save the Tokyo 2020 Olympics and a planned summit with Chinese President Xi Jinping.[13] This limited testing left the government shooting in the dark in trying to contain the outbreak while Abe's preoccupation with saving the Olympics slowed the government's response to the pandemic.

On April 7, nearly one month after most other countries around the world had already done so, Abe belatedly declared a national emergency in seven prefectures, and on April 16, extended it nationwide in the face of public pleas from prefectural governors and public opinion polls indicating broad dissatisfaction with his handling of the coronavirus outbreak. A mid-April poll found that 80 percent believed that Abe waited too long to declare a state of emergency, and his support rate dropped by 10 percentage points from early March to 40 percent.[14] A majority of Japanese became critical of Abe's crisis management, and in an April Mainichi poll, 70 percent thought that he waited too long to declare an emergency, losing precious time to manage the outbreak.[15] In the Asahi poll from April 18–19, 57 percent said Abe failed to provide leadership during the outbreak and 77 percent believed he should have declared a national emergency sooner.[16] Clearly, Abe's indecisiveness and shirking of his duties had a negative impact on public perceptions of his leadership qualities.

TESTING CONTROVERSIES AND THE JAPAN MODEL

On April 1st, a week before Abe declared a national emergency, the Japan Medical Association (JMA) declared a medical system crisis.[17] Health experts called for increased testing, noting that as of mid-April, Japan had conducted only 130,000 tests compared to 520,000 tests in South Korea, a nation with less than half the population.[18] Yet by mid-April, the number of people testing positive for the coronavirus in Japan exceeded the total in S. Korea, and Japan also recorded more deaths.[19] At that point, nobody was talking up the "Japan Model."

Nobel laureate Yamanaka Shinya, director of the Center for iPS Stem Cell Research Application at Kyoto University, warned that Tokyo's positive rate had become "very high" and called for more testing so that policymakers could better understand the scale of the outbreak before it overwhelmed the healthcare system.[20] Yokokura Yoshitake, the JMA president, also criticized the government's limited testing approach, focusing on clusters, asserting that by mid-March, "That policy should have been changed when more than half of the patients were those whose route of infection could not be traced."[21] Yokokura also acknowledged that the criteria for judging whether to test an individual were overly restrictive. One guideline required individuals with a fever of more than 37.5 degrees to stay at home for four days before administering a coronavirus test, unnecessarily risking community transmission.

Azby Brown, a lead researcher for Safecast, a citizen-science organization, notes that the government belatedly tried to make the case for limited testing in terms of not overwhelming hospitals and testing centers with the "worried well."[22] Some health professionals defend the cluster-based approach, arguing that it was pragmatic and effective by focusing on super-spreaders,[23] but as Brown notes, prominent epidemiologists remain quite critical of this limited testing approach. Moreover, by putting the understaffed National Institute for Infectious Diseases (NIID) in charge of producing PCR (polymerase chain reaction) test kits for diagnosing coronavirus infections, the government created a supply bottleneck and was slow to partner with private industry to expand testing capacity.[24] Thus, limited testing resulted from limited testing capacity.

As the number of infections surged in late July, Abe's crowing about the "Japan Model" in May came back to haunt him.[25] He is not the first leader to jump the gun on declaring mission accomplished, but Abe's extravagant claims about the "Japan Model" confronted a resurgence of infections in the summer of 2020. It seemed that Abe was overly keen to restart the economy and lifted the state of emergency too soon, conveying an unwarranted complacency about the pandemic. At the time of writing, much remains unknown about COVID-19, but it does seem certain that it will wax, wane, and linger longer than initially anticipated and that a rush to normalize is risky.

While Abe ruled out re-imposing a state of emergency in response to the second wave, Okinawan Governor Tamaki Denny decided to do so in July as his prefecture had the highest number of cases in the nation per 100,000 population, and the healthcare system was stretched to the limit.[26] The situation there was complicated by clusters of infections among U.S. military personnel. The number of reported cases among U.S. forces stationed there reached 143 by mid-July amid reports of lax enforcement of quarantine-on-arrival containment measures. This development reinforced anti-U.S. base sentiments and highlighted the lack of transparency that shrouds the U.S.

military presence in Okinawa.[27] U.S. forces are exempt from Japanese immigration regulations that banned travel from the United States, the global epicenter of the pandemic. The U.S. Department of Defense established a policy of non-disclosure for COVID-19 infected military personnel out of concern that it might compromise operations, but after the media reported about clusters of infections on U.S. bases in Okinawa, the commander of U.S. Forces in Japan granted Governor Tamaki special permission to disclose details of the outbreak. The United States also pledged to expand testing, strictly enforce quarantine protocols, and provide timely information to the Japanese government about infections. This sensible damage control underscored how insulated the U.S. military has been from local accountability, a lack of transparency that has fed rumor-mongering and bred resentment. Given Abe's strong support for expanding the U.S. military presence in Okinawa, despite public sentiments opposing the construction of a new base there, his image suffered further from the prefecture's coronavirus controversies.

OWN GOALS

There have been a series of own goals, including policy flip flops and poorly thought out initiatives that stoked public perceptions that Abe was not on top of the coronavirus situation. He was widely mocked over his pricey but inadequate policy of distributing two masks to every household, called "*Abenomasku*," that drew on public dissatisfaction with the sputtering range of policies called Abenomics.[28] This meager gesture costing taxpayers US$247 million was announced soon after NHK, Japan's public broadcaster, aired a documentary that showed how Taiwan distributes masks far more efficiently and has outperformed Abe's crisis response across the board.[29] Adding to the hapless messaging, there were massive recalls of Abe's masks after numerous complaints about mold, insects, eyelashes, and other signs of contamination. Abe's wife didn't help matters when she attended a cherry blossom viewing party while everyone else was told to stay home. Abe continued to dig himself a deeper hole when he tweeted a video of him coping with the lockdown by cuddling his dog, sipping tea, and channel surfing, provoking a torrent of criticism zinging his failure to lead and his apparent cluelessness about public anxieties and deprivations.[30] It was further damaging that his most popular policy response, blanket direct payments of 100,000 yen to everyone, took much longer than expected to come through.[31] While this was due to red tape beyond his control, his image took a beating when it emerged that ad giant Dentsu's subsidiary landed a massive 76.9 billion yen (US$ 700 million) contract to distribute aid to small- and medium-sized businesses amid allegations of inflated administrative costs.[32] The subsidiary then immediately subcontracted the project to Dentsu, pocketing 2 billion yen for its middle-man role. This was the largest outsourcing contract awarded by the government for COVID-19 countermeasures.[33] The Abe government's close ties with Dentsu are longstanding, thus media reports that the firm had an inside track on the SME bid appeared to fit a larger pattern of cronyism under Abe.[34] The constant stream of scandals implicating Abe in cronyism, cover-ups, corruption, and data tampering over the past few years have further eroded trust in him, especially the vote buying allegations involving his former Justice Minister Kawai Katsuyuki.[35] Abe also provoked strong criticism in 2020 for nominating a candidate to head the Tokyo Prosecutor's Office in violation of the mandatory age limit, and then trying to retroactively change the law to make this appointment legal. This blatant manipulation proved an embarrassing and damaging episode that ended when the media reported that the appointed prosecutor engaged in illegal gambling, causing him to resign.[36] Additionally, the 2017 Moritomo Gakuen scandal involving a dubious land deal implicating Abe roared back to life in 2020 when the wife of a Finance Ministry official released her husband's suicide note citing pressures to cover-up the wrongdoing of his superior.[37]

It appears that Abe prioritized reviving the economy over public health and treated the pandemic crisis more like a public relations challenge than a severe risk to the people. His inner circle of advisors on managing the pandemic were all elderly politicians who viewed the crisis through the prism of political implications rather than the science of epidemiology, a major contrast to President Tsai Ing-wen's crisis team in Taiwan.[38] At the end of June, Abe abruptly disbanded his Experts Group of scientific advisors in favor of a panel of celebrity scientists and others lacking a background in epidemiology. Apparently, the original Experts Group made awkward policy suggestions at odds with the prime minister's political agenda, recommending against, for example, easing constraints on business operations. With the economy tanking, Abe wanted to boost business activity while the Experts Group was warning of the risks of doing so. Yet again, Abe seemed complacent about mitigating public health risks. He also drew criticism over his strong arming of the bureaucracy to approve the domestically produced drug Avigan for treating COVID-19,[39] especially after the results of initial clinical trials proved disappointing.[40]

BRINK OF THE BRINK

Media reports warned that by mid-April, Japan's healthcare system was on the verge of collapse.[41] The governor of Osaka pleaded for the public to donate raincoats because doctors, facing acute supply shortages of personal protective equipment (PPE), had resorted to wearing trash bags as protective gear in dealing with COVID-19 patients,[42] and in response, the local Hanshin Tigers baseball team donated 4,000 ponchos. Perhaps not ideal, but it was still more than the central government had managed. Furthermore, at Tokyo's international gateway Narita Airport, after incoming travelers were tested, many were forced to stay quarantined in cardboard boxes for days before they got the results.[43]

Raincoats and cardboard boxes? This is not the meticulously prepared Japan most imagine. Cardboard boxes bring to mind the displacement centers in Tohoku back in March 2011, when people who had lost everything in the domino sequence of the earthquake, tsunami, and nuclear disaster created cardboard box villages to reestablish a semblance of order and community. At the time it seemed an inspiring sign of pluck and resilience, but in 2020, welcoming mostly Japanese returning from overseas to cardboard boxes wasn't nearly as uplifting. In contrast, travelers arriving in Hong Kong airport at the time were brought to a massive hangar quarantine facility, tested, and given their results within eight hours. If negative, they were released with an electronic tracking bracelet and told to remain at home for two weeks.

Many other nations also had PPE shortages, but the plea for raincoats was shocking given that Osaka Prefecture at the time had only 900 COVID-19 cases. How could that number overwhelm the healthcare system of the nation's third largest metropolis in a prefecture of 9 million residents? It turns out this was a problem shared nationwide, as hospitals in forty-three out of Japan's forty-seven prefectures reported running out of coronavirus-care capacity. The fact that Japan has a mere half of the intensive care unit (ICU) beds per 100,000 people as Spain does, while Germany has six times more and the United States seven times more, underlines the gravity of the problem.[44] Although the nightmare scenario of a swamped healthcare system did not materialize, projections for a shortage of ICU beds added to public anxieties.[45] Ignoring early warning signs, the government failed to prepare adequately, leaving frontline healthcare workers to face great personal risk as they scrambled to cope with an escalating outbreak.[46] In terms of public safety, a priority for any leader, Abe didn't mobilize with any sense of urgency. His complacency set the tone for the government's tardy response and poor preparations.

Finally, in declaring a nationwide state of emergency in April, Abe acknowledged the severity of Japan's healthcare crisis.[47] Compared to resolute regional leaders in the democracies of Taiwan, South Korea, New Zealand, and Australia, Abe dithered and failed the COVID-19 leadership stress test. Part of the problem was uncharacteristically poor messaging by Team Abe.

COMMUNICATING 101

In the government's crisis response, Abe lurked on the sidelines to the extent that in February the media accused him of being "missing in action."[48] After polls showed declining support, Abe tried to overcome negative perceptions but struggled to do so in part because he is a stiff and awkward communicator. Abe may be the Teflon premier, shrugging off numerous scandals that would have red-carded any other leader and bouncing back from imploding support rates, but 2020 was his *annus horribilis*.

In the face of Abe's shortcomings and blunders in responding to COVID-19, Tokyo Governor Koike Yuriko showed the Japanese public what a leader looks like.[49] Her frequent press conferences and no-nonsense style was well received by a public in desperate need of such clear-cut information. She tapped the mass media, social media, and YouTube to get her message out in Japanese and English while disseminating sensible advice about social distancing. She also funded a publicly accessible website to track and update relevant data in several languages on the coronavirus outbreak. By engaging the public, she earned their trust and support, winning reelection in July by a landslide. Her prominent position as head of a megapolis of nearly 14 million residents, together with national media attention, spread her message across the archipelago at a crucial time when cases and anxieties were rising. Abe's few press conferences were carefully stage managed and he could not match her media presence. Koike's experience from her time as a newscaster on television showed she understood both traditional media and social media in ways that Abe clearly does not.

The five-day Golden Week holidays began on May 2, but without the usual frenetic rush to the exits and transport overload. After a concerted campaign to get people to stay home and refrain from travel during the holidays, trains and planes were left empty, the streets eerily quiet. This self-restraint was exactly what was needed to curb transmission and showed that political leaders could cajole public compliance. Abe took his cue from Koike, and in the run-up to the Golden Week exodus, frequently reinforced her message to stay home. Earlier in April, the two leaders had been at odds as Koike lobbied for tougher shutdown measures while Abe fought a losing battle on behalf of business as usual. This contest made Abe look weak and beholden, while Koike looked resolute in supporting the public interest. There is much debate about the tradeoff between public health and economic distress, but in taking the high ground of public health, Koike emerged in the eyes of many as the people's champion, while Abe appeared somewhat craven.

Moreover, at a time when the public sought clarity, Abe sent a mixed message, stressing the need for social distancing to lessen transmission but in the same breath endorsing business re-openings, all while offering a stimulus package that left many disappointed and others forgotten.[50] His woes continued in the summer with an epic own goal.

"GO TO" TRAVEL CAMPAIGN BACKFIRES

With great fanfare, the government announced a roughly $16 billion (the budget provided for 1.35–2.7 trillion yen depending on popularity) travel subsidy campaign to provide relief to the battered tourism sector and to give families a summer break from the ennui of lockdown by paying up to half of travel and accommodation charges.[51] But as infections in Tokyo surged in July, some prefectural governors raised concerns about the heightened risk of transmission, and in the end, the government decided to exclude Tokyo residents without making preparations to cover cancellation charges.[52] Withdrawing the tax-funded holiday for Tokyoites triggered resentment and made the government look incompetent and ill-prepared. Furthermore, the planned stimulus for sectors battered by the pandemic was significantly curtailed as trips to Tokyo were declared ineligible while the capital's 14 million residents were told to stay at home. The "Don't Go" blowback was considerable, adding to public frustrations with Abe's overall handling of the pandemic.[53]

ABE REDUX

If leadership means taking charge in tackling critical challenges and making sure others are doing their jobs and taking responsibility for problems that arise, this is not the first time that the Japanese public has found Abe out of his depth. Back in September 2007, Abe resigned as prime minister, ostensibly due to ill health, but more likely because he was deeply unpopular and was essentially ousted from power by party elders after less than a year in office after leading the Liberal Democratic Party (LDP) to a thumping defeat in the July Upper House elections.[54] In response to reports about lost pension records before those elections, Abe remained nonchalant and downplayed the significance of the situation, doing little to assuage public anxieties. He paid the price at the polls for his lack of compassion or concern over the issue, which affected perceptions about his qualities as a leader. There was no serious backlash to his patriotic education initiative nor his controversial comments quibbling about the degree of coercion involved in recruiting "comfort women" (women and girls forced to provide sexual services to Japanese Imperial Army troops prior and during World War II), but his preoccupation with ideological issues such as constitutional revision seemed to overshadow his concern with public welfare and conveyed the impression he was out of touch about popular concerns. This was why he earned the derogatory nickname KY (*kuuki yomenai*), meaning someone who is unable to read the situation or, more bluntly, clueless. Given his blueblood political background—his grandfather was PM Kishi Nobusuke (1957–1960), his father was foreign minister, and PM Sato Eisaku (1964–1972) was his great uncle—Abe is also known as an *obochan*, a protected and privileged scion who knows little about harsh realities.

Abe's empathy deficit remains problematic. *Hibakusha* (atomic bomb survivors) complained to the press in 2020 that he brushed off their concerns and only went through the motions at the annual commemoration rites held in Hiroshima and Nagasaki, giving virtually the same speech at both ceremonies.[55]

LEGACIES?

According to Tobias Harris, who published a biography of Abe on the eve of his resignation, he has little to show for being Japan's longest serving prime minister and failed to deliver on most of his promises.[56] His signature policies on constitutional revision, security, secrecy, transparency, nuclear reactor restarts, arms exports, militarizing ODA, and labor deregulation were unpopular, while his "womenomics" ended in shambles along with Abenomics. There was no progress on territorial disputes with Russia, China, or South Korea, and he was marginalized from diplomatic initiatives with North Korea.

It is rather pitiable that Abe's shrinking legacy was seen by some to hinge on holding the Olympics.[57] The 2020 Tokyo Olympics were supposed to be Abe's crowning moment, a feel-good send-off, but COVID-19 laid waste to that scenario. Abe intervened personally in 2013 to secure Japan's bid for the Tokyo 2020 Summer Olympics, and the nation spent as much as $28 billion to prepare for the global spectacle in the hopes that the nation would have an opportunity to showcase its numerous strengths.[58] But in March 2020, due to the pandemic, Tokyo 2020 was postponed until 2021.[59] The government hoped to stage simplified games, but the Japanese public overwhelmingly favored cancellation.[60]

Knowing that the pandemic would influence how he is remembered, Abe proactively tried to shape his legacy. Leaders around the world are often prickly about criticism, but Abe fought back. Buried in the government's coronavirus stimulus package was US$22 million to fund AI monitoring of Abe's overseas critics so that the Ministry of Foreign Affairs could correct any "misunderstandings."[61] The Japanese Embassy in the United States also signed hefty contracts in 2020 with Seven Letter and Ogilvy, Washington,

D.C.-based public relations firms, to promote a positive spin on the Abe government's pandemic response. According to Mindy Kotler of Asia Policy Point, the goal is to influence the Japanese public's perceptions by generating a positive buzz in the U.S. media that will filter back to Japan.[62] Allocating taxpayer money to counter criticism is indicative of a government that handled COVID-19 more as a PR challenge than a profound public health crisis.[63]

There are lessons to be learned. While the pandemic may not have claimed as many lives in Japan as in other countries, PM Abe still successfully dug himself a deep hole by demonstrating poor crisis management and woeful messaging, appearing out of touch and erratic. It began with his AWOL February, and he never recovered. Japan is accustomed to disasters, and the public has very high expectations of leaders to manage them well. PM Murayama Tomiichi lost public support due to his woeful response to the twin disasters in 1995—the Kobe earthquake and the Aum Shinrikyo sarin gas terror attack. PM Kan Naoto arguably provided strong leadership in responding to the 2011 earthquake and tsunami, drawing on the lessons of Kobe, but stonewalling and scapegoating by the LDP and bureaucracy forced his ouster.[64] Abe's problems were self-inflicted, due to a toxic combination of arrogance, complacency, and insouciance that alienated the media and public. He seemed the shirker-in-chief and paid the price as public support cratered even as Japan suffered far less from the pandemic than other G7 nations. In responding to natural disasters, Japan's future leaders should know that the appearance of leadership matters very much, and the public is unforgiving of waffling and policy flip flops and expects transparency, a major issue for Abe in general. No minutes were disclosed for crucial COVID-19 countermeasures meetings, and he has been involved in cases of falsifying data, document shredding, and tampering. Institutionally, there seems a consensus that Japan needs something like the U.S. Center for Disease Control and that it needs to beef up ICU capacity. If just 900 cases can overwhelm Osaka, what might happen if the long anticipated Nankai Trough mega-quake strikes? The somewhat low-key approach to COVID-19 may have been due to the limited impact of SARS in 2003 and avian flu in 2007, but the 2020 coronavirus outbreak provides powerful reasons why this complacency should be abandoned going forward. Each disaster provides important lessons that Japanese people and institutions ignore at their peril, but the perennial problem of bureaucratic sectionalism is likely to persist and hamper disaster responses.

Back in 2013, Abe's three arrows and Abenomics entered the global lexicon, a promise of bold and decisive action to revive the economy and offer a vision of hope. That has not panned out. On Abe's watch, the public debt to GDP ratio surged to a whopping 266 percent and he left office with Japan's GDP at roughly the same level as it was when he started. Severe economic contraction carries stark implications for a recovery in consumer spending, government tax revenues, and public debt servicing.[65]

The Japanese economy was already in trouble before the pandemic due to Abe's ill-advised sales tax hike in 2019 that slashed fourth quarter growth by 7.3 percent, and Abenomics now seems little more than an exercise in branding than a coherent set of policy measures. But as Abenomics unravels, leaving a massive public debt in its wake and households disappointed by its limited benefits, reviving consumption is key. This will require unconventional policies. William Pesek suggests revoking the last two sales tax hikes, distributing debit cards to the public rather than cash, and having the Bank of Japan buy up local debt from prefectures and municipalities so they can borrow more to finance revitalization projects.[66] The BOJ could also fund a temporary basic income policy and do more to boost regional banks and small- and medium-sized firms to reverse the downward spiral. Such policies require bold and decisive action by a resolute leader, but Abe was not up to the task. Alas, he has inspired little confidence as in every NHK poll since 2013, only about 15 percent of the public admired his leadership qualities or his policies. Of those who supported Abe, typically 50 percent did so because they don't see a viable alternative.

Abe's counterparts in South Korea and Taiwan gained strength due to a competent handling of the coronavirus crisis in their nations, while Abe was diminished by the pandemic. South Korean President Moon won a landslide victory in the April parliamentary elections on the strength of his pandemic response.[67] Taiwan's President Tsai Ing-wen also won a landslide victory in January 2020 on the eve of Beijing's announcement about the Wuhan outbreak and has presided over a very effective pandemic containment strategy. In contrast, over the summer of 2020 there was mounting speculation about Abe's future. He looked like yesterday's man, haggard and listless, while ducking the media and Diet as much as possible.[68] His Holy Grail of revising the constitution was derailed by public opposition to this agenda, distrust of Abe even among supporters of this quest, and a pandemic that dominated Japan's political bandwidth. Due to ill health, facing a cascade of scandals and a daunting set of challenges, Abe handed the poisoned chalice to his Chief Cabinet Secretary Suga Yoshihide. Certainly, the pandemic downsized Abe, but even before that he had achieved far less than promised, and risks being remembered for achieving little despite enjoying considerable longevity in political power.

NOTES

1. *Shimbun Asahi*, "Aso: low virus death rate thanks to Japanese superiority," June 5, 2020. http://www.asahi.com/ajw/articles/13432875.

2. *Jiji Kyōdō*, "Abe administration bombs in global survey on coronavirus response," *Japan Times*, May 9, 2020. https://www.japantimes.co.jp/news/2020/05/09/national/abe-coronavirus-survey/.

3. Kasahara Shin, "Survey: Japanese less trusting of government in health crisis," *Asahi*, May 13, 2020. http://www.asahi.com/ajw/articles/13370715.

4. *Mainichi Shimbun*, "Majority say Abe bears responsibility over legislators' vote-buying scandal: Mainichi poll," June 22, 2020.

5. *Mainichi Shimbun*, "Q&A for July 2020 Mainichi poll on Abe Cabinet support, Japan's coronavirus response," July 24, 2020.

6. Jeff Kingston, "Japan's response to the coronavirus is a slow-motion train wreck," *The Washington Post*, February 22, 2020.

7. Murakami Hiromi, "A Japan divided over COVID-19 control," East Asia Forum, March 8, 2020. https://www.eastasiaforum.org/2020/03/08/a-japan-divided-over-covid-19-control/.

8. Linda Seig, "Where's Abe? Critics ask as coronavirus spreads in Japan," Reuters, February 25, 2020. https://www.reuters.com/article/us-china-health-japan-abe-idUSKCN20J16F.

9. Corey Wallace, "Abe departs from his own winning formula in battling COVID-19," Australia Institute for International Affairs, March 5, 2020.

10. Murata Atsushi, "70% of Japanese parents feel troubled by school closures," *Nikkei Asian Review*, March 14, 2020.

11. *Shimbun Asahi*, "Abe: No experts were consulted for my decision to close schools," March 3, 2020. http://www.asahi.com/ajw/articles/13182509.

12. *Jiji Kyōdō*, "Japan's single mothers and female workers hard hit by coronavirus," *Japan Times*, July 3, 2020. https://www.japantimes.co.jp/news/2020/07/03/national/social-issues/japan-single-mothers-female-workers-coronavirus/.

13. Jeff Kingston, "Goodbye, Tokyo 2020. It's time to start hoping for 2021," *The Washington Post*, March 22, 2020. https://www.washingtonpost.com/opinions/2020/03/21/goodbye-tokyo-2020-its-time-start-hoping-2021/.

14. *Jiji Kyōdō, Kyodo News*, "82% say government should compensate firms that shutdown for virus," April 13, 2020. https://english.kyodonews.net/news/2020/04/eea437e79b17-urgent-public-dissatisfied-with-abes-response-to-virus-outbreak-kyodo-poll.html.

15. *Mainichi Shimbun*, "Majority in Japan don't approve Abe govt's coronavirus response: Mainichi poll," April 20, 2020. https://mainichi.jp/english/articles/20200420/p2a/00m/0na/016000c.

16. *Shimbun Asahi*, "Survey: 57% say Abe not showing leadership in COVID-19 crisis," April 21, 2020. www.asahi.com/ajw/articles/13315219.

17. Takenouchi Takahiro, "Without vaccine for coronavirus, Tokyo Olympics in 2021 in doubt," *Asahi*, April 25, 2020. http://www.asahi.com/ajw/articles/13327110.

18. *Jiji Kyōdō*, "Experts in Japan call for more coronavirus tests as positive rate rises," *Japan Times*, April 23, 2020. https://www.japantimes.co.jp/news/2020/04/23/national/japan-coronavirus-tests-positive-rate-rises/#.XqT0kJMzab8.

19. *NHK World*, "Japan passes South Korea for coronavirus cases," April 23, 2020. https://www3.nhk.or.jp/nhkworld/en/news/backstories/1048/.

20. Obe Mitsuru and Ando Kiyoshi, "Nobel laureate Yamanaka frets over Japan's lax coronavirus fight," *Nikkei Asian Review*, April 19, 2020. https://asia.nikkei.com/Editor-s-Picks/Interview/Nobel-laureate-Yamanaka-frets-over-Japan-s-coronavirus-fight.

21. Takenouchi, "Without vaccine."

22. Azby Brown, "Information as the Key: Evaluating Japan's Response to COVID-19," *Asian Pacific Journal: Japan Focus*, Vol. 18, Issue 14, No. 11, July 15, 2020. https://apjjf.org/2020/14/Brown.html.

23. Haruka Sakamoto, "Japan's Pragmatic Approach to COVID-19 testing," *The Diplomat*, June 26, 2020. https://thediplomat.com/2020/06/japans-pragmatic-approach-to-covid-19-testing/.

24. Brown, "Information as the Key."

25. Lisa Diu and Rie Morita, "Japan Acted Like the Virus Had Gone. Now It's Spread Everywhere," *Bloomberg*, August 1, 2020. https://www.bloomberg.com/news/articles/2020-07-31/japan-acted-like-the-virus-had-gone-now-it-s-spread-everywhere.

26. *Asahi*, "Okinawa marks highest ratio of virus infection in all prefectures," August 3, 2020. http://www.asahi.com/ajw/articles/13603137.

27. John Feffer, "Okinawa: Will the pandemic transform US military bases?" *Responsible Statecraft*, July 17, 2020. https://responsiblestatecraft.org/2020/07/17/okinawa-will-the-pandemic-transform-u-s-military-bases/.

28. Gearoid Reidy, "From Abenomics to Abenonmask: Japan Mask Plans Meets with Derision," *Bloomberg*, April 2, 2020. https://www.bloomberg.com/news/articles/2020-04-02/from-abenomics-to-abenomask-japan-mask-plan-meets-with-derision.

29. NHK, "COVID-19: Fighting a Pandemic," Documentary, March 26, 2020. https://www3.nhk.or.jp/nhkworld/en/ondemand/video/5001289/.

30. *Mainichi Shimbun*, "Abe's 'stay home' message has fueled anger," April 13, 2020. https://mainichi.jp/english/articles/20200413/p2g/00m/0na/069000c.

31. *Mainichi Shimbun*, "Only 3% of Osaka families have received Japan gov't 100,000-yen cash handouts," June 27, 2020. https://mainichi.jp/english/articles/20200627/p2a/00m/0fp/015000c.

32. Reuters, "Japan stirs controversy with huge COVID aid contract for ad giant Dentsu," Reuters, July 28, 2020. https://www.reuters.com/article/us-health-coronavirus-japan-dentsu-insig-idUSKCN24S2PW.

33. Reuters, "Japan's Dentsu gets $700 million windfall from government SME aid scheme amid opposition criticism," Reuters, June 3, 2020. https://www.reuters.com/article/us-health-coronavirus-dentsu-idUSKBN23A18R.

34. *Mainichi Shimbun*, "給付金業務の委託 不透明さに疑念が深まる" [Editorial: Doubts deepen over murkiness in Japan's subcontracting of coronavirus subsidy], June 5, 2020. https://mainichi.jp/articles/20200605/ddm/005/070/082000c.

35. *Mainichi Shimbun*, "河井夫妻の裁判 政治とカネの実態解明を" [Editorial: Trial of Japan lawmaker couple must clear up money's ties to politics], August 27, 2020. https://mainichi.jp/articles/20200827/ddm/005/070/0910.

36. Kataoka Nobuyuki, "黒川元検事長不起訴 違法 法学者らが検察審査会に申し立て [Former Attorney General Kurokawa's non-indictment is 'illegal'

according to legal scholars], Shukan Kinyobi Online, August 20, 2020. http://www.kinyobi.co.jp/kinyobinews/2020/08/20/antena-777/.

37. *Shimbun Asahi*, "EDITORIAL: Fresh probe into land sale scandal is vital to restore trust in politics," June 25, 2020. http://www.asahi.com/ajw/articles/13488395.

38. Kasuya Yūko and Hans H. Tung, "Taiwan has a lot to teach Japan about coronavirus response," *Nikkei Asian Review*, April 20, 2020. https://asia.nikkei.com/Opinion/Taiwan-has-a-lot-to-teach-Japan-about-coronavirus-response.

39. Sakaguchi Yukihiro, "Abe's arm-twisting of bureaucrats paved way for Avigan blunder," *Nikkei Asian Review*, June 14, 2020. https://asia.nikkei.com/Politics/Abe-s-arm-twisting-of-bureaucrats-paved-way-for-Avigan-blunder2.

40. *Mainichi Shimbun*, "Avigan study fails to demonstrate benefit in COVID-19 treatment," July 10, 2020. https://mainichi.jp/english/articles/20200710/p2g/00m/0fe/107000c.

41. *Mainichi Shimbun*, "New wave of infections threatens to collapse Japan hospitals," April 18, 2020. https://mainichi.jp/english/articles/20200418/p2g/00m/0na/071000c.

42. Elaine Lies, "Lacking protective gear, Japan's Osaka pleads for plastic raincoats," Reuters, April 15, 2020. https://www.reuters.com/article/us-health-coronavirus-japan-raincoats-idUSKCN21X0RO.

43. Jesse Chase-Lubitz, "Cardboard boxes replace hotel rooms at Narita as Japan struggles with returnees," *Japan Times*, April 15, 2020. https://www.japantimes.co.jp/news/2020/04/15/national/cardboard-beds-narita-airport/#.XpvBF9MzZPM.

44. Maemura Akira, "Japan ranks below Italy and Spain in ICU bed capacity," *Nikkei Asian Review*, April 15, 2020. https://asia.nikkei.com/Spotlight/Coronavirus/Japan-ranks-below-Italy-and-Spain-in-ICU-bed-capacity.

45. Ju-min Park, Saitō Mari, and Yamamitsu Eimi, "On Japan's stretched frontline, doctors and nurses DIY a coronavirus response," Reuters, April 28, 2020. https://www.reuters.com/article/us-health-coronavirus-japan-icu-idUSKCN22A03L.

46. *Shimbun Asahi*, "Tokyo hospitals running on empty and sense of moral duty," April 17, 2020. http://www.asahi.com/ajw/articles/13305776.

47. *Kyodo News*, "Japan PM Abe declares state of emergency amid widespread virus infections," April 8, 2020. https://english.kyodonews.net/news/2020/04/ac4415709921-abe-to-declare-state-of-emergency-amid-widespread-virus-infections.html.

48. Seig, "Where's Abe?"

49. Kyodo, "Olympic delay and coronavirus add fuel to Abe-Koike rivalry," *Japan Times*, April 24, 2020. https://www.japantimes.co.jp/news/2020/04/24/national/politics-diplomacy/abe-koike-rivalry/#.XqU-3C9h21s.

50. Kajimoto Tetushi, "Japanese firms say government's $1 trillion coronavirus stimulus too little, too late: Reuters poll," Reuters, April 16, 2020. https://www.reuters.com/article/us-health-coronavirus-japan-companies/japanese-firms-say-governments-1-trillion-coronavirus-stimulus-too-little-too-late-reuters-poll-idUSKCN21Y04A.

51. Nagata Kazuaki, "After troubled start, Go to Travel campaign still likely to achieve some aims," *Japan Times*, July 22, 2020. https://www.japantimes.co.jp/news/2020/07/22/business/economy-business/go-to-travel-campaign-domestic-tourism-coronavirus/.

52. Murakami Sakura, "Japan's Abe faces anger over tourism subsidy as Tokyo COVID-19 cases hit record," Reuters, July 17, 2020. https://www.msn.com/en-us/news/world/japans-abe-faces-anger-over-backflip-on-coronavirus-spurred-tourism-subsidy/ar-BB16QbgT.

53. *Mainichi Shimbun*, "Go To事業見直し (混乱を招いた責任は重い" [Editorial: Japan gov't responsible for confusion over 'Go To' travel subsidy campaign], July 17, 2020. https://mainichi.jp/articles/20200717/ddm/005/070/106000c.

54. Onishi Norimitsu, "Prime Minister of Japan to step down," *New York Times*, September 12, 2007. https://www.nytimes.com/2007/09/12/world/asia/12cnd-japan.html.

55. *Shimbun Asahi*, "Dismay among hibakusha over Abe's perceived indifference," August 10, 2020. http://www.asahi.com/ajw/articles/13624165.

56. Tobias Harris, *The Iconoclast: Shinzo Abe and the New Japan*, Hurst: London, 2020.

57. *Jiji Kyōdō*, "Abe's legacy seen as hinging on holding delayed Tokyo Olympics," *Japan Times*, July 26, 2020. https://www.japantimes.co.jp/news/2020/07/26/national/politics-diplomacy/japan-shinzo-abe-legacy-tokyo-olympics/.

58. Jeff Kingston, "Tokyo's Diversity Olympics Dogged by Controversy," *Asia Pacific Journal: Japan Focus*, Vol. 18, Issue 4, No. 3, February 15, 2020. https://apjjf.org/2020/4/Kingston-2.html.

59. Kingston, "Goodbye, Tokyo 2020."

60. Kingston, "Tokyo Olympics 2020 Postponed," Australian Institute for International Affairs, July 24, 2020. http://www.internationalaffairs.org.au/australianoutlook/tokyo-olympics-2020-postponed/.

61. Simon Denyer, "Japan sets aside $22 million to buff government's global image amid pandemic struggles," *Washington Post*, April 15 2020. https://www.washingtonpost.com/world/asia_pacific/japan-coronavirus-image-abe/2020/04/15/73bf1dee-7f00-11ea-84c2-0792d8591911_story.html.

62. Personal communication, August 2020.

63. Jake Adelstein, "Japan Makes Saving Face a Priority Over Saving Lives," *The Daily Beast*, April 9, 2020. https://www.thedailybeast.com/japans-covid-19-state-of-emergency-locks-down-criticism.

64. Jeff Kingston, "Ousting Kan Naoto: The Politics of Nuclear Crisis and Renewable Energy in Japan," *Asia-Pacific Journal*, Vol. 9, Issue 39, No. 5, September 28, 2011. https://apjjf.org/2011/9/39/Jeff-Kingston/3610/article.html.

65. Shirakawa Masaki, "COVID-19's staggering economic impact forces deep macro policy rethink," *Nikkei Asian Review*, July 29, 2020. https://asia.nikkei.com/Opinion/COVID-19-s-staggering-economic-impact-forces-deep-macro-policy-rethink.

66. William Pesek, "Japan's COVID-19 relapse trumpets need for urgent economic action," *Nikkei Asian Review*, August 3, 2020. https://asia.nikkei.com/Opinion/Japan-s-COVID-19-relapse-trumpets-need-for-urgent-economic-action.

67. John Delury, "Opinion | How Democracy Won the World's First Coronavirus Election," *New York Times*, April 16, 2020. https://www.nytimes.com/2020/04/16/opinion/south-korea-election-coronavirus.html.

68. *Mainichi Shimbun*, "なぜ首相は「痛感」した責任を取らない？安倍流処世術、軽さの原点" [PM Abe evades responsibility over political scandals despite 'painfully aware' comments], July 17, 2020.

REFERENCES

Adelstein, Jake. "Japan Makes Saving Face a Priority Over Saving Lives." *The Daily Beast*, April 9, 2020. https://www.thedailybeast.com/japans-covid-19-state-of-emergency-locks-down-criticism.
Asahi Shimbun. "Abe: No experts were consulted for my decision to close schools." March 3, 2020. http://www.asahi.com/ajw/articles/13182509.
Asahi Shimbun. "Aso: low virus death rate thanks to Japanese superiority." June 5, 2020. http://www.asahi.com/ajw/articles/13432875.
Asahi Shimbun. "Dismay among hibakusha over Abe's perceived indifference." August 10, 2020. http://www.asahi.com/ajw/articles/13624165.
Asahi Shimbun. "EDITORIAL: Fresh probe into land sale scandal is vital to restore trust in politics." June 25, 2020. http://www.asahi.com/ajw/articles/13488395.
Asahi Shimbun. "Okinawa marks highest ratio of virus infection in all prefectures." August 3, 2020. http://www.asahi.com/ajw/articles/13603137.
Asahi Shimbun. "Survey: 57% say Abe not showing leadership in COVID-19 crisis." April 21, 2020. www.asahi.com/ajw/articles/13315219.
Asahi Shimbun. "Tokyo hospitals running on empty and sense of moral duty." April 17, 2020. http://www.asahi.com/ajw/articles/13305776.
Brown, Azby. "Information as the Key: Evaluating Japan's Response to COVID-19." *Asian Pacific Journal: Japan Focus*, Vol. 18, Issue 14, No. 11, July 15, 2020. https://apjjf.org/2020/14/Brown.html.
Chase-Lubitz, Jesse. "Cardboard boxes replace hotel rooms at Narita as Japan struggles with returnees." *Japan Times*, April 15, 2020. https://www.japantimes.co.jp/news/2020/04/15/national/cardboard-beds-narita-airport/#.XpvBF9MzZPM.
Delury, John. "Opinion | How Democracy Won the World's First Coronavirus Election." *New York Times*, April 16, 2020. https://www.nytimes.com/2020/04/16/opinion/south-korea-election-coronavirus.html.
Denyer, Simon. "Japan sets aside $22 million to buff government's global image amid pandemic struggles." *Washington Post*, April 15 2020. https://www.washingtonpost.com/world/asia_pacific/japan-coronavirus-image-abe/2020/04/15/73bf1dee-7f00-11ea-84c2-0792d8591911_story.html.
Diu, Lisa and Rie Morita. "Japan Acted Like the Virus Had Gone. Now It's Spread Everywhere." *Bloomberg*, August 1, 2020. https://www.bloomberg.com/news/articles/2020-07-31/japan-acted-like-the-virus-had-gone-now-it-s-spread-everywhere.
Feffer, John. "Okinawa: Will the pandemic transform US military bases?" *Responsible Statecraft*, July 17, 2020. https://responsiblestatecraft.org/2020/07/17/okinawa-will-the-pandemic-transform-u-s-military-bases/.
Harris, Tobias. *The Iconoclast: Shinzo Abe and the New Japan*. Hurst: London, 2020.
Jiji, Kyōdō. "Abe's legacy seen as hinging on holding delayed Tokyo Olympics." *Japan Times*, July 26, 2020. https://www.japantimes.co.jp/news/2020/07/26/national/politics-diplomacy/japan-shinzo-abe-legacy-tokyo-olympics/.
Jiji, Kyōdō. "Abe administration bombs in global survey on coronavirus response." *Japan Times*, May 9, 2020. https://www.japantimes.co.jp/news/2020/05/09/national/abe-coronavirus-survey/.

Kajimoto, Tetsushi. "Japanese firms say government's $1 trillion coronavirus stimulus too little, too late: Reuters poll." Reuters, April 16, 2020. https://www.reuters.com/article/us-health-coronavirus-japan-companies/japanese-firms-say-governments-1-trillion-coronavirus-stimulus-too-little-too-late-reuters-poll-idUSKCN21Y04A.

Kasahara, Shin. "Survey: Japanese less trusting of government in health crisis." *Asahi*, May 13, 2020. http://www.asahi.com/ajw/articles/13370715.

Kasuya, Yuko and Hans H. Tung. "Taiwan has a lot to teach Japan about coronavirus response." *Nikkei Asian Review*, April 20, 2020. https://asia.nikkei.com/Opinion/Taiwan-has-a-lot-to-teach-Japan-about-coronavirus-response.

Kataoka Nobuyuki. "黒川元検事長不起訴は　違法　法学者らが検察審査会に申し立て [Former Attorney General Kurokawa's non-indictment is 'illegal' according to legal scholars]. Shukan Kinyobi Online, August 20, 2020. http://www.kinyobi.co.jp/kinyobinews/2020/08/20/antena-777/.

Kingston, Jeff. "Goodbye, Tokyo 2020. It's time to start hoping for 2021." *The Washington Post*, March 22, 2020. https://www.washingtonpost.com/opinions/2020/03/21/goodbye-tokyo-2020-its-time-start-hoping-2021/.

Kingston, Jeff. "Japan's response to the coronavirus is a slow-motion train wreck." *The Washington Post*, February 22, 2020. https://www.washingtonpost.com/opinions/2020/02/21/japans-response-coronavirus-is-slow-motion-train-wreck/.

Kingston, Jeff. "Ousting Kan Naoto: The Politics of Nuclear Crisis and Renewable Energy in Japan." *Asia-Pacific Journal*, Vol. 9, Issue 39, No. 5, September 28, 2011. https://apjjf.org/2011/9/39/Jeff-Kingston/3610/article.html.

Kingston, Jeff. "Tokyo's Diversity Olympics Dogged by Controversy." *Asia Pacific Journal: Japan Focus*, Vol. 18, Issue 4, No. 3, February 15, 2020. https://apjjf.org/2020/4/Kingston-2.html.

Kingston, Jeff. "Tokyo Olympics 2020 Postponed." Australian Institute for International Affairs, July 24, 2020. http://www.internationalaffairs.org.au/australianoutlook/tokyo-olympics-2020-postponed/.

Kyodo. "Experts in Japan call for more coronavirus tests as positive rate rises." *Japan Times*, April 23, 2020. https://www.japantimes.co.jp/news/2020/04/23/national/japan-coronavirus-tests-positive-rate-rises/#.XqT0kJMzab8.

Kyodo. "Japan's single mothers and female workers hard hit by coronavirus." *Japan Times*, July 3, 2020. https://www.japantimes.co.jp/news/2020/07/03/national/social-issues/japan-single-mothers-female-workers-coronavirus/.

Kyodo. "Olympic delay and coronavirus add fuel to Abe-Koike rivalry." *Japan Times*, April 24, 2020. https://www.japantimes.co.jp/news/2020/04/24/national/politics-diplomacy/abe-koike-rivalry/#.XqU-3C9h21s.

Kyodo News. "Japan PM Abe declares state of emergency amid widespread virus infections." April 8, 2020. https://english.kyodonews.net/news/2020/04/ac4415709921-abe-to-declare-state-of-emergency-amid-widespread-virus-infections.html.

Kyodo News. "82% say government should compensate firms that shutdown for virus." April 13, 2020. https://english.kyodonews.net/news/2020/04/eea437e79b17-urgent-public-dissatisfied-with-abes-response-to-virus-outbreak-kyodo-poll.html.

Lies, Elaine. "Lacking protective gear, Japan's Osaka pleads for plastic raincoats." Reuters, April 15, 2020. https://www.reuters.com/article/us-health-coronavirus-japan-raincoats-idUSKCN21X0RO.

Maemura, Akira. "Japan ranks below Italy and Spain in ICU bed capacity." *Nikkei Asian Review*, April 15, 2020. https://asia.nikkei.com/Spotlight/Coronavirus/Japan-ranks-below-Italy-and-Spain-in-ICU-bed-capacity.

Mainichi Shimbun. "Abe's 'stay home' message has fueled anger." April 13, 2020. https://mainichi.jp/english/articles/20200413/p2g/00m/0na/069000c.

Mainichi Shimbun. "Avigan study fails to demonstrate benefit in COVID-19 treatment." July 10, 2020. https://mainichi.jp/english/articles/20200710/p2g/00m/0fe/107000c.

Mainichi Shimbun. "給付金業務の委託 不透明さに疑念が深まる" [Editorial: Doubts deepen over murkiness in Japan's subcontracting of coronavirus subsidy]. *Mainichi*, June 5, 2020. https://mainichi.jp/articles/20200605/ddm/005/070/082000c.

Mainichi Shimbun. "河井夫妻の裁判 政治とカネの実態解明を" [Editorial: Trial of Japan lawmaker couple must clear up money's ties to politics]. https://mainichi.jp/articles/20200827/ddm/005/070/0910.

Mainichi Shimbun. "Go To事業見直し 混乱を招いた責任は重い" [Editorial: Japan gov't responsible for confusion over 'Go To' travel subsidy campaign]. *Mainichi* July 17, 2020. https://mainichi.jp/articles/20200717/ddm/005/070/106000c.

Mainichi Shimbun. "Majority in Japan don't approve Abe govt's coronavirus response: Mainichi poll." April 20, 2020. https://mainichi.jp/english/articles/20200420/p2a/00m/0na/016000c.

Mainichi Shimbun. "Majority say Abe bears responsibility over legislators' vote-buying scandal: Mainichi poll." June 22, 2020. https://mainichi.jp/english/articles/20200622/p2a/00m/0na/002000c.

Mainichi Shimbun. "New wave of infections threatens to collapse Japan hospitals." April 18, 2020. https://mainichi.jp/english/articles/20200418/p2g/00m/0na/071000c.

Mainichi Shimbun. "Only 3% of Osaka families have received Japan gov't 100,000-yen cash handouts." June 27, 2020. https://mainichi.jp/english/articles/20200627/p2a/00m/0fp/015000c.

Mainichi Shimbun, "なぜ首相は「痛感」した責任を取らない？安倍流処世術、軽さの原点" [PM Abe evades responsibility over political scandals despite 'painfully aware' comments]. July 17, 2020.

Mainichi Shimbun. "Q&A for July 2020 Mainichi poll on Abe Cabinet support, Japan's coronavirus response." July 24, 2020. https://mainichi.jp/english/articles/20200723/p2a/00m/0na/013000c.

Murakami, Hiromi. "A Japan divided over COVID-19 control." East Asia Forum, March 8, 2020. https://www.eastasiaforum.org/2020/03/08/a-japan-divided-over-covid-19-control/.

Murakami, Sakura. "Japan's Abe faces anger over tourism subsidy as Tokyo COVID-19 cases hit record." Reuters, July 17, 2020. https://www.msn.com/en-us/news/world/japans-abe-faces-anger-over-backflip-on-coronavirus-spurred-tourism-subsidy/ar-BB16QbgT.

Murata, Atsushi. "70% of Japanese parents feel troubled by school closures." *Nikkei*, March 14, 2020.

Nagata Kazuaki. "After troubled start, Go to Travel campaign still likely to achieve some aims." *Japan Times*, July 22, 2020. https://www.japantimes.co.jp/news/2020/07/22/business/economy-business/go-to-travel-campaign-domestic-tourism-coronavirus/.

NHK. "COVID-19: Fighting a Pandemic." Documentary, March 26, 2020. https://www3.nhk.or.jp/nhkworld/en/ondemand/video/5001289/.

NHK World. "Japan passes South Korea for coronavirus cases." April 23, 2020. https://www3.nhk.or.jp/nhkworld/en/news/backstories/1048/.

Obe Mitsuru and Ando Kiyoshi. "Nobel laureate Yamanaka frets over Japan's lax coronavirus fight." *Nikkei Asian Review*, April 19, 2020. https://asia.nikkei.com/Editor-s-Picks/Interview/Nobel-laureate-Yamanaka-frets-over-Japan-s-lax-coronavirus-fight.

Onishi, Norimitsu. "Prime Minister of Japan to step down." *New York Times*, September 12, 2007. https://www.nytimes.com/2007/09/12/world/asia/12cnd-japan.html.

Park, Ju-min, Mari Saito, and Eimi Yamamitsu. "On Japan's stretched frontline, doctors and nurses DIY a coronavirus response." Reuters, April 28, 2020. https://www.reuters.com/article/us-health-coronavirus-japan-icu-idUSKCN22A03L.

Pesek, William. "Japan's COVID-19 relapse trumpets need for urgent economic action." *Nikkei Asian Review*, August 3, 2020. https://asia.nikkei.com/Opinion/Japan-s-COVID-19-relapse-trumpets-need-for-urgent-economic-action.

Reidy, Gearoid. "From Abenomics to Abenonmask: Japan Mask Plans Meets with Derision." Bloomberg, April 2, 2020. https://www.bloomberg.com/news/articles/2020-04-02/from-abenomics-to-abenomask-japan-mask-plan-meets-with-derision.

Reuters. "Japan stirs controversy with huge COVID aid contract for ad giant Dentsu." Reuters, July 28, 2020. https://www.reuters.com/article/us-health-coronavirus-japan-dentsu-insig-idUSKCN24S2PW.

Reuters. "Japan's Dentsu gets $700 million windfall from government SME aid scheme amid opposition criticism." Reuters, June 3, 2020. https://www.reuters.com/article/us-health-coronavirus-dentsu-idUSKBN23A18R.

Sakaguchi, Yukihiro. "Abe's arm-twisting of bureaucrats paved way for Avigan blunder." *Nikkei Asian Review*, June 14, 2020. https://asia.nikkei.com/Politics/Abe-s-arm-twisting-of-bureaucrats-paved-way-for-Avigan-blunder2.

Sakamoto, Haruka. "Japan's Pragmatic Approach to COVID-19 testing." *The Diplomat*, June 26, 2020. https://thediplomat.com/2020/06/japans-pragmatic-approach-to-covid-19-testing/.

Seig, Linda. "Where's Abe? Critics ask as coronavirus spreads in Japan." Reuters, February 25, 2020. https://www.reuters.com/article/us-china-health-japan-abe-idUSKCN20J16F.

Shirakawa, Masaki. "COVID-19's staggering economic impact forces deep macro policy rethink." *Nikkei Asian Review*, July 29, 2020. https://asia.nikkei.com/Opinion/COVID-19-s-staggering-economic-impact-forces-deep-macro-policy-rethink.

Takenouchi, Takahiro. "Without vaccine for coronavirus, Tokyo Olympics in 2021 in doubt." *Asahi*, April 25, 2020. http://www.asahi.com/ajw/articles/13327110.

Wallace, Corey. "Abe departs from his own winning formula in battling COVID-19." Australia Institute for International Affairs, March 5, 2020. www.internationalaffairs.org.au/australianoutlook/abe-departs-from-his-own-winning-formula-in-battling-covid-19/.

Chapter 4

Gender Policies and Conservative Values

Murakami Hiromi

INTRODUCTION

Despite the Abe administration's voiced emphasis on advancing female participation in various fields, Japan's global gender equality index ranking has worsened from 101st in 2012 to its lowest ever at 121st in 2020, and the fertility rate in 2019 hit its lowest in the past 12 years at 1.36. Despite setting a numerical target of 30 percent for female leadership positions, Abe strongly resisted discussing even the possibility of supporting a female heir to deal with the shrinking Japanese Imperial family (with females excluded from succession, those eligible to ascend the throne are now reduced to now reduced to a crown prince in his 50s with only one male heir and prince Hitachi in his 80s). Abe placed national priority on increasing childcare facilities, yet paid little attention to single mothers and issues of poverty. He has deliberately chosen policies that would fulfill his economic agenda and best stand by the core values of the conservatives and business community. The declining birth rate is the single most critical issue for Japan at present, yet no long-term vision to reverse such a trend has been provided. Gender equality has come a long way since 1986, when the equal employment law was enacted—nevertheless, Japan has yet to experience another breakthrough and is far from achieving its goals. Why is Japan so behind in advancing women in its society?

ABE, THE DEFENDER OF THE CONSERVATIVE VALUES

Abe's policies have generally been heavily influenced by conservative beliefs shared by his political supporters, such as core Liberal Democratic Party

(LDP) members and vocal conservative opinion leaders. Conservatives have been adamant in protecting their core values and are unwilling to accept any policies that might negate their principles. Examples of policies that are not acceptable to Japanese fundamental conservatives include separate legal surnames for married couples or discussion about promoting a female monarch. Abe himself has kept silent on these issues. What remained surprisingly consistent was Abe's avoidance of the phrase "achieving gender equality," which has never been desired by core conservatives; instead he used vague phrases, such as "a society where women shine" (*josei ga kagayaku shakai*). With only this vague slogan, it was unclear exactly what kind of society Abe hoped to achieve. To understand the priorities of Abe's women-focused policies, it is important to identify first the core conservative values at play.

What exactly are included in "core conservative values?" In Japan, their major pillars are "family," gender-based roles, and the Emperor system. Abe's core supporters share traditional views of the "family" with an emphasis on mutual help and the primacy of the family over the individual. The LDP proposed adding a new section under the Constitution's Article 24, which would determine that "the family is a natural unit to be respected in the society, and family members must help each other." This passage implies that the family members have a responsibility to take care of elders and raise children, along with other roles. Furthermore, in Japan's national conservatism, there are the unique features of a non-reciprocal relationship, where the state would give less while demanding citizens sacrifice for the sake of the state.[1] Based on this value, conservatives thus have less interest in supporting social welfare or offering help until citizens have exhausted self-help and their own family support systems.[2] A paternalistic family system is central to this concept, with gender-based roles built into it: as one of Abe's advisors Hasegawa Michiko was quoted saying in 2014, "Women's most important task is to raise children, and this should take priority over working outside the home, and men *must* earn money to feed wife and children."[3] Hand-in-hand with this traditional, paternalistic family unit that operates via mutual help, conservatives stress legitimate marriage, legitimate children within wedlock, eternal marriage, and have interventionist tendencies on private decisions to press for more babies.

These features are key in understanding Abe's preferences and policies. When the Koizumi administration was taking proactive steps toward gender equality, Abe Shinzō and his fellow conservatives expressed their concerns, referencing "the damage to family values and to Japanese culture that could result if men and women were treated equally."[4] In the conservative mind, women should stay at home, because women are "baby-making machines"[5] to produce more babies to recover Japanese demography. However, this rhetoric did not work, since more women resisted traditional norms by having fewer babies. In 2005, a cabinet office experts group found that there was a positive correlation between female labor participation and the birth rate based on twenty-four OECD nations" data (Figure 4.6).[6] However, these findings did not align with conservatives' theory that a stay-home wife would produce more children. The 2003 Basic Law for Society with Declining Number of Children (*Shōshika shakai taisaku kihon hō*)[7] says, essentially, that it is a citizen's "duty" to give birth and raise children and that both central and local authorities should conduct the necessary education to raise awareness of the importance of gender-based roles in the household, specifically regarding childbearing. It is increasingly evident that there is a perception of gap widening as conservatives press their values on citizens further and seek to "educate" them.

WOMEN'S AGENDA: WHAT HAS ABE DONE?

It was not Abe's original idea to promote women in the workplace; rather, it was his predecessor Koizumi Junichiro who had laid out comprehensive policies in 2003 to achieve 30 percent representation of women in various fields by 2020. Abe and other conservatives were not fully supportive of Koizumi's agenda at the time, and many perceived it as a setback for gender equality advancement when Abe succeeded him as prime minister. Although it was not a typical conservative move, Abe took on the catchy slogan of achieving 30 percent female representation in leading positions in various fields by 2020. It soon became evident that such a target was unachievable, so in 2015 it was substantially lowered from 30 percent to 10 percent,[8] and after approximately eight years of women's advancement policy, only 5.2 percent female executives had been achieved by 2019 (see table 4.1).[9] Not much attention was paid to women's representation in politics. Conversely, Abe consistently allocated major resources to increase the capacity of childcare centers. It did meet the 500,000 capacity increase target; however, as of April 2019, there are still 16,772 children waiting to find a place in nursery schools. In 2012, that number was 24,825 children. While this focus of Abe's did reduce the number of children waiting, it did not do so to a substantial extent.

Historically, the LDP has been very close to big businesses, and often adjusted laws in accordance with the desires of the business community. When the Gender Equal Opportunity Law for Recruitment (*Danjo koyō kintō hō*) was enacted in 1986, the LDP allowed corporations to get away with sidestepping the restrictions however they could. For example, because the law banned gender-based discrimination in recruitment, corporations immediately introduced two job tracks for women, *sōgoshoku* (career track) and *ippanshoku* (administrative), with the intention to navigate the majority of

Table 4.1 Have Abe's Targets Achieved?

	Politicians National (Lower House - LH, Upper House - UH) Prefectural level	Governors Mayors	Central government managers "Kachō"	Central government Directors "Shitsuchō"	Central government Executive "Shiteishoku"	Private firm managers "Kachō"	Private firm Directors "Buchō"	Private firm Executives "Yakuin"
Goal by 2020	30%	30%	30%→12%*	30%→7%*	30%→5%*	30%→15%*	30%→10%*	30%→10%*
2010-2012	LH 10.9% (2011) UH 18.2% (2011) Prefecture 8.6% (2010)	Governor 6.4% (2010)	5.8% (2010)	2.6% (2010)	2.2% (2010)	7.9% (2012)	4.9% (2012)	1.6% (2012)
2019	LH 17.8% UH 28.1% Prefectural 10%	Governor 4.2% Big city mayor 10% Mayor 1.8%	11.6%	5.3%	4.2%	11.4%	6.9%	5.2%
US 2019-2020	23.2% (House) 2020 26% (Senate) 2020	Governor 18% Big city mayor 27% Mayor 22%		Supervisor, manager 29% (2014)	34% (2014)	Manager/director 36%	VP 30%	Sr VP 26% F500 Board member 22%

Source: 2019 Gender White Paper, Gender Equality bureau, Cabinet office; Diversity Wins: How inclusion matters. McKinsey & Company May2020; Women Elected Officials by Position, Center for American Women and Politics 2019; Women in Federal Service: A Seat at Every Table, United States Office of Personnel Management, 2015.
* Goals were lowered in 2015.

women to administrative work. At the time, half of corporations with more than 5,000 employees introduced two track recruitment systems. By 2011, only 5.6 percent of the career track positions were filled by women,[10] even though women have entered tertiary education at a higher rate than men since 1988 (figure 4.2). Furthermore, the Worker Dispatching Law (*Rōdosha haken hō*) was revised to make it easier for corporations to continue hiring non-regular workers without shifting their status to regular workers. Abe continued to be easy on businesses: with the Act on Promotion of Women's Participation and Advancement in the Workplace (*Josei katsuyaku Suishin hō*) of 2015, he only asked corporations to disclose the situation of women employees for better transparency and didn't enforce the act with any penalties. By 2020, the Abe administration spoke less and less about the importance of promoting female managerial positions and, also in 2020, Abe postponed the target date, from "by 2020" for female management reaching 30 percent to "later in the 2020s"—a disgrace. Japan's figures for gender equality are substantially lower than the United States, which ranks 53rd in the Global Gender Gap Index of 2020 (see table 4.1), or France, which ranks 15th in GGGI where 44 percent of directorship positions are held by women (2019) and a quota system has been introduced.

Not Gender Equality, but Supplementing for Labor Shortage

Abe's target of 30 percent female leadership positions was quite unthinkable for a great number of conservatives, so why did Abe adopt such an unexpected policy? His true motivations may have been mixed, but gender equality was never his prime concern. In aligning with this policy, Abe might have wished to gain support from a wider range of women and the business community,[11] but at the same time, he had pure economic motivations, in that he wanted to the supplement severe labor shortage with women's labor, without achieving gender equality.[12] Matsuda Yasuko, a labor representative at the Labor Ministry's committee discussion also stated, "I feel very awkward because no one talks about the gender equality aspect of the issue, but the majority expressed a need for women to work for fulfilling the labor shortage."[13] Various pieces of evidence and government statements show that the administration did not necessarily advocate policies to advance women's positions in various fields but rather sought to utilize women to supplement the dwindling workforce "for overall revitalization and economic growth."[14]

> [T]he Government will aim to raise the women's labor participation rate to the world's highest level by providing childcare arrangements and other services so that working couples can raise their children with a sense of security and by

supporting women's return to the workplace following their childcare leave as well as promoting the proactive recruitment of women.[15]

Because of the labor shortage, conservatives agreed to allow women out from their homes before they considered the immigrant labor option. They considered women as a possible supplement to the male breadwinners of their households, and therefore imagined that women should consider a "work–life-balance" between work and childrearing. Abe's initial policies heavily reflected this view. Abe introduced a maternity leave policy that allowed for parents (mothers) to remain home to raise their babies for a full three years[16] and distributed a "Ladies' Maternal Handbook" which encouraged women to give birth at an "appropriate" age. Such interference was harshly criticized by women, who argued back that it was their own personal choice when and if they would raise children and that it was none of the government's business. These policies soon disappeared from Abe's agenda and revealed another gap in perception between the conservatives and working women.

Female labor participation has increased by 3.44 million during the Abe years of 2012 to 2019 (figure 4.3). However, the fact is that non-regular workers accounted for 2.26 million (two-thirds) of the increase.[17] The M-curve, representing women leaving jobs when they hit their child-raising period (figure 4.4), has been unchanged for many years (figure 4.5). Between the 1980s and 2009, approximately 60 percent of working women left their jobs, where now 45 percent of working women leave their job (2010–2014) when they have their first child (figure 4.1). For the latter period, it is most likely the 2008 economic crisis, rather than any of Abe's policies, that impacted their decisions.

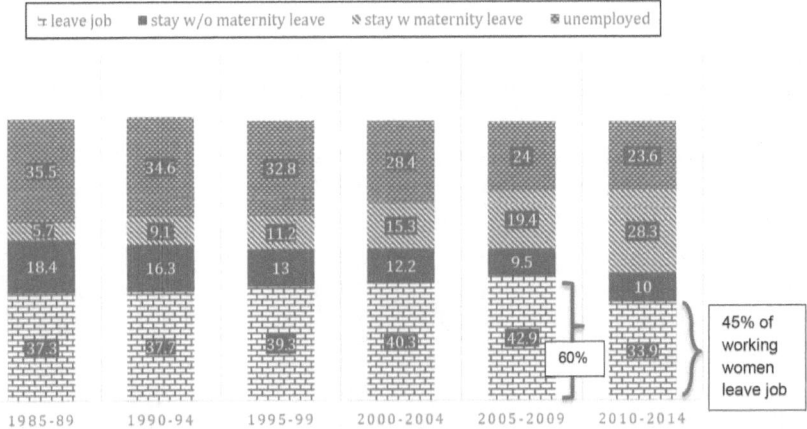

Figure 4.1 **Women Stay or Leave at the Birth of First Child (%).** *Source*: Danjo kyōdō sankakukyoku, Naikakufu, Shigoto to seikatsu no chōwa [Work-Life-Balance Report] (2018).

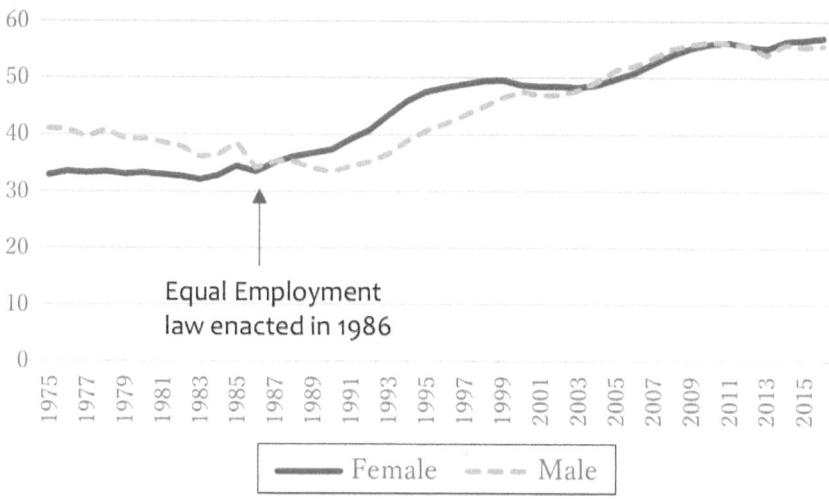

Figure 4.2 **Entrance to Tertiary Education (%).** *Source*: Danjo kyōdo sankakukyoku, Naikakufu, Danjo kyōdo sankaku hakusho (H29) [Gender Equality White Paper], 2017.

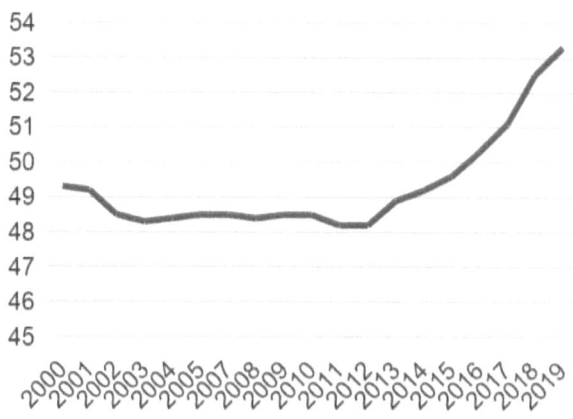

Figure 4.3 **Japan's Female Labor Participation (all ages, %).** *Source*: Sōmushō tokei-kyoku, Rōdōryoku chōsa Nenpō (R1) [Labor Statistics, 2019].

Never Intended to Increase the Amount of Women in Politics

Regarding female political representation, as of June 2020, Japan ranked 166th out of 193 nations in the Inter-Parliamentary Union's (IPU) Women in National Parliament ranking. The administration passed the Equal Opportunity Act for political candidates (*Kōhosha Danjo Kintō hō*) in May 2018, but the impact has been negligible as the law has no penalties to enforce it. According to the IPU ranking, only 9.9 percent of Japan's Lower House

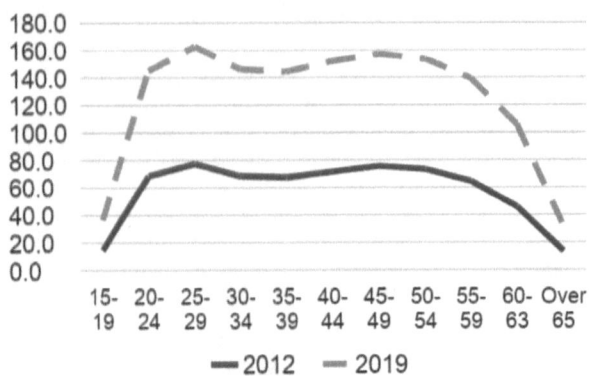

Figure 4.4 Japan's M-Curve 2012 and 2019 (point-basis). *Source*: Sōmushō, Rōdōryoku chōsa (kihon shûkei) (2012, 2019) [Workforce statistics, 2012, 2019].

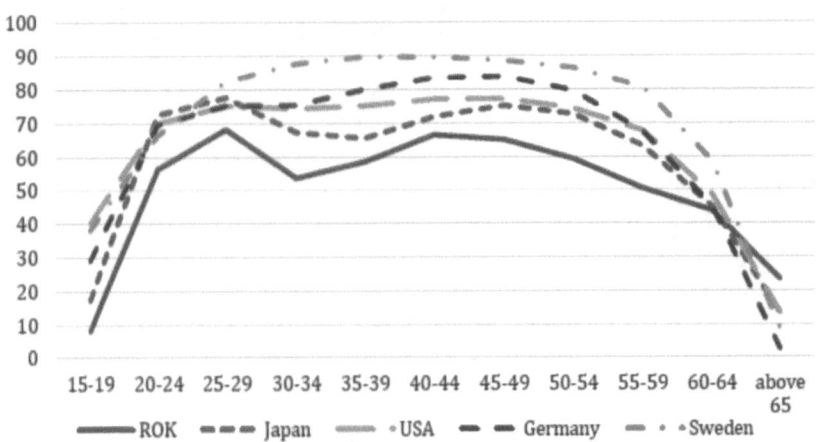

Figure 4.5 International "M-Curve" Comparison (%). *Source*: Danjo kyōdo sankaku-kyoku, Naikakufu, Danjo kyōdō sanau hakusho (H25) [Gender Equality White Paper], 2013.

members are female, a figure lower than those of both Congo and Botswana. While the Japanese Communist Party (25%) and Rikken Minshuto (22%) have higher female representation, the LDP boasts only 7.8 percent female members in the Lower House, the second lowest after Kokumin Minshuto (5.1%).[18] If Abe truly desired to increase the number of female parliament members, the LDP could have placed female candidates in the top of their proportional representation's shortlist, however, the 2017 general election result shows that the LDP did not, and so did most other parties. Studies show that in Japan, a male candidate has a 10 percent higher probability than a female candidate to be elected.[19] There are more reasons, it is difficult for

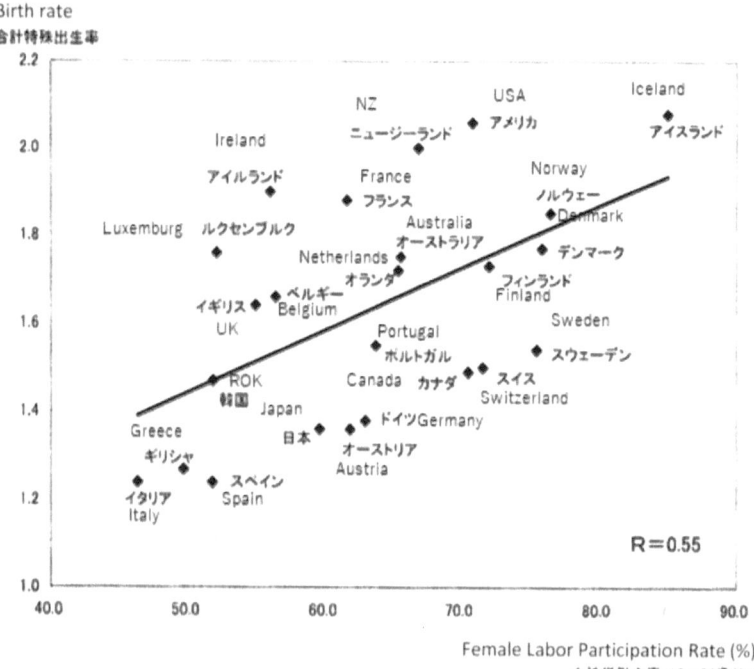

Figure 4.6 Positive Correlation: Birthrate and Female Labor Participation Rate.
Source: Danjo kyōdō sankaku kaigi, Shōshika to danjo Kyōdō sankaku ni kansuru senmon chōsakai [Gender Equality Bureau Cabinet Office, Declining Birthrate and Gender Equality Research Committee], Shōshika to danjo kyōdō sankaku ni kansuru shakai kankyō no kokusai hikaku hōkokusho (H17) [Social environment International Comparison for declining birthrate and gender equality (2005)].

women to run, too—for example, rural areas have more critical views toward female candidates because of their strong traditional view that women should stay home and raise children. Women also tend to have uncooperative husbands when they choose to run as candidates. A young parliament member Ogawa Junya stated that Japan's political culture is most conservative and that he was pressured to call his wife "*kanai*" (person in the house) rather than "*tsuma*" (wife) to get support from local senior constituents.[20] Furthermore, a majority of LDP leadership, dominated heavily by senior men, are reluctant to introduce a quota system that would support female membership. Therefore, it is unlikely that Japan's political scene will change anytime soon.

Productivity Rise and Working Style Change

The government is aware that while Japan needs to implement comprehensive and long-term measures to reverse the declining demographic trend, immediate measures to increase productivity is also necessary. In emphasizing the importance of increasing productivity and diversity in management, the Abe administration still remained passive in asking corporations to take action to this end. In 2013, Abe requested that major business leaders of "all stock-listed corporations should proactively hire female executives/directors to achieve the 30% target" and "all corporations hire one female executive."[21] However, without any penalties providing incentive to make good on these requests, corporations lacked motivation to respond and hire more women executives. Kathy Matsui argued in her *Womenomics* research that if Japan's gender employment gap were to be closed, Japan's GDP could rise by as much as 15 percent,[22] and advocated a "women-first" hiring policy that stipulated corporations should hire women first when there are candidates with similar backgrounds and skills for the position. However, no Japanese corporations were serious about adopting such a policy. Many corporations were skeptical of "Womenomics" and tried to find deficiencies in firms, such as Calbee Food, Inc., which strongly supported women's potential. Absurdly, Calbee Chairman of the Board & CEO Matsumoto Akira stated that it was his mission to increase Calbee's profits to prove to other firms that women could positively contribute to a firm's profit.

In order to achieve higher productivity, Japan needs to cut down on its long working hours style that has been a major barrier for women's advancement, as work is usually evaluated by the hours worked and not by outcome. The Abe administration passed a labor reform law (*Hatarakikata Kaikaku kanrenho*) in June 2018 to allow for a more flexible work style and to eliminate unfair conditions for non-regular workers. Despite this effort, Japan's inefficiency remains built into its own employment system. If the law could address other major hurdles for women, such as jobs without descriptions, seniority-based promotions, unequal opportunities for in-company promotions, and relocation transfer requirements for career track employees—all impediments on white-collar workers' productivity, the improvement in productivity and women's employment opportunities would be substantial. In a Japan where these inefficient customs were eliminated, achieving that 30 percent for women in leadership positions would sound more realistic.

Discriminatory Inheritance for Children Outside Wedlock Finally Corrected

While a majority of OECD nations have transformed their laws and rules in accordance with the gradual changes in modern family values over the years, Japan has remained almost unchanged. New forms of family, including civil unions, same-sex marriages, or partnerships without legal marriage are still not accepted. The Abe administration made only a few select changes, among which was the elimination of discrimination regarding inheritance for children born outside wedlock. The Supreme Court judged it unconstitutional in 2013 to differentiate the inheritance share for children born outside or inside wedlock, and one of the controversial articles of the Civil Code was finally modified based on the court judgment where political will had been absent in the past. Core conservatives remain upset with the decision. It is worth noting that while the Ministry of Justice was preparing the draft of the revised article in accordance with the court judgment, conservative members were reported to be disturbed, claiming that revising the law would destroy the "traditional family system." The prolonged 115 years of existence of this rule not only harmed unmarried mothers and their children financially but also stigmatized them, as criticisms over this issue were chiefly aimed at the women, not the men.

Minimal Changes to Spouse Tax Deduction Clause

The LDP has made it clear in the LDP Convention in both the 2012 and 2013 elections that it will maintain the spouse tax deduction clause, because it was critical for the LDP to defend the principle of household unity, where fulltime housewives get preferential status. However, Keidanren[23] and policy experts advocated for change; criticizing that the spouse deduction clause was akin to reducing women's incentive to work beyond the threshold set by the tax code.[24] Eliminating the spouse deduction meant allowing an eventual shift from household to individual taxation, but the Abe administration only made minimal changes as conservatives resisted. They agreed in 2018, however, to only eliminate the spouse reduction clause for higher income households earning more than 10 million yen, thereby upholding the deduction clause for the majority. In other words, conservatives would not accept any policy that might negate the "family system"—and the spouse tax deduction clause, only applicable to legally married couples, is an important aspect of it.

WHAT DID ABE NOT DO?

It was clear that the Abe administration had no intention to correct discriminatory rules against women. The United Nations Convention for Eliminating Discrimination Against Women (CEDAW) has condemned Japan for the absence of a clear legal definition and prohibition of discrimination against women and questions why Japan continues to have "unfair hierarchy and exclusion of women" despite having ratified the convention in 1985. The committee in 2016 pointed out the overall lack of progress and implementation of the 2009 recommendations into domestic legislations, as well as discriminatory legal provisions that remain within the Civil Code, Imperial Household Law, and the Anti-Prostitution Law.[25] The Abe administration made minimal changes, namely the raising of the legal marriage age for women from 16 to 18 years old to match with men, and equal inheritance for children born outside of wedlock. However, what was evident from the Abe administration's policies is that conservatives lacked the desire to eliminate discrimination against women, and only cherry-picked areas that were in line with the interests of businesses and themselves, carefully carving out the changes they considered unfavorable.

Restrictions on Newborn Registrations and Women for Remarrying

One of the controversial rules in the Civil Code is a discriminatory rule toward women who wish to remarry. A 100-day waiting period is imposed on women after divorce if they are suspected to be pregnant, while men can remarry immediately after a divorce. Women do not have to wait 100 days: (1) if she can prove that she was not pregnant when she filed a divorce (requires a doctor's certificate); (2) if the child's presumed father is the former husband; (3) if she is remarrying the formerly divorced husband; (4) if her husband was announced missing; (5) if divorced by court decision due to the husband being missing for more than three years; (6) if she submitted a doctor's letter indicating the abortion of the unborn child; or (7) if she does not have the ability to get pregnant (i.e., if her uterus was surgically taken out, or if she is too old to be pregnant). Instead of eliminating the waiting period, the Abe administration shortened it from six months to 100 days in 2016 in order to determine if the woman's pregnancy was from her former husband in response to repeated criticism of gender discrimination. A court case in 2011 triggered this: a woman in Okayama prefecture sued the Japanese government for her suffering through the unfair waiting period from her former domestic violence-convicted husband.

Another inflammatory issue is that of child registration. Under the Japanese Civil Code, it considers a child born within 300 days after the date of divorce to belong to the former husband, meaning the child would automatically be registered under the former husband's family registration tree (*koseki*), presuming that he is the father of that child. The Civil Code, being more than a century old, obviously does not require DNA testing. Many women who do not desire their babies to be forcefully registered under their former husband's family registration may end up choosing to not register their newborn child with the municipal authorities. As a result, the unregistered child is ineligible to receive what would normally be their entitled medical and educational benefits and public services, and additionally, the mother is not entitled to receive any financial assistance for that child. As long as the conservatives reign in Japan, this unfair discrimination against women is likely to continue, since conservatives lack any intention to change these long-standing laws any time soon.

Separate Surnames Destroying the "Family System"

The family system is one of the fundamental pillars of core conservative values. The family is united under one legal surname—therefore, having separate surnames within one family is simply not acceptable. Upon marriage, the couple can choose either the surname of the wife or husband as their legal surname, but the 2017 Census survey showed that more than 95 percent of the women were socially obliged to take their husbands' names. CEDAW pointed out that this was a violation of the convention, and warned the Japanese government that their legislation had to be consistent with Japan's international obligations. Nevertheless, Japan responded by saying it was difficult because the citizens' consensus was necessary to amend the Civil Code. Ironically, opinion surveys have increasingly shown Japanese citizens' profound support for having separate surnames; one survey reported more than 80 percent support separate surnames, and that 4 percent decided to not to marry because of their reluctance to share the same surname.[26] Despite this, in 2015, the Supreme Court rejected having separate legal surnames for married couples. The Tokyo District Court in 2019 rejected the proposal again, saying "the Civil Code provision stipulating a single surname for a husband and wife is constitutional and it is reasonable for the family register law not to allow separate surnames." Japan is the only one among developed nations that restricts married couples to the use of one legal surname. It is not "citizens," but the conservatives, who are strongly against having separate surnames, and therefore it makes sense that the Abe administration never took action regarding this issue.

Persistent Rejection for Female Heir of Imperial Throne

Core conservatives resolutely preserve male lineage-male emperor rule to protect the Imperial bloodline. One of the vocal conservative opinion leaders on this topic is Sakurai Yoshiko, who has said she is against the idea of having a female emperor because female lineage will lead to the switching of the Imperial family's bloodline from one family to the next.[27] The Koizumi administration's expert study group produced a report in November 2005 that recommended expanded eligibility for the throne, including female Imperial family members and/or female lineage for the Imperial throne, as the Meiji rule of male descendants from the male lineage is not a sustainable solution.[28] However, discussion of revising the Imperial House Law halted with the birth of a boy, Hisahito of the Akishino family, even though his birth did not actually solve the fundamental problem. Conservatives proposed to have male options by recovering "retired" royal families to take over after Hisahito's turn. In contrast with their rigid views, public opinion polls have shown more and more favor having a female emperor. A Kyodo News survey conducted on October 27, 2019 showed that 81.9 percent of respondents supported allowing for female emperors and 70 percent supported female lineage, while the percentage against having a female emperor was only 13.5 percent. Frustrated conservatives acted to limit any discussion that could lead to changing of the status and determined in February 2020 that the administration would neither hold any discussion regarding the Imperial Throne nor have any study groups by experts.[29] An editorial of the *Sankei Shimbun*, a conservative newspaper, also went forth advocating for the establishment of stable succession based on tradition and protecting the male line, "even [if] it may go against the principle of gender equality."[30] The NGO Japan Civil Liberties Union (JCLU) filed an issue to be listed under CEDAW in 2020[31] that Japan's Imperial House Act was in violation of the convention, as it excludes women from succeeding the Imperial Throne. When the Japanese government ratified CEDAW in 1985, the government viewed that "the Imperial throne was outside of the scope of the CEDAW Convention and, hence, the Imperial House Law needed no amendment." JCLU stated "it is deeply rooted in sexism, which reinforces discrimination against women in Japanese society."

WHAT REMAINED UNCHANGED OR UNSOLVED

Among other things, one striking fact is that the traditional gender-based division of labor continues to govern nearly half of the Japanese mindset. An unconscious bias continues to exist and is handed down to the following generations. Women are burdened with the duty of child rearing, while men continue to be very reluctant to take on housework or child rearing. Japanese husbands who have children under 6 years old spend on average eighty-three minutes on housework per day (while Japanese wives will spend 517 minutes on average), substantially lower in comparison with other OECD nations.[32] While there is a gradual shift occurring, a 2016 survey result indicated that 44.7 percent of Japanese men and 37 percent of women still support the traditional idea where the "husband works outside, wife stays at home" (see

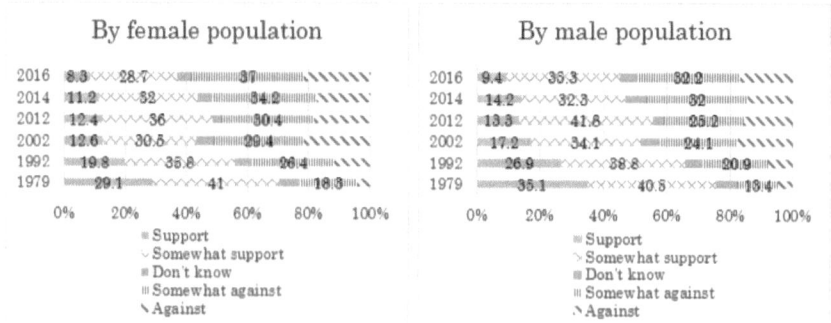

Figure 4.7 Do You Support the Notion of "Husband Works Outside and Wife Stays at Home"?. *Source*: Naikakufu, Danjo Kyodo Sankaku Shakai ni kansuru Yoron Chosa (H28, H26, H24, H14, H3, S54) Cabinet Office, Gender Equality Opinion Poll Survey (2016, 2014, 2012, 2002, 1992, 1979)

figure 4.7). Media reports were indeed surprised when minister of environment Koizumi Shinjiro announced in early 2020 that he would take two weeks paternity leave when his first baby was born. Abe's reform of the working environment to make it more family-friendly caused, in the end, only negligible change in the Japanese mindset, and hardly any noticeable impact on the fertility rate.

Single Mothers, Poverty, and Non-regular Workers

The poverty rate of Japanese single parents, the majority of whom are women, is more than 50 percent—the highest among OECD nations. Japan's social welfare and employment systems were designed to support the male breadwinners of the families, not mothers who happened to be single. As a result, single mothers tend to suffer with low levels of income support. Japan's social welfare system is based on "welfare through work,"[33] where medical expenses and pensions are supported through job security for male breadwinners. Furthermore, various public benefits and services are conducted through this de facto gender-biased system, meaning that benefit distributions are always given through the male head of household, leaving out individuals who ran away from their violent husbands. Mari Miura points out that public family benefits are kept low at the expense of maintaining male-privileged employment guarantees, which is why poverty levels remain high for single mothers who exist outside of the system.

Japan's 25 percent gender income gap also contributes to the poverty of single mothers, and is chiefly due to the disproportionately high number of women who are contracted into low-wage, non-regular jobs.[34] Single mothers tend to fall into this vicious cycle of insecure, low income work, leaving them in poverty. Despite the steady worsening of this situation, the Abe administration lacked adequate policies for these single mothers and usually excluded them, because they exist outside of the traditional family system. For example, when the 2020 fiscal year's tax code revision was discussed, Inada Tomomi, a core conservative member of Abe's group, persuaded key LDP members to make single mothers eligible for income tax reduction where it had originally only been available for widows and divorcees.[35] A majority of conservative members were against her proposal, because they believed making single mothers eligible would hurt their precious "traditional family system," as single mothers are those people who, in their view, intentionally "chose" to have children without getting married. Inada implored that it was unfair to exclude single mothers from tax code reductions for single women, because it may not have been their choice to raise a child alone, and that reasons and circumstances can vary. If Inada had not brought this up, single mothers would typically have been excluded from provisions.

Insufficient Measures: Women's Health, Domestic Violence, and Minimal Shelters

The Abe administration began to address domestic violence (DV), sexual harassment, and women's health in recent years, however, the comprehensive perspective required for protecting women was lacking, and larger problems remain unsolved. Japan retains a criminal code which punishes women for having an abortion without consent from their partner. Single mothers are treated with disgrace while access to oral contraceptives remains limited to only 1.1 percent of Japanese women (WHO, 2015), and morning-after pills require a prescription from a doctor. Japan legalized abortion in 1948, decades earlier than other nations, and Tiana Norgren (2001) pointed out that Japan's contradictory policies effectually encourage abortion over contraception. The male-dominated perspective in Japan becomes even more evident in realizing that birth control pills were finally made legal in 1999 after thirty-five years of debate and delay, while Viagra got approved within six months in 1999 and is now distributed nationwide. Women's health check rates are the lowest of OECD nations while men's annual health checks are done quite rigorously through the corporate health check system. According to OECD health data, the cervical cancer annual check rate is 26.5 percent[36] for women in their 20s, and sits at an average of 42.1 percent (2013) for all Japanese women in comparison to the rates of 74.6 percent–85.8 percent (2016, CDC) in the United States. Japan has severely insufficient support for DV victims as well. Despite a record high of 77,482 DV incidents reported in 2018, Japan has only 51 public DV shelters for women with a maximum capacity of 774 people, in addition to the 107 private shelters nationwide (Cabinet Office, 2018), numbers staggeringly low when compared to the 1,905 Intimate Partner Violence shelters (US Census, 2013) across U.S. programs. A majority of those privately run shelters are facing sustainability problems as subsidies are insufficient to cover the rent and their running relies heavily on unpaid volunteers. Abe's government allocated some additional budgeting for these shelters in 2020 due to the 2018 Cabinet Office survey, but that additional support is unlikely to be permanent. Women's labor is still insufficient to cover labor shortage, and Japan understands that it will need to rely more on foreign labor, yet there are no clear immigrant policies nor efforts at policy harmonization or even proper education for foreign-born children, since compulsory education applies only to Japanese children. Former Vice-Minister for Education Maekawa Kihei stated that this violates the Human Rights Convention, in which the right to education is guaranteed for every child. Japan ratified the convention in 1979, but the patriotic education framework continues to uphold prewar policies that exclude foreigners. Faced with rising truancy numbers, the government passed the Securing Education Opportunity Law (*Kyoiku kikai kakuhoho*) in 2016, but Maekawa said that political leaders across the board, from the LDP through the Communist Party, rejected the idea of including foreign-born children.[37] Thus, the issue of foreign-born children being denied a proper education in Japan has continuously been ignored.

CONCLUSION

Clearly, after almost eight years under the leadership of the Abe administration, Japan remains a male-dominated, chauvinistic country, where conservatives determine prevailing norms and values. Abe himself holds core conservative values and has made minimal effort to correct unfair conventions and achieve gender equality. In order to supplement the labor shortage, Abe successfully increased the number of women in the labor market, but two-thirds of the increase in female laborers was accounted for by low-paid, non-regular jobs. The Abe administration's passive stance toward businesses resulted in the achievement of neither the 30 percent women in leadership positions target nor a productivity increase led by a more efficient working style. The increase of women laborers was insufficient in mitigating the shortage, all while no clear immigrant policies or policy harmonization were pursued, meaning that there was no effort to systemically accommodate foreign families and incorporate them as community members. Big changes have finally begun to come, though not from any policy of Abe's but rather due to the COVID-19 crisis, which has forced corporations to change the ways they conduct business. Conservatives have continued to resist any change that would disturb their core values and have presented clear patterns of preferred policy decisions, averse to non-discrimination between men and women. Same-sex marriage is also another unthinkable issue for conservatives. Abe himself stated that such a union touches on the very fundamental existence of family values,[38] and therefore it is unlikely that the constitution could be revised to allow same-sex marriage. The gap between conservative values and global standards has widened under Prime Minister Abe in particular, seen acutely in CEDAW's consistent condemnation of the Japanese government for its lack of amendment of the discriminatory Civil Code that contains outdated and unfair rules against women.

Many discriminatory rules were established in the Meiji era, making them less than 200 years old, though conservatives claim to defend Japanese traditions drawing on 2,000 years of Japanese history. They are adamant in defending these outdated Meiji rules, which redefined Japan as a muscular nation with an emphasis on control and were modeled after European laws, though now they are somehow considered Japanese tradition. Even though we live now in a globalized society with rapidly developing technologies, Japan has been left behind by the rest of the world. Japanese women continue to suffer because conservatives lack the will to eliminate the discriminatory parts of the Civil Code which govern social norms.

It is ironic that corporations' and people's behaviors are made to change drastically not through Abe's policies, but because of COVID-19. The virus presented a situation where people found the new work-from-home style more efficient, which could be the beginning of a revolutionary shift from labor's value being determined by hours worked to being determined by job description, and further shift from a seniority-based system to a goals-oriented evaluation system. When such an evaluation system has become the norm, women will be less disadvantaged. Furthermore, an outcome-based flexible working style could allow women to gain financial security and sustainability, which could help them to feel stable enough to raise children, lending to a rise in the fertility rate, assuming Japan also follows the trends uncovered in the study on developed nations. As a result, overall productivity could increase. It is clear with the COVID-19 crisis that Japan no longer can afford to maintain conservative values in light of the unprecedented economic challenges.

In September 2020, newly appointed Prime Minister Suga Yoshihide announced that he will continue the policies of his predecessor Abe. However, it is not yet clear how he will advance gender equality or policies on women. Suga appointed only two women as cabinet members, and his speech sounded less than enthusiastic about the women's agenda. Mr. Suga did announce a new policy to financially support infertility treatment for those who want to have children, however, the scope of this policy is limited, and his approach lacks comprehensive vision. Because Suga had to ally with LDP faction seniors in order to secure his foundations within the party, it is unlikely that he would move to advance any agenda that promotes "gender equality" against core conservative values. What existed of Abe's positive legacy, in that he supported an increase in the female labor force has been turned upside down due to that population of female laborers, a majority of which are non-regular workers, becoming the most vulnerable population, as they are the most severely hit by COVID-19. If Suga is truly willing to tackle the fundamental problems faced by non-regular workers and break the cycle of poverty, he may be able to lift female workers to a more level playing field, even without giving voice to the term "gender-equality." So far, Suga is talking less about advancing women and instead emphasizing self-help, pushing for reform, and implying a desire to "abandon bad customs." Women's advancement may be possible if he chooses a pragmatic approach and steps away from fundamental conservative's values. With the pressure on due to COVID-19, it is time for Japan to truly transform from a nation under conservative norms to a more productive society.

NOTES

1. Kōichi Nakano, *Sengo Nihon no Kokka Hoshu Shugi* [Postwar Japan's National Conservatism], Tokyo: Iwanami, 2013.
2. Mari Miura, "*Shin jiyūshugi teki bosei – josei no katsuyaku seisaku no mujun*" [New liberalistic maternity: inconsistency of women advancement policies], *Gender Research* 18, (2015).
3. Michiko Hasegawa, Opinion Editorial, *Sankei Shimbun*, January 16, 2014.
4. "Holding back half the nation," *The Economist*, March 29, 2014.
5. Statement made by Minister of Health, Welfare & Labor Yanagisawa, January 27, 2007.
6. Gender Equality Bureau, "*Josei no rōdo ryoku-ritsu to gōkei tokushu shussei-ritsu*" [Female labor participation and birth rate], *Shoshika to danjo kyōdō sankaku ni kansuru senmon chōsakai* [Declining Number of Children and Gender Equality Special Research Committee], September 2005. http://www.gender.go.jp/kaigi/senmon/syosika/houkoku/pdf/honbun1.pdf.
7. Article 6 states "Citizens must try their best to realize a safe society where citizens give birth and raise children," and Article 17 states that national and local governments are to "provide education to raise awareness of the importance of male-female collaboration and roles of the household in raising children."
8. The government set breakdowns for each target: for central government directors 7%, prefectural government *kachō* (manager) 15%, private firms *kachō* 15%.

9. The increase from 1.6% in 2012 to 5.2% in 2019 is substantial, however, 5.2% is still very far from the stated goal. See more from the Gender Equality Bureau's site for female officers.

10. Miura, "*Shin jiyūshugi teki bosei.*"

11. Yuki Tsuji, "*Dainiji Abe naikaku ni okeru Josei suishin katsuyaku seisaku*" [Women empowerment promotion policies by the second Abe administration]. Kikan Kakei Keizai Kenkyu, 2015. http://kakeiken.jp/old_kakeiken/jp/journal/jjrhe/pdf/107/107_02.pdf.

12. Koji Horie, "*Seicho senryaku to shiteno josei*" [Women as a Growth Policy]. SYNODOS, July 19, 2016. https://synodos.jp/politics/17400/2.

13. 145th meeting memo of *Rōdo seisaku shingikai koyōkin tō bunka kai* [Labor policy committee regarding equal opportunity employment].

14. The MOFA (Ministry of Foreign Affairs) website states, "*Wagakuni no kihonteki Kangaekata*" [Our government's nation's basic stance]: "Women power is one of the most under-utilized resources in Japanese society, and therefore it is critical to realize full potential of women power for overall revitalization and economic growth" (provisional translation).

15. Prime Minister of Japan and His Cabinet, "Japan Revitalization Strategy -JAPAN is BACK-." June 14, 2013. https://www.kantei.go.jp/jp/singi/keizaisaisei/pdf/en_saikou_jpn_hon.pdf.

16. Prime Minister Abe mentioned this in his statement on April 19, 2013, as well as in the 2013 Japan Revitalization Strategy report.

17. Calculated from Labor Force Survey Historical data 10(2) Employed person by age group (five-year group), Employee by age group (five-year group), and Type of employment - Whole Japan, from the Statistics Bureau of Japan.

18. *Nippon.com*, "Gender Imbalance: Japan's Political Representation by Women Lowest in G20," March 9, 2019. https://www.nippon.com/en/japan-data/h00409/gender-imbalance-japan%E2%80%99s-political-representation-by-women-lowest-in-g20.html.

19. Kenji Suzuki, "*Naze nihon no josei giin ritsu wa sekai saitei reberu ka?*" [Why does Japan remain the lowest in political female representations?]. President Woman, August 7, 2019. https://president.jp/articles/-/29473?page=2.

20. Junya Ogawa, interview for the *Asahi Shimbun*, August 8, 2020.

21. Statements by Abe Shinzō on April 19, 2013 at a meeting with business leaders. See Abe Shinzō, "*Keizaikai to no iken kōkan-kai*" [Opinion exchange meeting with the business community], Prime Minister of Japan and His Cabinet, April 19, 2013.

22. Kathy Matsui, Hiromi Suzuki, and Kazunori Tatebe, "Womenomics 5.0: Progress, areas for improvement, potential 15% GDP boost," Portfolio Strategy Research by Goldman Sachs, April 18, 2019. https://www.goldmansachs.com/insights/pages/womenomics-5.0/multimedia/womenomics-5.0-report.pdf.

23. Josei Katsuyaku Action Plans 2014.

24. The spouse tax reduction clause only applies to legally married couples, with a threshold of 1.06 million yen for salary income and 1.3 million yen for spouse's total income. If the spouse's income exceeds these thresholds, they are not eligible for spouse tax reduction and spouse insurance.

25. UN Committee on the Elimination of Discrimination Against Women (CEDAW) reviewed Japan's reports 7 and 8.

26. A 2020 *Nishi Nihon Shimbun* survey showed 87.5% of women and 69.8% of men supported separate surnames. See *"Fūfu bessei, sansei 8-wari ankēto ni 'bessei erabezu kekkon dan'nen' 4-pāsento"* [Married couple's surnames, 80% in favor of 'I can't choose a different surname and give up marriage' 4%], *Nishi Nihon Shimbun*, March 8, 2020. https://www.nishinippon.co.jp/item/n/590242/.

Ogawa, Junya. Interview by the *Asahi Shimbun*, August 8, 2020.

27. Sakurai explains in an interview with *Shūkan Bunshun Digital* that she is concerned that if Aiko takes the throne, then Hisahito may lose the chance to succeed. See Yoshiko Sakurai, *"'Aiko tennō' wa zekahika] 'Hisahito-sama o sashioku koto de okoru jun'i gyakuten no kiken-sei',"* Interview by *Shūkan Bunshun Digital*, December 2, 2019. https://bunshun.jp/articles/-/15727.

28. 1947's revision restricting the throne to legitimate children made it difficult to maintain the Imperial line otherwise imperiled, according to the 2005 Advisory Council on Imperial House Law report.

29. Reported in the *Yomiuri Shimbun* on February 16, 2020.

30. The contents include: "A female emperor and female lineage succession will harm the tradition and argues that it is unconstitutional." Provisional translation by the author, from the *Sankei Shimbun*, *"[Shuchō] ten'nōheika go sokui shin jidai no go ketsui sasaetai dentō fumae antei keishō no kakuritsu o"* [Claim: His Majesty the Emperor's coronation, I want to support the determination of the new era, establish stable succession based on tradition], May 2, 2019. https://www.sankei.com/life/news/190502/lif1905020003-n1.html.

31. Japan's Imperial House Act stipulates that the Imperial Throne shall be succeeded only by a male offspring in the male line belonging to the Imperial Lineage (Article 1), thereby excluding women from succession (to become Empress). Information from JCLU.

32. Japanese husbands spend little time on childrearing and house work – there's only been a 16-minute increase in time they spend on average since 2011 (husbands spend 67 minutes on average). From results of the 2016 Social Life Basic Survey. See Gender Equality Bureau. *"'Heisei 28-nen shakai seikatsu kihon chōsa' no kekka kara ~ dansei no ikuji kaji kanren jikan ~"* [From the results of the '2016 Social Life Basic Survey' ~ Men's childcare / housework-related time ~]. October 2018. http://wwwa.cao.go.jp/wlb/government/top/hyouka/k_42/pdf/s1-2.pdf.

33. Miura, *"Shin jiyūshugi teki bosei."*

34. As of 2019, 56% of women are employed in non-regular positions, while only 21.9% of employed men are non-regular, according to the Statistics Bureau of Japan's historical data of 'employed person in age group.' See Statistics Bureau of Japan, "Historical data." http://www.stat.go.jp/english/data/roudou/lngindex.html.

35. From the conservative's view, widow or divorcees are "unfortunate," and therefore help should be offered because their circumstances may have been inevitable, but this logic does not extend to single mothers. From *Nikkan Gendai*'s Tomomi Inada interview.

36. Japan Medical Association, Accessed September 1, 2020. https://www.med.or.jp/forest/gankenshin/data/japan/.

37. Kihei Maekawa, "*Shugaku gimu gaikokuseki ni mo*" [Need Education opportunity for foreign-born children], Interview by Okuyama Haruna of the *Mainichi Shimbun*, August, 4, 2020.

38. Abe Shinzō stated at the Upper House Budget Committee, answering a question raised by Ishikawa Taiga, January 30, 2020.

REFERENCES

Abe Shinzō. "*Abe sōri 'seichō senryaku supīchi'*" [Prime Minister Abe 'Growth Strategy Speech']. Prime Minister of Japan and His Cabinet, April 19, 2013. http://www.kantei.go.jp/jp/96_abe/statement/2013/0419speech.html.

Abe Shinzō. "*Keizaikai to no iken kōkan-kai*" [Opinion exchange meeting with the business community]. Prime Minister of Japan and His Cabinet, April 19, 2013. http://www.kantei.go.jp/jp/96_abe/actions/201304/19keizaikai.html.

The Advisory Council on the Imperial House Law. "The Advisory Council on the Imperial House Law Report." November 24, 2005. http://japan.kantei.go.jp/policy/koshitsu/051124_e.pdf.

Center for American Women and Politics (CAWP). "Women in Elective Office 2019." https://cawp.rutgers.edu/women-elective-office-2019.

"*Fūfu bessei, sansei 8-wari ankēto ni 'bessei erabezu kekkon dan'nen' 4-pāsento*" [Married couple's surnames, 80% in favor of 'I can't choose a different surname and give up marriage' 4%]. *Nishi Nihon Shimbun*, March 8, 2020. https://www.nishinippon.co.jp/item/n/590242/.

Gender Equality Bureau. "'*Heisei 28-nen shakai seikatsu kihon chōsa' no kekka kara ~ dansei no ikuji kaji kanren jikan ~*" [From the results of the '2016 Social Life Basic Survey' ~ Men's childcare / housework-related time ~]. October 2018. http://wwwa.cao.go.jp/wlb/government/top/hyouka/k_42/pdf/s1-2.pdf.

Gender Equality Bureau. "*Josei no rōdo ryoku-ritsu to gōkei tokushu shusseiritsu*" [Female labor participation and birth rate]. *Shoshika to danjo kyōdō sankaku ni kansuru senmon chōsakai* [Declining Number of Children and Gender Equality Special Research Committee], September 2005. http://www.gender.go.jp/kaigi/senmon/syosika/houkoku/pdf/honbun1.pdf.

Gender Equality Bureau. *Josei yakuin jōhō saito* [Female officer information site]. http://www.gender.go.jp/policy/mieruka/company/yakuin.html.

Gender Equality Bureau. "White Paper on Gender Equality 2019." June 2019. https://www.gender.go.jp/english_contents/about_danjo/whitepaper/pdf/ewp2019.pdf.

Hasegawa, Michiko. Opinion Editorial. *Sankei Shimbun*, January 16, 2014.

"Holding back half the nation." *The Economist*, March 29, 2014.

Horie, Koji. "*Seicho senryaku to shiteno josei*" [Women as a Growth Policy]. SYNODOS, July 19, 2016. https://synodos.jp/politics/17400/2.

Inada, Tomomi. "*Jimintō inada tomomi-shi mikon hitori oya katei no shien kakudai kara henka o*" [Liberal Democratic Party's Tomomi Inada changes from expanding support for unmarried single-parent families]. Interview by *Nikkan Gendai*, January 27, 2020. https://www.nikkan-gendai.com/articles/view/news/268024.

JCLU Letter to the UN Committee on the Elimination of Discrimination Against Women. "RE: List of Issues Prior to Reporting (JAPAN)." February 28, 2020. http://jclu.org/wp-content/uploads/2020/03/1f05968ea8e23e78810b4d5a7333d860.pdf.

Japan Medical Association. Accessed September 1, 2020. https://www.med.or.jp/forest/gankenshin/data/japan/.

Maekawa, Kihei. "*Shugaku gimu gaikokuseki ni mo*" [Need Education opportunity for foreign-born children]. Interview by Okuyama Haruna of the *Mainichi Shimbun*, August, 4, 2020.

Matsui, Kathy, Hiromi Suzuki, and Kazunori Tatebe. "Womenomics 5.0: Progress, areas for improvement, potential 15% GDP boost." Portfolio Strategy Research by Goldman Sachs, April 18, 2019. https://www.goldmansachs.com/insights/pages/womenomics-5.0/multimedia/womenomics-5.0-report.pdf.

McKinsey & Company. "Diversity wins: How inclusion matters." May 2020. https://www.mckinsey.com/~/media/mckinsey/featured%20insights/diversity%20and%20inclusion/diversity%20wins%20how%20inclusion%20matters/diversity-wins-how-inclusion-matters-vf.pdf.

Miura, Mari. "*Shin jiyūshugi teki bosei – josei no katsuyaku seisaku no mujun*" [New liberalistic maternity: inconsistency of women advancement policies]. *Gender Research* 18, (2015).

MOFA. "*Josei ga kagayaku shakai*" [A Society where Women Shine]. Accessed on June 25, 2020. https://www.mofa.go.jp/mofaj/gaiko/women/index.html.

Nakano, Kōichi. *Sengo Nihon no Kokka Hoshu Shugi* [Postwar Japan's National Conservatism]. Tokyo: Iwanami, 2013.

Nippon.com. "Gender Imbalance: Japan's Political Representation by Women Lowest in G20." March 9, 2019. https://www.nippon.com/en/japan-data/h00409/gender-imbalance-japan%E2%80%99s-political-representation-by-women-lowest-in-g20.html.

Ogawa, Junya. Interview by the *Asahi Shimbun*, August 8, 2020.

OHCHR. "Committee on the Elimination of Descrimination Against Women examines reports of Japan." 2016. https://www.ohchr.org/EN/NewsEvents/Pages/DisplayNews.aspx?NewsID=17052&LangID=E.

Prime Minister of Japan and His Cabinet. "Japan Revitalization Strategy -JAPAN is BACK-." June 14, 2013. https://www.kantei.go.jp/jp/singi/keizaisaisei/pdf/en_saikou_jpn_hon.pdf.

Statistics Bureau of Japan. "Historical data." http://www.stat.go.jp/english/data/roudou/lngindex.html.

"*[Shuchō] ten'nōheika go sokui shin jidai no go ketsui sasaetai dentō fumae antei keishō no kakuritsu o*" [Claim: His Majesty the Emperor's coronation, I want to support the determination of the new era, establish stable succession based on tradition]. *Sankei Shimbun*, May 2, 2019. https://www.sankei.com/life/news/190502/lif1905020003-n1.html.

Sakurai, Yoshiko. "*['Aiko tennō' wa zekahika] 'Hisahito-sama o sashioku koto de okoru jun'i gyakuten no kiken-sei'*" Interview by *Shūkan Bunshun Digital*, December 2, 2019. https://bunshun.jp/articles/-/15727.

Suzuki, Kenji. "*Naze nihon no josei giin ritsu wa sekai saitei reberu ka?*" [Why does Japan remain the lowest in political female representations?]. President Woman, August 7, 2019. https://president.jp/articles/-/29473?page=2.

Tsuji, Yuki. "*Dainiji Abe naikaku ni okeru Josei suishin katsuyaku seisaku*" [Women empowerment promotion policies by the second Abe administration]. Kikan Kakei Keizai Kenkyu, 2015. http://kakeiken.jp/old_kakeiken/jp/journal/jjrhe/pdf/107/107_02.pdf.

Unites States Office of Personnel Management (OPM). "Women in Federal Service: A Seat at Every Table." 2014. https://www.opm.gov/fevs/reports/special-reports/women-in-the-federal-service-a-seat-at-every-table-2014.pdf.

Chapter 5

Prime Minister Abe's Security Policy

A Broader Spectrum

Guibourg Delamotte

INTRODUCTION

Prime Minister Abe Shinzō was among the most active prime ministers in the field of national security and foreign affairs. In the balancing act between liberal and conservative groups, which accession to power requires, the 2006 Abe was a fervent promoter of a "beautiful Japan," staunch advocate of a revision of the pacifist constitution, a conservative on history issues, who nevertheless refrained from visiting the Yasukuni shrine while in office and made China the destination of his first trip overseas after taking office. In 2012, while pushing for a minimal revision to the constitutional, he undertook a reform of the national security policy legal framework and thereby remained in the "incremental revisionism" inaugurated by Yoshida Shigeru. He did visit the Yasukuni shrine in 2013, but emphasized a relatively consensual vision of history in his speeches abroad or at home, upon the 70th anniversary of the end of World War II. While eager to engage with China (and relations indeed improved until the COVID-19 and Hong Kong crises), he consistently strengthened partnerships with "like-minded countries," seeking to counterbalance Chinese power.

In the field of defense and security, he established a more efficient security-related legal system and expanded some heretofore underdeveloped aspects of defense, such as space, cyber defense, and intelligence. He undertook reforms which stretched constitutional interpretation further than his predecessors had, and probably as far as it will need to go, short of a reconsideration of the willingness to accept more risk and the loss of SDF life. Furthermore, his administration took a global outlook on the world, adopted a wider and more strategic perspective.

This chapter will explain Japan's perception of its security context and its approach to security in order to highlight what changes Abe made as well as their long-term significance.

JAPAN'S PERCEPTION OF THE SECURITY CONTEXT UNDER PRIME MINISTER ABE

What Security Risks or Threats Does Japan Face? How Does It Perceive Global Security Challenges?

A Volatile Regional Context

President Xi Jinping has taken power projection and political control further than his predecessor, and relations with Japan have generally been unfriendly. In November 2013, China established an Air Defense Identification Zone covering contested waters and granting Chinese authorities unusual law enforcement powers. From the end of 2012, maritime incursions into what Japan considers its territorial waters or contiguous zone by Chinese government-owned vessels occurred almost daily. Efforts were made in 2014 and a Foreign Ministers Summit meeting was held, the first in two years and the first since Xi's ascent to power, on the margins of the APEC summit, so working-level dialogues could resume. In the "favorable" context of the trade war with the United States, 2017 marked the 45th anniversary of the establishment of diplomatic relations between the two countries, an opportunity to enhance a "mutually beneficial relationship based on common strategic interests." Incursions by Chinese vessels (generally the coast guards) decreased substantially in 2018, though they picked up again from January 2019. China's approximately 2,000 intermediate-range missiles near Taiwan could strike Japanese land. Japan finds itself in a state of constant vigilance and knows even positive signs can be easily reversed in the Chinese autocratic context.

The regional context provides further challenges. Russia ranks second after China for incursions into Japan's territorial airspace and Abe's efforts could not bring about the return of the "Northern Territories," annexed by Russia in the aftermath of Japan's surrender. Abe watched closely as President Trump met Kim Jong-un in June 2018 following the Pyeongchang Olympics. The Japanese government agreed with President Trump's insistence on a "complete, verifiable, irreversible" denuclearization, though it held reservations on the possibility of achieving this. It was not surprised by the standoff in the coming-up to the U.S. elections.

South Korea requires a delicate balancing act. Abe made gestures but he, or more likely the administration, could not help itself. Abe could bring himself to overcome a likely reluctance, but his efforts failed to produce the expected results, because they did not go quite a far as they should have. Abe agreed to provide renewed compensation to the "comfort women" (a term which refers to the sex slaves—some of whom were also Japanese—of the frontline brothels used by the Japanese Imperial Army), yet the 2015 Ministry of Foreign Affairs agreement mentioned the South Korean government should try and tackle the issue of the statues built in front of Japanese consulates worldwide to commemorate them—where the government was bound to fail. In 2019, four months after the South Korean government froze the assets of the Japanese companies condemned to pay damages to former "forced laborers" in contradiction with the wording of the 1965 treaty, according to Japan, Japan lifted South Korea's privileged export status for three chemical components, which South Korea interpreted as sanctions for the former and to which retaliated on a range of issues, from trade to security. Anti-Japanese sentiment is an important component of national identity in the divided nation and young democracy of South Korea. President Lee Myung-bak attempted in June 2012 to circumvent the National Assembly and have an intelligence-sharing bilateral agreement (GSOMIA) approved in a cabinet meeting; he ultimately had to backtrack, and a couple of months later became the first president to visit Dokdo/Takeshima (known in English as the Liancourt Rocks), which Japan considers its own. Before her administration signed a new compensation scheme with Japan to benefit "comfort women," in December 2015, President Park Geun-hye undertook an international campaign publicizing the issue so as to strengthen her credibility. It was also she who signed the GSOMIA in November 2016. Left-wing president Moon Jae-in dissolved the foundation set up to provide new compensation to the former prostitutes in June 2019, in effect suspending the agreement, and came close to denouncing the GSOMIA in August 2019. Given the volatility of South Korean politics, Japan must be reproachless.

Beyond Northeast Asia: A Precarious International Situation

Japan's contribution to international security has expanded as new international challenges arose. It provided some help in fighting piracy in the 1990s in the Strait of Malacca and in the 2010s in the Gulf of Aden, where it participates in the joint international effort (though the SDF are not integrated into the combined command). It contributes to the fight against proliferation through the Proliferation Security Initiative, set up by President George W. Bush in 2003, and has applied UN resolutions (and more) in relation to North Korea. It suffered losses in Algeria (January 2013) when Japanese employees working on an industrial project were killed during an attack by Islamist fighters opposed to the Algerian government and applied collective sanction mechanisms (such as the freezing of terrorists' assets), but has mainly sought to deal with terrorism economically through its Official Development Assistance (in Afghanistan or Iraq).

The SDF were sent to the Indian Ocean (2001–2010 with a brief interruption) and Iraq (2003) on the basis of *ad hoc* legislation. Japan endeavored to meet the needs of international cooperation expressed by international organizations or the United States, yet preserve Article 9 for legal and political purposes, though the article's limits were expanded by the cabinet and the Cabinet Legislation Bureau (the government agency which advices the government on bills and ensures their compatibility with existing laws) to allow any policy adjustment needed and insure that the legal rationale would remain consistent.[1] Japan now uses its SDF overseas in an array of non-combat operations, yet Japan's policy of not exposing them to life-threatening danger has remained untouched under Abe.

Japan also deployed diplomatic mediation efforts, most recently between Iran, the United States, and Saudi Arabia, from the Osaka G20 in June 2019 to Abe's visit to three Middle Eastern countries in January 2020), though to no avail.

Beyond those issues, Japan, like Western democracies, faces a wider challenge: China's worldwide investments and their associated influence, which Japan has sought to counterbalance diplomatically.

JAPAN'S APPROACH TO SECURITY

In this Environment, How Can Japan's Interests Be Defended, and How Are they Defined?

Japan's Leaders Have Had to Strike a Balance between Idealism and Realism

Immediately postwar, the new constitution by which Japan renounced the use of force and all military potential was adopted. The government's interpretation initially was that Japan could only revert to diplomacy to defend itself. This, however, was not a line which it found particularly attractive, and indeed it believed that it would at some stage depart from it. The Ashida Amendment to Article 9 left open a possibility to do so. Soon, the Cold War began. It became quite clear to the United States that it needed a strong Japan, and to Japan that the United States may not want to leave the region. Japan needed to think about the means by which it could defend itself given this new context, and American bases provided the solution. The 1952 Security Treaty (which was replaced in 1960 by a new agreement, still in force) served this purpose.

Since then, the government has found itself on a tightrope, juggling the constitution, to which nationalists were hostile, and the Security Treaty, which most on the left rejected and nationalists also disliked due to its restriction on Japan's autonomy. U.S. demands were just as contradictory: the constitution must be upheld, yet Japan must rearm. The "Yoshida line" sought to emphasize economic recovery and limit defense spending, while rearming to the extent necessary for self-defense only—the limits of which can be very rhetorical.

This paradigmatic framework created by two sets of norms born in different historical contexts has given Japan's defense and foreign policies their characteristics, which remain to this day.

A second consequence followed from this situation. Japan's defense and security policy emerged incrementally. In 1960 (upon the ratification of the new Security Treaty), the right became aware that a *status quo* had been reached, the lines of which would be difficult to shift. Therefore, any change was accompanied by "principles" (the non-deployment overseas principle, the ban on arms exports, the non-nuclear principles, which were not completely upheld) which served as guarantees to the left and to the United States that the pacifist spirit of the constitution was unaffected. The limits of international cooperation likewise shifted after 1992, away from strictly bilateral, and activities were added to the SDF's missions and some degree of involvement in international peace-keeping cooperation activities became acceptable.

Prime Minister Abe remained in the incremental realm, and the reforms he undertook will require adaptation and interpretation themselves. However, they provide a more stable framework than most of the laws adopted hitherto for the purpose of international cooperation.

The International Warranty Provided by the UN Framework Was Emphasized

Japan has based its foreign and security policy decisions on an adherence to the international order, to show that it was no longer a challenger to the *status quo*. It became a member of the United Nations in 1956, and the first document setting principles to the recently reestablished armed forces (officially called the Self-Defense Forces), the Basic Policy for National Defense, referred to the UN as the ultimate guarantor of Japan's security in 1957 (though few in Tokyo were naïve enough to think this would ever be possible on the part of the organization, which was no longer made of "united nations"). Yet, this idealism was always balanced by realism—as was the constitution's Article 9 by the Security Treaty. Pending the UN's ability to effectively defend Japan, Japan would procure limited armament based on the Japan–U.S. agreements on which it depended.

The mention of the UN has not been simply formal. It has been considered as providing legitimacy for the purposes of international and domestic law alike. When Japan ventured to take part in international peace cooperation activities from 1992, it always deployed its SDF in undebatable accordance with UN resolutions including in Iraq in 2004 (the SDF were deployed after the adoption of resolution 1511[2]).

Though the UN remains the ultimate guarantor of the legitimacy of an international operation, Japan ensured in the 2015 reform of its security system (*infra*) that its assistance in an international operation would not be hampered by a Chinese veto.

Japan Took a Broad Approach to Security

Early on, Japan took a broad approach to security, when the world was deep in the Cold War and its derived realist notions of security. Beyond its military dimension, Japan emphasized the social and economic dimensions. Perhaps inspired by John Galtung's seminal article on the sources of violence,[3] advisers to the future prime minister Ōhira Masayoshi—academics Inoki Masamichi, Kōtaka Masataka, Sato Seizaburō—came up with the notion of "comprehensive security" in 1978, stressing that Japan should be internally safe from the economic, educational, cultural points of view, and diplomatic efforts should be pursued in those economic and cultural directions.

This approach to security has been embraced by International Theory.[4] It has also been welcomed by the UN, which drew on it to give birth to "human security,"[5] and has appeared as the societal lever to fight terrorism. Japan's 2003 ODA Charter refers to "human security" as a key-concept. The term was kept, as indeed was the philosophy, in the 2015 Charter (Development Cooperation Charter), which also places emphasis on self-help efforts.

Prime Minister Abe could not question the fundamental parameters of Japan's approach to security; thus, he built upon them.

PM ABE'S UNDERTAKINGS

Abe Shinzō had hoped to achieve constitutional revision in 2020.[6] In 2018, a 4-point revision proposal was put forward with a view (*a*) on ensuring the constitutional compatibility of the SDF (diverging views were expressed: keep Article 9 entirely and add a mention of the SDF, or delete paragraph 2 banning all war potential and replacing it with one on the SDF; in addition, LDP members considered adding civilian control); (*b*) on establishing institutional workings under emergency situations (there are no provisions on the prolongation of the Diet mandate if elections cannot be held, or on concentrating powers in the executive under such circumstances); and two other points which did not concern security or defense.[7] This was very low-key by comparison to the LPD's 2004 proposals. In view of the lack of popular support, Prime Minister Abe stopped short of attempting constitutional reform. Instead, he pushed Article 9's interpretation further still, to ensure that Japan could better defend itself and cooperate more efficiently with partners in an international crisis and undertook a reform of the security legal framework to this effect.

The three elements listed above remain, yet the balance between idealism and realism has shifted further toward realism. A UN Security Council resolution is no longer the sole basis for international deployment of the SDF which may be requested by other international organizations; Japan's approach to security was broadened.

There are uncertainties resulting from the 2015 security system legal reform, but this left the government room for maneuver in the assessment of a future crisis situation. Abe allowed collective self-defense and logistic support to be provided in international crises; in theory, hostages can be rescued, but the government can still keep the SDF out of danger. Nonetheless the benefits of the new system are substantial. It is more predictable for the public, therefore more satisfactory from perspective of democratic requirements, and slightly more predictable for allies too (they still can't be sure to have support, but will know which support they could get).

Abe made numerous changes with respect to Japan's national defense policy as well. Let us start from there, before we turn to the international security-related changes.

The National Defense Legal Framework

In 2013, a number of changes were made. A National Security Council was created to provide the prime minister with advice in crisis situations and strategic analysis stemming from the key intelligence organizations, and encourage officials from the Ministry of Foreign Affairs, Ministry of Defense, and the National Police Agency to exchange intelligence. It can meet in different formats and receives the support of the cabinet secretariat's national security team.

The National Security Strategy (2013) was the first such document since the 1957 Basic Policy on National Defense to state principles along six axes—strengthening Japanese defense capabilities, the Japan–U.S. alliance, emphasizing diplomacy and security cooperation with partners, taking a "proactive approach" to international cooperation, defending certain values (human security, free trade, the protection of the environment, among others), and raising the Japanese public's awareness of security issues. One such principle is the idea of a "highly effective and joint defense force" to ensure "flexibility and readiness."

Two new documents were released soon after: the National Defense Program Guidelines (NDPG) for FY 2014 and beyond[8] and the accompanying Mid-Term Defense Program (MTDP), which presented the objectives based on the strategy and the means to achieve them. The philosophy was to adapt in the event of a "severe security situation" and capabilities in a variety of areas including missile defense, intelligence, cyber and space capabilities, deployment, and international cooperation.[9]

The 2019 Guidelines mention "grey-zone situations" and new threats (through the social media, cyberthreats).[10] National defense objectives are defined as: improving the security environment; deterring threats through the potential to inflict enough damage; having the capacity to counter the threat should it occur nevertheless, and minimizing damage. From these considerations derive the three pillars of Japan's national defense: self-help efforts, international partnerships, the U.S.–Japan alliance (the "cornerstone" of Japan's defense). In addition, Japan is expected to contribute to international peace.

Based on this assessment, the MTDP for FY 2019–2023 reorganizes SDF units and ensures equipment quality and quantity is improved. Japan under Prime Minister Abe has continued to invest in projection and amphibious capabilities to protect the small southwestern islands. Missile defense was to be upgraded with the introduction of "Aegis Ashore" (the Aegis missile detection system, on land) in the FY 2018 budget, but it appeared that North Korean ballistic know-how had already outpaced the system and in June 2020, the government announced its decision to halt its deployment.

Missile capabilities were improved with the acquisition of Kongsberg's Joint Strike Missile (JSM), a sea- and land-target missile for F-35 stealth fighters, Lockheed–Martin's Joint Air-to-Surface Standoff Missile-Extended Range (JASSM-ER) and its variant, the Long Range Anti-Ship Missile, for the F-15 fighter jets, and the development of Mitsubishi's improved, supersonic ASM-3s. The new Hypersonic Cruise Missile and Hyper Velocity Gliding Projectile announced at the end of 2019 is to be ready for deployment in 2024–2028.

Simultaneously, in 2015, the Basic Plan on Space Policy based on the Fundamental Law on Space (2008) improved Japan's ability to detect missile launches, its reconnaissance capabilities, and ensured that JAXA, the space agency hitherto devoted to science for civilian purposes, would integrate security objectives. Cyber defense received increased attention too, with private partnerships to be developed in the future.

The network of defense attachés (which was deemed insufficient after the In-Amenas hostage crisis of January 2013) was developed. Intelligence exchanges with the United States required a better regime for the protection of classified information, and for that purpose the Act on the Protection of Specially Designated Secrets (2013) was passed. The General Security of Military Information Agreement (GSOMIA) was signed with South Korea in 2016, after a four-year negotiation and an agreement on "comfort women" providing individual compensation from the Japanese state. Intelligence further benefited from defense dialogues with Australia and European countries (*infra*).

Defense spending, which had declined between 2005 and 2012 to 4.68 trillion yen, increased steadily to 5.31 trillion yen in FY 2019–2020 (approximately US$48 billion).[11] Given budget constraints, due consideration was given to rationalization and industrial cooperation. To raise Japanese military capabilities through international industrial cooperation, the ban on defense or dual-material exports was lifted in 2014, and "three principles on transfer of defense equipment and technology" were adopted instead, to the effect that Japan can now export technology equipment if it serves its security interests. Furthermore, to reduce cost, the Acquisition, Technology & Logistics Agency was created as an external organ of the Ministry of Defense in October 2015. It replaced the separate organizations, which existed in the three forces, and is responsible for the acquisitions and development of weapons.

The defense doctrine was also altered by a cabinet decision to allow collective self-defense in July 2014, allowing Japan to use force when one of its allies is attacked and as a result Japan's survival (存立, *sonritsu*) is under threat, or the people's right to life, liberty, and pursuit of happiness is in clear danger (though use of force should be minimal). This enables Japan to show the reciprocity which the United States had long been requesting from Tokyo, yet Japan really retains full discretion in the use of force, which has been linked to Japanese survival, or to clear danger to constitutional rights (the wording refers to Article 13 of the Constitution[12]). This measure was inserted in the legislation on armed-attack or threat-to-survival situations (*buryoku kōgeki jitai hō*, as amended to cover *sonritsu kiki jitai*), though use of force could be used in international-cooperation deployments, provided the criteria were met.

Lastly, the SDF can now free Japanese expatriates who are taken hostage overseas (they could only repatriate them before 2015), though this can only be done with the approval of the state where the Japanese are held. In addition, to do so without casualties among the hostages would require advanced special-operations know-how, which very few countries have—and Japan is not among them yet.

The New International Security Cooperation Legal Framework

The 2013 National Security Strategy also makes Japan a "proactive contributor to peace." Use of the term "proactive pacifism" (積極的平和主義, *sekigyokuteki heiwa shugi*) has implied that Japan is prepared to get more involved in international security efforts.

The 2015 legislative reform allows Japan to provide logistic support and Search and Rescue (SAR) services:

- to foreign armed forces engaged in activities which contribute to Japan's security, in crisis situations worldwide which "have an important impact on Japan's peace and security" (*jūyō eikyō jitai*).
- to armed forces engaged in collective action to further the objectives of the Japan–U.S. Security Treaty and address a situation which threatens international peace and security. The collective action in question must be based on a United Nations Security Council resolution, which recognizes that the situation constitutes a threat to peace or breach of peace and requests member-states to take measures.

The nature of the goods, which can be supplied in both instances, has been expanded from the previous legal bases to include ammunition (along with oil, fuel, tents, medical supplies, and more), which can be transported for the United States and other forces, pursuant to the SDF law revision). Aircraft taking off to take part in combat can be refueled. However, logistic support cannot be provided if combat operations (*sentō kōi*) are taking place (though the SDF can carry out SAR if the situation has deteriorated, provided they can do so safely). The commander of the operation also can now decide to suspend an operation if he sees the situation deteriorating. The Minister of Defense is responsible for ensuring the deployment zone is safe and to alter it, if need be. Diet approval is required in principle, but can be sought retroactively after deployment in case of emergency.

Therefore, legal precautions have been taken to avoid Japan finding itself party to an international conflict without having been attacked. Admittedly, Japan would find it diplomatically difficult, when providing logistic support or SAR, not to invoke collective self-defense to reply on behalf of an ally who was under attack and struggling to retaliate. To avoid being in an precarious position legally, the government would likely avoid deployment altogether. The political hurdle of facing a dangerous deployment, where SDF forces could be put in danger or put in a position where they might create casualties in an international conflict, is too great at this stage.

Maritime inspections can occur in the context of crisis situations "bearing important consequences for Japan's peace and security." They can also take place to further international peace-keeping efforts.

Indeed, aside from this set of interventions in mildly dangerous situations, Japan can take part in international peace-keeping efforts.

Japan can send SDF members on a peace-keeping mission on an expanded legal basis (*kokusairengō heiwa kyōryoku*) provided that there has been a ceasefire and the operation is non-partisan; the operation should cease if it becomes dangerous. It must have been requested by a neighboring country or based on a request from the UNSC or (this is new) another international body. This avoids being held hostage to a possible Chinese veto. Use of force should still be minimal, but rules of engagement have been leveled with international standards, meaning that the SDF can use their weapons to accomplish their mission (a possibility first inserted in the 2010 Anti-Piracy Act). The use of weapons used to be allowed for self-defense or the protection of equipment only. The SDF also can take part in a broader range of missions and protect local populations (*kaketsuke keigo*). The Diet's approval is required (though approval can be sought *a posteriori* if the Diet is not in session or the Lower House is inter-mandate).

In practice, little has changed with respect to peace-keeping operations (PKOs). Japan currently has none, and two were ended while Prime Minister Abe was in office, to shield the SDF from danger. The operation on the Golan Heights (which had started in 1996) ended in January 2013, and the one to South Sudan, in July 2017 (it had started in 2008). The latter provided insight into current government thinking on PKO deployment. Though the SDF were deployed after a ceasefire had been declared, they remained in spite of a deteriorated security environment after 2013. They were deployed in an area which was not shielded from combat in itself, but where risk of loss of life appeared limited enough,[13] though leaks led to their repatriation and to the resignation of the Minister for Defense in July 2017. The Golan Heights deployment ended due to the deteriorating situation in Syria. The government will take no chances where SDF lives are at stake, regardless of the consequences in terms of reputation or the resulting lack of experience in emergency situations and danger.

Further activities in relation to international cooperation can take place outside a UN PKO framework (*kokusai heiwa shien*). They require a UN resolution (from the General Assembly or the Security Council) requesting, welcoming or acknowledging action against a state and condemning its actions as a threat or breach of international peace. In such a context, Japan can undertake ship inspections, as well as provide logistic support (excluding the provision of ammunitions) and SAR. Use of weapons is limited to individual self-defense. There can be no "association with the use of force," and the commander can stop the operation even if under way, with the Minister of Defense required to redefine the deployment zone if it becomes dangerous. Diet approval is mandatory prior to deployment though its members must attempt to deliver a resolution in seven days. Approval must be renewed after two years (it can then come *a posteriori* if the Diet is not in session or is inter-mandates[14]).

Lastly, "grey-zone" situations (which do not amount to an aggression) were given new attention. The SDF are able under the SDF Law to back the coastguards in their police missions if the latter's capacities appear to be insufficient. A cabinet decision in May 2015 established a simplified procedure to allow the government to deploy the SDF on a public order operation at sea (*chian shutsudō, kaijō keibi kōdō*) without a cabinet meeting by collecting ministers' approvals over the phone. This concerns three situations in particular: when a vessel does not meet the requirements of the right of innocent passage under International Law, the illegal landing of armed individuals even if not officially members of a military force, and the need to protect civilian vessels in the open seas. In December 2019, the government sent a helicopter-equipped destroyer and two P-3C maritime patrol planes to the Arabian Sea, the Gulf of Aden, and the Gulf of Oman (not the Persian Gulf or the Strait of Hormuz, which were deemed too dangerous) on a fact-finding mission, which would not have required a cabinet decision, but sought one nevertheless, under the normal procedure. The simplified emergency one has not yet been used.

Diplomatic Efforts

In the 2013 National Security Strategy, diplomacy, too, received attention. Prime Minister Abe was active in two main directions: to ensure good relations with the United States in spite of the Trump administration's "America first" focus and counter the effects of the latter wherever possible, as well as to balance China's expansionism through partnerships while still preserving dialogue.

Obama's "Asian pivot" (2011) implied containment yet engagement of China via the Trans-Pacific Partnership (TPP) to which, it was hoped, China would later adhere. Japan, who sought new markets to promote growth, saw advantages to the mega-trade deals. When President Trump announced the United States' withdrawal from the TPP, Japan took the lead in negotiations in this reduced format and the TPP11 was signed in March 2018. Abe then managed to strike a reasonable deal with Trump in the bilateral negotiations that followed, ensuring that Japan made no further concessions in the bilateral deal than it had under the TPP11. Indeed, rice was left out of the bilateral deal—the trade-off was that the question of quotas for Japanese car imports to the United States remains open. Japan also signed a "mega-trade treaty" and a Strategic Partnership Agreement with the EU, in the middle of the trade war launched by Trump on China and the EU. Furthermore, Japan offered (to no avail) its mediation in the conflict with Iran over the 2015 nuclear deal, from which the United States had withdrawn in May 2018.

The second direction was hedging China. Under the "Pivot", U.S. allies were encouraged to establish relations to develop their cooperation and thereby counterbalance China's rise. The Middle East kept the Obama administration busier than expected, but Japan pursued diplomatic efforts to establish links with "like-minded countries" (a term meaning nations which, like Japan, were concerned about China). Abe expressed the idea of a "Democratic Security Diamond" before taking office in December 2012, and a few years later, announced his "Free and Open Indian Ocean vision" (FOIP) during the Sixth Tokyo International Conference on African Development (TICAD VI) in August 2016. The FOIP displays an opening of Japan's strategic horizon from the Asia-Pacific to the Indian Ocean, a willingness to develop partnerships and promote democratic values and the rule of law through increased prosperity.

From this standpoint derived, first, an array of new security relationships and related diplomatic adjustments (on history and territorial issues), and second, a new security-focused assistance policy placing emphasis on connectivity. Notwithstanding those efforts, Japan sought to engage, or rather not to antagonize, China.

From 2007, Japan established security links (albeit on different levels) with Australia, India, Indonesia, Malaysia, Vietnam; from 2012, with France and the United Kingdom, and with the EU and NATO. (Cooperation with South Korea was briefly mentioned above, cooperation with Russia receives limited attention here—both are addressed in separate chapters of this volume.)

Leaving the United States aside, Japan now has "2+2" dialogues (in Ministers of Defense and Foreign Affairs formats) with Australia (since 2007), which has the status of a "special strategic partner," as well as with Russia, France (a "partnership of exception"), and the United Kingdom. It has signed ACSAs (Acquisitions and Cross Servicing Agreement) with Australia, the United Kingdom, France, and Canada (with two more close to completion with India and Russia). Japan and Australia have agreed on the terms of a Reciprocal Access Agreement (RAA), which Abe and Scott Morrison should sign in July 2020, opening the door for SDF operations in and around Australia, and *vice versa*. The *ad referendum* agreement provides access to facilities in a reciprocal fashion and covers such issues as taxation, basing, entry and exit procedures, and criminal jurisdiction. For the first time since the signing of the Status of Forces Agreement of 1960 with the United States, foreign troops are allowed to station in Japan. Conversely, the agreement allows the SDF to station overseas (after the precedent of Djibouti in 2009) and displays Japan's willingness to play a more active role in international security in the region. The agreement, which will require ratification, makes Australia Japan's closest ally after the United States.

Furthermore, industrial cooperation is carried on with France (on drones) and the United Kingdom (on missiles). Intelligence-sharing is taking place with the United States, United Kingdom, Canada, Australia, New Zealand, France, and Germany, in particular on cyber defense.[15]

With Southeast Asian countries, cooperation continued on the track set in 2005 under Koizumi. Japan had developed a variety of dialogues and cooperation based on personnel or student exchanges, regular visits, and aid in the form of decommissioned coast guard vessels from 2005 (to Indonesia) with those countries which share concern over China due to similar maritime border issues.

Security cooperation with the EU was strengthened with the signing, along with that of an EPA, of a Strategic Partnership Agreement (SPA) (both entered into force in February 2019). The SPA provides a foundation for enhanced cooperation in many areas. Japan is also a partner country of the EU's Action Plan entitled "EU Security Cooperation in and with Asia" adopted in October 2019. Furthermore, an EU–Japan Framework Partnership Agreement (FPA), under discussion, would create the legal framework for Japanese institutionalized contributions to EU Common Security and Defense Policy (CSDP) missions.[16]

Cooperation between NATO and Japan was stepped-up with the signature in April 2013 of a joint political declaration and, from May 2014, of individual partnership and cooperation programs. Japan's ambassador to Belgium is also representative to NATO. Japan now has liaison officers at the Supreme Headquarters Allied Powers Europe (in Belgium) and the Maritime Command (in the United Kingdom). It also contributes a staff officer on "Women, Peace and Security." Cooperation takes place in cyber defense, maritime security, humanitarian assistance, and disaster relief or non-proliferation, for instance.

This surge in a defense and security-motivated diplomacy under Abe Shinzō (from 2007) was accompanied (from the mid-2010s) by an effort to settle history issues with partners— Australia (prisoners of war), the United States (Hiroshima/Pearl Harbor), Southeast Asia—and neighbors (South Korea) alike. In Canberra in July 2014, Prime Minister Abe mentioned the lives lost and survivors of the Kokoda Trail battles and Sandakan "death marches." Upon the 70th anniversary of the end of the World War II, he addressed all those on whom "our country inflict[ed] immeasurable damage and suffering." With South Korea, Japan, whose stance is that the 1965 treaty rules out claims from citizens against either state, agreed in December 2015 the state would compensate "comfort women" individually (Moon

Jae-in later walked out of this agreement). Abe was the first Japanese prime minister to visit Pearl Harbor and offer condolences in December 2016, after President Obama came to Hiroshima and met survivors in May 2016. On territorial issues, Abe was uncompromising over the Senkaku, non-provocative yet consistent on Dokdo/Takeshima, and he attempted in vain to solve the Northern Territory issue with Russia. The government stance on textbooks was changed in 2014, after which they have been required to reflect the government's official position, no longer needing to take into account neighboring countries' sensitivities, which indeed Japan does in its official positions.

Furthermore, Abe's Japan sought to offer alternatives to China's investments and assistance through different channels, such as its official development assistance, the Asian Development Bank, the TICADs, and the FOIP. Japan's ODA is directed to capacity-building efforts in the ASEAN countries[17] and Africa (with a "training trainers" program in Djibouti for instance). Connectivity promotion is an important aspect of the FOIP. The Japan–Indian Asia–Africa Growth Corridor (2017) aims to promote quality infrastructure, and digital and institutional connectivity. "Quality infrastructure to enhance connectivity" are part of the economic pillar of TICADs VI and VII. The EU and Japan have paved the way for enhanced cooperation in the field with their Partnership on Sustainable Connectivity and Quality Infrastructure (September 2019).[18]

In parallel, Abe Shinzō sought to engage China (cf. chapter 8 on China) and was milder than the United States, the United Kingdom, or Australia in blaming China regarding the pandemic and the new Security Law adopted to extend mainland security practices to Hong Kong. Upon the COVID-19 outbreak, the government was criticized for belatedly closing its borders with China (it stopped traffic with South Korea at the same time). In May 2020, Japan joined the call for an international investigation on the COVID-19 outbreak, which the WHO rallied. With EU Council President Charles Michel, Abe called for respect for democracy, an improvement of international organizations' functioning to avoid the spread of pandemics, and both leaders called on China to respect Hong Kong's autonomy. Japan (like New Zealand) would not join the strongly worded Five Eyes statement released that month,[19] but issued one separately,[20] and submitted a draft statement at the Group of Seven (G7) foreign ministers' meeting convened in June, which expressed the "grave concern" of the G7 leaders and the EU.[21]

THE CHALLENGES AHEAD

Where does Japan stand after Abe's near decade in power? While Abe remained along the incremental path of the Yoshida doctrine, he succeeded in setting up a system which should prove relatively long-lasting, though it will continue to adapt (in June 2020, the LDP was considering admitting preemptive strike capability in view of the obsolete character of the missile defense system). Abe set new conditions to the legitimate use of force, general frameworks for overseas deployments, and reformed the areas where the defense and security policies were unsatisfactory (costly, detrimental to the SDF's image, and to Japan's safety in preventing industrial cooperation). Japan can now defend itself better (with U.S.'s help), and it can contribute to international crisis resolution more straightforwardly than it could before. The government can now do, in terms of international security, more than what it has been doing since 1998, with greater efficiency and more transparent conditions (the range of possibilities being known), under the Diet's control, but not at the mercy of the opposition. The situation is more manageable for the prime minister, who has the legal basis to act swiftly, or for MOFA officials, who know what they can offer, and international partners, who know what the Japanese government can provide—if they are willing to.

The Abe administration has upheld the pacifist principle of non-intervention in a war though the admission of collective self-defense could open breaches. Use of force will be up to a democratically elected government to decide. Japanese voters now have a better vision of their future leader's powers in this field and of what their SDF could be asked to do. They should vote according to their opinions not just on economic and social policies but also on security issues. For the Japanese voters to become security-alert is possibly the first challenge facing Japan.

At least four others remain. First, Abe has had to stick to the Yoshida Doctrine, the benefits of which have been tremendous. The contradiction between the constitution and the 1960 Japan–U.S. Security Treaty remains. There would be a need to revise either the constitution or the Security Treaty to suppress the ambivalence. A limited revision of the constitution would help clarify the situation from a legal and intellectual point of view. For this to take place in a serene domestic and international environment, history controversies must cease entirely on the Japanese side. Abe has taken this direction. It would not clarify the situation from a political point of view. The uneasy relation to strategic considerations and weak eminent-domain laws, which inhibit the deployment of military assets, have created a political culture so embedded that even revision of Article 9 would not suffice to uproot it.[22] Furthermore, today, acceptance of danger, risk and pain inflicted on the SDF or by the SDF, is the real limit to Japan's security commitments. At this stage, the Japanese see in the constitution a symbol of its pacifism and in its revision a danger, and do not want to see their SDF take any combat role in an international war. Meanwhile, Japan can provide for its safety, and take part in the international cooperation activities which it wishes, on its own terms.

The second challenge is a more recent one. The limits of multilateral institutions, of multilateralism as it has been practiced since the 1990s, with faith in the power of free trade to bring benefits to populations worldwide and create tightly knit interests that would ensure the system's stability, appeared clearly in 2019. The lack of interest on the part of Donald Trump for multilateral organizations, partly fueled by Xi Jinping and Vladimir Putin's abuse or disregard of their rules, those institutions' budgetary frailty and the power games they are caught in, imperil their continued workings. To contribute and succeed in influencing the renewal of the international system, further cooperation between Japan and its partners appears essential.

A third challenge is public finances. With a declining population, Japan finds itself with limited resources and increased social welfare and pensions costs. Convincing Japanese voters to accept a policy which would entail devoting more resources to the SDF would be all the more difficult.

A fourth challenge one may point out is how to ensure a lower dependency on China and its rare earth metals when relying ever more on innovation, artificial intelligence, and technologies to make up for a shrinking population and generate growth in Japan, or to open new markets to Japanese firms and promote sustainable development goals based on increased interconnectivity abroad. Abe's successors will have much to grapple with in the days ahead.

NOTES

1. Richard Samuels, "Politics, Security and Japan's Cabinet Legislation Bureau: Who Elected These Guys Anyway?" *JPRI Working Paper*, No. 99, March 2004.
2. UN Security Council, Resolution 1511. 2003.
3. John Galtung, "Violence, Peace, and Peace Research," *Journal of Peace Research*, 6(3), 1969, 167–191.
4. Barry Buzan, *People, States and Fear*, London: Wheatsheaf Books, 1983, 262.
5. United Nations, *UN Development Report*, 1994.
6. Shinzō Abe, Message on constitutional amendment, Transcript from *Nikkei*, May 3, 2017. https://www.nikkei.com/article/DGXLASFK03H16_T00C17A5000000/.
7. Jimintō, "Kenpō kaisei ni kansuru ronten torimatome," and Murohashi, "Abe seiken ga mezasu kenpōkaisei wo tetteiteki kaisetsu."
8. The NDPG (*taikō*) have come to be revised every 5 years, in general, but can be updated according to need.
9. *Defense White Paper 2016*, Chapter 2 section 1.
10. Ministry of Defense, "National Defense Program Guidelines," December 18, 2018. https://www.mod.go.jp/j/approach/agenda/guideline/2019/pdf/20181218_e.pdf.

11. See Ministry of Defense, *White Book for Defense 2019*. The figure excludes SACO [Special Action Committee on Okinawa]-related expenditures, US-Forces alignment-related expenditures (portion allocated to the mitigation of their impact on local communities), expenses for the acquisition of a new government aircraft, expenses for the three-year emergency measures for emergency prevention, reduction, and national resilience. Including those, defense-related spending was 5.25 trillion yens in FY2019.

12. Article 13 reads as follows: "All of the people shall be respected as individuals. Their right to life, liberty, and the pursuit of happiness shall, to the extent that it does not interfere with the public welfare, be the supreme consideration in legislation and in other governmental affairs."

13. Michael Bosack, "What did Japan learn in South Sudan?" *The Diplomat*, June 10, 2017. https://thediplomat.com/2017/06/what-did-japan-learn-in-south-sudan/.

14. For a summary of the changes, see Cabinet Secretariat, "'Heiwa anzen hosei' no gaiyō" [Overview of "Peace and Security Legislation"], http://www.cas.go.jp/jp/houan/150515_1/siryou1.pdf.

15. *Mainichi Shimbun*, "Five Eyes intel group ties up with Japan, Germany, France to counter China in cyberspace," February 4, 2019. https://mainichi.jp/english/articles/20190204/p2a/00m/0na/001000c.

16. Axel Berkofsky, "Moving Beyond Rhetoric? The EU-Japan Strategic Partnership Agreement (SPA)," April 2020. https://isdp.eu/publication/the-eu-japan-strategic-partnership-agreement/.

17. Ministry of Defense, "Vientiane Vision: Japan's Defense Cooperation Initiative with ASEAN," 2016. https://www.mod.go.jp/e/d_act/exc/vientianevision/.

18. EEAS, "The Partnership on Sustainable Connectivity and Quality Infrastructure between the European Union and Japan," September 27, 2019. https://eeas.europa.eu/headquarters/headquarters-homepage/68018/partnership-sustainable-connectivity-and-quality-infrastructure-between-european-union-and_en. Accessed March 13, 2020.

19. For the statement on May 29 stressing the "deep concern" of the Four and the "direct conflict" of the new Security Law with China's international obligations, see Government of the United Kingdom, "China's proposed new security law for Hong Kong: Joint statement," May 28, 2020. https://www.gov.uk/government/news/joint-statement-from-the-uk-australia-canada-and-united-states-on-hong-kong. Accessed 1 June 1, 2020. New Zealand did not join either, but issued a similarly-worded statement separately.

20. The Chief Cabinet Secretary Suga Yoshihide declared his strong anxiety (*tsuyoi kenen*) on May 27th and the Press Secretary Ōtaka Masato stated Japan was "deeply concerned" (*fukaku yūryō shiteimasu*) on 28th May.

21. Ministry of Foreign Affairs of France, "G7 Foreign Minister's Statement on Hong Kong (17 Jun. 2020)," June 17, 2020. https://www.diplomatie.gouv.fr/en/country-files/china/news/article/g7-foreign-ministers-statement-on-hong-kong-17-jun-2020 Accessed June 20, 2020.

22. Michael Bosack, "The impact of compensation politics on Japan's defense," *Japan Times*, May 28, 2020. https://www.japantimes.co.jp/opinion/2020/05/28/commentary/japan-commentary/impact-compensation-politics-japans-defense/.

REFERENCES

Abe, Shinzō. Message on constitutional amendment. Transcript from *Nikkei*, May 3, 2017. https://www.nikkei.com/article/DGXLASFK03H16_T00C17A5000000/.

Berkofsky, Axel. "Moving Beyond Rhetoric? The EU–Japan Strategic Partnership Agreement (SPA)." April 2020. https://isdp.eu/publication/the-eu-japan-strategic-partnership-agreement/.

Bosack, Michael. "The impact of compensation politics on Japan's defense." *Japan Times*, May 28, 2020. https://www.japantimes.co.jp/opinion/2020/05/28/commentary/japan-commentary/impact-compensation-politics-japans-defense/.

Bosack, Michael. "What did Japan learn in South Sudan?" *The Diplomat*, June 10, 2017. https://thediplomat.com/2017/06/what-did-japan-learn-in-south-sudan/.

Buzan, Barry. *People, States and Fear*. London: Wheatsheaf Books, 1983, 262.

Cabinet Secretariat, "'Heiwa anzen hosei' no gaiyō" [Overview of "Peace and Security Legislation"]. http://www.cas.go.jp/jp/houan/150515_1/siryou1.pdf.

EEAS. "The Partnership on Sustainable Connectivity and Quality Infrastructure between the European Union and Japan." September 27, 2019. https://eeas.europa.eu/headquarters/headquarters-homepage/68018/partnership-sustainable-connectivity-and-quality-infrastructure-between-european-union-and_en. Accessed March 13, 2020.

Galtung, John. "Violence, Peace, and Peace Research." *Journal of Peace Research*, 6(3), 1969, 167–191.

Government of the United Kingdom. "China's proposed new security law for Hong Kong: Joint statement." May 28, 2020. https://www.gov.uk/government/news/joint-statement-from-the-uk-australia-canada-and-united-states-on-hong-kong. Accessed 1 June 1, 2020.

Mainichi Shimbun. "Five Eyes intel group ties up with Japan, Germany, France to counter China in cyberspace." February 4, 2019. https://mainichi.jp/english/articles/20190204/p2a/00m/0na/001000c.

Ministry of Defense. "National Defense Program Guidelines." December 18, 2018. https://www.mod.go.jp/j/approach/agenda/guideline/2019/pdf/20181218_e.pdf.

Ministry of Defense. "Vientiane Vision: Japan's Defense Cooperation Initiative with ASEAN." 2016. https://www.mod.go.jp/e/d_act/exc/vientianevision/.

Ministry of Defense. *White Book for Defense 2019*. 2019.

Ministry of Foreign Affairs of France. "G7 Foreign Minister's Statement on Hong Kong (17 Jun. 2020)." June 17, 2020. https://www.diplomatie.gouv.fr/en/country-files/china/news/article/g7-foreign-ministers-statement-on-hong-kong-17-jun-2020 Accessed June 20, 2020.

Murohashi, Yuki. "Abe seiken ga mezasu kenpōkaisei wo tetteiteki kaisetsu." *Business Insider*, January 8, 2018. https://www.businessinsider.jp/post-159342.

Samuels, Richard. "Politics, Security and Japan's Cabinet Legislation Bureau: Who Elected These Guys Anyway?" *JPRI Working Paper*, No. 99, March 2004.

United Nations. *UN Development Report*. 1994.

UN Security Council. Resolution 1511. 2003.

Chapter 6

Japanese Military Diplomacy
Abe's Security Legacy?
Alessio Patalano

On July 14, 2020, the *London Times* ran an article in which it was revealed that senior British military leadership was contemplating plans to forward-base one of the new aircraft carriers in East Asia.[1] As the Royal Navy's fleet commander had observed during a webinar the previous day, the navy indeed had the ambition to operate persistently in the region.[2] The announcement prompted, shortly thereafter, strong reactions from Defence Secretary Ben Wallace, who discouraged senior officers from further commenting on the matter.[3] The plans pointed to an idea of the United Kingdom as a "resident power" in the Indo-Pacific that was not entirely new.[4] What was truly remarkable about this episode, however, was the notion that, according to the leaked plans, Japan would play a central role in the U.K.'s ability to shape regional affairs. One key assumption in these plans was that British and Japanese military capabilities were to be mobilized in a coordinated fashion to deliver a diplomatic effect.

This chapter engages with the above assumption and focuses on explaining how Japanese military diplomacy has changed to the point that countries like the United Kingdom today consider Tokyo to be a vital partner in their defence engagement plans with the region. This chapter has two particular objectives. First, it investigates the ways in which Japanese military power has been reintegrated within the tools of statecraft under Prime Minister Abe Shinzō, with a specific focus on his second period as Prime Minister after a landslide electoral victory in 2012. The chapter builds upon a strategic studies methodology to argue that the Abe government has been instrumental in expanding two critical areas of Japanese military diplomacy: its geographic reach—with the specific widening of activities from Southeast Asia to the Indian Ocean region and its intended influence—by leveraging in a more systematic fashion military activities in support of the country's foreign and security policy objectives.

The second aim is to address a legacy question about whether and to what extent such an expanded military diplomatic agenda will continue now that the Abe era has drawn to a close. In this regard, the chapter leverages recent literature examining the impact of reforms promoted under the Abe government on Japanese foreign and security policy to make the case that military diplomacy will continue.[5] In particular, the establishment of the National Security Secretariat (NSS) has contributed to the placement of military diplomacy at the heart of the country's diplomatic statecraft. This option of using military diplomacy will remain available to Japanese governments in Abe's aftermath. In this respect, the chapter argues that military diplomacy represents one of the most important legacies of the second Abe cabinet. It specifically suggests that Abe adopted what *de facto* could be regarded as a proactive-or 'shaping' -defence engagement strategy in which military diplomacy was a primary tool in support of the government's signature Free and Open Indo-Pacific (FOIP) initiative. Such an approach to military diplomacy marks a clear development from the past use of defence capabilities in a more passive way, chiefly to manage bilateral ties with the United States.

The chapter makes an original contribution to the debate over how Japanese military power has changed under Prime Minister Abe, by highlighting the importance of shifting the analytical focus away from assessments of military capabilities to better understand the nature of change in Japanese military posture.[6] In so doing, the chapter also expands the current understanding of the importance of Abe's reforms on policy-making in security matters by adding a military diplomatic dimension to it.[7] The chapter builds upon existing findings on the role of naval diplomacy to Japanese foreign policy[8] to suggest that military diplomacy is a significant part of how Japanese military power has evolved under Abe, one that requires researchers to look beyond Japan's reliance on American hard capabilities for its security.[9] Under Abe's leadership, Japan has been conducting activities shaping regional stability in a fashion that enhanced the country's profile as a security provider. In so doing, the chapter specifically expands similar conclusions in the literature concerning Japan's activities in Southeast Asia, suggesting that under Prime Minister Abe, military diplomacy has expanded beyond Southeast Asia into the Indian Ocean and, more recently, in the South Pacific.[10] The chapter tests its argument against case studies based on a variety of primary sources, including new and previously unexplored data from the Japan Maritime Self-Defence Force (JMSDF) and the Japan Ministry of Defence (JMOD).

DEFENCE ENGAGEMENT AND MILITARY DIPLOMACY: A STRATEGY TO SHAPE AND INFLUENCE

In Spring 2002, just a few months after Prime Minister Koizumi Jun'ichirō had committed Japanese capabilities to the international naval coalition operating in the Indian Ocean, the National Institute for Defence Studies (NIDS) in Tokyo conducted a significant internal study on peacetime uses of military power.[11] The study was designed to reflect upon two questions. First, it sought to review the debate of the previous decade regarding the impact of Japanese contributions on United Nation-sponsored multinational activities. Second, it aimed at developing an understanding of the implications of that debate in light of the evolving regional and international security landscapes after 9/11. In engaging with both questions, the study focused on examining the U.K.'s approach to defence engagement. It did so to explore the political uses of military power to enhance national influence internationally in addition to stabilization and crisis response, as a possible model for Japan.[12]

What was, then, the model that Japanese defence researchers assessed? A brief examination into the British context is helpful to understand the framework informing the evolution of the Japanese debate. In the United Kingdom, defence engagement concerns—in the words of the latest version of the U.K.'s international defence engagement strategy (IDES)—"the use of our people and assets to prevent conflict, build stability, and gain influence."[13] In the first iteration of this strategy, defence engagement was similarly defined as the "means by which we use our defence assets and activities short of combat operations to achieve influence."[14] Crucially, in the British context, defence engagement included a "shaping" component, one aimed at improving stability to prevent crises, not merely through crisis response and stabilization activities.[15] Military diplomacy was a central pillar of defence engagement. It involved the planning and coordinating of peacetime military activities so that they support and enhance the projection of influence and the promotion of national prosperity.[16] Establishing and improving defence ties bilaterally and multilaterally, developing cooperation and operational interoperability, as well as enhancing security and industrial collaborations to increase agency on international affairs were key aspects of how military diplomacy could support defence engagement.[17]

It is certainly important to stress that within the U.K. official literature on military diplomacy, the conduct of non-warfighting functions by the armed forces included activities to signal, deter, and coerce potential adversaries.[18] Indeed, specialized literature—especially on navies—has long held that military (and especially naval) diplomacy incorporates activities aimed at building and maintaining relationships as much as actions that are more competitive in nature. In the latter category, actions classed under what James Cable labeled "gunboat diplomacy" and those pertaining to nuclear deterrence represent the most consequential conventional and strategic manifestations.[19] However, in the aftermath of the 1998 Strategic Defence Review (SDR), military diplomacy was recast as a component of a broader "defence diplomacy" agenda. This "new" mission was the intellectual brainchild of an interventionist foreign policy posture spearheaded by Prime Minister Tony Blair that linked defence, security, and development.[20] This was designed to "build and maintain trust and assist in the development of democratically accountable armed forces, thereby making a significant contribution to conflict prevention and resolution."[21] A decade later, defence engagement relied on this intellectual tradition to further consolidate the link between engagement and the shaping potential of military diplomacy.

The reconstruction of the above framework matters because in the years following the original NIDS study, the Japanese debate too evolved to take the first steps in an approach that integrated defence engagement activities in national strategy. Indeed, the second Abe cabinet took stock of this debate and sought to develop a military diplomatic agenda that reflected a broader defence engagement strategy. The Japanese government's first National Security Strategy adopted in 2013—just one year after Abe's return to power—incorporated much of the language and the logic informing the British approach to defence engagement as a tool to implement national security. Crucially, the Council on Security and Defence Capabilities, the committee of experts set up by Abe with the task to draft the National Security Strategy, specifically aimed at setting the ground for Japan to contribute more to international stability.[22] For this reason, the strategy emphasized international cooperation as a key ambition for Japan to pursue as part of its national security policy.[23]

In the National Security Strategy, a clear understanding of the role that military power had to play in peacetime complemented the absence of direct reference to defence engagement. As the document pointed out, "the key to national security is to create a stable and predictable international environment, and prevent the emergence of threats."[24] More importantly, it stressed that:

> Japan must have the power to take the lead in setting the international agenda and to *proactively advance* its national interests, without being confined to a reactionary position to events and incidents after they have already occurred. In doing so, it is necessary to *enhance diplomatic creativity* and negotiating power to deepen the understanding of and garner support for Japan's position in the international community, *through effectively utilizing all strengths and features of the nation.*[25] (emphasis added)

Thus, the Japanese National Security Strategy sought to shift the policy focus from reacting to international crises to shaping an international environment in a way that promoted stability and prosperity. For the Japanese, this meant first and foremost enhancing maritime security, which in turn raised the question of how Japan could influence and contribute to the process of creating a stable regional environment consistent with the notion of a rule-based maritime order.[26] Port visits, joint exercises, interactions to foster maritime security represented all inherent components of a contribution to strengthen relations and enhance stability. Shortly thereafter, new vocabulary was introduced to more clearly reflect the correlation between military diplomacy and its wider security role. Notably, both the JMOD and the Japanese Ministry of Foreign Affairs started using the notion of "strategic port calls" (*senryaku tekini kikō*) to qualify the nature of a key peacetime military diplomatic activity.[27] The role of the NSS in promoting the coordination across various ministries was instrumental in this process.

A key question that needed to be addressed concerned how and what a defence engagement strategy would prioritize in order to enhance Japanese security. This required an ideational framework that could elucidate a way to prioritize efforts and resources. Within this context, cooperation with a variety of key strategic partners located along the main sea-lanes connecting Asia to Europe via the Indian Ocean aimed at capacity-building and capability build-ups represented two ways in which Japan could be more proactive. In the words of the national security strategy, maritime capacity-building could strengthen the ability of coastal states in Southeast Asia to maintain the rule of law and reward Japan's efforts in developing relationships.[28] In this regard, the Japanese approach, while falling short of being formally part of a "defence engagement strategy," it did not differ in substance from the U.K.'s IDES on matters of objectives and methods.[29]

FOIP as a Defence Engagement Strategy: Commitment by Presence in the Indian Ocean

Prime Minister Abe delivered the wider ideational framework within which defence engagement and military diplomacy were to be implemented through a worldview that explained Japan's role in international affairs. Formally announced in 2016, Tokyo's "Free and Open Indo-Pacific" (FOIP) initiative represented the ultimate manifestation of a political project that had started in 2006. FOIP included elements of geopolitical anxiety vis-à-vis the need to propose alternative visions to China's Belt and Road Initiative.[30] Yet, it was an attempt to propose a specific worldview that Abe developed over time and that he distilled in three key speeches: the 2007 "Confluence of the Two Seas," delivered in India; the 2013 "The Bounty of the Open

Seas" intervention delivered in Jakarta, and Abe's keynote at TICAD in 2016.

Abe's FOIP was a powerful statement about how Japan sees the world. In it, the future rested on how Africa and Asia sought to "connect" to shape economic and social development. FOIP had three pillars, the first being about "connectivity" and the prosperity that it creates.[31] This was understood first and foremost as physical connectivity, promoting infrastructural projects—from ports to roads and railways. FOIP's second and third pillars unfolded from the first. The second pillar was about values—in particular, the respect of rule of law, liberal economies, and open societies. Under Abe's premiership, the stability of the maritime order (including the values of freedom of navigation and over flight) and of "rule of law," the normative frameworks governing both the management of the oceans and approaches to disputes resolution, represented a clear example of this second pillar. Abe articulated its essence in a keynote address at the Shangri-La Dialogue in 2014.[32] The third pillar was about security. Prosperity is informed by values and depends on security, and security in the Indo-Pacific related to the stability resulting from capacity and capability-building, as well as by enhanced coordination in preventing and addressing disaster relief.

FOIP placed the Indian and Pacific oceans at the heart of Japanese national policy and in doing so it also provided a clear geographical space for defence engagement.[33] From the perspective of a "proactive" role, the prime minister had emphasized throughout the decade prior to the formal adoption of FOIP how, from his perspective, Japan had to start looking at shaping the security environment. Shortly after he came back to power in 2012, Abe specifically stated that he expected Japan to "play a greater role in preserving the common good" in the Indo-Pacific area.[34] While the Prime Minister fell short of specifically defining the content of Japan's "greater role," his views recognized the importance of Japan taking action beyond Northeast Asia to address the potential impact of security issues in theaters relevant to international sea-lanes connecting Japanese waters to the Indian Ocean and the Middle East. Specifically, he later stated that Japan would commit to what was "necessary to protect the sea under international law as a public good shared by all of humanity."[35] Still, given the wide area FOIP was intended to cover, and provided that Japanese military resources for defence engagement remained relatively limited—cooperation with other partners, especially in the Indian Ocean region, remained a central feature of how Japan would be proactive in security matters.[36]

By the time FOIP became an official policy initiative, Abe's ambitions for Japanese defence engagement were already part of the fabric of military planning. Since Abe's speech in India in 2007, defence policy circles had started to assess how Japan could engage more in defence cooperation. Notably, in

2008, a senior Japanese naval defence planner, Admiral Tomohisa Takei—later appointed as chief of maritime staff—was the first author of a service strategy that went on to become aligned with the aims of the second Abe cabinet. Takei's strategy considered the stability of the four "areas" (Northeast Asia, Southeast Asia, South Asia, and Middle East) of transit of Japan's main sea-lanes as a key objective. In each of them, the Japan Maritime Self-Defence Force's "commitment" to regional security had to be developed on the basis of the specific potential threats and the available resources to tackle them. In Southeast and South Asia as well as in the Middle East, the "commitment strategy" was to prioritize defence exchanges, capacity-building, multilateral exercises, port calls, and international relief missions, in other words military diplomacy.[37] Starting with port calls and simple exercises and up to the level of senior military visits and complex exercises, military diplomacy would be able to articulate in a nuanced fashion the character of Japanese commitments in Southeast Asia and in the Indian Ocean, as well as establish a pattern for the development of partnerships.

By 2013, this was no longer just a naval strategy. On the basis of the new National Security Strategy, JMoD was fully committed to provide for a wider defence engagement agenda. Indeed, Japan's dialogue and exchange activities were broadening "from neighboring countries to encompass partners across the globe" with the aim to deepen interaction "to achieve more concrete, practical cooperation, (. . .) including building regional order and common norms and standard."[38] Some eight years later, this function had grown to the point that it constituted one of the pillars of Japanese defence policy. By 2020, FOIP was the overarching umbrella driving security cooperation, and defence engagement across the Indo-Pacific was organized along four areas: Pacific Island countries, Southeast Asia, South Asia, and Middle East and Africa.[39] Maritime security and capacity-building were still leading the military diplomatic agenda as they played to the strengths of the ability of naval assets to tailor interactions to achieve specific effects, but exchanges were expanding to include different forms of military interactions.

Japanese Military Diplomacy Explained: Shaping through Tailored Engagement

The centrality of the maritime domain to Japanese foreign and security policy has meant that naval diplomacy has led the way in which Japanese military diplomacy has evolved ever since Prime Minister Ikeda sent the fleet training squadron to Europe in 1963.[40] In this section, some of the key examples draw upon Japanese naval diplomacy, but they are not limited to it. In addition, while a comprehensive review of all military diplomatic activities is beyond this chapter's scope, this section focuses on examining three types of diplomatic activities that can better allow exploring both the geographic expansion and content development of military diplomacy under PM Abe. These encompass: the deployment patterns of the JMSDF training squadron, the program for the "Ship Rider" initiative undertaken to favor capacity-building in the ASEAN region, and changes in bilateral exercises patters with key partners in the Indo-Pacific. Given the longstanding and well-established patterns of cooperation with the United States, this section specifically focuses on actors other than the United States to make a wider case for military diplomacy to serve a broader defence engagement strategy.

The deployment patterns of the JMSDF training squadron offer a very relevant way to assess changes in how peacetime military activities evolve to support changing diplomatic agendas. As a dataset, deployments of the training squadrons offer a coherent way to assess changes in the geographic reach of Japanese diplomacy. These deployments have occurred consistently since the first class of midshipmen graduated from the JMSDF academy in 1957. Every year the training squadron conducts an overseas cruise before young officers are assigned to their first posts. As senior JMSDF officers maintain, while the time of the year for the overseas cruise remains constant—starting at the end of March after graduation and lasting some five months—the selection of the destinations changes every year. These are decided on the combination of a rotational approach and the diplomatic requirements provided by the Ministry of Foreign Affairs.[41] Indeed, from the JMSDF's perspective, the cruise has a "double" diplomatic function: it aims to support Japanese foreign policy through official visits and to develop young officers' cosmopolitan outlook to help them engaging with civilian and uniformed counterparts the world over throughout their career.[42]

Tables 6.1 and 6.2 provide an overview of the characteristics of the overseas cruise in terms of number of days, distances covered, and—crucially—number of port calls during the period 2002–2018. The chosen period corresponds to the cruises taking place after 9/11, since in October 2001, for the first time, the Japanese government authorized the deployment of naval assets in the Indian Ocean in support of the international coalition effort to support the

Table 6.1 JMSDF Training Squad Deployments, 2002–2010

	2002	2003	2004	2005	2006	2007	2008	2009	2010
Training Squadron	Kashima Matsuyuki Shimayuki	Kashima Hamayuki Sawagiri	Kashima Hamagiri Umigiri	Kashima Murasame Yuugiri	Kashima Amagiri Yamagiri	Kashima Shimayuki Sawagiri	Kashima Asagiri Umigiri	Kashima Shimayuki Yuugiri	Kashima Yamagiri Sawayuki
Days	141	138	151	155	140	155	158	141	156
Miles	27.662	25.128	29.883	31.998	27.836	32.419	32.190	24.349	28.514
No. Port Calls	10	13	13	14	12	11	13	14	15

Data provided by the Japan Maritime Command and Staff College, Japan Ministry of Defense.

Table 6.2 JMSDF Training Squad Deployments, 2011–2018

	2011	2012	2013	2014	2015	2016	2017	2018
Training Squadron	Kashima Asagiri Mineyuki	Kashima Shimayuki Matsuyuki	Kashima Shirayuki Isoyuki	Kashima Asagiri Setoyuki	Kashima Yamagiri Shimayuki	Kashima Asagiri Setoyuki	Kashima Harusame	Kashima Makinami
Days	156	154	162	156	160	169	164	163
Miles	32.889	28.458	32.744	33.091	31.533	31.000	35.418	36.039
No. Port Calls	13	15	19	14	16	16	13	12

Data provided by the Japan Maritime Command and Staff College, Japan Ministry of Defense.

United States' efforts in the War on Terror. This commitment expanded the requirements for military—and especially naval—diplomatic engagement to include the Indian Ocean and consolidated opportunities for interactions along the primary naval arteries connecting Japan to the theater of operations in this basin, notably across Southeast Asia. It is also important to stress that while the mission was interrupted in 2007 for three months and was discontinued in January 2010, in 2009 Japan started operating regular deployments in the Gulf of Aden to support the international coalition in fighting piracy off the coast of Somalia. This mission continues to the present day.

A glance at tables 6.1 and 6.2 shows that during the period under examination, the length of the cruises has increased consistently, together with the areas covered by the squadron—with a little less than a third of the nautical miles covered in 2002 added by 2018. The number of port calls also expanded considerably: cruises in 2013, 2015, and 2016 conducted more than a 50 percent increase in number of stops compared to 2002. On this point, in some of the later years, for example in 2017 and 2018, the increase in number of port calls was less stark, but this was in part due to longer transits from one destination to another.

This leads to table 6.3, which details the locations of the port calls conducted by the training squadron. As a general observation, the patterns of deployments clearly highlight the importance of the United States for the JMSDF, given that port calls in the country are included every year—the only country in that position—except for 2009 and 2012. What is equally remarkable is the shift to include more regularly Middle Eastern and Western Indian Ocean locations in the deployment patterns. In 2008, the overseas cruise stretched from the United Kingdom to Hawaii and the U.S. West Coast, through Egypt, Senegal, Panama, and Brazil. The following year, however, the bulk of the cruise focused on Southeast Asia and, for the first time, a full schedule of stops across the Indian Ocean, including stops along Africa and the Middle East. Since 2009, areas of deployment for the cruise have settled on an expanded routine more markedly including stops in the Indian Ocean—especially in the Western Indian Ocean. This suggests that the Indian Ocean has come to represent an area of systematic engagement for this key asset in the Japanese naval diplomatic toolkit.

Table 6.3 Training Squadron Port Calls, 2002–2018

	Europe	MENA	Southeast Asia	Oceania/SP	Hawaii	N America	C America	S America
2002					Pearl Harbor	Anchorage Esquimalt New Orleans Halifax Norfolk	Quetzal Balboa Santo Domingo Manzanillo	
2003			Suba Manado Jakarta Bangkok Changi Manila	Wellington Auckland Sidney Melbourne Port Moresby	Pearl Harbor			
2004					Pearl Harbor Honolulu	San Diego	Balboa Port of Spain Manzanillo	Recife (x2) Montevideo Buenos Aires Santos Rio de Janeiro Cartagena
2005	Portsmouth Oslo St Petersburg Hamburg Brest Istanbul	Port Said	Mumbai Sihanoukville		Pearl Harbor	Norfolk	Manzanillo Balboa	
2006					Pearl Harbor	Anchorage Esquimalt Baltimore Boston Tampa Galveston San Diego	Manzanillo Panama City Santo Domingo Puerto Cortes	
2007			Port Klang Incheon	Papeete Wellington Darwin	Pearl Harbor	San Diego	Manzanillo Acajutla	Callao Valparaiso
2008	Portsmouth Amsterdam Ruen	Port Said Dakar	Bombay (Mumbai) Singapore		Pearl Harbor	San Diego	Panama City	Recife Rio de Janeiro Santos
2009	Piraeus Istanbul Constanta	Al Fugaira Abu Dhabi Bahrain Jeddah Muscat	Karachi Goa Manado Singapore Muara (Brunei) Port Klang					
2010	Lisbon Napoli	Alexandria Djibouti Muscat	Jakarta Mersin			San Francisco San Diego Baltimore	Acapulco Chiapas Santo Domingo	
2011					Pearl Harbor	Vancouver Halifax Anchorage Seattle San Francisco Suffolk Tampa	Manzanillo Veracruz Panama City	Callao Valparaiso

Table 6.3 Training Squadron Port Calls, 2002–2018 (*Continued*)

	Europe	MENA	Southeast Asia	Oceania/SP	Hawaii	N America	C America	S America
2012	Marmaris	Djibouti Jeddah	Chittagong Karachi Bombay (Mumbai) **Malé (Maldives)** Colombo Singapore Bangkok Manila Victoria Darussalam Salalah					
2013	Portsmouth Kiel Helsinki Gdynia St Petersburg Brest Barcelona Taranto Split	Djibouti	Colombo Yangon Sihanoukville Da Nang		Pearl Harbor	Halifax Newport	Manzanillo Panama City	
2014			Jakarta Manado Muara	Honiara	Pearl Harbor	San Diego	Manzanillo Acapulco Panama City Havana Kingston Port of Spain	
2015					Pearl Harbor Hilo	San Diego	Manzanillo Quetzal Puerto Cortes Corinto Santo Domingo	Cartagena Callao Valparaiso Recife Rio de Janeiro Santos Montevideo Buenos Aires
2016	Brest London Klaipeda Rostock Antwerp Valletta Civitavecchia	Djibouti Mombasa Colombo	Manila		Pearl Harbor	San Diego Jacksonville Baltimore	Panama City	
2017	Vladivostok		Pyeongtaek		Pearl Harbor	San Diego Newport Fort Lauderdale Anchorage Vancouver	Chapas Manzanillo Havana	Valparaiso Guayaquil
2018	Barcelona Stockholm Helsinki Portsmouth	Abu Dhabi Fujairah Bahrain Jeddah	Jakarta		Pearl Harbor	Norfolk	Manzanillo	

Data provided by the Japan Maritime Command and Staff College, Japan Ministry of Defense.

Another significant example of military diplomacy serving a wider defence engagement strategy concerns the "Ship Rider" initiative. In 2016, Japanese Defence Minister Tomomi Inada launched at the second ASEAN–Japan Defence Ministers' Informal Meeting in Vientiane, the "Vientiane Vision."

Japanese authorities regarded the program as inherently linked to the principles promoted by the FOIP initiative and later, linked it to ASEAN's own principles as outlined in the "ASEAN Outlook on the Indo-Pacific."[43] Within this context, the Japanese "vision" aimed at promoting practical and enduring cooperation with the organization, in addition to its established bilateral ties with ASEAN's member-states. Its aim was to promote a common understanding of the basic principle of international law, to foster practices in maritime security as a mean to enhance regional prosperity, and to offer capacity and capabilities building and multilateral training opportunities as means to maintain stability.[44]

From 2017 to 2019, Japan conducted three Ship Rider activities during the summer period, each featuring a major surface combatant deployment, including the flagship *JDS Izumo* in 2017 and 2019. Participants from all ASEAN countries joined the warship for about a week to conduct a series of practical activities, from ship handling, to ship communication using frameworks, such as the Code for Unintended Encounters at Sea (CUES). They also experienced some capacity-building programs and training focusing particularly on search and rescue, and also HADR activities. The initiative was well received in Southeast Asia in that it witnessed the deployment of major Japanese naval capabilities to offer practical assistance to countries located in the contested waters of the South China Sea.[45] Capacity-building focused on cooperation through practical activities represented one innovative way in which Japanese military diplomacy offered a clear and tangible contribution to Abe's FOIP initiative in a space central to Japanese national security. Crucially, it did so in a way that was positive and proactive, engaging with actors looking to develop their own capacity, seeking to promote Japanese influence through the empowerment of ASEAN.

Last but by no means least, the third example focuses on senior military leadership visits and military exercises to promote stronger bilateral ties, another crucial function of military diplomacy. Senior military visits are indicative of a political will to develop defence ties, while exercises provide an indication of the level of military-to-military interactions. As such, visits and training exercises offer insights on how military diplomacy is evolving in regards to a wider defence engagement strategy. In the past, senior uniformed personnel visits and military exercises were predominantly a means to nurture U.S.–Japan defence cooperation, and this empowered Japanese officials with a wealth of transferable experience that could be relatively quickly applied to implement Abe's FOIP initiative. Crucially, this wealth of experience in working closely with the United States has not been motivated by an ambition to move away from the United States,[46] but rather by a willingness to diversify security ties in addition to the alliance with the

United States, especially through initiatives that reinforced the Japanese narrative around the core principles of the FOIP initiative.[47]

An examination of visits by the four services' chiefs (ground, maritime, air, and joint) and military and security exercises conducted by the Japanese armed forces during the period under examination confirm the trends outlined above. Ties with Australia and especially India stand out as developing a strong bilateral engagement agenda. In particular, India has certainly emerged during the Abe years as a key defence engagement partner, with a particular emphasis on maritime cooperation. In December 2013, the two countries conducted the second bilateral exercise—covering basic maneuver and security training—only to see the opportunities for training growing in frequency and scope on a very short order. The following year, Japan joined India's Malabar exercise (conducted with the United States) and a permanent member of it in 2015.[48] This is India's prime military exercise covering missions from high-end warfare to maritime security and interdictions operations.[49] By 2016, the two countries added regular counter-piracy bilateral exercises, comparing practices and command structures. In a similar fashion, visits by Japanese uniformed chiefs became a regular occurrence, and certainly the increased defence engagement contributed to the development of other formats, such as trilateral cooperation with the United States and the multilateral Quad initiative (with Australia).

Defence engagement with Southeast Asian countries, especially Indonesia, the Philippines, Vietnam, and Singapore, followed a similar pattern with uniformed chiefs visiting the country first and small scale exercises kick-starting shortly thereafter. Within this context, remarkable developments occurred with island states in the Indian Ocean and South Pacific. Starting with Sri Lanka, in 2014, the chief of maritime staff visited the country heralding an intense defence engagement era, with some thirteen "goodwill exercises" conducted from 2015 to 2020. These activities were certainly facilitated by Japan's continuous presence in the Gulf of Aden, but also indicate the importance that key strategic actors along the Indo-Pacific main sea arteries have for Japan. On a similar note, since 2014, Japanese military diplomacy was deployed to develop "goodwill" with the Maldives, with four exercises taking place in the following five years, with Oman (three exercises from 2018–2019), and with the United Arab Emirates (one visit by Chief of Air Staff, 2 flight training exercises, and one maritime exercise). In 2019, Japanese military diplomacy started to expand toward a new trajectory, with the first visit by a chief of staff to Papua New Guinea, and port calls to South Pacific islands. Against the backdrop of Japan's FOIP initiative, military diplomacy would appear to have been systematically mobilized to practically implement a broader national strategy to advance and develop key relationship through defence engagement.[50]

CONCLUSIONS: MILITARY DIPLOMACY—ABE'S SECURITY LEGACY?

When Prime Minister Abe stepped down in August 2020, the *New York Times* noted that, judged by the ambitious agenda Prime Minister Abe set out when he returned to power in 2012, on security matters his results were somewhat limited.[51] This view contains seeds of truth, in the sense that one of Abe's chief objectives, which was to revise the Japanese Constitution, was not achieved. Yet, this type of assessment is particularly narrow and prevents to appreciate a core change that was inherent to the wider goal of constitutional revision. As this chapter has shown, Abe Shinzō has brought back the use of military power as a tool of statecraft in Japan, and he has done so in a way that defence engagement is an inherent component of Japan's proactive behavior in security affairs.

Abe's reforms to enhance coordination among the primary stakeholders in foreign and security policy and the publication of a strategy overseen by the National Security Secretariat provided them with guidance on how to mobilize their resources to pursue specific objectives. Similarly, the development of a complex vision, which culminated with the formal presentation of FOIP in 2016, centered on a commitment to the wider Indo-Pacific region as a way to prioritize partners and develop ties, offered a framework for military diplomacy. Within this context, the chapter has shown that the maritime-centric nature of the FOIP as a vision put the spotlight on naval interactions in many key partnerships, notably in the development of defence cooperation with India. At the same time, a closer inspection at military diplomacy reveals patterns of engagement that stress the growing importance of the Indian Ocean in Japanese foreign and security policy, as well as engagement with key state actors within this space, from Oman, to Sri Lanka and the Maldives, and the South Pacific Islands.

The nature of Abe's reforms, and the way in which they have been implemented by the Japanese Self-Defence Forces clearly suggest that these changes are here to stay, and they remain at the disposal of Japan's new Prime Minister Suga Yoshihide. In 2020, it was clear that security cooperation was now one of Japan's three pillars in defence matters. Thus, military diplomacy is likely to remain active and centered on a defence engagement strategy aimed at shaping the stability of the wider Indo-Pacific region. In this respect, while Prime Minister Abe has certainly failed to deliver a constitutional change, he has certainly succeeded in changing how military power—and diplomacy—contributed to project Japan's influence internationally. In terms of statecraft, that is a more substantive legacy than any constitutional change could have guaranteed. Whether and to what extent other prime ministers will follow on his footsteps and take this legacy forward remains something to be seen.

NOTES

1. Lucy Fisher, "Britain Set to Confront China with New Aircraft Carrier," *The Times*, 14 July 2020. https://www.thetimes.co.uk/article/britain-set-to-confront-china-with-new-aircraft-carrier-v2gnwrr88.

2. International Institute for Strategic Studies, "A New Era for UK Maritime Air Power: Testing Times, Testing Waters," 13 July 2020. https://www.iiss.org/events/2020/07/uk-maritime-air-power.

3. Alessio Patalano, *UK Defence from the 'Far East' to the 'Indo-Pacific,'* London: Policy Exchange, 2019, https://policyexchange.org.uk/publication/uk-defence-from-the-far-east-to-the-indo-pacific/.

4. Lucy Fisher, "Top Armed Forces Officers Gagged by Defense Secretary Ben Wallace over Aircraft Carrier Discussion," *The Times*, 17 July 2020, thetimes.co.uk/article/top-armed-forces-officers-gagged-by-defence-secretary-ben-wallace-over-aircraft-carrier-discussion-jgsf29rc2.

5. Guilio Pugliese and Alessio Patalano, "Diplomatic and Security Practice under Abe Shinzō: The Case for Realpolitik Japan," *Australian Journal of International Affairs*, 22 June 2020; Alessio Patalano, *Shinzō Abe and Japan: Strategic Reset: The Rise of the Kantei and Why It Matters to the UK Integrated Review*, London: Policy Exchange, 2020, https://policyexchange.org.uk/wp-content/uploads/Shinzō-Abe-and-Japan%E2%80%99s-Strategic-Reset.pdf.

6. Christopher W. Hughes, *Japan's Remilitarisation*, Abingdon, OX: Routledge, 2009; Sheila Smith, *Japan Rearmed: The Politics of Military Power*, Cambridge, MA: Harvard University Press, 2019.

7. Adam P. Liff, "Japan's Defense Policy: Abe the Evolutionary," *The Washington Quarterly*, Vol. 38, 2015:2, 79–99; Adam P. Liff, "Japan's Security Policy in the 'Abe Era': Radical Transformation or Evolutionary Shift?" *Texas National Security Review*, Vol. 1, 2018:3, 8–34.

8. Alessio Patalano, "Commitment by Presence: Naval Diplomacy and Japanese Defense Engagement in Southeast Asia," *Japan's Foreign Relations in Asia*, edited by Jeff Kingston and James Brown. Abingdon, OX: Routledge, 2018, 100–113.

9. Smith, *Japan Rearmed*, 190–205.

10. Corey Wallace, "Leaving (north-east) Asia? Japan's Southern Strategy," *International Affairs*, Vol. 94, 2018:4, 883–904; Corey Wallace, "Japan's Strategic Contrast: Continuing Influence despite Relative Power Decline in Southeast Asia," *The Pacific Review*, Vol. 32, 2019:5, 863–897; John F. Bradford, "Japanese Naval Activities in Southeast Asian Waters: Building on 50 Years of Maritime Security Capacity Building," *Asian Security*, 25 May 2020.

11. Author's interview with senior research official, NIDS, Tokyo, 22 May 2018.

12. Ibid.

13. Ministry of Defence (MoD), Foreign & Commonwealth Office (FCO), *International Defence Engagement Strategy*, London: MoD, 2017, 1.

14. Ministry of Defence (MoD), *International Defence Engagement Strategy*, London: MoD, 2013, 1.

15. Ministry of Defence (MoD), *Shaping a Stable World: The Military Contribution*, JDP 05, Shriveham, Swindon: The Development, Concepts and Doctrine Centre, 2016, 31–54.

16. MoD & FCO, *International Defence Engagement Strategy*, 11–12; MoD, *International Defence Engagement Strategy*, 2.

17. MoD & FCO, *International Defence Engagement Strategy*, 12–18; MoD, *International Defence Engagement Strategy*, 3.

18. MoD, *Shaping a Stable World*, 87–89.

19. Ibid., 65; See also James Cable, *Gunboat Diplomacy, 1919-1991: Political Applications of Limited Naval Force*, London: Palgrave, 1994; Geoffrey Till, *Seapower: A Guide for the Twenty-first Century* (2nd edition), Abingdon, OX: Routledge, 2004, 253–285.

20. Tony Blair, "The Blair Doctrine," *Global Policy Forum*, 22 April 1999. https://www.globalpolicy.org/component/content/article/154/26026.html; Lawrence Freedman, "Force and the International Community: Blair's Chicago Speech and the Criteria for Intervention," *International Relations*, Vol. 3, 2017:2, 107–124.

21. Alice Hills, "Defence Diplomacy and Security Sector Reform," *Contemporary Security Policy*, Vol. 21, 2000:1, 47.

22. Shin'nichi Kitaoka, "'Proactive Contribution to Peace' in context: The Long Path to Normalisation," *Japan's World Power: Assessment, Outlook, and Vision*, edited by Guibourg Delamotte. Abingdon, OX: Routledge, 2018, 82–84.

23. Ibid., 83.

24. Japan Cabinet Secretariat, *National Security Strategy*, 2013, 14. http://www.cas.go.jp/jp/siryou/131217anzenhoshou/nss-e.pdf.

25. Ibid., 14–15.

26. Ibid., 16–17.

27. Alessio Patalano, "Japanese Naval Power," *Oxford Handbook of Japanese Politics*, edited by Robert and Saadia Pekkanen. Oxford: Oxford University Press: forthcoming 2021, https://www.oxfordhandbooks.com/view/10.1093/oxfordhb/9780190050993.001.0001/oxfordhb-9780190050993-e-40.

28. Japan Cabinet Secretariat, *National Security Strategy*, 28–29.

29. Ministry of Defence, *Joint Doctrine Note 1/15: Defence Engagement*, OX: DCDC, 2015, 19–23.

30. Yûichi Hosoya, "FOIP 2.0: The Evolution of Japan's Free and Open Indo-Pacific Strategy," *Asia-Pacific Review*, Vol. 26, 2019:1, 18–28.

31. For a formal overview of FOIP, see Ministry of Foreign Affairs, "Free and Open Indo-Pacific," https://www.mofa.go.jp/files/000430632.pdf.

32. Shinzō Abe, "Keynote Address, 13th IISS Asian Security Summit 'Shangri-La Dialogue'," Ministry of Foreign Affairs, 30 May 2014. https://www.mofa.go.jp/fp/nsp/page18e_000087.html.

33. Shin'nichi Kitaoka, "Vision for a Free and Open Indo-Pacific," *Asia-Pacific Review*, Vol. 26, 2019:1, 7–8.
34. Shinzō Abe, "Asia's Democratic Security Diamond," *Project Syndicate*, 2012. https://www.project-syndicate.org/onpoint/a-strategic-alliance-for-japan-and-india-by-Shinzō-abe?barrier=accesspaylog.
35. Shinzō Abe, "Message from Prime Minister Shinzō Abe on the Occasion of 'Marine Day'," Tokyo, 18 July 2016.
36. Michito Tsuruoka, "Competing Visions of Japan's International Engagement: Japan First vs Global Japan," *The International Spectator*, Vol. 55, 2020:1, 34–47; Michito Tsuruoka, "Japan's Indo-Pacific Engagement: The Rational and Challenges," *ISPI Online*, 4 June 2018. https://www.ispionline.it/en/pubblicazione/japans-indo-pacific-engagement-rationale-and-challenges-20691.
37. Tomohisa Takei, "Kaiyou Shinkindai ni okeru Kaijoujieitai" [The JMSDF in the New Maritime Era], *Hatou*, 2008:11, 2–29.
38. Japan Ministry of Defense (JMoD). *Defense of Japan*, Tokyo: 2012, 267.
39. Japan Ministry of Defense (JMoD), *Defense of Japan*, Tokyo: 2020, 32.
40. Patalano, *Post-war Japan as a Sea Power: Imperial Legacy, Wartime Experience, and the Making of a Navy*, London, Bloomsbury, 2015, 70.
41. Author's interview with a senior JMSDF flag officer, retired, London, 15 October 2019.
42. Ibid.
43. Japan Ministry of Defence (JMoD), "Updating the 'Vientiane Vision: Japan's Defense Cooperation Initiative with AASEAN.'"
44. Ibid.; Also, Japan Ministry of Defence (JMoD), "Vientiane Vision: Japan's Defense Cooperation Initiative with ASEAN."
45. Mike Yeo, "Much to China's Ire, Japan's Regional Influence is Becoming the Norm," *Defense News*, 31 May 2019. https://www.defensenews.com/global/asia-pacific/2019/05/31/much-to-chinas-ire-japans-regional-influence-is-becoming-the-norm/.
46. Adam P. Liff, "Unambivalent Alignment: Japan's China Strategy, the US Alliance and the 'Hedging' Fallacy," *International Relations of the Asia-Pacific*, Vol. 19, 2019:3, 453–491.
47. Wilhem V. Vosse, "Learning Multilateral Military and Political Cooperation in the Counter-Piracy Missions: A Step Towards De-Centering of Japan's Security Policy?" *The Pacific Review*, Vol. 31, 2018:4, 480–497; Thomas S. Wilkins, "After a Decade of Strategic Partnership: Japan and Australia 'Decentering' from the US Alliance?" *The Pacific Review*, Vol. 31, 2018:4, 498–514.
48. Japan Ministry of Defense (JMoD), *Defense of Japan*, Tokyo: 2016, 453–454; Franz-Stefan Gady, "India, US, and Japan to Hold 'Malabar' Naval War Games This Week," *The Diplomat*, 5 June 2018. https://thediplomat.com/2018/06/india-us-and-japan-to-hold-malabar-naval-war-games-this-week/.
49. Ankit Panda, "India-Japan-US Malabar 2017 Naval Exercises Kick Off with Anti-Submarine Warfare in Focus," *The Diplomat*, 10 July 2017. https://thediplomat.com/2017/07/india-japan-us-malabar-2017-naval-exercises-kick-off-with-anti-submarine-warfare-in-focus/.
50. Japan Ministry of Defense (JMoD), *Defense of Japan*, Tokyo: 2020, 530–542.

51. Motoko Rich, "Shinzō Abe, Japan's Longest-Serving Prime Minister, Resigns Because of Illness," *New York Times*, 28 August 2020. https://www.nytimes.com/2 020/08/28/world/asia/Shinzō-abe-resign-japan.html.

REFERENCES

Abe, Shinzō. "Asia's Democratic Security Diamond." *Project Syndicate*, 2012. https ://www.project-syndicate.org/onpoint/a-strategic-alliance-for-japan-and-india-by -Shinzō-abe?barrier=accesspaylog.

Abe, Shinzō. "Keynote Address, 13th IISS Asian Security Summit 'Shangri-La Dialogue.'" Ministry of Foreign Affairs, 30 May 2014. https://www.mofa.go.jp/fp /nsp/page18e_000087.html.

Abe, Shinzō. "Message from Prime Minister Shinzō Abe on the Occasion of 'Marine Day.'" Tokyo, 18 July 2016.

Blair, Tony. "The Blair Doctrine." *Global Policy Forum*, 22 April 1999. https://www .globalpolicy.org/component/content/article/154/26026.html.

Bradford, John F. "Japanese Naval Activities in Southeast Asian Waters: Building on 50 Years of Maritime Security Capacity Building." *Asian Security*, 25 May 2020.

Cable, James. *Gunboat Diplomacy, 1919-1991: Political Applications of Limited Naval Force*. London: Palgrave, 1994.

Fisher, Lucy. "Britain Set to Confront China with New Aircraft Carrier." *The Times*, 14 July 2020. https://www.thetimes.co.uk/article/britain-set-to-confront-china-with-new-aircraft-carrier-v2gnwrr88.

Fisher, Lucy. "Top Armed Forces Officers Gagged by Defense Secretary Ben Wallace over Aircraft Carrier." *The Times*, 17 July 2020, https://www.thetimes.co.uk/article/top-armed-forces-officers-gagged-by-defence-secretary-ben-wallace-over-aircraft-carrier-discussion-jgsf29rc2.

Freedman, Lawrence. "Force and the International Community: Blair's Chicago Speech and the Criteria for Intervention." *International Relations*, Vol. 3, 2017:2, 107–124.

"Discussion." *The Times*, 17 July 2020. https://www.thetimes.co.uk/article/top-a rmed-forces-officers-gagged-by-defence-secretary-ben-wallace-over-aircraft-carri er-discussion-jgsf29rc2.

Gady, Franz-Stefan. "India, US, and Japan to Hold 'Malabar' Naval War Games This Week." *The Diplomat*, 5 June 2018. https://thediplomat.com/2018/06/india-us -and-japan-to-hold-malabar-naval-war-games-this-week/.

Hills, Alice. "Defence Diplomacy and Security Sector Reform." *Contemporary Security Policy*, Vol. 21, 2000:1, 47.

Hosoya, Yûichi. "FOIP 2.0: The Evolution of Japan's Free and Open Indo-Pacific Strategy." *Asia-Pacific Review*, Vol. 26, 2019:1, 18–28.

Hughes, Christopher W. *Japan's Remilitarisation*. Abingdon, OX: Routledge, 2009.

International Institute for Strategic Studies. "A New Era for UK Maritime Air Power: Testing Times, Testing Waters." 13 July 2020. https://www.iiss.org/events/2020 /07/uk-maritime-air-power.

Japan Cabinet Secretariat. *National Security Strategy*. 2013. http://www.cas.go.jp/jp/siryou/131217anzenhoshou/nss-e.pdf.
Japan Ministry of Defense (JMoD). *Defense of Japan*. Tokyo: 2012, 267.
Japan Ministry of Defense (JMoD). *Defense of Japan*. Tokyo: 2016, 453–454.
Japan Ministry of Defense (JMoD). *Defense of Japan*. Tokyo: 2020.
Japan Ministry of Defence (JMoD). "Updating the 'Vientiane Vision: Japan's Defense Cooperation Initiative with AASEAN.'" November 2019. https://www.mod.go.jp/e/d_act/exc/admm/06/vv2_en.pdf.
Japan Ministry of Defence (JMoD). "Vientiane Vision: Japan's Defense Cooperation Initiative with ASEAN." https://www.mod.go.jp/e/d_act/exc/vientianevision/.
Kitaoka, Shin'ichi. "'Proactive Contribution to Peace' in context: The Long Path to Normalisation." In *Japan's World Power: Assessment, Outlook, and Vision* edited by Guibourg Delamotte. Abingdon, OX: Routledge, 2018, 82–84.
Kitaoka, Shin'ichi. "Vision for a Free and Open Indo-Pacific." *Asia-Pacific Review*, Vol. 26, 2019:1, 7–8.
Liff, Adam P. "Japan's Defense Policy: Abe the Evolutionary." *The Washington Quarterly*, Vol. 38, 2015:2, 79–99.
Liff, Adam P. "Japan's Security Policy in the 'Abe Era': Radical Transformation or Evolutionary Shift?" *Texas National Security Review*, Vol. 1, 2018:3, 8–34.
Liff, Adam P. "Unambivalent Alignment: Japan's China Strategy, the US Alliance and the 'Hedging' Fallacy." *International Relations of the Asia-Pacific*, Vol. 19, 2019:3, 453–491.
Ministry of Defence (MoD). *International Defence Engagement Strategy*. London: MoD, 2013.
Ministry of Defence. *Joint Doctrine Note 1/15: Defence Engagement*. Shrivenham, OX: DCDC, 2015, 19–23.
Ministry of Defence (MoD), Foreign & Commonwealth Office (FCO). *International Defence Engagement Strategy*. London: MoD, 2017.
Ministry of Defence (MoD). *Shaping a Stable World: The Military Contribution*. JDP 05, Shriveham, Swindon: The Development, Concepts and Doctrine Centre, 2016.
Ministry of Foreign Affairs. "Free and Open Indo-Pacific." https://www.mofa.go.jp/files/000430632.pdf.
Panda, Ankit. "India-Japan-US Malabar 2017 Naval Exercises Kick Off with Anti-Submarine Warfare in Focus." *The Diplomat*, 10 July 2017. https://thediplomat.com/2017/07/india-japan-us-malabar-2017-naval-exercises-kick-off-with-anti-submarine-warfare-in-focus/.
Patalano, Alessio. "Commitment by Presence: Naval Diplomacy and Japanese Defense Engagement in Southeast Asia." In *Japan's Foreign Relations in Asia*, edited by Jeff Kingston and James Brown. Abingdon, OX: Routledge, 2018, 100–113.
Patalano, Alessio. "Japanese Naval Power." In *Oxford Handbook of Japanese Politics*, edited by Robert and Saadia Pekkanen. Oxford: Oxford University Press, 2021. https://www.oxfordhandbooks.com/view/10.1093/oxfordhb/9780190050993.001.0001/oxfordhb-9780190050993-e-40

Patalano, Alessio. *Post-war Japan as a Sea Power: Imperial Legacy, Wartime Experience, and the Making of a Navy*. London, Bloomsbury, 2015, 70.

Patalano, Alessio. *Shinzō Abe and Japan: Strategic Reset: The Rise of the Kantei and Why It Matters to the UK Integrated Review*. London: Policy Exchange, 2020. https://policyexchange.org.uk/wp-content/uploads/Shinzō-Abe-and-Japan%E2%80%99s-Strategic-Reset.pdf.

Patalano, Alessio. *UK Defence from the 'Far East' to the 'Indo-Pacific.'* London: Policy Exchange, 2019, https://policyexchange.org.uk/publication/uk-defence-from-the-far-east-to-the-indo-pacific/.

Pugliese, Giulio and Alessio Patalano. "Diplomatic and Security Practice under Abe Shinzō: The Case for Realpolitik Japan." *Australian Journal of International Affairs*, published online, 22 June 2020; Alessio Patalano, *Shinzō Abe and Japan: Strategic Reset: The Rise of the Kantei and Why It Matters to the UK Integrated Review* (foreword by Jeremy Hunt, MP, and introduction by Nobukatsu Kanehara, London: Policy Exchange, 2020), https://policyexchange.org.uk/wp-content/uploads/Shinzō-Abe-and-Japan%E2%80%99s-Strategic-Reset.pdf.

Rich, Motoko. "Shinzō Abe, Japan's Longest-Serving Prime Minister, Resigns Because of Illness." *New York Times*, 28 August 2020. https://www.nytimes.com/2020/08/28/world/asia/Shinzō-abe-resign-japan.html.

Smith, Sheila. *Japan Rearmed: The Politics of Military Power*. Cambridge, MA: Harvard University Press, 2019.

Takei, Tomohisa. "Kaiyou Shinkindai ni okeru Kaijoujieitai" [The JMSDF in the New Maritime Era]. *Hatou*, 2008:11, 2–29.

Till, Geoffrey. *Seapower: A Guide for the Twenty-first Century* (2nd edition). Abingdon, OX: Routledge, 2004, 253–285.

Tsuruoka, Michito. "Competing Visions of Japan's International Engagement: Japan First vs Global Japan." *The International Spectator*, Vol. 55, 2020:1, 34–47

Tsuruoka, Michito. "Japan's Indo-Pacific Engagement: The Rational and Challenges." *ISPI Online*, 4 June 2018. https://www.ispionline.it/en/pubblicazione/japans-indo-pacific-engagement-rationale-and-challenges-20691.

Vosse, Wilhem V. "Learning Multilateral Military and Political Cooperation in the Counter-Piracy Missions: A Step Towards De-Centering of Japan's Security Policy?" *The Pacific Review*, Vol. 31, 2018:4, 480–497.

Wallace, Corey. "Leaving (north-east) Asia? Japan's Southern Strategy." *International Affairs*, Vol. 94, 2018:4, 883–904.

Wallace, Corey. "Japan's Strategic Contrast: Continuing Influence despite Relative Power Decline in Southeast Asia." *The Pacific Review*, Vol. 32, 2019:5, 863–897.

Wilkins, Thomas S. "After a Decade of Strategic Partnership: Japan and Australia 'Decentering' from the US Alliance?" *The Pacific Review*, Vol. 31, 2018:4, 498–514.

Yeo, Mike. "Much to China's Ire, Japan's Regional Influence is Becoming the Norm." *Defense News*, 31 May 2019. https://www.defensenews.com/global/asia-pacific/2019/05/31/much-to-chinas-ire-japans-regional-influence-is-becoming-the-norm/.

Chapter 7

Japan–U.S. Relations

Tosh Minohara

It is without doubt that the current global coronavirus pandemic will become a defining event of the first half of this century. Thus, 2020 will surely be etched in our minds as a year that delineates the pre-COVID and post-COVID eras. The world underwent a significant transformation between these two epochs, but the future historian will surely notice a distinct shift from the perspective of Japanese politics as well. In other words, the final decade of the pre-COVID era, the 2010s, will be recognized as one which the domestic political landscape was dominated by the presence of a single leader: Abe Shinzō.

To be sure, Japan has had its share of powerful postwar political leaders, such as Yoshida Shigeru, Satō Eisaku, Nakasone Yasuhiro, and most recently Koizumi Jun'ichiro.[1] However, in the period between Nakasone and Koizumi and during the post-Koizumi period, Japan had a succession of prime ministers that lacked strong leadership and were quickly replaced. One can recall that the first prime minister succeeding Koizumi was Abe, but during his first stint as prime minister, he was in office a mere 366 days. Despite this, the resilient Abe achieved the rare feat of a successful political comeback by acheiving a non-consecutive second term. Furthermore, he also ended up becoming the longest serving prime minister in Japanese parliamentary history, surpassing the long-held record of Prime Minister Katsura Tarō who was in power from June 1901 to January 1906, and again from July 1908 to August 1911.[2]

Thus, it can be seen that Abe's second term lasting nearly eight years, from December 26, 2012 to September 16, 2020, was not only a rare moment in postwar Japanese history but also one that would become definitive based on its longevity. Many aspects of Japan changed under his strong political stewardship, but part of this reason was because Japan too was adapting to a rapidly changing geostrategic environment, as can be witnessed by the rise of China and the great recession of 2008.

With this as a backdrop, this chapter will track the main events of U.S.–Japan relations under Prime Minister Abe from his second term that began on December 2012. Just by the length of his tenure, Abe played an outsized role in policy formulation and implementation; arguably, he also had the greatest impact on foreign and defense policy of any recent Japanese leader. Furthermore, this chapter will examine and assess Abe's legacy within the context of U.S.–Japan relations. As such, key events during his tenure will be highlighted as well as the key policies that facilitated closer bilateral relations. In this process, this chapter will show what Abe was able to change, as well as where he fell short in managing Japan's most important bilateral relationship.

Abe's tenure as prime minister is unique, in that he dealt with two American presidents not only with different party affiliations but also with a vastly divergent political style and personality. Therefore, it is practical that the chapter be divided into two sections, the first examining U.S.–Japan relations, under President Barack Obama, and the second examining U.S.–Japan relations, under President Donald Trump. In conclusion, the chapter will assess the overall state of U.S.–Japan relations during Abe's tenure at the political helm of Japan in addition to examining his political legacy.

ABE'S U.S. POLICY DURING THE OBAMA ADMINISTRATION

It is conventional wisdom that the 46th lower house elections on December 16, 2012 became the catalyst for Abe's return to the Japan's top job.[3] Showing not only their incompetence but also grossly ineffective leadership amid the Great East Japan Earthquake and Tsunami of March 11, 2011, swaths of Japanese voters turned their backs on the Democratic Party of Japan (DPJ). They showed their dissatisfaction at the polls and dealt the ruling party a decisive blow, toppling them from power.[4] Although the DPJ was initially embraced by many as proof that Japan's democracy was maturing by bringing a decisive end to the longstanding one-party dominant system, the party's lack of experience became its death knell, as after a mere three years, it was replaced by the former ruling party, the Liberal Democratic Party (LDP). The LDP was in search of a new soul amid the post-Koizumi years, but the growing public discontent toward the DPJ allowed the LDP to stage a political comeback under their new leader, Abe. His campaign slogan, "Take Japan Back" (*Nihon wo torimodosu*), resonated with the Japanese voters who had become utterly disillusioned by the DPJ. Thus, the LDP was awarded with a landslide victory that gave LDP the control of the lower house, and with it, the position of the prime minister. The stage was set for the birth of the Second Abe Cabinet. The new prime minister aptly coined his government, "Breaking through the crisis cabinet" (*Kiki toppa naikaku*).[5] A proud Abe proclaimed his ambition to build a nation that Japanese people could be proud to be born in, but aside from this rhetoric, his foremost policy goal was to revive the economy and bring forth economic growth after many years of deflation. Of course, Abe was keenly aware that this was much easier said than done, as he himself claimed that this would be no simple feat, considering Japan's rapidly aging and dwindling population. But the enormity of the challenge was not going to dissuade him from his quest, and he made it clear that he firmly believed that a nation that had either given up on its quest of economic growth, or had abandoned the spirit of striving for economic prosperity, had no future whatsoever.

It was this conviction which formed the backbone for his signature "Abenomics," or the three arrows policy of financial deregulation, government spending, and growth strategy, which he announced in February.[6] Unlike the previous DPJ governments, Abe acted with speed and decisiveness; it was apparent to all that he was going to seize the moment in full stride. In accomplishing this policy goal, his first concrete step was to announce Japan's participation in the ongoing Trans Pacific Partnership (TPP) agreement. Japan's agricultural sector had traditionally been an important support base of the LDP, and thus just one year prior, the party had disseminated posters throughout Japan proclaiming, "We won't lie. We are opposed to TPP. We will not diverge."[7] However once in power, Abe showed no hesitation in proceeding with a significant policy *volte face*. The single most important element of the TPP was that it brought the world's largest—the United States—and third largest—Japan—economies together in a high-quality free trade agreement. No doubt, President Barack Obama also took considerable political risk by actively pursuing a trade policy that was clearly unpopular among his working-class support base, but the benefits that could be gained by bringing the two economies together outweighed any political costs.

In June, Abe finally secured cabinet approval for his economic growth strategy known as "Japan revival strategy" (*Nihon saikō senryaku*) where he reiterated the need for speed and agility in pressing for the implementation of an ambitious policy that would smash existing barriers.[8] The prime minister's decisive actions toward reforming Japan gained wide support from the electorate and as a result, Abe emerged victorious in the 23rd upper house elections held on July 21, 2013.[9] This victory solidified Abe's power base, in that the LDP now had become the majority party in the Diet, taking back control of the upper house as well. In this manner, Abe's primary focus was on Japanese domestic politics. But this did not mean that he was not paying attention to international relations—it was at this juncture that China formally announced its "One Belt, One Road" policy with much fanfare.[10]

A More Robust Japan

To Abe's credit, he recognized not only the significance of the rise of China but also the threat that it posed much earlier than most European leaders. His first iteration of this menace was uttered during a speech that he gave at the Hudson Institute on September 25, 2013.[11] In this speech, Abe referred to China's rapid militarization and announced that Japan's military expenditures will grow for the first time in eleven years (albeit a mere 0.8%). Uncharacteristic of a Japanese leader, his tone was defiant, exclaiming, "so call me, if you want, a right-wing militarist."[12] It was readily apparent that this marked a significant departure from the traditionally meek posture on national security issues. Abe used the slogan, "Proactive Contributor of Peace" (*Sekkyokyuteki heiwashugi*), to refer to this new stance.[13] As an institution to realize his vision, the National Security Council (NSC) was established on December 4, 2013, marking an important milestone in postwar Japanese security policy. But Abe did not stop there. In rapid succession, he also passed Japan's Specified Secret Protection Law (*Tokutei himitsu hogo-hō*) which would allow the government to share and receive sensitive intelligence from its allies. Although Japanese public opinion was not supportive of its enactment, the strength of the revived economy served to mitigate any serious political repercussions. This, of course, would form the basis for any future discussion regarding Japan's possible entry in to the "Five Eyes" intelligence group. The act was followed on December 17 by the Abe cabinet signing off on the National Security Strategy (NSS) which affirmed, under the banner of proactive pacifism that U.S.–Japan alliance would be further strengthened to enhance deterrence.[14] In this manner, Abe took key steps in not only managing U.S.–Japan relations but also forging stronger ties in the area of national security. To be sure, at this moment in time, the threat perception was clearly geared more toward North Korea than China.

Unfortunately, the U.S.–Japan relationship suffered a setback when Abe followed through on his decision to pay respects to Japan war's dead—including convicted Class A war criminals —by making an official visit to the controversial Yasukuni shrine on December 26, 2013.[15] As Abe had openly commented about regretting not being able to visit the Yasukuni shrine during his first term as prime minister, he was essentially making good on his previous words. This enabled him to solidify his political support base on the right, giving him more leeway to pursue progressive domestic policies. The international outcry following his visit was not small, as China and South Korea immediately lodged protests, but the most painful rebuttal was dealt by the United States, as Washington quickly released a statement of disappointment that essentially was a rebuke of Abe.[16]

Such an official rebuke coming from an American government led by the Democratic Party perhaps helps to explain why many Japanese conservatives continue to hold strong animosity toward that particular party as witnessed by their vocal support for the incumbent Donald Trump during the 2020 presidential elections. Conversely, Abe's visit to Yasukuni prompted left-leaning political commentators and academics in the United States to view Abe as a dangerous right-wing nationalist, which even led to a petition to censure his actions. However, further damage to U.S.–Japan relations were contained, as a more pragmatic Abe refrained from making another visit to Yasukuni during his remaining tenure as prime minister. In fact, he would visit again only after he had left office on September 19, 2020. But this visit did not elicit a response from the U.S. government, which no doubt further cemented support for President Trump by the Japanese right.

Enhancing the U.S.–Japan Alliance

A more substantial bilateral issue in terms of national security, and one which remains unresolved, was the issue of U.S. bases in Okinawa. In February 2013, the Okinawan governor agreed to begin landfill work in Henoko in order to phase out the Marine Corps Air Station Futenma, but the ensuing change in the prefectural political leadership the following year did not allow any further progress.[17] In the meantime, the debate over the base issue was replaced by the upcoming plan to increase the consumption tax. Although the LDP braced itself for a major political backlash, nothing came as the DPJ no longer functioned as an alternative to the LDP. This lack of a viable political counterweight meant that the Japanese voters had no real choice but to go along with a prime minister that at least provided economic growth and political stability. Thus, it can be said that the staying power of Abe was to a large part due to the lack of a strong opposition.

Another important issue, although not directly relevant to U.S.–Japan relations per se, was Abe's decision to reverse the longstanding policy of prohibiting arms exports (*Buki yushutsu sangensoku*) and implemented a new guideline for permitting foreign military sales.[18] The self-imposed ban had long been a hallmark policy of Japan's pacifism, but it was no longer tenable in a rapidly changing and increasingly hostile global security environment. From a practical perspective, Japan also desired to export arms in order to lower the unit cost of its military hardware so that it could procure more. Under the new rules, once certain conditions had been met, Japan could now export arms and military equipment to its allies. However, a vastly more significant policy decision was taken on July 1, 2014. For the first time since

1972, Abe and his cabinet reinterpreted Japan's regulations to allow for collective self-defense.[19] Undoubtedly, this marked a paradigm shift in postwar Japanese security policy and is perhaps a key legacy of Prime Minister Abe. This decision not only allowed Japan to alter its existing security identity, it also paved the path for forging a much more formidable alliance between the two powers across the Pacific. Surprisingly, despite this important change in interpreting Japanese security policy, the LDP fared well in the 47th lower house elections that were held on December 14, 2014, losing a mere four seats.[20]

2015 would be a key year in U.S.–Japan relations. On April 27th, the Guidelines for Japan–U.S. Defense Cooperation were revised for the first time since 1997 to better reflect the new security realities. And two days later, Abe became the first Japanese prime minister to address the Joint Session of Congress on April 29. In his speech, the prime minister not only proclaimed his support for Obama's rebalance, or Asia pivot policy, but also embraced the importance of America in maintaining peace and stability in the Asia Pacific region (the "Indo-Pacific" concept would emerge after this speech).[21] Additionally, on August 14, Abe made an important speech marking the 70th anniversary of the conclusion of the Pacific War, but also stated that this would be the last of such speeches.[22] In the following month, Abe was chosen to continue leading the LDP without a formal vote, clearly attesting his vast political clout within the party.

Looking back, one will surely note September 19 as being a pivotal date in postwar Japanese history. It was on this day that the national security related act (*Anzenhoshō kanren hōan*)—a combination of the Peace and Security Maintenance act which included ten bills including the JSDF law, and the International Peace Support Act which made JSDF missions in overseas deployment during peacetime permanent—was passed, to take effect from March 29 of the following year.[23] Although many Japanese constitutional scholars deemed it to be unconstitutional, Abe's strong resolve in the face of the rapidly changing international security situation allowed its passage after much deliberation that began from shortly after he was reappointed prime minister in 2013. Of course, strong public support in addition to strong political will was what ultimately brought this result. Many Japanese recognized the need for strengthening the U.S.–Japan alliance and furthering the integration of the JSDF and the U.S. military to enhance deterrence capabilities amid an increasingly menacing North Korea as well as growing Chinese maritime ambitions.

An oft overlooked aspect of U.S.–Japan security relations is that in the end it was Japanese public opinion that allowed for the forging of stronger bonds. This was in part a rational reaction to the repeated missile firing tests conducted by North Korea as well as Chinese encroachment upon the Senkaku

Islands. Using this change in public opinion as a powerful gust of wind in his sails, Abe was able to pursue a security policy that would have otherwise been difficult to attain. Among the two threats, undeniably the greater one was with China, with its huge economic presence. China overtook Japan in 2010 to become the world's second largest economy, and in a span of five years, it had vastly widened the gap with Japan. With newly gained economic prowess came enlarged confidence which in turn led to greater national aspiration to revise the status quo so that it would better reflect its national interests. Naturally, this meant that China would emerge as a challenger to the existing world order led by the United States as evinced by the launch of the Asia Infrastructure Investment Bank (AIIB) in December 2015.[24] Faced with this new reality, Japan and the United States acted in lockstep and refrained from entering the AIIB despite key European allies and Canada showing initial interest and then eventual membership; astonishingly, even Australia became a founding member.

Coming on the heels of the national security act, Abe hosted the G7 Summit meeting in Ise Shima, Mie prefecture, in late April. President Obama was the last to arrive at the venue, and the nationally televised image of Abe standing alone patiently waiting the president's arrival was a poignant reminder to many Japanese of the asymmetrical nature of U.S.–Japan relations. Any negative emotion was effectively erased, however, by the first ever visit by a sitting U.S. president to Hiroshima after the summit. This time, it was the widely viewed image of Obama gentling embracing an A-Bomb survivor that reflected American compassion as well as showing how far U.S.–Japan relationship had evolved.[25] With U.S.–Japan relations on a vastly more solid footing—some pundits would refer to it as a coming of "New Age" in U.S.–Japan relations—and the Japanese economy humming along, if not exactly taking off, the ideal stage was set for the 24th upper house elections on July 10. As such, it was no surprise that the LDP, along with its coalition partner the Kōmeitō, cruised to an easy victory which allowed it to successfully secure a two-thirds majority in the upper house, enough to initiate a national referendum on constitutional revision.[26] The LDP campaign slogan during the election was "Boldly advance in this path with strength" (*Kono michi wo, chikarazuyoku maee*), but unfortunately as we will see in the next section, this path toward constitutional revision would consist of a lot more rhetoric than reality.

ABE'S U.S. POLICY DURING THE TRUMP ADMINISTRATION

The outcome of the November 2016 U.S. presidential election surprised many. The overwhelming favorite, Hilary R. Clinton, despite gaining nearly

2.8 million more popular votes than Donald J. Trump, the Republican candidate, was soundly defeated in the electoral college. In a stunning upset, it was Trump who would be elected as the 45th U.S. president. A reality TV star/real estate mogul with no prior political experience had essentially taken over the Republican machine under such slogans as "Drain the Swamp," "Make America Great Again," and "America First." The latter slogan understandably had foreign policy implications, and the Japanese government watched warily to see what the ramifications would be in the context of U.S.–Japan relations.

In the meantime, Abe relentlessly pursued policies that would further enhance Japan's defense posture. In this vein, on November 15, the Abe cabinet approved the JSDF to utilize force when necessary in protecting others during its peace-keeping operation (PKO) in South Sudan. With this small albeit important move, the rules of engagement of the Japanese peace-keeping force had been fundamentally altered. No doubt, Abe perceived this as a crucial step in normalizing the role of the JSDF so that it could eventually be transformed into a full-fledged military. Despite these changes, foremost on the mind of Abe was U.S.–Japan relations, as the new American president brought with him much uncertainty. Thus, a mere two days later, the prime minister was in New York, gifts in hand, to pay his respects to "president-elect" Trump at his private residence in Manhattan.[27] No doubt this was an awkward moment in U.S.–Japan relations as the current president was still in Washington D.C. This clearly showed the reality of how dependent Japan was upon the United States; the striking parallelism to the days when Japan had made tributary visits to China did not go unnoticed.

In the press conference after his meeting with Trump, Abe remarked with confidence that President-elect Trump would surely be a "trustworthy leader."[28] However, the very fact that the Japanese bureaucrats wasted no time in organizing this unconventional meeting with Trump indicated there were in fact some serious concerns about the incoming president. It was evident from the presidential campaign that Trump was in no way like that of any other modern president, and it was also certain that he did not subscribe to any traditional Republican ideology. Trump being a large unknown factor made the Japanese uneasy, and thus the decision was made for Abe to make a visit in order to impress upon the incoming president the importance of Japan. In retrospect, Abe's flattering of Trump, although undeniably shameless, most likely did pay handsome dividends as U.S.–Japan relations remained generally turbulence-free over the next four years.

However, in the following month, Abe was once again at the side of the outgoing president, Obama, during a ceremony commemorating the 75th anniversary of the attack on Pearl Harbor.[29] This was to reciprocate the president's visit to Hiroshima, but it was sight to behold: the leaders of Japan and the United States standing next to each other at the very spot that U.S.–Japan relations had been shattered in December 1941 was not only profoundly symbolic but also demonstrated how far U.S.–Japan relations had matured after the day of informy.

U.S.–Japan Relations as the Core Axis

As the contours of the Trump administration began to take shape, Abe proudly announced in his annual policy speech that the "US–Japan alliance was firmly grounded on principles that never change," and added that the "US–Japan alliance will remain steadfast as the core axis of Japan's foreign and national security policy."[30] Gaining further political strength through the support of Japanese public opinion, the LDP realized that they were presented with an opportune moment to revise party guidelines that would enable Abe to head the party for a third term. Facing no serious challenges from within party ranks, on May 3, 2017, Abe was now confident enough to announce that he would strive for the implementation of a new constitution by 2020.[31] The goal was symbolic, in that it marked the 70th anniversary of the promulgation of the current constitution. Moreover, he became the first prime minister to openly state that Article 9 had to be revised so that it would legally recognize the existence of the JSDF.[32]

The timing could not have been better. In July, an increasingly recalcitrant Kim Jong-un announced that North Korea had successfully developed an ICBM that placed the continental United States within striking range. As this dramatically increased the threat posed by North Korea, Abe moved quickly to seize the moment by striking a hard tone and stating that these actions were "totally unacceptable."[33] He was resolute in his view that a traditional diplomacy-centered approach was no longer effective in dealing with Kim Jong-un. Abe further commented that history showed that nations needed to work closer together and apply concerted pressure on dictatorial regimes in order to change their behavior. Such comments presented Abe as a strong leader who would not back down in the face of an adversary—Japan would be no push over. Capitalizing on this bold public image, snap elections were called on September 28, 2017, and during the 48th lower house elections on October 22, the LDP, alongside its coalition partner Kōmeitō, were able to maintain their two-thirds majority by securing 310 seats.[34]

On November 29, North Korea escalated the situation further by test firing an ICBM. The direct Japanese reaction to this was to initiate the so-called "Aegis Ashore" program that consisted of building two anti-ballistic missile sites in Akita and Yamaguchi prefectures on the side that faced the Sea of Japan. This highly expensive program would eventually be scrapped in late 2020 upon Abe's departure from office, but it did impress upon the average

Japanese that the government was not standing idly as North Korea threatened Japan. However, in an ironic twist of events, Kim's threatening posture toward the United States actually paid off. The initially bellicose Trump—his angry "Rocket Man" speech at the United Nations where he threatened that the United States would "totally destroy" North Korea, echoed Nikita Khrushchev's famous "We will bury you" speech—toned down his rhetoric. And in a remarkable about-face, he was now willing to sit down and meet his arch nemesis, Kim Jong-un.[35]

The first ever bilateral meeting between the two countries took place in Singapore on June 12, 2018. Just a few weeks earlier, it had been unthinkable that a sitting U.S. president would be meeting Kim Jong-un, thereby handing him the legitimacy that he so greatly sought. The world watched as the U.S. and North Korean leaders made their historic appearances. On the sidelines, Abe used this moment to pass laws that would be necessary in forming the new TPP sans the U.S., officially known as the Comprehensive and Progressive Trans-Pacific Partnership (CPTPP; also referred to as TPP 11).

Managing Trump and U.S.–Japan Trade Relations

Although the new trade agreement was launched lacking American membership, the formation of the CPTPP is arguably one of the crowning achievements of Prime Minister Abe. On the other hand, the absence of the United States from this free trade framework necessitated the negotiation of an alternative "bilateral" trade agreement between the two countries. This became the starting point of the ensuing discussion that would eventually culminate in the U.S.–Japan trade agreement. The trade negotiation gained a sense of urgency, because Trump had made it abundantly clear that he was displeased with the existing trade deficit vis-à-vis Japan. Thus, in addition to Japan acquiescing to a new trade agreement, the president demanded that Japan commit itself to making large purchases of U.S. military equipment. Japan was more than willing to abide on both points as it did not want to risk alienating a U.S. administration that clearly placed less value upon alliances. Another important reason was that Tokyo saw this as a way in which the door could be left ajar for the eventual reentry of the United States into the CPTPP. On the other hand, this meant that Japan did not want to agree to a trade deal that was so comprehensive that it would negate any incentive for the United States to rejoin in the future. As such, the Japanese government chose to refer to the final agreement simply as a bilateral trade agreement (TAG), whereas Vice President Mike Pence made it no secret that he viewed it as a Free Trade Agreement (FTA) during his speech on October 4, 2018.[36]

During this period, Abe also displayed prudence in managing Sino-Japan relations. He made it a point to attend the commemorating ceremony of the 40th anniversary of the signing of the peace and amity treaty between the two nations on October 26, 2018. It had been seven years since a sitting Japanese prime minister had made a visit to China, and on this occasion, Abe proclaimed that he would endeavor to begin a "new era of Sino-Japanese relations" that would be marked by "cooperation, and not competition."[37] The reason behind such an overtly pro-Chinese position was that Abe had become cognizant of how inextricably linked the Japanese economy was with China's, and with a record number of Chinese tourists flocking to Japan, it made practical sense that relations remain positive so that Japanese businesses could capitalize on this opportunity.

Of course, in no way did this mean that Japan had let its guard down. As a matter of fact, Abe further left his mark on Japan's defense policy through his National Defense Program Guidelines (*Bōeitaikō*) that would serve as a basic policy for the next decade or until revised by a future government.[38] In addition to the traditional defense domains of air, sea, and land, outer space and cyber space were recognized as new areas in which Japan would strive to bolster its defense as a way to effectively deal with hybrid warfare. Abe also made the decision to convert two JMSDF *Izumo*-class helicopter carriers into aircraft carriers in addition to committing to the purchase of 105 F-35 fighter jets—approved by the U.S. Congress on July 9, 2020—and upgrading 99 current F-15Js to F-15EXs.[39] A favorable side effect of the purchasing of this military hardware from the United States was that it ameliorated Trump's concerns about Japan's trade surplus. Thus, Abe increased Japan's defense budget to its highest levels ever, outlaying an expenditure plan of nearly ¥27.5 trillion in a span of five years. Clearly, this was Japan's way of reacting to the dual geostrategic threats posed by Chinese and North Korea, as well as making sure that the leader of its closest ally was placated.

As Japan was taking steps to shore up its own defenses, it also took a symbolic step in moving away from the stance of international cooperation which had the added effect of pleasing Abe's right-wing supporters. On December 26, the Japanese government announced that it would withdraw from the International Whaling Commission (IWC) and resume commercial whaling from July of the following year.[40] Interestingly, while this surely would have led to protest during the Obama's administration, the Trump administration did not even bat an eye. In this way, the Japanese authorities calculated the leeway that they possessed in implementing policies under the new government in Washington. Since Trump did not have an iota of enthusiasm for conservation issues, or for that matter even the global climate, Japan realized that it could leave the IWC without having to endure the ire of America.

Another tool that Tokyo used effectively was Abe's personal relationship, or rather personal diplomacy, with Trump. Flattery, unwavering attention, multiple and frequent phone calls, and a juicy hamburger with a Diet Coke, comprised the key ingredients of Abe's personal diplomacy with Trump as witnessed during the president's four-day official State visit to Japan from May 25, 2019.[41] Of course, this could at times cause embarrassment, such as the time when Trump shamelessly boasted that Abe had informed him that he would be pleased to nominate him for the Nobel Peace Prize.[42] One can perhaps argue that Abe went a bit overboard in his approach to Trump, but the result that appeasement had was readily apparent. Trump was clearly elated when he spoke to reporters about Abe providing him a copy of the nomination letter that the prime minister had written to the commission, referring to it gleefully as a "most beautiful letter."[43]

The Coming of Reiwa and U.S.–Japan Relations

Abe's term as prime minister coincided with the end of the Heisei era, which lasted nearly thirty-three years. The new era of Reiwa began on April 1, 2019, but this was the first time in postwar Japanese history that a new reign began not by the death of the previous emperor, but by his abdication, one which Abe himself had helped facilitate. But the new era did not bring about any drastic changes in Japan, and it was essentially the continuation of Heisei under a different label. In late June, Trump attended the G20 summit in Osaka, but it was apparent that his heart was not in Japan but rather at his next stop, Seoul, where he planned to meet Kim Jong-un at Panmunjom and become the first American president to set foot on North Korean soil. As the world witnessed this historical event, Japan held its 25th upper house elections on July 21.

The voter turnout was dismal at 48.8 percent, the second lowest in the postwar period. However, it was this very political apathy shown by the Japanese voters that allowed Abe to remain in power and limit his losses to a mere nine seats.[44] It certainly appeared to most that he would have no problem serving out his final term as prime minister, and most questions revolved around whether the LDP would extend his tenure for another term. At the same time, it was difficult to deny that the strains and stresses of being prime minister was taking a heavy toll on Abe's health, which was easily visible in his fatigued facial expression. Thus, it was logical to think that Abe was planning to resign upon the conclusion of the 2020 Tokyo Olympic Games, the perfect final touch to his grand exit. Problems, however, were later to intervene.

In August, the South Korean government announced that it would not renew the annual General Security of Military Information Agreement (GSOMIA), which had first been signed on November 2016 at the behest of the Obama administration. Washington was quick to release a statement conveying disappointment and worked to apply pressure on Seoul behind the scenes. As a result, the South Koreans suddenly agreed to extend the agreement.[45] Fortunately, U.S.–Japan relations continued to be on firmer ground, and on September 25, after a year-long negotiation, the two countries finally wrapped up a new trade agreement. As part of the deal, Japan agreed to reduce tariffs on ¥780 billion worth of U.S. agricultural products and promised to further open its markets. Although rice was excluded completely from the trade deal, Japan had to pay a steep price for this concession, and as a result Japan did not obtain any tariff reductions for both automobiles and automobile parts.[46] All in all, it was a good deal for the United States, which Trump wasted no time in proudly boasting. Perhaps this can be a case study in which the Japanese adage of "losing is winning" is quite appropriate. Had the Japanese played hard ball and the negotiations had dragged on without results, this surely would have incurred Trump's wrath, possibly to the detriment of U.S.–Japan security relations. As a matter of fact, Host Nation Support (HNS) discussions were about to begin over Japanese financial contributions, so the fall out of a failed trade discussion had ample possibility of spilling over to this arena as well.

In hindsight, 2019 was a relatively uneventful year in U.S.–Japan relations, although from the vantage point of U.S. politics, the impeachment of Trump would dominate the headlines. In contrast, 2020 would be vastly different as the global stage would be dominated by two major events. The first was novel coronavirus epidemic in Wuhan, China, that soon expanded from an epidemic to a pandemic by February despite repeated WHO assurances to the contrary. The other was the U.S. presidential election in November in which Trump faced-off with his Democratic opponent, Joseph R. Biden. The two events became linked as the outcome of the presidential race was profoundly affected by the pandemic had never occured if the COVID-19 pandemic had never occurred, the incumbent, Trump, certainly would have prevailed. The pandemic not only sank the U.S. economy, but Trump's lackluster response and inability to contain the spread of the virus turned the political tide decidedly against him.

As witnessed, popular support for Trump was far from insignificant, but in the end, even more Americans had lost their confidence in him. Interestingly, there were many Japanese conservatives who were unabashedly pro-Trump based on his anti-China position and their general disdain of the Democratic Party. The pro-Trump rally that took place in Hibiya, Tokyo, on January 6, 2021, were particularly revealing as it showed how a certain segment of Japanese had become so outspoken in favoring one president over another during a presidential election.[47] It remains to be seen whether this phenomenon will have larger political consequences in future of U.S.–Japan relations.

With the exit of Trump and the arrival of a new president who places greater emphasis on alliance management and international cooperation, there is little doubt that U.S.–Japan relations will once again enter a new phase. Japan will wholeheartedly embrace the new U.S. position on global climate issues, but problems can again resurface on the national security front. For one, the Okinawa base relocation process has virtually halted, and in April 2020, it was made public that that the new base on Henoko would not be completed for another twelve years at the earliest.[48] Second, Japan–ROK relations are in a midst of downward spiral, and it remains to be seen if and how the Biden administration will intervene. The United States serves as a lynchpin between these two key allies in Northeast Asia, and there is no denying that bickering among these allies only serves to benefit China. Third, increasing American willingness to stand up to China, whether it be on human rights, technology, trade, or geopolitical issues, such as in the East and South China Seas, will lead to an increasingly unfamiliar and tense security environment for Japan that will require adroit maneuvering on the part of Japan's leadership as it navigates these perilous waters.

What surely cannot continue is Japan's current policy of placing itself between the United States and China—that is, relying on China for its economic well-being, but being dependent on the United States for its security. Can Japan rise to this challenge in order to ensure its survival? These will be the key issues that will need to be resolved within this decade, if not sooner, and ultimately it will be Japan's policy decisions that will play a large role in shaping the future course of U.S.–Japan relations. For example, for how long will the United States allow Japan in not carrying its burden toward increased regional security, including the revision of Article 9, so that the U.S.–Japan alliance can evolve into a mutual defense pact? What is clear, however, as the capability gap between China and the United States further shrinks, is that Washington will have much less incentive to continue a security policy of "strategic tolerance" toward Japan.

THE END OF AN ERA: LOOKING BACK ON ABE'S LEGACY

All things must come to an end, and so too has the tenure of the longest serving Japanese Prime Minister Abe Shinzō. If his first term is included as well, he was at the helm of Japan's political leadership for nearly nine years; astoundingly, this means that he was in power longer than any postwar U.S. president. Such political staying power also means that Abe had ample time to establish a solid legacy. Conversely, this means that critics abound. In Abe's case, one can make a strong case that he failed in achieving or resolving his three foreign policy goals of the North Korean abduction issue, the Northern Territories issue with Russia, and the constitutional revision of Article 9, which is a domestic issue with profound external implications. Surely, it cannot be denied that attaining each of these goals was a tall order to begin with, and therefore it is possible to make the criticism that Abe, despite being a self-proclaimed pragmatist, lacked adequate realism when setting his goals in the first place. As a result, he left these issues to his successor without making any significant headway in any one of them.

Furthermore, his much-touted Abenomics also fell short of its lofty aims, although Abe did bring about an era of much needed economic growth for Japan—in fact it was Japan's second longest period of economic growth in the postwar period. Credit also needs to be given for his adroit handling in not allowing the Tran-Pacific Partnership (TPP) to falter amid the withdrawal by the United States. However, his overall economic legacy is clouded because growth was stymied in part because of his decision to raise the consumption tax not once, but twice, and nearly all the economic gains made during his tenure were wiped clean by the recent pandemic. Moreover, he was also never truly able to clear his name from the major political scandals that embroiled him, including allegations of favoritism. Moreover, the first lady who was always out of touch with the general public also became a political liability that tarnished his image, however slightly. Finally, toward the end of his tenure, there were numerous resignations by his cabinet ministers due to serious political scandals, including one involving his justice minister who was indicted on bribery charges.[49]

Despite these shortfalls, future historians will surely heap praise on Abe in the following three areas. First, his longevity as Japan's political leader gave a strong face to Japanese diplomacy. Whether liked or disliked, the world knew Abe. Thus, unlike past Japanese leaders, the leaders of the G7 summit could be certain that Japan's leader would be back again the following year. Ultimately, Abe would become the second longest attending member of the G7 behind Angela Merkel of Germany. This considerably bolstered Japan's presence as well as visibility not only among the G7 nations, but also on the global stage.

Second, Abe was able to nudge Japan away from the Yoshida Doctrine, which steadfastly defined Japan's security identity from the early 1950s as being one of one-sided reliance on the United States. Abe paved the way toward reinterpretation of Japan's national security laws so that it would finally permit collective self-defense with the United States. Considering the future of the U.S.–Japan alliance, the revision was overdue and also pure commonsense, but Japan's past leaders lacked the political will and capital to bring about change. Putting aside the changes to Japan's security environment, it was the political determination of Abe and the concrete results that followed that not only made the U.S.–Japan alliance more robust but also gave it a fresh set of sturdy legs that will carry it further, if not indefinitely, into the future. Ironically, it was the success achieved in this reinterpretation that took away the momentum from constitutional revision, the real prize. This also would have been the most decisive way in which Abe could have surpassed the legacy of his grandfather, Kishi Nobusuke, whose own legacy was forged in his successful revision of the U.S.–Japan Security Treaty in 1960. Eventually, Japan's future leaders must bring about constitutional revision, as only through this action can Japan truly alter its security identity to one that will enable it to transform itself into a regional security provider. This single action alone will signify the final passing of the Yoshida Doctrine. Only then will Japan finally be able to chart new waters as a proactive player in the realm of security with a real military that will be able to strike first in order to defend regional like-minded powers if necessary.

Lastly, Abe was able to forge a strong working relationship with his American counterpart, Donald Trump, a person that is not known for his generosity nor amicability. Not only did Abe swallow his pride to visit Trump when he was still "president-elect," he made sure that he kept in touch with him as much as possible by calling him more often than any other G7 leader. This level of attention and flattery, along with the numerous rounds of golf that served to bolster the personal relationship, in turn provided stability for state-to-state relations. Although this "Don-Shinzō" relationship was by no means a relationship based on genuine friendship nor mutual admiration, such as the one between Ronald Reagan and Nakasone Yasuhiro—the "Ron–Yasu" relationship—it was nevertheless a relationship that served to bolster the U.S.–Japan bilateral relations from top to bottom. As one high-ranking U.S. official commented to the author, Abe's project-like approach of "working on" Trump rather than "working with" Trump, proved to function rather well. In the end, it was Abe's effective management of the "Trump project" that allowed the bilateral relationship to steer clear of the turbulence that severely affected other American allies.[50] Therefore, from the standpoint of U.S.–Japan relations, Abe should be given high marks for his statesmanship in maintaining and strengthening the alliance that will most assuredly contribute to the peace and stability of Indo-Pacific in the years to come.

NOTES

1. For an excellent study that deals with the earlier postwar prime ministers, see Akio Watanabe ed., *Sengo nihon no saishō tachi* [Postwar Japanese Prime Ministers], Tokyo: Chuōkōronshinsha, 1995.

2. Katsura served as prime minister for 2,866 days, while Abe is the current record holder at 3,188 days. Interestingly, the top four prime ministers in terms of length in office all are from the former Chōshū clan and include Satō Eisaku (2,798 days) and Itō Hirobumi (2,346). See Kantei, Information on Cabinet Generations, https://www.kantei.go.jp/jp/rekidai/ichiran.html.

3. Jiji Tsūshin, "46th House of Representatives Election-December 16 Voting-," https://www.jiji.com/jc/election?g=2012syuin&l=top.

4. The election ended in a landslide defeat for the DPJ, as they slid from 231 seats to 57. The big winners were the LDP which went up from 118 seats to 294 and the Japan Restoration Party (now known as the Japan Innovation Party) which went up from 11 to 54 seats. The Kōmeitō also won 10 seats. Ibid. The election brought an end to the DPJ's position as the ruling party.

5. The term was coined from a phrase in Abe's inauguration speech that outlined his policy goals. See Zenichiro Tanaka, "Crisis Breakthrough Cabinet," *Imidas*, March 2013. https://imidas.jp/genre/detail/C-109-0602.html.

6. Daisuke Karakama, "Abenomikusu towa nandattanoka" [What was Abenomics?], *Business Insider*, September 4, 2020. https://www.businessinsider.jp/post-219621.

7. Upper House Diet member Yamada Toshio, a politician supported by Japan's agricultural interests, details the LDP position against TPP in his digital magazine. See Toshio Yamada, "Liberal Democratic Party decides to oppose participation in TPP negotiations," Toshio Yamada E-mail Magazine No. 255, March 9, 2012. https://www.yamada-toshio.jp/mailmagazine/backnumber/no00255.

8. See Japan Economic-Industrial Committee Research Report, September 9, 2013.

9. The LDP won 65 seats (for a net gain of 31) while the coalition partner Kōmeitō won 11 (net loss of 1). See *Jiji Tsushin*, "Number of seats won," 2013. https://www.jiji.com/jc/2013san.

10. Benjamin Robbins, "One Belt, One Road and the History of the Maritime Silk Route," *E-International Relations*, March 26, 2017. https://www.e-ir.info/2017/03/26/one-belt-one-road-and-the-history-of-the-maritime-silk-route/.

11. Shinzō Abe, "Remarks by Prime Minister Shinzo Abe on the occasion of accepting Hudson Institute's 2013 Herman Kahn Award, September 25, 2013. The Pierre Hotel, New York City." (Speech transcript), https://www.japan.go.jp/tomodachi/2013/winter2013/hudson.html.

12. Ibid.
13. Ibid.

14. Kantei, "About 'National Security Council' (Explanatory Material)," https://www.kantei.go.jp/jp/singi/ka_yusiki/dai6/siryou1.pdf.

15. Reiji Yoshida and Mizuho Aoki, "Abe visits Yasukuni, angering Beijing and Seoul," *Japan Times*, December 26, 2013. https://www.japantimes.co.jp/news/2013/12/26/national/abes-surprise-visit-to-yasukuni-sparks-criticism/.

16. George Nishiyama, "Abe Visit to Controversial Japanese Shrine Draws Rare U.S. Criticism," *The Wall Street Journal*, December 26, 2013. https://www.wsj.com/articles/japan8217s-abe-to-visit-yasukuni-shrine-1388023074.

17. *Ryuku Shinpō*, 「新知事に翁長氏 仲井真氏に１０万票差」 [New mayor to be Onaga, setting apart Nakaima by 100,000 votes], November 17, 2014. https://ryukyushimpo.jp/photo/prentry-234626.html.

18. Reuters News Editorial Department, "Cabinet decision on new rules to replace the three principles of arms exports, Exports are permitted if certain conditions are met," *Reuters*, March 31, 2014.

19. *Nihon Keizai Shimbun*, "Cabinet decision to change the interpretation of the Constitution allows the exercise of collective self-defense rights," July 1, 2014. https://www.nikkei.com/article/DGXNASFS0103O_R00C14A7MM8000/.

20. *Jiji Tsūshin*, "47th House of Representatives Election-December 14 Voting-," https://www.jiji.com/jc/2014syu?j1.

21. Shinzō Abe, "'Toward an Alliance of Hope' – Address to a Joint Meeting of Congress by Prime Minister Shinzo Abe" (Speech transcript), Kantei, April 29, 2015.

22. Shinzō Abe, "Statement by Prime Minister Abe Shinzo" (Speech transcript), Kantei, August 14, 2015. https://www.kantei.go.jp/jp/97_abe/discource/20150814danwa.html.

23. *Nihon Keizai Shimbun*, "Security bill reorganized the whole picture," May 15, 2015. https://www.nikkei.com/article/DGXZZO76056900T20C14A8000028/.

24. *Financial Times*, "AIIB launch signals China's new ambition," June 29, 2015. https://www.ft.com/content/5ea61666-1e24-11e5-aa5a-398b2169cf79.

25. Jonathan Soble, "Hiroshima Survivor Cries, and Obama Gives Him a Hug," *New York Times*, May 27, 2016.

26. See *Jiji Tsushin*, "25th House of Counselors Election 2019," https://www.jiji.com/jc/2019san. This was the first national election that was held with the new voter age limit of 18. Previously, the age limit was 20.

27. Steve Holland and Kiyoshi Takenaka, "Japan's PM Abe meets Trump, says confidence can build trust," *Reuters*, November 16, 2016. https://www.reuters.com/article/us-usa-trump-japan-idUSKBN13C0C8.

28. Steve Holland and Kiyoshi Takenaka, "UPDATE 12-Japan's Abe says after meeting with Trump he is confident of building trust," *Reuters*, November 17, 2016. https://jp.reuters.com/article/usa-trump-abe/update-12-japans-abe-says-after-meeting-with-trump-he-is-confident-of-building-trust-idUSL4N1DI3VQ.

29. *Kyodo*, "Abe's Pearl Harbor visit hailed in Japan, but some question lack of apology," *Japan Times*, December 28, 2016. https://www.japantimes.co.jp/news/2016/12/28/national/abes-pearl-harbor-visit-hailed-japan-question-lack-apology/.

30. Shinzō Abe, "Policy speech by Prime Minister Shinzo Abe to the 193rd Session of the Diet" (Speech transcript), Kantei, January 20, 2017.

31. *Nihon Keizai Shimbun*, "Full text of Prime Minister's message on constitutional amendment," May 3, 2017.

32. *Mainichi Shimbun*, "Self-Defense Forces specified in Article 9, Aiming for constitutional amendment by 2020," May 3, 2017.

33. Takashi Hirokawa and Yuki Hagiwara, "North Korea announces successful ICBM launch- 'absolutely unacceptable,' Secretary of State Suga," *Bloomberg*, July 4, 2017. https://www.bloomberg.co.jp/news/articles/2017-07-04/OQWH416S972901.

34. *Jiji Tsūshin*, "48th House of Representatives election, Liberal Democratic victory = constitutional breakthrough, hope 'complete defeat'," October 23, 2017. https://www.jiji.com/jc/movie?p=j000940.

35. Scott Horsley, "Trump to UN: North Korea's 'Rocket Man' Kim Jong Un on a suicide mission," *NPR*, September 19, 2017. https://www.npr.org/2017/09/19/551229652/trump-addresses-u-n-general-assembly-for-the-first-time.

36. *Japan Press Weekly*, "Abe gov't refers to new trade talks with USA as TAG, not FTA," October 10-16, 2018. https://www.japan-press.co.jp/s/news/?id=11772.

37. Ministry of Foreign Affairs (MOFA), "Prime Minister Abe's visit to China (overview)," October 26, 2018. https://www.mofa.go.jp/mofaj/a_o/c_m1/cn/page4_004452.html.

38. Ministry of Defense (MOD), "National Defense Program Guidelines for FY 2019 and beyond," December 18, 2018. https://www.mod.go.jp/j/approach/agenda/guideline/2019/pdf/20181218_e.pdf.

39. *AFP BB News,* "US, F35 sale approval to Japan 105 aircraft 2.48 trillion yen," July 10, 2020. https://www.afpbb.com/articles/-/3293063.

40. National Resource Defense Council, July 1, 2019.

41. *Jiji Tsūshin*, "[Illustration/International] US President Donald Trump's visit to Japan (May 2019)," May 22, 2019. https://www.jiji.com/jc/graphics?p=ve_int_america20190522j-04-w430.

42. Chris G. Pope, "Trump for the Nobel Peace Prize? Japan's nomination is part of a strategic plan," *The Conversation*, May 14, 2019. https://theconversation.com/trump-for-the-nobel-peace-prize-japans-nomination-is-part-of-a-strategic-plan-114484.

43. Tsuyoshi Nagasawa, "Trump says Abe nominated him for Nobel in 'beautiful' letter," *Nikkei Asia*, February 16, 2019. https://asia.nikkei.com/Politics/International-relations/Trump-says-Abe-nominated-him-for-Nobel-in-beautiful-letter.

44. *Jiji Tsūshin*, "25th House of Counselors Election 2019."

45. *Asahi Shimbun*, "Last minute GSOMIA extension, What moved the Korean government," November 23, 2019. https://www.asahi.com/articles/ASMCQ56Z4MCQUHBI038.html.

46. Ministry of Agriculture, Forestry and Fisheries (MAFF), "About the Japan-US Trade Agreement," January 1, 2020. https://www.maff.go.jp/j/kokusai/tag/index.html.

47. Asaka Yutaka, "January 6: Pay attention to Trump's counterattack (Yutaka Asaka's theory of Japan's revival)," *Daily Will*, January 5, 2021. https://web-willmagazine.com/international/4yEpp.

48. *Sankei Shimbun*, "A more polite explanation is needed than the extension of the construction period of Henoko," December 31, 2019. https://www.sankei.com/column/news/191231/clm1912310003-n1.html.

49. Ippo Saou, "Why are Abe Cabinet members resigning one after another?" *President*, November 1, 2019. https://president.jp/articles/-/30545.

50. Tosh Minohara, "Japan's new leader unlikely to confront China," *Nikkei Asia*, October 8, 2020. https://asia.nikkei.com/Opinion/Japan-s-new-leader-unlikely-to-confront-China.

REFERENCES

Abe, Shinzō. "Policy speech by Prime Minister Shinzo Abe to the 193rd Session of the Diet" (Speech transcript). Kantei, January 20, 2017. https://japan.kantei.go.jp/97_abe/statement/201701/1221105_11567.html.

Abe, Shinzō. "Remarks by Prime Minister Shinzo Abe on the occasion of accepting Hudson Institute's 2013 Herman Kahn Award, September 25, 2013. The Pierre Hotel, New York City." (Speech transcript). https://www.japan.go.jp/tomodachi/2013/winter2013/hudson.html.

Abe, Shinzō. "Statement by Prime Minister Abe Shinzo" (Speech transcript). Kantei, August 14, 2015. https://www.kantei.go.jp/jp/97_abe/discource/20150814danwa.html.

Abe, Shinzō. "'Toward an Alliance of Hope' – Address to a Joint Meeting of Congress by Prime Minister Shinzo Abe" (Speech transcript). Kantei, April 29, 2015. https://japan.kantei.go.jp/97_abe/statement/201504/uscongress.html.

AFP BB News, "US, F35 sale approval to Japan 105 aircraft 2.48 trillion yen." July 10, 2020. https://www.afpbb.com/articles/-/3293063.

Asahi Shimbun. "Last minute GSOMIA extension, What moved the Korean government." November 23, 2019. https://www.asahi.com/articles/ASMCQ56Z4MCQUHBI038.html.

Financial Times. "AIIB launch signals China's new ambition." June 29, 2015. https://www.ft.com/content/5ea61666-1e24-11e5-aa5a-398b2169cf79.

Hirokawa, Takashi and Hagiwara Yuki. "North Korea announces successful ICBM launch- 'absolutely unacceptable,' Secretary of State Suga." *Bloomberg,* July 4, 2017. https://www.bloomberg.co.jp/news/articles/2017-07-04/OQWH416S972901.

Holland, Steve and Takenaka Kiyoshi. "Japan's PM Abe meets Trump, says confidence can build trust." *Reuters,* November 16, 2016. https://www.reuters.com/article/us-usa-trump-japan-idUSKBN13C0C8.

Holland, Steve and Kiyoshi Takenaka. "UPDATE 12-Japan's Abe says after meeting with Trump he is confident of building trust." *Reuters,* November 17, 2016. https://jp.reuters.com/article/usa-trump-abe/update-12-japans-abe-says-after-meeting-with-trump-he-is-confident-of-building-trust-idUSL4N1DI3VQ.

Horsley, Scott. "Trump to UN: North Korea's 'Rocket Man' Kim Jong Un on a suicide mission." *NPR,* September 19, 2017. https://www.npr.org/2017/09/19/551229652/trump-addresses-u-n-general-assembly-for-the-first-time.

Japan Economic-Industrial Committee Research Report. September 9, 2013.

Japan Press Weekly. "Abe gov't refers to new trade talks with USA as TAG, not FTA." October 10-16, 2018. https://www.japan-press.co.jp/s/news/?id=11772.

Jiji Tsūshin. "[Illustration/International] US President Donald Trump's visit to Japan (May 2019)." May 22, 2019. https://www.jiji.com/jc/graphics?p=ve_int_america20190522j-04-w430.

Jiji Tsūshin. "Number of seats won." 2013. https://www.jiji.com/jc/2013san.

Jiji Tsūshin. "25th House of Counselors Election 2019." https://www.jiji.com/jc/2019san.

Jiji Tsūshin. "46th House of Representatives Election-December 16 Voting-." https://www.jiji.com/jc/election?g=2012syuin&l=top.
Jiji Tsūshin. "47th House of Representatives Election-December 14 Voting-." https://www.jiji.com/jc/2014syu?j1.
Jiji Tsūshin. "48th House of Representatives election, Liberal Democratic victory = constitutional breakthrough, hope 'complete defeat'." October 23, 2017. https://www.jiji.com/jc/movie?p=j000940.
Kantei. "About 'National Security Council' (Explanatory Material)." https://www.kantei.go.jp/jp/singi/ka_yusiki/dai6/siryou1.pdf.
Kantei. Information on Cabinet Generations. https://www.kantei.go.jp/jp/rekidai/ichiran.html.
Karakama, Daisuke. "Abenomikusu towa nandattanoka" [What was Abenomics?]. *Business Insider,* September 4, 2020. https://www.businessinsider.jp/post-219621.
Kyōdō. "Abe's Pearl Harbor visit hailed in Japan, but some question lack of apology." *Japan Times,* December 28, 2016. https://www.japantimes.co.jp/news/2016/12/28/national/abes-pearl-harbor-visit-hailed-japan-question-lack-apology/.
Mainichi Shimbun. "Self-Defense Forces specified in Article 9, Aiming for constitutional amendment by 2020." May 3, 2017. https://mainichi.jp/articles/20170504/k00/00m/010/077000c.
Ministry of Agriculture, Forestry and Fisheries (MAFF). "About the Japan–US Trade Agreement." January 1, 2020. https://www.maff.go.jp/j/kokusai/tag/index.html.
Ministry of Defense (MOD). "National Defense Program Guidelines for FY 2019 and beyond." December 18, 2018. https://www.mod.go.jp/j/approach/agenda/guideline/2019/pdf/20181218_e.pdf.
Ministry of Foreign Affairs (MOFA). "Prime Minister Abe's visit to China (overview)." October 26, 2018. https://www.mofa.go.jp/mofaj/a_o/c_m1/cn/page4_004452.html.
Minohara, Tosh. "Japan's new leader unlikely to confront China." *Nikkei Asia,* October 8, 2020. https://asia.nikkei.com/Opinion/Japan-s-new-leader-unlikely-to-confront-China.
Nagasawa, Tsuyoshi. "Trump says Abe nominated him for Nobel in 'beautiful' letter." *Nikkei Asia,* February 16, 2019. https://asia.nikkei.com/Politics/International-relations/Trump-says-Abe-nominated-him-for-Nobel-in-beautiful-letter.
National Resource Defense Council. July 1, 2019.
Nihon Keizai Shimbun. "Cabinet decision to change the interpretation of the Constitution allows the exercise of collective self-defense rights." July 1, 2014. https://www.nikkei.com/article/DGXNASFS0103O_R00C14A7MM8000/.
Nihon Keizai Shimbun. "Full text of Prime Minister's message on constitutional amendment." May 3, 2017. https://www.nikkei.com/article/DGXLASFK03H16_T00C17A5000000/.
Nihon Keizai Shimbun. "Security bill reorganized the whole picture." May 15, 2015. https://www.nikkei.com/article/DGXZZO76056900T20C14A8000028/.
Nishiyama, George. "Abe Visit to Controversial Japanese Shrine Draws Rare U.S. Criticism." *The Wall Street Journal,* December 26, 2013. https://www.wsj.com/articles/japan8217s-abe-to-visit-yasukuni-shrine-1388023074.

Pope, Chris G. "Trump for the Nobel Peace Prize? Japan's nomination is part of a strategic plan." *The Conversation*, May 14, 2019. https://theconversation.com/trump-for-the-nobel-peace-prize-japans-nomination-is-part-of-a-strategic-plan-114484.

Reuters News Editorial Department. "Cabinet decision on new rules to replace the three principles of arms exports, Exports are permitted if certain conditions are met." *Reuters*, March 31, 2014. https://www.huffingtonpost.jp/2014/03/31/three-principles-on-arms-exports_n_5066440.html.

Robbins, Benjamin. "One Belt, One Road and the History of the Maritime Silk Route." *E-International Relations*, March 26, 2017. https://www.e-ir.info/2017/03/26/one-belt-one-road-and-the-history-of-the-maritime-silk-route/.

Ryūkyū Shinpō. 「新知事に翁長氏 仲井真氏に１０万票差」 [New mayor to be Onaga, setting apart Nakaima by 100,000 votes]. November 17, 2014. https://ryukyushimpo.jp/photo/prentry-234626.html.

Saou, Ippo. "Why are Abe Cabinet members resigning one after another?" *President*, November 1, 2019. https://president.jp/articles/-/30545.

Sankei Shimbun. "[Claim] A more polite explanation is needed than the extension of the construction period of Henoko." December 31, 2019. https://www.sankei.com/column/news/191231/clm1912310003-n1.html.

Soble, Jonathan. "Hiroshima Survivor Cries, and Obama Gives Him a Hug." *New York Times*, May 27, 2016. https://www.nytimes.com/2016/05/28/world/asia/hiroshima-obama-visit-shigeaki-mori.html.

Tanaka, Zen.ichirō. "Crisis Breakthrough Cabinet." *Imidas*, March 2013. https://imidas.jp/genre/detail/C-109-0602.html.

Watanabe, Akio, ed. *Sengo nihon no saishō tachi* [Postwar Japanese Prime Ministers]. Tokyo: Chuōkōronshinsha, 1995.

Yamada, Toshio. "Liberal Democratic Party decides to oppose participation in TPP negotiations." Toshio Yamada E-mail Magazine No. 255, March 9, 2012. https://www.yamada-toshio.jp/mailmagazine/backnumber/no00255.

Yoshida, Reiji and Aoki Mizuho. "Abe visits Yasukuni, angering Beijing and Seoul." *Japan Times*, December 26, 2013. https://www.japantimes.co.jp/news/2013/12/26/national/abes-surprise-visit-to-yasukuni-sparks-criticism/.

Yutaka, Asaka. "January 6: Pay attention to Trump's counterattack (Yutaka Asaka's theory of Japan's revival)." *Daily Will*, January 5, 2021. https://web-willmagazine.com/international/4yEpp.

Chapter 8

Japan's Diplomacy toward China under the Abe Shinzō Administration

Soeya Yoshihide

INTRODUCTION

On August 28, 2020, Prime Minister Abe Shinzō announced his resignation from office due to a chronic health problem. The next day, a deputy spokesperson of the Ministry of Foreign Affairs of China issued a statement saying, "In recent years, China–Japan relations have returned to a normal track and achieved a new development. We appraise important endeavors by Prime Minister Abe and wish early recovery of health."[1]

The Chinese intent behind this visibly positive attitude toward Abe appears strategic, in that it is employed as an effort to balance China against the United States. On the day of Abe's resignation announcement, *Global Times*, an affiliate of *People's Daily*, said in its editorial as follows:[2]

> China is a major power and faced with strategic containment from the US. China must win the support of countries like Japan. Although Japan is a US ally, China is its largest trading partner. China can work to make Japan keep a certain distance from Washington's China policy, which is becoming increasingly radical. China can also persuade Japan to cooperate less with Washington in attacking China. This is more significant than the disputes between China and Japan.

From sometime in 2018, Abe Shinzō indeed improved relations with China. As discussed in detail below, in October of 2018, Abe paid an official visit to China for the first time in seven years in his full capacity as Japanese Prime Minister, where he and Xi Jinping confirmed that the two countries' bilateral relationship was now back on a normal track.

Abe, however, has been known as a nationalist as well as an alarmist against the expansion of Chinese influence and military presence in Asia and beyond.

He has increased Japan's defense spending, consolidated security policies, and strengthened Japan's alliance with the United States. The pronounced rationale behind these assertive moves was the worsening of the security environment in the Northeast Asian neighborhood, pointing at Chinese military expansion and assertive behaviors, and the threat posed by North Korean missile development.

Abe holds strong ideological beliefs that could have caused friction with China, but had to put them aside to take into account insurmountable realities, such as the policies of China, the two countries' economic interdependence, and other aspects of the external environment, such as the policies of key regional countries and the postwar premises of Japanese diplomacy including historical baggage, the peace constitution, and the security ties with the United States.

Abe indeed had ideologically based ambitions central to his agenda, most importantly the revision of the postwar constitution, particularly regarding the war-renouncing Article 9, and putting an end to the politics of apology over history, both domestically and vis-à-vis Japan's neighbors. Abe dubbed these core elements of his agenda as "departure from the postwar regime," the ultimate goal of which was to "recover true independence by allowing the recreation of the core structure of the state from scratch, by the Japanese people themselves."[3] Some of Abe's foreign policy agenda reflected these beliefs and was bound to cause friction with Japan's immediate neighbors, China and South Korea, specifically over the history problem and misperceptions of the "remilitarization" of Japan.

Other policies that did not clash so much with this core ideological agenda were pursued more or less within typical postwar parameters of Japanese diplomacy. Many observers therefore characterized Abe as being realistic rather than ideological. Such slogans as "proactive contribution to peace" and "diplomacy with a bird's eye view of the globe" bore no ideological inclinations. Still, a third type of Abe diplomacy took a middle stance, bearing an ideological motive, but pursuing a realistic outcome in the sense that it remained within the framework of postwar diplomacy. The Free and Open Indo-Pacific initiative and the 2015 Security Legislation under the second administration are the clearest examples of such policies.

Using these three perspectives by which to analyze Abe's foreign policy, this chapter will examine three areas of importance in reflecting upon Abe's China policy: the history problem, defense and security policy, and the Free and Open Indo-Pacific (FOIP) initiative.

WHERE ABE SHINZŌ STARTED

Since diplomatic normalization in 1972, Japan's China policy had been built around the following key assumptions: one, that the economic development of China would lead to its social stability and eventually to its political stability, and two, that a stable Japan–China relationship would be the key to the stability of East Asia and eventually that of the world. Massive ODA and FDI flows were justified by these assumptions.

The year 1992, however, became a key turning point in Japan–China relations. Japanese Emperor Akihito's China visit, realized in October as a symbolic event to commemorate the 20th anniversary of diplomatic normalization, turned out to be the high point of the so-called "1972 regime" of Japan–China relations. At the time, China was recovering from the aftermath of the Tiananmen Square Massacre (事件 in Japanese) of June 1989, and in embarking on its path to rise as a great power, began to show its assertiveness more externally. In February 1992 for instance, the Standing Committee of the National People's Congress adopted the so-called Territorial Law, which declared that "The land territory of the People's Republic of China includes the mainland of the People's Republic of China and its coastal islands; Taiwan and all islands appertaining thereto including the Diaoyu islands; "[4] The specific reference to the "Diaoyu" (hereafter Senkaku, a set of islets administered by Japan since 1895 and claimed by China since the 1970s as being part of Taiwan) alarmed the Japanese, and in the course of the 1990s, various developments caused the perception of China as a threat to grow gradually, including the fall of the Soviet Union, the democratization of Taiwanese politics and Chinese intimidation there, China's behavior in the South China Sea, its moves to acquire an aircraft carrier, and so forth.[5] In the meantime, Prime Minister Koizumi Junichiro's annual visits to Yasukuni Shrine from 2001 to 2006 strained the Japan–China relationship further.

The worsening of relations with China and the associated deterioration of the security environment surrounding Japan were conducive to the rise of Abe Shinzō as Japanese prime minister, a leader among the Japanese conservative nationalists who had been voicing their alarmist views toward China since the 1990s. Subsequently, the central postwar assumptions of Japan's China policy stated previously have virtually vanished under the leadership of Abe.

At the end of July 2006, two months before Abe was elected the prime minister of Japan on 26 September, Abe published a book titled *Utsukushii Kuni e (Towards a Beautiful Country)* in which he explained the "thinking at the root of my identity as a politician."[6] Chapter 5 of the book is devoted to "Asia and China."[7] Abe approaches the topic of anti-Japanese sentiments of Chinese people deriving from the memories of the past history by saying that Japan has already apologized a total of twenty-one times (though without mentioning specific cases) and implies his interest in putting an end to the politics of apology. Abe then refers to the principle of "separation of politics and economy" and argues that reciprocal economic relations between

Japan and China cannot be cut off. He goes on to introduce the concept of what would later come to be known as "Quad" among Japan, the United States, Australia, and India. There, conversely, Abe emphasizes the importance of universal values, such as freedom, democracy, basic human rights, and the rule of law, and names the quadrilateral framework as "Asia-Pacific Democratic G3 plus the United States."

It is interesting that most of the elements and thinking central to Abe's China policy had therefore been explicitly expressed as early as 2006, before he became the youngest prime minister of Japan in the postwar era at the age of 52. Since the first Abe administration turned out to be short-lived (September 2006–September 2007), the examination in the following section will focus mostly on the second administration of Abe Shinzō (December 2012–September 2020).

YASUKUNI AND 70TH ANNIVERSARY STATEMENT

Yasukuni Controversy

Abe Shinzō visited Yasukuni Shrine on December 26, 2013, the first visit by an incumbent prime minister since Koizumi Junichiro went in 2006. Abe had said upon his first resignation in 2007 that he deeply regretted not having visited Yasukuni while in office, which he rectified upon returning to prime ministership in December 2012.[8] After the visit, Abe stated:[9]

> Regrettably, it is a reality that the visit to Yasukuni Shrine has become a political and diplomatic issue. Some people criticize the visit to Yasukuni as paying homage to war criminals, but the purpose of my visit today, on the anniversary of my administration's taking office, is to report before the souls of the war dead how my administration has worked for one year and to renew the pledge that Japan must never wage a war again.
>
> It is not my intention at all to hurt the feelings of the Chinese and Korean people. It is my wish to respect each other's character, protect freedom and democracy, and build friendship with China and Korea with respect, as did all the previous prime ministers who visited Yasukuni Shrine.

As was expected by Abe, China reacted by saying that the visit was "absolutely unacceptable to the Chinese people." Seoul expressed "regret and anger." Even the U.S. embassy in Tokyo issued a statement saying that "the United States is disappointed that Japan's leadership has taken an action that will exacerbate tensions with Japan's neighbors."[10]

At the time, there was a debate among observers whether Abe, like Koizumi before him, would make annual visits to Yasukuni. In the end, Abe was pragmatic enough to realize that such a practice would be detrimental to his diplomacy. Nonetheless, given his inner beliefs, he could not have accepted the official record of him not visiting Yasukuni at all as the Japanese prime minister. Visiting once, therefore, was acceptable, if not satisfactory. In doing so, Abe chanced Japan's relations with both China and South Korea. Somewhat ironically, from the time of Abe's Yasukuni visit and into 2014, Xi Jinping was consolidating his power and reaching for ways to improve relations between China and Japan, which had soured significantly since the "nationalization" of the Senkaku Islands by the Noda Yoshihiko administration in 2010. Equally ironically, perhaps Abe had thought that December 2013 would be his only chance to visit Yasukuni, just before the relationship with China would begin to improve.

Thus, while the bilateral relationship experienced a temporary shock, momentum for improved relations was not entirely lost. The immediate question that attracted public attention was if an Abe–Xi bilateral meeting would happen during the APEC Economic Leaders' Meeting, which was to be held in Beijing in November 2014. Entrusted by Abe, former Prime Minister Fukuda Yasuo and secretary general of the National Security Secretariat of the *Kantei* (prime minister's office) Yachi Shotaro visited China in July 2014 to lay the groundwork. Later in October, Yachi made a secret visit to China to confer with State Councilor Yang Jiechi on the preparations for an Abe–Xi summit. Then on November 7, three days before the APEC summit meeting, Yachi and Yang agreed on a document titled "Regarding Discussions toward Improving Japan–China Relations," consisting of the following four points:[11]

1. Both sides confirmed that they would observe the principles and spirit of the four basic documents between Japan and China, and that they would continue to develop a mutually beneficial relationship based on common strategic interests.
2. Both sides shared some recognition that, in the spirit of facing history and advancing toward the future, they would overcome political difficulties that affect their bilateral relations.
3. Both sides recognized that they had different views as to the emergence of tense situations in recent years in the waters of the East China Sea, including those around the Senkaku islands, and shared the view that, through dialogue and consultation, they would prevent the deterioration of the situation, establish a crisis management mechanism and avert the rise of unforeseen circumstances.
4. Both sides shared the view that, by utilizing various multilateral and bilateral channels, they would gradually resume dialogue in political,

diplomatic, and security fields and make an effort to build a political relationship of mutual trust.

Thus, the first Abe–Xi meeting was realized on November 10, preceding the APEC summit meeting. Abe proposed the concept of a "Mutually Beneficial Relationship based on Common Strategic Interests," to which Xi agreed. Xi did not forget to point out the importance of the "four items of common ground" stipulated in the November 7 document.[12] As a result of this summit, the commotion over Abe's Yasukuni visit subsided within a year.

70th Anniversary Abe Statement

The year 2015 presented another chance for the history controversy to complicate the relationship. Abe intended to issue a statement for the 70th anniversary of the end of World War II which would overwrite previous postwar statements, especially that of former Prime Minister Murayama Tomiichi from August 1995, on the 50th anniversary of the end of the war. Murayama had said, "in the not too distant past, Japan, . . . through its *colonial rule* and *aggression*, caused tremendous damage and suffering to the people of many countries, particularly to those of Asian nations. . . . I regard, in a spirit of humility, these irrefutable facts of history, and express here once again my feelings of *deep remorse* and state my *heartfelt apology*" (emphasis added).[13] Abe has long been an outspoken critic of the Murayama Statement, and many had expected the four words (emphasized in italics) would be dropped from the Abe Statement.

The actual outcome was a typical compromise of Abe's. He did not formally nullify the Murayama Statement and did include the four words in his statement, but in entirely different contexts, effectively refusing to honor the spirit of the Murayama Statement. The relevant parts said as follows (emphasis added):[14]

> Incident, *aggression*, war—we shall never again resort to any form of threat or use of force as a means of settling international disputes. We shall abandon *colonial rule* forever and respect the right of self-determination of all peoples throughout the world. . . . Japan has repeatedly expressed the feelings of *deep remorse* and *heartfelt apology* for its actions during the war. . . . Such positions articulated by the previous cabinets will remain unshakable into the future.

Thus, while the worst case scenario was avoided, many sensed Abe's shrewdness in his presented rhetoric. Nonetheless, the following paragraph of the statement was perhaps enough to alleviate China's concerns prior to the announcement:

How much emotional struggle must have existed and what great efforts must have been necessary for the Chinese people who underwent all the sufferings of the war and for the former POWs who experienced unbearable sufferings caused by the Japanese military in order for them to be so tolerant nevertheless?

Thus, China's response to the Abe Statement was rather moderate. The spokesperson of the Ministry of Foreign Affairs of China repeated its usual phrase of "taking history as a mirror to guide the future," but did not criticize the statement itself.[15]

2015 Security Legislation

Constitutional Revision Going Astray

The motive behind Prime Minister Abe Shinzō's enthusiasm for building up Japan's defense capabilities were essentially ideological and deeply connected with his interest in regaining "true independence" from the occupation reforms. One of his personal proposals for revision of the postwar constitution was to give the Japanese Self Defense Force (SDF) explicit "national military" status. On an ideological level, the motive behind this proposal was similar to the one behind his desire to change Article 9: removing constraints on Japanese autonomy that derived from the defeat in the war as well as the occupation reforms.

Nonetheless, actual policy changes, if achieved, were sure to have deep implications for Japan's security policy, in general, and its China policy, in particular. Upon returning to power in December 2012, Abe posted a column advocating the formation of a "democratic security diamond" comprised of Japan, the United States, Australia, and India. As mentioned previously, Abe had expressed this idea already in 2006 before moving into Japan's top office the first time. In his opinion column, Abe also brought up the idea of connecting the Pacific Ocean and the Indian Ocean. By introducing these policy ideas, Abe clearly displayed his alarmist stance toward China:[16]

> Peace, stability, and freedom of navigation in the Pacific Ocean are inseparable from peace, stability, and freedom of navigation in the Indian Ocean. Developments affecting each are more closely connected than ever. Japan, as one of the oldest sea-faring democracies in Asia, should play a greater role in preserving the common good in both regions.... Yet, increasingly, the South China Sea seems set to become a "Lake Beijing," which analysts say will be to China what the Sea of Okhotsk was to Soviet Russia: a sea deep enough for the People's Liberation Army's navy to base their nuclear-powered attack submarines, capable of launching missiles with nuclear warheads. Soon, the PLA

Navy's newly built aircraft carrier will be a common sight—more than sufficient to scare China's neighbors.

It was natural, therefore, that China and observers of Abe's policy took Abe's move to revise postwar constitution as motivated by and directed at mitigating the increasing power of China. Although the China factor may not necessarily have been the central drive of Abe's agenda, were these changes implemented, the outcomes for Japan's China policy would be rather substantial. However, the outcome of Abe's initiatives were not revolutionary at all— even as the longest serving prime minister in history since the Meiji Restoration (one year in his first stint, plus seven-years-and-eight months in the second, totaling eight-years-and-eight months), Abe could not change a single word in the constitution. He did, however, manage to realize the exercise of the right of collective self-defense without touching Article 9.

The changes spearheaded by Abe's ideological motives still remain within the postwar parameters of defense and security policy of Japan. Whether consciously or unconsciously, perhaps China came to understand this, which is why Abe's security policy did not halt the improvement of Japan–China relations under Abe and Xi Jinping.

As is well known, constitutional revision, particularly the revision of Article 9, was of utmost importance for Abe's departure from the "postwar regime" from the beginning of his first administration in 2006. Becoming prime minister once again in 2012, he began to float the idea of changing Article 96 first. Article 96 stipulates that proposing revision of the constitution in Japan requires a two-thirds majority vote in both houses of the Diet before being put to a national referendum. Abe proposed changing the required two-thirds majority vote to a simple majority vote in the Diet, but this proved unpopular among most of the constitutional experts, as well as liberal intellectuals and the interested public. Seeing little chance of success, Abe dropped the idea and sought to legalize the exercise of the right to collective self-defense without touching Article 9. In doing this, Abe contradicted himself. While the main rationale in changing Article 9 had long been to legalize the right of collective self-defense and participation in collective security, as stipulated in the U.N. Charter, Abe achieved the former only and justified it in the name of Article 9. He ended up preserving the core of the very "postwar regime" he had set out to unmake.

Even more ironically, once the exercise of the right of collective self-defense was reinterpreted as constitutional, both theoretically and realistically, the need to revise Article 9 for this purpose dissipated. For Abe, however, constitutional revision continued to be important, amply demonstrating that this was an ideological issue for him rather than a strategic one. Abe, in continuing to pursue editing Article 9, proposed an addition of a third clause to legitimize the SDF while still leaving the first and second clauses intact. This way, Abe argued in May 2017, while there would be no change to Japan's defense and security policies, the debate about whether or not the SDF is constitutional would be resolved.[17]

Constitutional revision under the Abe administration, while potentially inflammatory to bilateral relations, proved to be almost harmless to the Japan–China relationship. However, the implications of Japanese collective self-defense were mixed and more complex.

The Logic of Collective Self-Defense

Prior to the introduction of the 2015 Security Legislation, the Japanese government maintained the interpretation formalized in 1972 that Japan, as a sovereign state, has the right to collective self-defense, but its own constitution does not allow the exercise of that right.[18] Collective self-defense refers to the right of a country to use military force to defend other states from attack. At the same time, the Japanese government has interpreted since the 1950s that self-defense is an innate right of a sovereign state and that Article 9 does not deny the right to self-defense, therefore making the SDF constitutional as long as it was maintained strictly for Japan's own self-defense purposes and not "as means of settling international disputes."

Pushed forward by the desires of Prime Minister Abe Shinzō, the 2015 Security Legislation justified the exercise of the right to collective defense by new logic that collective self-defense is included within the definition of "self-defense" permitted by Article 9. The cabinet decision of July 1, 2014 argued as follows:[19]

> As a matter of course, Japan's "use of force" must be carried out while observing international law. At the same time, a legal basis in international law and constitutional interpretation need to be understood separately. In certain situations, the aforementioned "use of force" permitted under the Constitution is, under international law, based on the right of collective self-defense. Although this "use of force" includes those which are triggered by an armed attack occurring against a foreign country, they are permitted under the Constitution only when they are taken as measures for self-defense which are inevitable for ensuring Japan's survival and protecting its people, in other words for defending Japan.

Accordingly, Article 76 of the Self-Defense Law was revised so that the prime minister, as supreme commander of the SDF, can now order the deployment and dispatch of the SDF to assist a friendly country under attack, but only when the threat to the country endangers Japan's survival.[20]

Up until the 2015 revision, the conditions for the use of force in the name of self-defense were: (1) when an armed attack against Japan occurs; (2) when there are no other appropriate means available to repel the attack and ensure Japan's survival and protect its people; (3) use of force should be limited to the minimum extent. Now, condition (1) reads as follows (emphasis added):[21]

> When an armed attack against Japan occurs *or when an armed attack against a foreign country that is in a close relationship with Japan occurs, and as a result threatens Japan's survival and poses a clear danger to fundamentally overturn people's right to life, liberty, and pursuit of happiness.*

Despite the legal justification for the exercise of the right to collective self-defense, an important question remains: is Japan ready to use the right in real security contingencies? To argue that the 2015 Security Legislation adds to deterrence, as the Japanese government often stresses, is one thing, but putting it into practice in a real scenario is another. The likely case in which Japan could actually consider invoking the right would be over conflict on the Korean peninsula. For various reasons, however, the Japanese prime minister ordering deployment of SDF in such a contingency is almost unthinkable.

If intervening in the case of conflict in Korea is unrealistic, what about situations involving China and its People's Liberation Army (PLA) either in Taiwan or the South China Sea? Just like in a Korean contingency, the U.S. military operations would likely form the bulk of a collective response, while the SDF's role would be limited to logistical support.

As far as the right of collective self-defense itself is concerned, therefore, it is fair and safe to conclude that the issue was primarily an item on Abe's ideological agenda, not necessarily the outcome of serious consideration of security policy either vis-à-vis China or North Korea. The issue of logistical support for the United States is, however, a different story.

Logistical Support for the United States

The 2015 Security Legislation involved the revision of regulations in two other areas on top of general reinterpretation to include collective self-defense, that is, "important influence situations" and "international peace cooperation." The former expanded the roles and missions of the SDF covered by the "Guidelines of Defense Cooperation between Japan and the United States" initially agreed upon in 1978 and revised in 1997, as well as the "Law Concerning Measures to Ensure the Peace and Security of Japan in Situations in Areas Surrounding Japan" enacted in May 1999. In addition, the

Japan's Diplomacy toward China 159

SDF is now able to provide support not only to the United States but also to other foreign countries with whom Japan has close relations.

As for the specific measures that Japan can provide for the United States, the law prohibits the use of force by the SDF, limiting support efforts to logistic support, search and rescue operations, and vessel inspection.[22] An "important influence situation" is defined as "a situation that has an important influence on Japan's peace and security in that it could lead to a direct armed attack against Japan if left unattended." The relevant law, therefore, does not deal with any case relating to collective self-defense.

More strikingly, the so-called "Law Concerning Measures relating to Actions by the Militaries of the United States and Other Countries" specifically stipulates that support measures of the SDF apply only to Clause 1 of Article 76 of the SDF Law (examined above) and excludes the case of Clause 2, which is about contingencies invoking the exercise of the right to collective self-defense.[23] This means that Japan is not yet ready to enter scenarios that require working with the United States by actually exercising the right of collective self-defense. Nonetheless, the expansion of Japan's roles and missions in providing SDF support for the United States and other friendly nations would mean important changes, a welcome development from the United States' perspective. This is indeed what is meant by the strengthening of the U.S.–Japan alliance, which could work as a deterrent against Chinese assertive behaviors to the extent that the U.S. military preparedness would be made more robust via the integration of the SDF into U.S. military planning.

Concerning the defense of the Senkaku Islands, the islands themselves and the territorial waters surrounding them are under the administrative control of Japan, meaning that the Japanese government regards their issue as a matter of self-defense, with no restrictions on the use of force. The United States also regards the area as under the administrative control of Japan, and thus stipulates that Chinese military aggression toward the islands would be responded to according to Article 5 of the U.S.–Japan Security Treaty, which says that "Each Party recognizes that an armed attack against either Party in the territories under the administration of Japan would be dangerous to its own peace and safety and declares that it would act to meet the common danger in accordance with its constitutional provisions and processes." The defense of the Senkaku islands, in light of them being under Japanese administration, is then a separate issue from those concerning the right of collective self-defense or SDF support in U.S. military operations. The U.S. military and the Japanese SDF must have contingency planning for defending Senkaku, although it should naturally be highly classified.

Free and Open Indo-Pacific (FOIP)

From Strategy to Vision

As discussed previously, as soon as Abe Shinzō was reelected as prime minister in December 2012, he published his concept of a "security diamond," a four-point network formed between Japan, the United States, Australia, and India, which included in its scope an approach that considered the Pacific Ocean and the Indian Ocean as integral geopolitical and economic spaces. These ideas were intended as a counterbalance against China.

The "Quad," as this security diamond is called, became the basis of Abe's regional outlook and strategy to be aimed at the Chinese Belt and Road Initiative (BRI) launched by President Xi Jinping (originally known as "One Belt One Road") in 2013. In August 2016, at the Sixth Tokyo International Conference on African Development (TICAD VI), held in Nairobi, Prime Minister Abe declared, "Japan bears the responsibility of fostering the confluence of the Pacific and Indian Oceans and of Asia and Africa into a place that values freedom, the rule of law, and the market economy, free from force or coercion, and making it prosperous."[24]

Sometime in 2018, however, the Japanese government stopped calling FOIP a strategy, and re-named it a "vision" at a time when relations with China were reaching the warmest they'd been in many years. Japan's relations with China had steadily improved since Abe met Xi in November 2014 for the first time, as a side event on the occasion of the APEC Summit in Beijing. Then, in October 2018, Abe Shinzō paid an official visit to China for the first time in seven years as Japanese prime minister.

On October 26, Abe met Chairman Li Zhanshu of the National People's Congress Standing Committee, Premier Li Keqian, and President Xi Jinping. The matters discussed were wide-ranging. Of utmost significance was the mutual confirmation of a willingness to advance cooperation in economic domains as the two most developed economies in Asia and indeed as "equals." It was symbolic, therefore, that in his meeting with Li and Xi, Abe conveyed the decision of the Japanese government to end all new official development assistance (ODA) to China, and the Chinese leaders expressed gratitude for the past assistance of Japan to Chinese economic modernization. Equally symbolically, they agreed to "coordinate towards the holding of dialogues and personnel exchanges in the area of development cooperation as bilateral cooperation at a new stage."[25]

At the same time, the Abe administration began to show some conciliatory postures to China's BRI. In fact, if joint development cooperation were realized in third countries, they might see an overlapping area between BRI and FOIP. There was also a quiet, but significant shift in the Abe administration's stance toward the Asian Infrastructure Investment Bank (AIIB), established in late 2015 with the Chinese initiative. In October 2019, Hatoyama Yukio of the Democratic Party's administration, was replaced by Katô Takatoshi, a former vice-minister of finance for international affairs of the Ministry of Finance, as the Japanese member of the AIIB's International Advisory Panel. Reportedly, the nomination of Katô was approved by the prime minister's office beforehand.[26]

An important factor behind the shift in the Japanese approach was a set of moves by regional countries to present their own responses and approaches toward the emerging "Indo-Pacific" concept. Almost all the countries in the Indo-Pacific region have been pursuing a nuanced policy toward China, endorsing an ASEAN-centered approach in one way or another. Then, in June 2019, ASEAN itself adapted the "ASEAN Outlook on the Indo-Pacific (AOIP)," which articulated clearly that it cannot take sides between BRI and FIOP. The AOIP turned out to be the virtual reconfirmation of the ASEAN way and its principles in organizing multilateral cooperation in the Indo-Pacific region.[27]

Following these regional developments, in mid-2019, the Ministry of Foreign Affairs of Japan summarized the principles of the FOIP vision in three domains: (1) promotion and establishment of the rule of law, freedom of navigation, and free trade; (2) pursuit of economic prosperity (by improving three sets of connectivity: physical connectivity through quality infrastructure; people-to-people connectivity through education, training and friendship; and institutional connectivity through harmonization and common rules including EPA/FTA); and (3) commitment to peace and stability (by such means as capacity-building, humanitarian assistance and disaster relief, anti-piracy, counter-terrorism, non-proliferation, and peace keeping operations). MOFA then said that "FOIP is an open and inclusive concept" and that "no single country can maintain and enhance the rules-based international order alone. Japan cooperates with a broad range of partners which share the vision of FOIP; no country is excluded for partnership."[28]

Thus, the Japanese vision for the FOIP has come to mean an updated version of the long-held Japanese regional policies which have evolved during the last three decades after the end of the Cold War, emphasizing non-exclusive multilateralism by respecting the central role ASEAN plays.

Quadrilateral Consultations (Quad)

The idea of the Quad followed a similar transformation process as FOIP toward a less exclusive and less confrontational conceptualization vis-à-vis China. The notion that Quad is an anti-China grouping led by the United States and Japan is, therefore, a myth that can be empirically confirmed by following its evolutionary process. Quite significantly, trilateral dialogues among

Japan, Australia, and India preceded Quad dialogues involving the United States. Australia and India's China policies are nuanced and often try to avoid direct confrontation with China while supporting the ASEAN way, which then became the foundation of trilateral dialogue among the three countries.

The first Japan–Australia–India Trilateral Dialogue by senior officials (administrative vice-ministers of foreign affairs) was held in New Delhi in June 2015, followed by the second Dialogue in Tokyo in February 2016, the third Dialogue in Canberra in April 2017, and the fourth Dialogue in New Delhi in December 2017. Then, after involving the United States, the first Japan–Australia–India–U.S. Consultations on the Indo-Pacific occurred in Manila in November 2017 and was attended by senior officials (Director-Generals) of foreign affairs as a side event on the occasion of ASEAN-related meetings. This was followed by the second Quad Consultations in Singapore in June 2018, the third consultations in Singapore in November 2018, the fourth consultations in Bangkok in May 2019, the fifth consultations in Bangkok in November 2019, and most recently the sixth consultations via video-conferencing in September 2020 (by which time, Japan was under the Suga Yoshihide administration).

A significant change in the evolution of the Quad began to manifest itself at the second consultations, where explicit reference was made to the importance of ASEAN centrality in the Indo-Pacific as well as the inclusive nature of the regional order. The press release after the consultations said as follows:[29]

1. On June 7, the Japan–U.S.–Australia–India Consultations were held in Singapore. The four countries reaffirmed shared support for a free, open, and inclusive Indo-Pacific region where all countries respect sovereignty and international law, freedom of navigation and overflight, and sustainable development.
2. The four countries confirmed a common commitment to uphold and strengthen the rules-based order in the Indo-Pacific, with shared democratic values in mind. The four countries discussed ways to achieve shared goals, including development and connectivity; good governance; regional security, including counterterrorism and nonproliferation; and maritime cooperation.
3. The four countries strongly supported ASEAN centrality in the Indo-Pacific region and reaffirmed that ASEAN-led mechanisms, such as East Asia Summit (EAS) and ASEAN Regional Forum (ARF) play an indispensable role in the region. The four countries also noted that they each have an important role to play in safeguarding and strengthening the open, transparent, inclusive, and rules-based regional order in the Indo-Pacific region.

4. The four countries agreed to partner with countries and institutions in the region to promote the shared vision of rendering the Indo-Pacific region peaceful and prosperous and to hold consultations on a regular basis.

Building on the achievements made at the senior official level, the first Quad Ministerial meeting, which foreign ministers attended, was held on September 26, 2019 in New York on the occasion of the General Assembly of the United Nations. The Quad Ministerial essentially endorsed the aforementioned points agreed to by the senior officials, including a reference to "a free, open, prosperous, and inclusive Indo-Pacific" and "strong support for ASEAN centrality and an ASEAN-led regional architecture."[30] The ASEAN way emphasizes the "inclusive" nature of a regional order, which reveals its strong propensity for not antagonizing China. At the second "Japan–Australia–India–U.S. Foreign Ministers' Meeting" held in Tokyo on October 6, 2020, the baseline of respecting the principle of ASEAN centrality was maintained. Behind the scenes, however, there were some differences in opinion among the participants, and they failed to issue a joint statement. The press release issued by the Japanese MOFA emphasized the importance of realizing "a Free and Open Indo-Pacific," while reaffirming strong support for ASEAN centrality.[31] The media release by the Australian Minister for Foreign Affairs, however, did not mention "Free and Open" in referring to the Indo-Pacific, and reaffirmed commitment to "promote stable, resilient and inclusive Indo-Pacific." She also mentioned explicitly "support for ASEAN centrality, and the important role of ASEAN and ASEAN-led architecture."[32]

While the shared concerns among the four countries regarding China's assertive and often aggressive behaviors in the region are the common glue encouraging the four countries to get united under the banner of the Quad, at this point, the "security diamond" is still at the embryonic stage, and it is hard to know what its actual impact could be as a coordinated China-facing strategy. If the United States and Japan emphasize a confrontational logic toward China, both Australia and India, as well as ASEAN countries, will resist out of their desire to remain out of the polarizing conflict between the United States and China. The emphasis on ASEAN centrality, therefore, signifies the limited role and function of the Quad at present.

CONCLUSION

China policy under the leadership of Prime Minister Abe Shinzō was not as anti-China as some have come to think, given his conservative bent. If Abe's ideological side had swayed his China policy, Japan–China relations might have walked a collision course due to the history issue and Abe's security policy. In the end, Abe had to compromise with reality, but sought to do so without discarding his deeply held ideology and other beliefs. This compromise is why much of his China policy appears ambiguous. Despite this, Abe still had to face China itself.

During much of the Abe administration's second tenure, China's policy toward Japan was largely conciliatory, aside from what China defines as its core values: Taiwan, the South China Sea, and the Senkaku islands. For Abe, just as for any leader of Japan, there was no option but to rebuff Chinese positions. Here, Abe's commitment to the "separation of politics and economy," which has long been the baseline of Japan's China policy throughout much of the postwar era, informed Abe's approach toward China, particularly in emphasizing the importance of economic relations. There was a popular argument that the Ministry of Economy, Trade, and Industry had influence over Abe, but where China policy was concerned, the phenomenon was more a congruence of perspectives rather than the effect of any one influence.

Another reality that Abe was unable to escape was that of the regional environment, including policies of regional countries toward China and the region, as well as the concept of the Indo-Pacific. In order for a regional initiative (in Abe's case, the Indo-Pacific strategy or vision) to succeed, it must be built on some extent of consensus among the relevant countries and actors. Here, Abe's ideology presented an obstacle between Japan and the other regional countries, including Australia and India. Eventually, Abe's Indo-Pacific and Quad initiatives were pushed back to the baseline of regional consensus, that is, the inclusive nature of the regional order and the principle of ASEAN centrality.

Having said this, however, due to a series of self-centered and coercive behaviors from China—including their actions regarding climate change, military expansion into the South China Sea, the destruction of democracy in Hong Kong, frequent intrusions into the Senkaku waters, initial mishandling of COVID-19, and so forth—antagonism aimed at China in Japan and the Asian region, as well as the rest of the world, is reaching new heights.

Under these circumstances, Prime Minister Suga Yoshihide, who took office on September 16 to replace Abe Shinzō, proclaims that, being a non-expert in foreign policy, he will inherit and follow the footsteps of Abe's diplomacy which, being built on his personal ideological beliefs and forced to compromise with reality, was complex and ambiguous. The challenge posed by China, however, is greater than ever, and there is a dire need for reconstruction of a comprehensive China strategy in the present post-Abe phase of Japanese diplomacy.

NOTES

1. *Mainichi Shimbun,* August 30, 2020.
2. "Abe resignation complicates China ties: Global Times editorial," *Global Times*, August 28, 2020. https://www.globaltimes.cn/content/1199204.shtml.
3. Abe Shinzō, *Utsukushī Kuni e* (Towards a Beautiful Country), Tokyo: Bunshun-Shinsho, 2006, 29.
4. "Law of the People's Republic of China on the Territorial Sea and the Contiguous Zone," Standing Committee of the National People's Congress, February 25, 1992. http://www.asianlii.org/cn/legis/cen/laws/lotprocottsatcz739/.
5. Kokubun Ryōsei, Soeya Yoshihide, Takahara Akio, and Kawashima Shin, "Japan-China Relations of the 1990s – Rise of China and Increase of Frictions," in *Japan-China Relations in the Modern Era*. Translated by Keith Krulak. London and New York: Routledge, 2017.
6. Abe, *Utsukushī Kuni e*, 232.
7. *ibid.*, 145–161.
8. "*Shushō, Yasukuni Sanpai ni Iyoku Dai 1-ji Seiken de Miokuri 'Tsūkon'*" [Prime Minister eager to visit Yasukuni, saying putting off the visit in the first administration 'grief'], *Nihon Keizai Shimbun*, October 19, 2013. https://www.nikkei.com/article/DGXNASFS1901W_Z11C13A0PE8000/.
9. Abe Shinzō, "Statement by Prime Minister Abe – Pledge for everlasting peace," December 26, 2013. https://japan.kantei.go.jp/96_abe/statement/201312/1202986_7801.html.
10. U.S. Embassy and Consulates in Japan, "Statement on Prime Minister Abe's December 26 Visit to Yasukuni Shrine," December 26, 2013. https://japan2.usembassy.gov/e/p/2013/tp-20131226-01.html.
11. MOFA, "Regarding Discussions toward Improving Japan-China Relations," November 7, 2014. https://www.mofa.go.jp/a_o/c_m1/cn/page4e_000150.html.
12. Kokubun, Soeya, Takahara, and Kawashima, *Japan-China Relations in the Modern Era*, 193–194.
13. MOFA, "Statement by Prime Minister Murayama Tomiichi 'On the occasion of the 50th anniversary of the war's end'," August 15, 1995. https://www.mofa.go.jp/announce/press/pm/murayama/9508.html.
14. "Statement by the Prime Minister Shinzo Abe – Cabinet Decision," August 14, 2025. https://japan.kantei.go.jp/97_abe/statement/201508/0814statement.html.
15. Kokubun, Soeya, Takahara, and Kawashima, *Japan-China Relations in the Modern Era*, 196.
16. Abe Shinzō, "Asia's Democratic Security Diamond," *Project Syndicate*, December 27, 2012. https://www.project-syndicate.org/onpoint/a-strategic-alliance-for-japan-and-india-by-Shinzô-abe.
17. "*Kenpō-kaisei ni kansuru Shushō-messeji Zenbun*" [Full Text of a Message by the Prime Minister Concerning Constitutional Revision], *Nihon Keizai Shimbun*, May 3, 2017. https://www.nikkei.com/article/DGXLASFK03H16_T00C17A5000000/.

18. Cabinet Legislation Bureau, "*Shūdanteki Jieiken to Kenpō no Kankei ni tsuite*" [Relationship between the Right of Collective Self-Defense and the Constitution] October 14, 1972. in *Bōei Handobukku* (Defense Handbook), Tokyo: Asagumo Shimbunsha, 2011, 665–666.

19. Cabinet Secretariat, "Cabinet Decision on Development of Seamless Security Legislation to Ensure Japan's Survival and Protect its People," July 1, 2014. https://www.cas.go.jp/jp/gaiyou/jimu/pdf/anpohosei_eng.pdf.

20. Ministry of Defense, *Jieitaihō (Saishū Kaisei: Heisei 27-nen 9-gatsu 30-nichi)* [Self-Defense Forces Law: Last revised on September 30, 2015]. https://www.mod.go.jp/j/presiding/law/.

21. Cabinet Secretariat, "Cabinet Decision on Development of Seamless Security Legislation."

22. "*Juyō-eikyō-jitai ni saishite Wagakuni no Heiwa oyobi Anzen wo Kakuho-suru tameno Sochi ni kansuru Hōritsu*" [Law Concerning Measures to Ensure Japan's Peace and Security in Important Influence Situations], March 29, 2016. https://elaws.e-gov.go.jp/search/elawsSearch/elaws_search/lsg0500/detail?lawId=411AC0000000060.

23. "*Buryoku-kōgeki Jitai-tō oyobi Sonritsu-kiki Jitai niokeru Amerika-gasshukoku-tōno Guntai no Kodō ni tomonai Wagakuni ga Jisshi-suru Sochi ni kansuru Hōritsu*" [Law Concerning Measures Japan Would Undertake Relating to Actions by the Militaries of the United States and Other Countries in Cases of an Armed Attack and Existential Crisis Situations], March 29, 2016. https://elaws.e-gov.go.jp/search/elawsSearch/elaws_search/lsg0500/detail?lawId=416AC0000000113.

24. MOFA, "Address by Prime Minister Abe Shinzō at the Opening Session of the Sixth Tokyo International Conference on African Development," August 27, 2016. https://www.mofa.go.jp/afr/af2/page4e_000496.html.

25. MOFA, "Prime Minister Abe Visits China," October 26, 2018. https://www.mofa.go.jp/a_o/c_m1/cn/page3e_000958.html.

26. Yoshioka Keiko, "*Chūgoku shudō no AIIB ni naze sekkin?*" [Why is Japan coming close to AIIB led by China?], *Asahi Shimbun*, October 30, 2019.

27. "ASEAN Outlook on the Indo-Pacific," ASEAN, June 23, 2019. https://asean.org/storage/2019/06/ASEAN-Outlook-on-the-Indo-Pacific_FINAL_22062019.pdf.

28. MOFA, "Japan's Effort for a Free and Open Indo-Pacific," May 2020. https://www.mofa.go.jp/mofaj/files/100056243.pdf.

29. MOFA, "Japan-Australia-India-U.S. Consultations," June 7, 2018. https://www.mofa.go.jp/press/release/press4e_002062.html.

30. MOFA, "Japan-Australia-India-U.S. Ministerial," September 26, 2019. https://www.mofa.go.jp/fp/nsp/page3e_001112.html.

31. MOFA, "The Second Japan-Australia-India-U.S. Foreign Ministers' Meeting," October 6, 2020. https://www.mofa.go.jp/press/release/press6e_000244.html.

32. Marise Payne, "Australia-India-Japan-United States Quad Foreign Ministers' Meeting," Minister for Foreign Affairs, Minister for Women, Senator the Hon website, October 6, 2020. https://www.foreignminister.gov.au/minister/marise-payne/media-release/australia-india-japan-united-states-quad-foreign-ministers-meeting.

REFERENCES

"Abe resignation complicates China ties: Global Times editorial." *Global Times*, August 28, 2020. https://www.globaltimes.cn/content/1199204.shtml.
Abe Shinzō. "Asia's Democratic Security Diamond." *Project Syndicate*, December 27, 2012. https://www.project-syndicate.org/onpoint/a-strategic-alliance-for-japan-and-india-by-Shinzô-abe.
Abe Shinzō. "Statement by the Prime Minister Abe Shinzô." Cabinet Decision, August 14, 2015. https://japan.kantei.go.jp/97_abe/statement/201508/0814statement.html.
Abe Shinzō. "Statement by Prime Minister Abe – Pledge for everlasting peace." December 26, 2013. https://japan.kantei.go.jp/96_abe/statement/201312/1202986_7801.html.
Abe Shinzō. *Utsukushī Kuni e* [Towards a Beautiful Country]. Tokyo: Bunshun-Shinsho, 2006.
"ASEAN Outlook on the Indo-Pacific." ASEAN, June 23, 2019. https://asean.org/storage/2019/06/ASEAN-Outlook-on-the-Indo-Pacific_FINAL_22062019.pdf.
"*Buryoku-kōgeki Jitai-tou oyobi Sonritsu-kiki Jitai niokeru Amerika-gasshukoku-touno Guntai no Kodou ni tomonai Wagakuni ga Jisshi-suru Sochi ni kansuru Horitsu*" [Law Concerning Measures Japan Would Undertake Relating to Actions by the Militaries of the United States and Other Countries in Cases of an Armed Attack and Existential Crisis Situations]. March 29, 2016. https://elaws.e-gov.go.jp/search/elawsSearch/elaws_search/lsg0500/detail?lawId=416AC0000000113.
Cabinet Legislation Bureau. "*Shudanteki Jieiken to Kenpō no Kankei ni tsuite*" [Relationship between the Right of Collective Self-Defense and the Constitution] October 14, 1972. in *Bōei Handobukku* (Defense Handbook), Tokyo: Asagumo Shimbunsha, 2011.
Cabinet Secretariat. "Cabinet Decision on Development of Seamless Security Legislation to Ensure Japan's Survival and Protect its People." July 1, 2014. https://www.cas.go.jp/jp/gaiyou/jimu/pdf/anpohosei_eng.pdf.
"*Juyō-eikyō-jitai ni saishite Wagakuni no Heiwa oyobi Anzen wo Kakuho-suru tameno Sochi ni kansuru Hōritsu*" [Law Concerning Measures to Ensure Japan's Peace and Security in Important Influence Situations]. March 29, 2016. https://elaws.e-gov.go.jp/search/elawsSearch/elaws_search/lsg0500/detail?lawId=411AC0000000060.
"*Kenpō-kaisei ni kansuru Shushō-messeji Zenbun*" [Full Text of a Message by the Prime Minister Concerning Constitutional Revision]. *Nihon Keizai Shimbun*, May 3, 2017. https://www.nikkei.com/article/DGXLASFK03H16_T00C17A5000000/.
Kokubun Ryōsei, Soeya Yoshihide, Takahara Akio, and Kawashima Shin. "Japan-China Relations of the 1990s – Rise of China and Increase of Frictions" in *Japan-China Relations in the Modern Era*. Translated by Keith Krulak. London and New York: Routledge, 2017.
"Law of the People's Republic of China on the Territorial Sea and the Contiguous Zone." Standing Committee of the National People's Congress, February 25, 1992. http://www.asianlii.org/cn/legis/cen/laws/lotprocottsatcz739/.

Ministry of Defense. *Jieitaihō (Saishū Kaisei: Heisei 27-nen 9-gatsu 30-nichi)* [Self-Defense Forces Law: Last revised on September 30, 2015]. https://www.mod.go.jp/j/presiding/law/.

MOFA. "Address by Prime Minister Abe Shinzō at the Opening Session of the Sixth Tokyo International Conference on African Development." August 27, 2016. https://www.mofa.go.jp/afr/af2/page4e_000496.html.

MOFA. "Japan–Australia–India–U.S. Consultations." June 7, 2018. https://www.mofa.go.jp/press/release/press4e_002062.html.

MOFA. "Japan-Australia-India-U.S. Ministerial." September 26, 2019. https://www.mofa.go.jp/fp/nsp/page3e_001112.html.

MOFA. "Japan's Effort for a Free and Open Indo-Pacific." May 2020. https://www.mofa.go.jp/mofaj/files/100056243.pdf.

MOFA. "Prime Minister Abe Visits China." October 26, 2018. https://www.mofa.go.jp/a_o/c_m1/cn/page3e_000958.html.

MOFA. "Regarding Discussions toward Improving Japan-China Relations." November 7, 2014. https://www.mofa.go.jp/a_o/c_m1/cn/page4e_000150.html.

MOFA. "Statement by Prime Minister Murayama Tomiichi 'On the occasion of the 50th anniversary of the war's end.'" August 15, 1995. https://www.mofa.go.jp/announce/press/pm/murayama/9508.html.

MOFA, "The Second Japan–Australia–India–U.S. Foreign Ministers' Meeting." October 6, 2020. https://www.mofa.go.jp/press/release/press6e_000244.html.

Payne, Marise. "Australia–India–Japan–United States Quad Foreign Ministers' Meeting." Minister for Foreign Affairs, Minister for Women, Senator the Hon website. October 6, 2020. https://www.foreignminister.gov.au/minister/marise-payne/media-release/australia-india-japan-united-states-quad-foreign-ministers-meeting.

"*Shushō, Yasukuni Sanpai ni Iyoku Dai 1-ji Seiken de Miokuri 'Tsūkon'*" [Prime Minister eager to visit Yasukuni, saying putting off the visit in the first administration 'grief']. *Nihon Keizai Shimbun*, October 19, 2013. https://www.nikkei.com/article/DGXNASFS1901W_Z11C13A0PE8000/.

U.S. Embassy and Consulates in Japan, "Statement on Prime Minister Abe's December 26 Visit to Yasukuni Shrine," December 26, 2013. https://japan2.usembassy.gov/e/p/2013/tp-20131226-01.html.

Yoshioka Keiko. "*Chūgoku shudō no AIIB ni naze sekkin?*" [Why is Japan coming close to AIIB led by China?]. *Asahi Shimbun,* October 30, 2019.

Chapter 9

Recriminations and Deepened Distrust

Assessing PM Abe's Legacy of Mismanaging Japan–ROK Relations

David H. Satterwhite, PhD and Laney Bahan

Inheriting fractious Japan–ROK relations steeped in historical enmity and distrust, Prime Minister Abe Shinzō had multiple opportunities to move the relationship in positive directions and sought to do so on his own terms, for instance in a 2015 agreement with since-impeached South Korean President Park Geun-Hye that was to "irrevocably" solve the "Comfort Women" issue. However, his administration's deeper commitment to a nationalist agenda, articulated by and within, we argue, the highly influential *Nippon Kaigi,* has inflamed rather than resolved tensions with the Republic of Korea (ROK) public. Furthermore, a tit-for-tat over other pressing issues, reflecting a lack of statesmanship and poor judgment, has similarly damaged Japan–ROK governmental relations. Abject failure to more effectively deal diplomatically with the Moon Jae-In presidency, which has reflected and harnessed popular sentiments in the ROK on a range of contentious issues, prevented PM Abe from achieving a lasting legacy of improved relations, despite the geopolitical logic of democratically elected regimes standing firmly together in the face of NE Asian threats to those shared democratic principles.

PM Abe's hardline stance vis-à-vis the DPRK, furthermore—focused on the dual agenda of solving the abductee issue and enforcing uncompromising sanctions to force DPRK denuclearization—impeded what could have been a closer working relationship with the Moon Administration's efforts at reconciliation and eased tensions on the Korean Peninsula. Analyzed together, PM Abe's approach was an inherently flawed one from its inception, badly out of touch with sentiments and perceptions in both the ROK and Japan.[1] Prior to his resignation, relations between the two countries had hit their lowest level since Korea's liberation from Imperial Japan—the very Japan that Abe and his *Nippon Kaigi* cohort hold such nostalgia for.

STEPS TOWARD A FLAWED LEGACY: MISSED OPPORTUNITIES TO END AN INHERITED ENMITY

A year prior to his unexpected resignation in late August 2020, Prime Minister Abe Shinzo had warned his close aides to expect a "'chill' in [Japan's] South Korea ties," articulating what was described as a "widespread consensus" in his administration that "relations with Seoul are unlikely to improve while President Moon Jae-In remains in office" and that "Japan should focus on diplomacy elsewhere, 'instead of wasting effort with a country that can't be trusted'."[2] This stark recognition of how far relations with the ROK had deteriorated by 2019 reverberated in Seoul as well, with the sense that relations with Japan were unlikely to improve while PM Abe remained in office.

Much as Japan and the ROK should be close allies with overlapping priorities as liberal democracies facing illiberal regimes in their East Asian neighborhood, PM Abe leaves behind a woefully mismanaged Japan–ROK relationship. While the pendulum-swing transition in political leadership in 2017 from impeached President Park Geun-Hye to President Moon Jae-In resulted in a shift in the conduct of ROK relations with the Abe administration, PM Abe appears not to have recognized that it was precisely the unpopular "Comfort Women" Agreement with Japan that contributed to President Park's downfall and Moon's subsequent election. Whether oblivious or impervious to how his administration's revisionist stance on key bilateral issues, including that agreement, had compounded damages to the relationship, in the end PM Abe failed to craft a statesmanlike legacy. He leaves behind a deepened conundrum for his successor—a like-minded *Nippon Kaigi* member, PM Suga Yoshihide—to solve.

From Abe's brief first stint as Prime Minister (2006–2007) came his *Toward a Beautiful Country: My Vision for Japan* book, aptly critiqued as a "reactionary vision for the future . . . caught in a pre-1945 time warp, drawing on the values that prevailed in Imperial Japan that are out of touch with contemporary Japan."[3] We would add that those values are also dramatically out of touch with public sentiment in Japan's neighbor Korea—which was liberated in 1945 from its oppressive 36-year colonial domination by Japan—and PM Abe's revisionist stance has been monitored closely and reported on in the ROK over the years.[4]

PM Abe set the tone early for a notably unapologetic nationalist agenda, which both included his and the LDP's long-cherished dream of revising the 1947 Constitution as well as a turning-back of the clock on the entire postwar understanding of Japan as an aggressor in Asia.[5] As early as 2007, he openly considered a disavowal of the official apology articulated in the 1993 Kono Statement which had stated that the wartime government and military had been directly complicit in the establishment and running of the wartime "Comfort Stations" and the coerced recruitment of women, the majority of whom were Korean. Astutely deciding not to formally retract the Kono Statement's official apology, PM Abe has nonetheless made clear that it did not reflect his views, which deny official wartime complicity and argue that such apologies were and continue to be unnecessary.[6]

His much-touted "comeback kid" return to the prime ministerial position in 2012 signaled at the outset a focus on economic recovery, with what seemed at the time a toned-downed emphasis on the revisionist agenda that had marked his first round in office.[7] Within a year, however, his visit to Yasukuni Shrine in his official capacity as prime minister in November 2013 seemed to show his true colors to international watchers, touching off a maelstrom of outrage from China and the ROK, as well as criticism from the United States.[8] Together with the revisionist vision outlined in his first term, his words and actions within the first year of his second iteration in office from 2012 signaled further steps toward flawed relations and were presciently noted by commentary from within the ROK indicating a deep distrust of his pledges to improve the bilateral relationship.[9] What, then, are PM Abe's "true colors" vis-à-vis Korea, and how does that ill-advised visit to Yasukuni—combined with his actions and statements since 2006 onward— illustrate him "playing to his base" in a manner that would render improved relations virtually impossible? Several dimensions explored in this chapter seek to answer these questions we consider crucial to assessing the Abe legacy of fractured relations with Japan's closest neighbor.

We begin with an inventory of key incidents between the two countries that occurred during PM Abe's almost 8-year tenure in office:

- The "Comfort Women" tragedy of sexual slavery (the preferred term of the ROK government, though rejected by Japan), and the ROK Supreme Court's rulings in October and November 2018 determining that Japanese firms must pay compensation for the slave-labor conditions of colonial and wartime Korean workers—closely related issues illustrating the contentious debate over both the applicability and finality of the 1965 treaty that normalized relations between the two countries.
- The existing dispute over Dokdo/Takeshima and the dispute over a dangerous air/naval encounter between ROK and Japanese armed forces in 2018, each illustrating the tenacity of contentious territorial claims.

- Looming security concerns, specifically regarding the DPRK, highlighting the contrast between the hardline approach insisted upon by the Abe administration and the Moon presidency's prioritization of reconciliation and dialogue, along with the ROK's August 2019 stated intent to withdraw from (and then last-minute decision to remain in) the Japan–ROK General Security of Military Information Agreement (GSOMIA).
- The Abe administration's controversial decision to remove the ROK from its "whitelist" of trusted trading nations, paired with the termination by Japan of exports to Korea of key components for the semiconductor industry, which not only triggered a similar response from the ROK government and widespread boycott of Japanese goods and tourism to Japan but also unnecessarily decoupled complementary economies and— counterproductive for Japanese manufacturers—reduced ROK reliance on key Japanese products.

The confluence of these issues saw the disastrous plummeting of the ROK public's approval rating of Japan—and specifically of PM Abe himself.[10] Any improvement in bilateral ties will take considerable effort to repair and achieve in years to come.[11] Will Abe's successors rise to the challenge of building back from an absolute nadir in ROK–Japan bilateral relations?

Underlying the foregoing inventory of incidents are deep-seated political cultures in each country. In PM Abe's Japan, this has been most clearly represented by the revisionist *Nippon Kaigi* as his philosophical and political "base." In South Korea, the complex political culture has seen a combination of an enduring enmity and distrust of Japan by the public, on the one hand, and, on the other, by the shift from the conservative Park Geun-Hye regime, to her successor, President Moon Jae-In—a progressive with his ear closely attuned to a vibrant civic "base." This "base," while not without its own internal concerns and challenges, reflects a political culture comprised of a public highly critical of autocratic rule on the domestic front, as well as any appearance of collaborative subservience to Japanese revisionist interests.[12]

The impeachment of Park Geun-Hye, PM Abe's counterpart in negotiating the 2015 "Comfort Women" Agreement, signaled a tectonic shift in the ROK that pulled the carpet out from under his apparent success. The potential of a legacy of improved relations with the ROK was, in the end, doomed both by PM Abe's own inability to grasp the Korean public's distaste for his revisionist approach to the "Comfort Women" issue and by the historical timing of having negotiated a flawed agreement with an unpopular ROK president, herself out of touch with the sentiments of her people and, soon after, toppled by the Candlelight Revolution of 2016–2017.

WHERE DO COMFORT WOMEN "FIT" IN PM ABE AND THE NIPPON KAIGI'S VISION FOR JAPAN?

As Japan's largest conservative, ultra-right political organization, the *Nippon Kaigi* ("Japan Conference") carries considerable weight. The popular Governor of Tokyo and former Defense Minister Koike Yuriko is a notable member, as were nearly 90 percent of PM Abe's cabinet members, and the prime minister himself served as special advisor to the group's Parliamentary Discussion Group. Furthermore, an astonishing 60 percent of the Diet's 480 members are said to belong to the *Nippon Kaigi*.[13] How that weight has been instrumental in PM Abe's decisions and accomplishments in office has been well-researched by others;[14] here we explore the most crucial elements as the keys to unlocking Abe's legacy of failure vis-à-vis the ROK.

At its core, the goals of the *Nippon Kaigi* have been closely reflected in the statements and positions taken by the prime minister and can be seen both to directly and indirectly impact the key "sticking point" in PM Abe's turbulent relationship with the ROK: the "Comfort Women" issue. Established in 1997 as an amalgam of earlier nationalist and Shinto organizations, the *Nippon Kaigi* has articulated six goals that, combined, would see a Japan returned to its previous era of ill-conceived chauvinism and exceptionalism.[15] Its members value conservative traditions and a Japanese identity linked to nationalistic pride in such a way that they project and nurture a nostalgic longing for what Imperial Japan sought to accomplish—"liberating" Asia from the shackles of Western colonialism—rather than recognizing the aggressive realities of the "Greater East Asia Co-Prosperity Sphere" or comprehending and respecting what it means to be Japanese today.

The *Nippon Kaigi* is denialist in nature, and its representation in such large numbers in the Japanese Diet sends chills of concern through careful Japan watchers and the public in "most important neighbor" South Korea.[16] As such, at the heart of its positions that most damage relations with the ROK is the denial that the wartime Japanese government and military were responsible for or involved in forcibly recruiting Korean and many other women into "Comfort Stations."[17]

In seeking a revival of the Emperor System, a relaxation of the separation of state and religion, the strengthening of nationalist content in textbooks and education while excising reference to historically embarrassing or "negative" issues, the *Nippon Kaigi* seeks to overturn the core finding of the Tokyo War Crimes Tribunal that Japan was an aggressor.[18] The *Nippon Kaigi* builds on the denialist ideology University of Tokyo professor of education Nobukatsu Fujioka—the founder of two nationalist organizations focused on revising popular understanding of "masochistic" modern history—shared in his interview for the investigative documentary on the "Comfort Women" controversy, *Shusenjo*. He explained: "It is a fundamental proposition for a nation not to apologize ... even if a nation did those things, a nation ends once it apologizes."[19] Including this unapologetic approach, each of these core goals of the *Nippon Kaigi* strikes directly at the foundations of an improved relationship as perceived by the ROK:

1) Japan fought WWII in the name of the Emperor; reviving elements of the Emperor System—the "establishment of a clear national polity linked to [elsewhere, 'centered on'] the Emperor"[20]—would be a sign of danger from the Korean perspective, as they had once been a victim of that all-consuming Japanese loyalty to the Emperor;
2) The Korean people were, among other disdainful measures, made to worship at Shinto shrines during the colonial period. Re-legitimizing "State Shinto" in any form—the barely hidden agenda behind "loosening the separation of religion and state" of an organization founded in part by Shinto associations—would be anathema from a Korean point of view;
3) A more proactive state role in "suppressing critical views of Japanese history" and of inculcating nationalist patriotism through increased state control of textbooks would be a victory for those who deny the culpability of the wartime Japanese government and military in the "Comfort Women" issue. In the face of first-person accounts of Korean women who survived and have testified to their coerced sexual enslavement at the hands of the Imperial military, the denialists are both an insult and a looming danger. Additionally, PM Abe's 2006 legislation requiring patriotic education, together with other textbook-approval regulations, has already removed any reference to the "Comfort Women" issue from approved textbooks, reversing the mention of the topic that by 1997 became incorporated in most textbooks following the 1993 Kono Statement.[21]
4) Although *Nippon Kaigi* members fret over what they refer to as a "masochistic" Japan for having repeatedly apologized, the notion that a nation's apology signifies weakness, too, strikes at the heart of Korean hopes for a truly sincere apology from Japan. Rather than obfuscating and systematically denying, the Korean people wish to see Japan as a neighbor that can conduct a thorough accounting of and take responsibility for having created, systematized, and operated the wartime military "Comfort Stations," directly coercing and enslaving Korean women in the process. The efforts or desires of the *Nippon Kaigi* and PM Abe to overturn or abandon the apologies to Korea thus far, rather than embrace those as key elements in moving the relationship forward, casts a dark shadow on prospects for improving relations.

Apologies have been front-and-center in two key dimensions: first, the depth, breadth, and sincerity of apologies by Japan—such as in acknowledgements of its direct complicity in establishing, recruiting for, and running the so-called "Comfort Stations"—are crucial barometers for genuinely improved relations with the people of Korea. The fact that the apologies that have already been made, which have gone a long way toward the yardstick of sincerity, are repeatedly criticized[22] undermines the sense of sincerity required for rapprochement. Second, PM Abe and others have openly suggested that the key apologies made thus far (from Kono, Maruyama, and Kan Naoto) should be amended or retracted entirely.[23] Regardless of PM Abe's ultimate decisions not to retract the Kono statement and to continue upholding the Murayama statement, these initial sentiments, combined with the entwining of his administration with the *Nippon Kaigi* ideation of Japan, are considered a show of his "true colors," and paint him an untrustworthy denialist from a South Korean's view.[24]

"LIKE FATHER LIKE DAUGHTER": COMING TO TERMS WITH THE FLAWED 1965 AND 2015 AGREEMENTS

It was felicitous for PM Abe, and a deep historical irony, that the 2015 Japan–ROK Agreement regarding the "Comfort Women" was made possible by the election in 2013 of Park Geun-Hye, pairing two staunchly conservative leaders to reach a "win-win" that suited their respective political ends. The achievement was, for PM Abe, monumental—until it came undone with Park's impeachment. Her elected successor Moon Jae-In had campaigned for the presidency on a platform promising renegotiation of the highly unpopular agreement, and soon after his inauguration in May 2017, set in motion efforts to render it unenforceable.[25]

The 2015 Agreement marked exactly fifty years since Park's father, military dictator Park Chung-Hee, had overridden enormous popular opposition to push through the 1965 *Basic Treaty on Relations between Japan and The Republic of Korea*. Economic development had been one of Park Chung-Hee's six plank's justifying the coup d'etat by which he had come to power in 1961, reflecting the failure of the Syngman Rhee government (1948–1960) to wean the ROK from America's foreign aid largess.[26] The United States, in turn, had worked diligently behind the scenes to have Japan and the ROK normalize diplomatic relations, seeking to harness Japan's postwar economic prowess and investment funds in support of the ROK's palpable needs for its developmental goals.[27] Popular opposition to the treaty was fierce, targeted both at the military-dominated regime of pro-Japanese players (both Park

Chung-Hee and his coup co-conspirator Kim Jong-P'il had served in Japan's Kwantung Army) and at the prospect of Japanese involvement in Korea's affairs yet again.

For her part, daughter Park Geun-Hye's agenda was quite different, but did involve, as had her father's, negotiating and reaching an agreement with the intensely disliked Japanese government. Indications were that Park Geun-Hye had "tilted" heavily toward China since her election in 2013, rebuffed earlier efforts by Japan to receive PM Abe's personal emissary, and was aware of the anti-Japanese sentiment surrounding the "Comfort Women" and other issues. However, when faced with U.S. pressure to solve the seemingly unending recriminations over contentious historical interpretations,[28] and perhaps more importantly to show a united front by which to pressure the DPRK, President Park chose to acquiesce. Her father had made his name on the international stage, despite his regime's egregious human rights' violations, as the architect of the ROK's post-Korean War transformation from "basket case" economy to "Asian Tiger" status—a transition not all his own doing[29] and financially underwritten by Japan's aid as part of the 1965 Treaty. Following in his footsteps and elected to the presidency on his economic success track record, Park Geun-Hye may have seen the agreement as a diplomatic milestone for which she too would gain accolades.[30]

Her own leadership style—quasi-authoritarian, hostile to the democratization successes that had denigrated her father's accomplishments, and aloof from the public—led to a negotiated agreement on the highly charged "Comfort Women" issue without once consulting the victims of that system of sexual slavery. This included, for South Koreans, accepting financial contribution (not compensation) from the Japanese government and taking steps to resolve the issue of the "Comfort Women" statue in front of the Japanese embassy in Seoul, as well as for both countries to refrain from criticizing each other over this particular issue and accept the agreement as an irreversible solution. The public's outcry was fierce and, combined with other unforgivable dimensions of her presidency, brought her down.

Abe's "success" in having achieved the 2015 Agreement could be seen to have validated both the 1965 Treaty and the 2015 Agreement in historical tandem. Neither were acceptable to the people of the ROK. For Japan to cite both as "irrevocable" finalities, without the buy-in of the Korean public and over their strenuous objections, comes across as unabashed revisionism and a return to Japan's colonialist mindset.[31]

It is richly ironic, then, to note that the very negotiations on the "Comfort Women" Agreement created a precedent—the Japanese government's "line" thus far, repeated as recently as concerning the "slave-labor reimbursement" rulings by the ROK Supreme Court in late 2018, has been that all issues were solved by the 1965 Treaty.[32] By coming to an agreement with Park

Geun-Hye, PM Abe effectively acknowledged that the "Comfort Women" were not covered and needed a separate agreement, thus opening the argument that the slave labor of Koreans in wartime mines and factories, too, were not covered by the whitewashing brush of the 1965 Treaty.

How has this conundrum played in Japan? This can be seen in two important dimensions: "apology fatigue" and fierce criticism of the ROK's decisions to not honor its pledged commitments, notably the 1965 Treaty and 2015 Agreement. A clear subtext from the *Nippon Kaigi* is that Japan was mistreated by "victor's justice" in the Tokyo War Crimes Tribunal and has no need to apologize for the noble cause of having liberated Asia from Western (if not Japan's own) colonialism. According to the *Nippon Kaigi* playbook, apology signals weakness. Thus, apologies that have been made based on "erroneous" facts or interpretations should be retracted or annulled. Beyond this vehement resistance to contrition lies the perception that the ROK government and public have not been satisfied by the apologies extended thus far and are always pushing for yet another apology.[33]

That the apologies given are "never enough" is both a circular and duplicitous argument. Whether in the nationally televised name-calling by then-Diet Member Abe of then-Prime Minister Kan Naoto as "*baka*" ("you fool") in 2010 when PM Kan read his eloquent, humble, and sincere apology to the Korean people in marking the 100th anniversary of Japan's colonization, or in the efforts to retract the carefully considered national, official apologies of 1993 and 1995—the Kono Statement and the Maruyama Statement—the spirit of the original apologies has been undermined and called into serious question by PM Abe, the *Nippon Kaigi*, and by its predecessor organizations. Viewed from Korea and other Asian nations, statements from PM Abe and others that detract from the spirit of earlier apologies quite naturally lead to calls for a more sincere admission to Japan's wartime behavior rather than the obfuscation and outright denial of that history that came to dominate thinking during the tenure of PM Abe.

There are serious issues surrounding both the 1965 Treaty that normalized diplomatic relations and the 2015 Agreement that sought to lay to rest claims regarding the "Comfort Women" controversy. Each document contains wording that the respective issues taken up therein are "settled completely and finally" (in the 1965 Basic Treaty) and are "resolved finally and irreversibly" (in the 2015 Agreement), and it is in this wording that the true aim of the agreements is revealed. In brushing aside the voices of the South Korean public, the resolution of these issues in each case clearly works to the advantage of Japan. The Korean people, as victims, are forever denied cathartic justice in the absence of genuine apologies, effectively belittling the historical wrongs against Korea which the 1965 Treaty and 2015 Agreement ostensibly sought to address. Japan, the perpetrator both of colonialism and of the wartime forced-labor exploitation of workers and sexual slavery of Korean women, is protected from further recrimination from its victims by the "final and irreversible" settlements.

When the Moon Jae-In administration said that it would not interfere in the ruling by the ROK Supreme Court requiring Japanese firms to pay damages to former Korean slave-labor employees, for instance, the Japanese government insisted that this violated the 1965 Treaty, which had stipulated any additional claims should be handled through government-to-government arbitration.[34] The response from the ROK government was crystal clear—that to interfere in a ruling that had worked its way through the courts would have undermined the crucial constitutional principle of separation of powers among the executive, legislative, and judicial branches of government.[35] Similarly, PM Abe and the Japanese Ministry of Foreign Affairs reacted vehemently when the Moon Jae-In administration dismantled the mechanism agreed upon in the 2015 Agreement by which "Comfort Women" would receive financial payments from funds provided by the Japanese government—a central component of that agreement. PM Abe went so far as to say that the ROK "risked damaging relations" by "breaking international pledges," "urging South Korea to act responsibly" as "this commitment made between our two countries forms the cornerstone of our bilateral relationship."[36] President Moon made clear his response, pointing out both that Japan was in no position to press such a demand, as the "perpetrator of wartime crimes against humanity,"[37] and that the 2015 Agreement was fundamentally flawed.

While insisting that the ROK was violating the principle of international agreements in these instances, the Japanese government found itself on the wrong side of history in the evolution of policies, politics, and state structure in the ROK. The wartime slave laborers in Japanese mines and factories had not been heard nor represented in the 1965 Treaty entered into by the authoritarian regime of Park Chung-Hee, and took their quest for justice through the now-independent courts, winning their cases in the Supreme Court. Similarly, the twenty-seven surviving "Comfort Women" registered with the ROK government[38] had not been "at the table" nor consulted by the Park Geun-Hye regime fifty years after her father pushed through the controversial normalization treaty in 1965.

Coming to office on his pledge to rectify the wrongs of the 2015 Agreement, there was no way that President Moon could uphold an agreement with Japan deemed to have been both flawed and a product of Park Geun-Hye's inappropriate representation of the ROK on the world stage. In short, it had not, in the eyes of the South Korean public or the successor government, "finally and irreversibly resolved" the "Comfort Women" issue. Rather than a centerpiece accomplishment of PM Abe's revisionist agenda, the 2015 Agreement became one piece of the tattered tapestry of mismanaged ROK–Japan relations.

AN INVENTORY OF ISSUES POORLY HANDLED: PM ABE'S FAILURES WITH JAPAN'S CLOSEST AND MOST VALUABLE NEIGHBOR

Warning bells had started to ring in South Korea during Abe Shinzo's first iteration as prime minister, watching for the impact of his revisionist proclivities. His outburst from the opposition's bench in the Diet against PM Kan's 2010 contrite and sincere apology to Korea had confirmed South Korean fears of what his political stripes stood for. Within the first year of his come-back prime ministership, he had emerged as a committed nationalist, publicly stating his administration's intent to implement an agenda that the ROK would find worrisome. We recap here the sequence of issues and actions by PM Abe that illustrate a fundamental mismatch in outlook that led to seriously damaged relations with erstwhile ally and closest neighbor South Korea.

On his ascension to the office in late December 2012, PM Abe announced his intent both to review Article 9 of the Constitution and to visit Yasukuni Shrine. As noted, exactly a year later and in commemoration of the day, PM Abe became the first prime minister since Koizumi to visit Yasukuni in his official capacity. Acknowledging the immediate and vociferous reaction from China and Korea, PM Abe claimed to have been misunderstood, and that he was reporting to the souls enshrined there his firm commitment to ensure Japan would never again engage in such war.[39] He has also said that "Yasukuni is Japan's equivalent of Arlington Cemetery."[40] However, given the enshrinement of convicted war criminals—after which the Emperor himself refused to pay his respects at Yasukuni[41]—and the militarist tenor of the Yushukan museum within the shrine's precinct, PM Abe had not been misunderstood at all.[42] That the *Nippon Kaigi* has called for a "loosening of the separation of religion and politics," moreover, and with key Shinto shrines and associations as active members of the *Nippon Kaigi* itself, PM Abe's visit rubbed salt in the wounds of Korean victims of wartime Japan.

We have focused heavily on the "Comfort Women" Agreement of 2015, illustrating how it was, and remains, a crucial failure in PM Abe's self-proclaimed goal of improved relations with the ROK. In June of that year, the two nations commemorated the 50th anniversary of the 1965 normalization treaty in upbeat tones, foregoing the opportunity to assess the roller-coaster of bilateral relations. Not all was rosy in the intervening decades, but on the surface, 2015 seemed to bode well for PM Abe, agreeing with President

Park Geun-Hye in late autumn to hasten negotiations for an agreement to be reached within the anniversary year.

Just weeks prior to the official 50th anniversary events, however, an incident marred the quiet interlude. There was the prime minister, smiling in the cockpit of a T-4 Air Self-Defense Forces' training jet numbered 731. It is likely PM Abe was not even aware of the notorious Unit 731 that, in the wartime years of 1937–1945, had carried out biological warfare testing on live prisoners, including those from Korea, China, and the Soviet Union. Being ignorant of or genuinely oblivious to the past was no excuse, for the outcry against such an insulting reminder of wartime Japan was loudest in the ROK, where PM Abe had already earned negative marks with the public.[43]

The aftermath of the "Comfort Women" Agreement, combined with the tragic sinking of the ferry Sewol previously in 2014, had a further negative impact on Park Geun-Hye's popularity. Domestic opposition rose to a crescendo as revelations of her corruption and abuse of power came to light, culminating in the succession of peaceful Candlelight demonstrations from October 2016 until the spring of 2017, when she was impeached in March. With the ruling party in disarray, the leading opposition candidate, Moon Jae-In, was elected president and assumed office in May 2017, with one of his key campaign promises to renegotiate the agreement in order to reflect input from the survivors.[44]

The remainder of 2017 was one of considerable turmoil surrounding the Korean Peninsula, with Japan a concerned bystander as newly elected President Trump and the DPRK's Kim Jong-Un ratcheted up tensions and armed conflict appeared possible. The tide turned in early 2018, however, starting with a conciliatory New Year's Address by Kim Jong-Un, the successful hosting by the ROK of the Winter Olympics in February, and in April, the first of three summits between Moon Jae-In and Kim Jong-Un to be held that year, followed in June by the first-ever U.S.–DPRK summit held in Singapore. PM Abe joined the summit rush, exploring a chance to meet with Kim Jong-Un in the second half of the year. A third ROK–DPRK summit was held in September, with President Moon traveling to Pyongyang. These events serve as the backdrop for a series of controversial, negative developments impacting Japan's relations with the ROK in the last three months of 2018.

The first occurred in early October, when Japan canceled its planned participation by Maritime Self-Defense Force vessels in an ROK-hosted international fleet review of thirteen other nations. Although both Japan and the ROK had insisted that they would "continue military exchanges and efforts to strengthen [their] friendship," the cancelation came in response to ROK requests that the Japanese vessel not fly its "Rising Sun" flag, which is the official ensign of the Japanese Maritime Self-Defense Forces. Where earlier instances in 1998 and 2008 had permitted the flag on Japanese naval vessels, sentiment had dramatically shifted in the ROK, and in the wake of the 2015 Agreement there were popular calls to not permit the "war-crime flag" being flown in Korea.[45]

In quick succession, four more events took place. In October, the ROK Supreme Court upheld a lower court ruling requiring leading Japanese firms to compensate Korean workers who had suffered under slave-like conditions working in wartime factories—a ruling immediately challenged by Japan as a violation of the 1965 normalization treaty. In November, over strenuous Japanese government objections that the 2015 Agreement was being violated as well, the ROK announced that the foundation set up by the agreement to disburse Japanese government funds to the surviving "Comfort Women" would be disbanded. Also in November, elected members of the ROK's National Assembly made a visit to the disputed Dokdo/Takeshima islands, claimed by both countries, but administratively under ROK control. Finally, in late December, an event took place in which a Japanese reconnaissance plane reported being targeted by a South Korean naval vessel's "lock-on" radar—a harrowing moment, if proven true, as "lock-on" can be followed on moment's notice by a live-fire attack. Both governments and their militaries produced evidence to support their respective claims, but the incident ended without agreement, deepening recriminations on both sides in the process.

2019, too, saw a further deterioration in relations, with a series of events mid-year. In July, in tandem with the ongoing ROK–Japan tit-for-tat, the Abe administration announced that the ROK would be taken off the "whitelist" of trusted nations engaged in trade with Japan and, on flimsy evidence that the ROK was potentially sharing trade secrets with the DPRK, Japan prohibited the export of chemicals important in semiconductor manufacturing, a sector crucial to the ROK economy. Within six weeks, the ROK announced that Japan, too, would be removed from its "whitelist" of trusted trade partners.

Two weeks later, in late August 2019, a bombshell announcement signaled a near-rupture in ROK–Japan relations, when President Moon indicated the ROK would withdraw from the General Security of Military Information Agreement (GSOMIA) by which the military forces of both nations shared intelligence directly relevant to a joint readiness posture vis-à-vis the DPRK. Signed just three years earlier in 2016, GSOMIA was a landmark indication (strongly promoted by the United States) that Japan and the ROK could cooperate in the timely sharing of confidential intelligence. Under intense urging by the United States, President Moon reversed the decision to withdraw at the last minute, rescuing the annually renewed agreement amidst a climate of severely damaged mutual trust. With its concerns over the perceived DPRK threat, Japan hopes for a recurring renewal, asserting that GSOMIA "strengthens Japan–South Korea cooperation and coordination, and contributes to regional peace and stability."[46] Although Abe Shinzo will not be at the helm, the question remains whether the deterioration of relations between Japan and the ROK on his clock will continue to have an impact on such a fundamental pledge for security cooperation and whether GSOMIA will be renewed each year.

CONCLUDING REFLECTIONS: TWO ROADS DIVERGING IN A TENSE NE ASIAN NEIGHBORHOOD

In the decades preceding Abe Shinzo's first stint at the helm of the Liberal Democratic Party and Japan, and in the five-year interim until he would return as prime minister in 2012, fully a dozen others served in that capacity, steering the Japanese ship of state through turbulent times. Despite short terms for many, some left their mark on Japan's diplomacy and others, including the populist PM Koizumi, made pilgrimages to Yasukuni Shrine, incurring the wrath of China and Korea before PM Abe did so with his 2013 visit. Some in Abe's LDP leadership signaled that they would not visit—Fukuda Yasuo, who succeeded as prime minister after Abe's first term, stands out in this regard. Prime ministers in the 3-year Democratic Party's leadership from 2009 to 2012 made it explicitly clear that neither they nor their cabinet members would visit Yasukuni, in private or public capacities. What was different with Abe at the helm, and how did he create a legacy of deeply damaged relations with the Republic of Korea?

We have discussed the expressed goals of the *Nippon Kaigi*, Japan's largest and most influential nationalist organization, and have shown that PM Abe not only associated with the group, but consistently articulated as his own agenda and beliefs the ideological platform espoused by the *Nippon Kaigi*, selecting the majority of his cabinet from the *Nippon Kaigi's* membership ranks. In characterizing this as his political "base," we point out that Japan's East Asian neighbors —notably South Korea and China—have analyzed PM Abe's every move and have placed him squarely in the explicitly revisionist camp the *Nippon Kaigi* so powerfully represents. Abe came to the prime minister's position as a known quantity in this regard, going on to prioritize the denial of wartime culpability in the coerced sexual slavery of the so-called "Comfort Women," and made efforts to amend, retract, or cast doubts upon his predecessors' carefully articulated apologies to the people of Asia, and of Korea specifically. This consistent reading from the *Nippon Kaigi's* playbook is the key difference in how PM Abe has been perceived and received by the Moon administration and civil society in the Republic of Korea.

The statement issued in 1993 by then-Chief Cabinet Secretary Kono Yohei is a remarkable read, leaving no doubt about both the findings of the government's report on the "Comfort Women" or the sincerity of the official apology extended on behalf of Japan. The 1995 Murayama Statement, too, while addressed to the wider audience of victims of Japan's war across Asia, articulates a genuine apology and strikes a fully believable tone of repentance and humility. The 2010 statement by then-prime minister Kan Naoto captured in eloquent terms an understanding of the Korean people's enduring pain and shame at having been brutalized by Japan's colonization that started a century earlier. These and other efforts have illustrated that Japan can nurture closer relations with the people and government of the ROK and have created a legacy to that end—a legacy that PM Abe and the *Nippon Kaigi* he has so explicitly represented in his long political career have sought to erase. PM Abe succeeded in replacing that foundation of improved relations with a legacy of revisionist denial that has reaped distrust, making it imminently more difficult to foster mutual respect and genuinely improved relations with the government and people of South Korea.

That the LDP remains firmly in control, that many in parliament align their ideological approach to the *Nippon Kaigi's* goals, and that PM Abe's immediate successor is not only a member of *Nippon Kaigi* but has vowed to carry on the policies of his predecessor, do not bode well for an immediate turnaround in approaches to South Korea nor to the rebuilding of trust going forward. While the political pendulum in the ROK could very well swing yet again when President Moon's single term ends in 2022, the astounding display of civil society's resolve in the 2016–2017 Candlelight Revolution signals a public determination not to permit a repeat subservience to Japan's interests or revisionist design. If Japan truly wishes for improved relations with the ROK moving forward—mutually advantageous in the face of illiberal neighbors in East Asia—it will need to acknowledge and jettison the Abe legacy's damage inflicted on an earlier legacy of sincerity and mutual trust.

NOTES

1. Nikkei, 『韓国世論調査、慰安婦合意 評価せず54％ 評価する」26％』 [Korea public opinion poll, Comfort Women Agreement 'Not favorably evaluated' 54% 'Favorably evaluated' 26%], January 8, 2016. https://www.nikkei.com/article/DGXLASDE08H07_Y6A100C1PP8000/.

2. Gaku Shimada, "Abe tells aides to brace for 5-year chill in South Korea ties," *Nikkei Asia*, October 19, 2019. https://asia.nikkei.com/Politics/Inside-Japanese-politics/Abe-tells-aides-to-brace-for-5-year-chill-in-South-Korea-ties.

3. Jeff Kingston, "Under Abe, are we heading toward a beautiful Japan or an ugly future?" *Japan Times*, May 27, 2017. https://www.japantimes.co.jp/opinion/2017/05/27/commentary/abe-heading-toward-beautiful-japan-ugly-future/.

4. Rising Powers Initiative, "Return of Japan's LDP and Shinzo Abe Draws Mixed Reactions from Asian Powers," December 2012. https://www.risingpowersinitiative.org/publication/return-of-japans-ldp-and-shinzo-abe-draws-mixed-reactions-from-asian-powers/.

5. David McNeill, "Nippon Kaigi and the Radical Conservative Project to Take Back Japan," *The Asia-Pacific Journal*, Vol. 13, Issue 50, No. 4, December 14, 2015; See also Tawara Yoshifumi, "What is the Aim of Nippon Kaigi, the Ultra-Right Organization that Supports Japan's Abe Administration," *Asia Pacific Journal: Japan Focus*, Vol. 15, Issue 21, No. 1 (2017). https://apjjf.org/2017/21/Tawara.html; Andrew Salmon, "Why South Korea likes Shinzo Abe less than Kim Jong-un," *South China Morning Post*, November 8, 2015. https://www.scmp.com/news/asia/east-asia/article/1876571/why-south-korea-likes-shinzo-abe-less-kim-jong-un.

6. Kingston, "Under Abe, are we heading toward a beautiful Japan or an ugly future?"

7. "Yohei Kono, a moderate former president of the Liberal Democratic Party who retired in 2009, said that Abe may turn more nationalist after a victory: 'He is restraining his remarks and actions only because of the election.'" See Min-sik Yoon, "Japan's Abe may push nationalism after elections," *Korea Herald*, July 19, 2013. http://www.koreaherald.com/view.php?ud=20130719000405&ACE_SEARCH=1.

8. George Nishiyama, "Abe Visit to Controversial Japanese Shrine Draws Rare U.S. Criticism," *Wall Street Journal*, December 26, 2013. https://www.wsj.com/articles/japan8217s-abe-to-visit-yasukuni-shrine-1388023074.

9. Rising Powers Initiative, "Return of Japan's LDP."

10. Jeong Chan, "Gallup Korea poll: 'Favorable rating of Putin at 17%; Trump & Xi Ji-Ping 15%; Kim Jong-Un 9%; Abe 3%'," *Polinews*, November 11, 2019. https://polinews.co.kr/news/article.html?no=435359.

11. Abe himself predicted to his inner circle that improvement would take at least 5 years, and could not happen within Moon Jae-In's tenure as president. See Shimada, "Abe tells aides to brace for 5-year chill in South Korea ties."

12. Korea's long history of suzerain subservience to China led to a pejorative term shared on the Korean Peninsula—*sadaejui*—"kowtowing to the powerful." Combined with a ubiquitous disdain for Japan's colonial rule, any appearance of *sadaejui*-like subservience to Japanese interests is fiercely criticized to this day.

13. Yoshifumi, "What is the Aim of Nippon Kaigi."

14. Tomomi Yamaguchi, "The 'History Wars' and the 'Comfort Women' Issue: The Significance of Nippon Kaigi in the Revisionist Movement in Contemporary Japan," in *The Transnational Redress Movement for the Victims of Japanese Military Sexual Slavery*, edited by Pyong Gap Min, et al., 233–260. Walter de Gruyter, 2020; See also Yoshifumi, "What is the Aim of Nippon Kaigi."

15. Nippon Kaigi, 「日本会議が目指すもの」 [Aims of the Nippon Kaigi], http://www.nipponkaigi.org/about/mokuteki.

16. The Ministry of Foreign Affairs (MOFA) of Japan and PM Abe himself repeatedly refer to the ROK as their "most important neighbor."

17. Yoshifumi, "What is the Aim of Nippon Kaigi."

18. Ibid.

19. *Shusenjo*, directed by Miki Dezaki (2018; No Man Productions LLC), Screening at Foreign Correspondents Club of Japan (FCCJ), 2019.
20. Yoshifumi, "What is the Aim of Nippon Kaigi," 6–7.
21. Jeff Kingston, "On 'Comfort Women' and Japan's war history, Abe's historical amnesia is not the way forward," *South China Morning Post*, August 4, 2018. https://www.scmp.com/comment/insight-opinion/asia/article/2157956/comfort-women-and-japans-war-history-abes-historical.
22. *Shusenjo*, dir. Miki Dezaki.
23. S. Nathan Park, "Abe Ruined the Most Important Democratic Relationship in Asia," *Foreign Policy*, September 4, 2020. https://foreignpolicy.com/2020/09/04/shinzo-abe-japan-south-korea-war-nationalism/.
24. Salmon, "Why South Korea likes Shinzo Abe less than Kim Jong-un."
25. Robin Harding and Edward White, "Divided by History: Why Japan-South Korea Ties Have Soured," *Financial Times*, October 24, 2019. https://www.ft.com/content/13a3ff9a-f3ed-11e9-a79c-bc9acae3b654. Accessed on September 19, 2020; See also Wooyoung Lee, "South Korea disbands 'comfort women' foundation," UPI World News, November 20, 2018. https://www.upi.com/Top_News/World-News/2018/11/20/South-Korea-disbands-comfort-women-foundation/2581542772145/.
26. David Satterwhite, "The Politics of Economic Development: Coup, State, and the ROK's First Five-Year Economic Development Plan (1962–1966)," (Ph.D. dissertation, University of Washington), author's interview with the late Kim Jong-P'il, coup co-instigator with Park Chung-Hee, March 6, 1987; See also U.S. Director of Central Intelligence, "Current Situation in South Korea," May 18, 1961 [OCI-2298-61]—"The American Embassy reports that the revolutionary [SCNR government] presently lacks personnel capable of dealing with economic problems and has no real economic program"—an assessment two days after the coup.
27. Satterwhite, "The Politics of Economic Development," dissertation research interview with the late Edwin O. Reischauer, August 6, 1988. Prof. Reischauer, the late U.S. Ambassador to Japan, was directly involved in facilitating ROK–Japan negotiations.
28. In Salmon, "Why South Korea likes Shinzo Abe less than Kim Jong-un" – "A Washington insider said there is 'Korea fatigue' in the capital over Seoul's prioritization of historical issues."
29. Satterwhite, "The Politics of Economic Development," (Ph.D. dissertation, University of Washington), Chapters 5 & 6, Passim.
30. Kangkyu Lee, "The Comfort Women Agreement: An Analysis of the Motivations that led to Park Geun-hye's Acquiescence," (Master's thesis, Georgetown University, 2017), 14–15. https://repository.library.georgetown.edu/bitstream/handle/10822/1043803/Lee_georgetown_0076M_13544.pdf?sequence=1&isAllowed=y.
31. Harding and White, "Divided by History."
32. MOFA Japan, "Failure of the Republic of Korea to comply with obligations regarding arbitration under the Agreement on the Settlement of Problems concerning Property and Claims and on Economic Co-operation between Japan and the Republic of Korea (Statement by Foreign Minister Taro Kono)," Press releases, July 19, 2019. https://www.mofa.go.jp/press/release/press4e_002553.html.

33. Harding and White, "Divided by History."

34. MOFA Japan, "Failure of the Republic of Korea to comply with obligations."

35. Xu Aiying and Kim Minji, "Cheong Wa Dae [ROK Presidential 'Blue House'] rejects Japan's arbitration committee proposal," Korea.net, July 19, 2019. http://www.korea.net/NewsFocus/policies/view?articleId=173190.

36. Tim Kelly and Hyonhee Shin, "South Korea risks ties by disbanding 'comfort women' fund: Japan PM," Reuters, November 21, 2018. https://www.reuters.com/article/us-southkorea-japan-comfortwomen-abe/south-korea-risks-ties-by-disbanding-comfort-women-fund-japan-pm-idUSKCN1NQ0CH; See also The Prime Minister and his Cabinet, "Visit to the Republic of Korea: Day One," February 9, 2018. https://japan.kantei.go.jp/98_abe/actions/201802/9article2.html.

37. Kelly and Shin, "South Korea risks ties."

38. Ibid.

39. The Prime Minister and His Cabinet, "Statement by Prime Minister Abe - Pledge for Everlasting Peace -," December 26, 2013. http://japan.kantei.go.jp/96_abe/statement/201312/1202986_7801.html.

40. Abe Shinzo as keynote speaker at a luncheon hosted by the American Chamber of Commerce in Japan (ACCJ), attended by author David Satterwhite (sitting with MP Abe at the head table), prior to his first stint as PM.

41. *The Japan Times*, "Hirohito visits to Yasukuni stopped over war criminals," July 21, 2006. https://www.japantimes.co.jp/news/2006/07/21/national/hirohito-visits-to-yasukuni-stopped-over-war-criminals/.

42. Antoni Slodkowski and Linda Sieg, "Japan's Abe visits shrine for war dead, China, South Korea angered," Reuters, December 23, 2013, https://www.reuters.com/article/us-japan-shrine-abe-idUSBRE9BP00Q20131226.

43. AFP, "Abe training jet photo sparks outrage in South Korean media," *South China Morning Post*, May 16, 2013. https://www.scmp.com/news/asia/article/1238533/abe-training-jet-photo-sparks-outrage-south-korean-media.

44. *The Korea Herald*, "What Moon Jae-in pledged to do as president," May 11, 2017. http://www.koreaherald.com/view.php?ud=20170509000521.

45. Mari Yamaguchi, "Japan withdraws from fleet review over flag spat with South Korea," *Navy Times*, October 5, 2018. https://www.navytimes.com/news/your-navy/2018/10/05/japan-withdraws-from-fleet-review-over-flag-spat-with-south-korea/.

46. Jiji, "Japan stresses significance of GSOMIA intel pact with South Korea," *The Japan Times*, August 24, 2020. https://www.japantimes.co.jp/news/2020/08/24/national/japan-south-korea-gsomia/.

REFERENCES

AFP. "Abe training jet photo sparks outrage in South Korean media." *South China Morning Post*, May 16, 2013. https://www.scmp.com/news/asia/article/1238533/abe-training-jet-photo-sparks-outrage-south-korean-media.

Chan, Jeong. "Gallup Korea poll: 'Favorable rating of Putin at 17%; Trump & Xi Ji-Ping 15%; Kim Jong-Un 9%; Abe 3%.'" *Polinews*, November 11, 2019. https://polinews.co.kr/news/article.html?no=435359.

Harding, Robin, and Edward White. "Divided by History: Why Japan-South Korea Ties Have Soured." *Financial Times*, October 24, 2019. https://www.ft.com/content/13a3ff9a-f3ed-11e9-a79c-bc9acae3b654. Accessed on September 19, 2020.

The Japan Times. "Hirohito visits to Yasukuni stopped over war criminals." July 21, 2006. https://www.japantimes.co.jp/news/2006/07/21/national/hirohito-visits-to-yasukuni-stopped-over-war-criminals/.

Jiji. "Japan stresses significance of GSOMIA intel pact with South Korea." *The Japan Times*, August 24, 2020. https://www.japantimes.co.jp/news/2020/08/24/national/japan-south-korea-gsomia/.

Kelly, Tim and Shin Hyonhee. "South Korea risks ties by disbanding 'comfort women' fund: Japan PM." Reuters, November 21, 2018. https://www.reuters.com/article/us-southkorea-japan-comfortwomen-abe/south-korea-risks-ties-by-disbanding-comfort-women-fund-japan-pm-idUSKCN1NQ0CH.

The Korea Herald. "What Moon Jae-in pledged to do as president." May 11, 2017. http://www.koreaherald.com/view.php?ud=20170509000521.

Kingston, Jeff. "On 'Comfort Women' and Japan's war history, Abe's historical amnesia is not the way forward." *South China Morning Post*, August 4, 2018. https://www.scmp.com/comment/insight-opinion/asia/article/2157956/comfort-women-and-japans-war-history-abes-historical.

Kingston, Jeff. "Under Abe, are we heading toward a beautiful Japan or an ugly future?" *The Japan Times*, May 27, 2017. https://www.japantimes.co.jp/opinion/2017/05/27/commentary/abe-heading-toward-beautiful-japan-ugly-future/.

Lee Kangkyu. "The Comfort Women Agreement: An Analysis of the Motivations that led to Park Geun-hye's Acquiescence." Master's thesis, Georgetown University, 2017, 14–15. https://repository.library.georgetown.edu/bitstream/handle/10822/1043803/Lee_georgetown_0076M_13544.pdf?sequence=1&isAllowed=y.

Lee, Wooyoung. "South Korea disbands 'comfort women' foundation." UPI World News, November 20, 2018. https://www.upi.com/Top_News/World-News/2018/11/20/South-Korea-disbands-comfort-women-foundation/2581542772145/.

McNeill, David. "Nippon Kaigi and the Radical Conservative Project to Take Back Japan." *The Asia-Pacific Journal*, Vol. 13, Issue 50, No. 4, December 14, 2015.

MOFA Japan. "Failure of the Republic of Korea to comply with obligations regarding arbitration under the Agreement on the Settlement of Problems concerning Property and Claims and on Economic Co-operation between Japan and the Republic of Korea (Statement by Foreign Minister Taro Kono)." Press releases, July 19, 2019. https://www.mofa.go.jp/press/release/press4e_002553.html.

Nikkei. 『韓国世論調査、慰安婦合意「評価せず」54%「評価する」26%』 ["Korea public opinion poll, Comfort Women Agreement 'Not evaluated' 54% 'Evaluated' 26%"] January 8, 2016. https://www.nikkei.com/article/DGXLASDE08H07_Y6A100C1PP8000/.

Nippon Kaigi. 「日本会議が目指すもの」 ["Aims of the Nippon Kaigi"]. http://www.nipponkaigi.org/about/mokuteki.

Nishiyama, George. "Abe Visit to Controversial Japanese Shrine Draws Rare U.S. Criticism." *Wall Street Journal*, December 26, 2013. https://www.wsj.com/articles/japan8217s-abe-to-visit-yasukuni-shrine-1388023074.

Park, S. Nathan. "Abe Ruined the Most Important Democratic Relationship in Asia." *Foreign Policy*, September 4, 2020. https://foreignpolicy.com/2020/09/04/shinzo-abe-japan-south-korea-war-nationalism/.

The Prime Minister and His Cabinet. "Statement by Prime Minister Abe - Pledge for Everlasting Peace -." December 26, 2013. http://japan.kantei.go.jp/96_abe/statement/201312/1202986_7801.html.

The Prime Minister and his Cabinet. "Visit to the Republic of Korea: Day One." February 9, 2018. https://japan.kantei.go.jp/98_abe/actions/201802/9article2.html.

Rising Powers Initiative. "Return of Japan's LDP and Shinzo Abe Draws Mixed Reactions from Asian Powers." December 2012. https://www.risingpowersinitiative.org/publication/return-of-japans-ldp-and-shinzo-abe-draws-mixed-reactions-from-asian-powers/.

Salmon, Andrew. "Why South Korea likes Shinzo Abe less than Kim Jong-un." *SCMP*, November 8, 2015. https://www.scmp.com/news/asia/east-asia/article/1876571/why-south-korea-likes-shinzo-abe-less-kim-jong-un.

Satterwhite, David. "The Politics of Economic Development: Coup, State, and the ROK's First Five-Year Economic Development Plan (1962-1966)." Ph.D. diss., University of Washington.

Shimada, Gaku. "Abe tells aides to brace for 5-year chill in South Korea ties." *Nikkei Asia*, October 19, 2019. https://asia.nikkei.com/Politics/Inside-Japanese-politics/Abe-tells-aides-to-brace-for-5-year-chill-in-South-Korea-ties.

Shusenjo, directed by Miki Dezaki (2018; No Man Productions LLC). Screening at Foreign Correspondents Club of Japan (FCCJ), 2019.

Slodkowski, Antoni and Linda Sieg. "Japan's Abe visits shrine for war dead, China, South Korea angered." Reuters, December 23, 2013, https://www.reuters.com/article/us-japan-shrine-abe-idUSBRE9BP00Q20131226.

U.S. Director of Central Intelligence. "Current Situation in South Korea." May 18, 1961 [OCI-2298-61].

Xu Aiying and Kim Minji. "Cheong Wa Dae [ROK Presidential 'Blue House'] rejects Japan's arbitration committee proposal." Korea.net, July 19, 2019. http://www.korea.net/NewsFocus/policies/view?articleId=173190.

Yamaguchi, Mari. "Japan withdraws from fleet review over flag spat with South Korea." *Navy Times*, October 5, 2018. https://www.navytimes.com/news/your-navy/2018/10/05/japan-withdraws-from-fleet-review-over-flag-spat-with-south-korea/.

Yamaguchi, Tomomi. "The 'History Wars' and the 'Comfort Women' Issue: The Significance of Nippon Kaigi in the Revisionist Movement in Contemporary Japan." In *The Transnational Redress Movement for the Victims of Japanese Military Sexual Slavery*, edited by Pyong Gap Min, et al., 233–260. Walter de Gruyter, 2020.

Yoon, Min-sik. "Japan's Abe may push nationalism after election." *Korea Herald*, July 19, 2013. http://www.koreaherald.com/view.php?ud=20130719000405&ACE_SEARCH=1.

Yoshifumi, Tawara. "What is the Aim of the Nippon Kaigi, the Ultra-Right Organization that Supports Japan's Abe Administration?" *Asia Pacific Journal: Japan Focus,* Vol. 15, Issue 21, No. 1 (2017). https://apjjf.org/2017/21/Tawara.html.

Chapter 10

Abe Shinzō and the Securitization of Japan–North Korea Relations

Benoît Hardy-Chartrand

While post-war Japan has maintained fraught ties with neighboring China, South Korea, and Russia, its relationship with the Democratic People's Republic of Korea (DPRK, or North Korea) has been the most antagonistic. Plagued by seemingly intractable issues, the bilateral relationship has constituted since the early 1990s a vexing political and security quagmire for Tokyo. In spite of numerous efforts deployed by successive Japanese prime ministers to pressure—and at times engage—the DPRK, Japan today finds itself no closer to a satisfactory resolution of its grievances.

From his first short-lived stint in office in 2006–2007, Prime Minister Abe Shinzō made North Korea an important focus of his entrepreneurial foreign policy. In fact, no other leader in modern Japanese history demonstrated such resolve in addressing the country's two primary concerns with regard to North Korea: the abduction of Japanese citizens in the 1970s and 1980s and the relentless development of the North's nuclear and missile capabilities. Although Abe was ultimately unable, during his eventual record-breaking tenure as prime minister, to achieve a breakthrough on either of these matters, his approach to the "North Korea problem" will leave a lasting legacy, especially in the security sphere.

This chapter will explore Abe Shinzō's North Korea policy and the influence that it will have on Japan–DPRK relations beyond his prime ministership. Under his leadership, Japan tended to pursue a hardline approach toward North Korea, in line with its American ally, while at times also attempting to engage the Kim regime. Due in large part to growing North Korean military capabilities, underscored by missile tests that directly threatened Japanese territory, Prime Minister Abe adopted a more active defense posture than his predecessors. I will argue that his hardened stance on North Korea and the progressively securitized bilateral relationship are likely to hamper future efforts to normalize bilateral ties.

In addition, an underlying argument of this chapter is the necessity of recalibrating the relative importance of Japan in the geopolitics of Korea. Despite its proximity to North Korea, its involvement in multilateral negotiations on Pyongyang's nuclear program, and its long history of interactions with Korea, Japan has been traditionally seen as a minor actor on the Korean peninsula.[1] Indeed, in the academic literature and the media's coverage of regional diplomacy, the United States, China, and South Korea have taken precedence over Japan. Yet, it remains a central actor whose relations with North Korea have repercussions that go beyond the peninsula. Tokyo's responses to developments in Pyongyang impact the geostrategic landscape in Northeast Asia, most specifically its relations with Beijing and Seoul.

I will first provide a brief overview of Japan's relations with North Korea in the post-Cold War era. Then, the nature of Abe Shinzō's approach to North Korea will be examined, with an initial focus on the abductions issue, followed by an analysis of Tokyo's stance on Pyongyang's nuclear and missile ambitions. Finally, I turn to his legacy and analyze how his North Korea policy will impact the future direction of Tokyo's relations with Pyongyang.

MISTRUST AND TENSION: THREAT PERCEPTION IN JAPAN–DPRK RELATIONS

The bilateral relationship between Japan and North Korea is arguably the most contentious in the East Asian region. Although Tokyo and Pyongyang cautiously engaged in embryonic and generally non-confrontational relations following the American occupation of Japan,[2] they have had few periods of sustained engagement and never came close to normalizing their relationship. Distrust and resentment have persistently permeated their interactions,[3] dogging overtures and attempts from both sides to engage on specific matters.

Although the North Korean regime maintains an inimical posture toward the majority of liberal democratic states, it reserves special opprobrium for Japan and its leaders. Its propaganda, both targeting its citizens and an international audience, depicts Japan as a country bent on remilitarizing and that has not properly atoned for the suffering it wrought on Korea[4] when it colonized the peninsula from 1910 to 1945.[5] Moreover, the DPRK frequently accuses Japan of exhibiting an adventurist and hostile policy toward it, threatening its interests.[6] Conversely, since Pyongyang's nuclear program was revealed in the early 1990s, Japan has perceived North Korea as a rogue state, a destabilizing actor whose increasingly capable arsenals of nuclear weapons and ballistic missiles pose a direct threat to its security. The danger became more salient in 1998, when Pyongyang launched a three-stage intermediate range ballistic missile that flew over Japanese territory. This event shook the long-held assumption of Japanese pacifists that, as one scholar put it, "the nation (was) immune to attack,"[7] resulting in greater public support for a stronger defense.[8] The kidnapping by the North of numerous Japanese citizens in the 1970s and 1980s, admitted to by former leader Kim Jong-Il in 2002, has only served to further impress upon the Japanese public and political class the magnitude of the North Korean threat. The severely degraded image of North Korea among Japanese citizens and the demonization of the country and its leaders[9] have since buttressed the government's hardline attitude toward Pyongyang.

"FOR THEIR IMMEDIATE RETURN!": ABE SHINZŌ AND THE CENTRALITY OF THE ABDUCTION ISSUE

When Abe Shinzō took office for the first time as prime minister in 2006, the DPRK had already been looming large on his radar. His long-standing involvement in North Korean affairs, more specifically his handling of the sensitive abduction issue, had solidified his hawkish views of the North, to the extent that by the beginning of his first term, he was already seen as an "emblematic critic of the regime in Pyongyang."[10]

One of Abe's first major steps in his rise to prominence occurred when, in his capacity as deputy chief cabinet secretary, he traveled to Pyongyang with then-Prime Minister Koizumi Junichiro in September 2002 for a historic summit with then-North Korean leader Kim Jong-Il. In this first trip to North Korea by a Japanese leader, Koizumi was to tackle with his counterpart a host of issues in the hopes of paving the way for an eventual normalization of bilateral ties. As part of his agenda, the prime minister was determined to press Kim regarding Japan's suspicions on the kidnappings. In Pyongyang, Abe took an uncompromising stance, advocating pressure, both behind the scenes and publicly.[11] He encouraged Koizumi to walk out without signing a joint declaration if his counterpart refused to disclose details and apologize for any wrongdoings, despite the political risks that a failed summit might entail.[12]

When Kim Jong-Il acknowledged that North Korean agents had kidnapped a number of Japanese citizens, the matter became a national emergency and captured the public's imagination. Up to that point, the unproven claims of kidnappings by the DPRK had taken a backseat to strategic considerations and were even treated by some as a mere conspiracy theory.[13] Kim Jong-Il's admission paved the way to the signing of the Pyongyang Declaration, in which Japan apologized for the "tremendous damage and suffering" caused by its colonial rule and both sides agreed to work toward "early normalization of the relations."[14] On October 15, 2002, a month after the Koizumi–Kim summit, five abductees were allowed to visit Japan and reunite with their families for what both sides had initially agreed would be a "temporary return." While some in the Japanese government insisted that the deal be kept and abductees be sent back, Abe was adamant that they remain in Japan, a view that the prime minister agreed with.[15] The eight other Japanese citizens that the North admitted to kidnapping were declared dead by Kim Jong-Il, which, in the absence of conclusive evidence, the Japanese delegation refused to believe.

From the groundbreaking 2002 summit in Pyongyang, Abe's handling of this thorny matter helped to raise his profile nationally and solidified his standing within the Liberal Democratic Party (LDP). Once he succeeded Koizumi and became prime minister on September 26, 2006, he continued to deploy the same energy to the cause. He quickly established a "Headquarters on the Abduction Issue"[16] in the cabinet secretariat dedicated to coordinating policy on the matter. In a speech to the Diet three days after his inauguration, he vowed to pursue a policy of "dialogue and pressure" and to "strongly demand the return of all abductees assuming that they are all still alive."[17]

However, in a baptism of fire, his plans were to soon be further complicated. A mere two weeks after reaching the highest echelon of Japanese politics, Abe Shinzō faced a major security crisis when on October 9, 2006, North Korea detonated a nuclear device for the first time. At a moment when some in Japan were already questioning the ban on possessing nuclear weapons,[18] this episode threw into stark relief the emerging threat, immediately forcing the new prime minister to demonstrate resolve on North Korea. From Seoul, where on the same day he had held a summit meeting with South Korean President Roh Moo-Hyun, Abe announced that he had instructed his government to request consultations with the United Nations Security Council (UNSC) "with a view to taking firm action on North Korea."[19] Two days later, Tokyo imposed unilateral sanctions, banning all trade with the DPRK and denying its vessels entry to all Japanese ports. The nuclear test and the sharp rise in tensions that ensued greatly undermined efforts to engage Pyongyang on the abductions issue. Plagued by scandals and health problems, Abe Shinzō abruptly resigned after exactly a year in office, with little progress to show for on the abductions front.

After Abe Shinzō was elected prime minister in December 2012 thanks to a resounding LDP victory in the general election, he promised once more to pursue the resolution of the abductions issue. Soon after, his government secretly re-engaged North Korea behind the scenes,[20] eventually leading to the Intergovernmental Consultations on Abductions in March 2014, the first in a series of meetings on the matter. Two months later, Abe finally obtained an apparent breakthrough: on the occasion of consultations in Stockholm, Sweden,

Pyongyang agreed to conduct a full-scale investigation on the kidnappings, in return for a partial lifting of Japanese unilateral sanctions. The two sides continued to meet off and on for the rest of the year, before hopes of further progress were dashed in early 2016. In February of that year, Pyongyang announced that it was putting an end to all investigations into the issue, in reaction to new Japanese sanctions following North Korea's fourth nuclear test a month earlier.

All previous Japanese prime ministers since Koizumi Junichiro had endeavored to resolve the abductions issue. In contrast to his predecessors, however, starting with his 2002 trip to Pyongyang as Deputy Chief Secretary, Abe seemed to make it his personal mission to reach a breakthrough and expanded a greater amount of political capital and energy on the matter. From his first term as prime minister, he brought up the abduction issue at every juncture, to the point where it often eclipsed denuclearization as a government priority.[21] Abe addressed the abductions at the UN General Assembly and in various other multilateral settings. He tried to enlist the support of other foreign leaders, most notably U.S. President Donald Trump, who promised at his behest to bring up the question during the June 2018 summit with Kim Jong-Il in Singapore.

Abe was so determined to make progress that he was willing to jeopardize the six-party talks on North Korean denuclearization by raising the issue despite Pyongyang's opposition. In fact, his position on the abductions was so strong that at times it left him isolated from South Korea, China, and Russia during the nuclear negotiations, even complicating coordination with the United States.[22] For instance, during the February 2007 round of six-party talks, Tokyo made clear that it would not contribute financially to the assistance package promised to the DPRK by the other parties unless the abductions issue was resolved.[23] At various points, Abe has used a mix of carrots (normalization, partial lifting of sanctions, investments) and sticks (unilateral and multilateral sanctions) to induce Pyongyang to come clean and conduct a full investigation. The lack of tangible results highlighted the fact that the DPRK remains a difficult target, vulnerable to pressure and sanctions only under very specific circumstances.[24] In the end, the Abe administration's tough stance on the matter, buoyed by clear popular support,[25] did not bear fruit. On August 28, 2020, when Abe announced his resignation due to health concerns, he cited his failure to resolve the abductions issue as one of his biggest regrets.[26]

IN THE LINE OF FIRE: ABE SHINZŌ'S RESPONSES TO THE NORTH KOREAN NUCLEAR AND MISSILE THREATS

Although it was the abduction issue that originally made Abe Shinzō a household name in Japan, his response to the North Korea nuclear and missile threats will ultimately define his legacy. As a result of the Kim dynasty's development of a nuclear deterrent and its attendant advances in ballistic missile technology, the reclusive state has been perceived by Japan as the most immediate threat to its national security. Is the perception justified?

Since North Korea's first nuclear test in 2006, shortly after the beginning of Abe's first term, its nuclear and missile technology has made considerable advances.[27] Starting from a test that many experts believed to be a fizzle in 2006, Pyongyang's September 2017 test had an estimated yield of up to 271 kilotons,[28] almost twenty times the explosive power of the bomb that was used on Hiroshima in 1945. This estimate renders plausible North Korea's claims that it has developed a hydrogen bomb, a much more potent weapon. More importantly for the operationalization of the DPRK's nuclear arsenal, Japanese intelligence now believes that Pyongyang has successfully miniaturized warheads to fit them on ballistic missiles.[29]

Notwithstanding the nuclear threat, the North's increasingly capable missile forces have caused much greater alarm in Japan. The North Korean regime has at its disposal a wide range of short- and mid-range missiles that can hit Japanese territory. In only seven years since taking over the reins of the country in December 2011, Kim Jong-Un has presided over more than a hundred missile tests, a much greater number than both his father and grandfather.[30] While some questions remain about the reliability of certain classes of missiles, the greatly improving success rate of their test launches highlights the seriousness of the threat. In another technological milestone, the country's engineers have developed a submarine-launched ballistic missile, which was tested with apparent success in October 2019. These missiles are particularly problematic from the perspective of Japanese defense, given how difficult it is to detect submarines in surrounding waters.

The aforementioned developments underscore the multipronged nature of the North Korean threat. In the event of an armed conflict, Japan could suffer enormous damage from artillery units, short- and mid-range ballistic missiles, and medium-range submarine-launched nuclear missiles.[31] The probability of Pyongyang using force unprovoked against Japan remains low, due to the overwhelming retaliation that it would face from both the United States and Japan, thus jeopardizing the Kim regime's survival. In the first days of a conflict, however, it is likely that Pyongyang would target U.S. forces based in Japan and South Korea.

Any leader faced with a threat of that nature would be compelled to take steps to reinforce his country's defenses. However, Abe's changes in Japan's defense posture and his responses to North Korea over the duration of his administration have been particularly consequential. Under the banner of making a "proactive contribution to peace," Abe came to power promising that the country would play a greater global role in order to secure "peace, stability and prosperity of the international community."[32] In order to better respond to an "increasingly severe security environment (. . .) and grave national security challenges,"[33] the prime minister took a number of measures to loosen long-standing restrictions on Japan's Self-Defense Forces (SDF) and make Japan a more assertive regional player. Many of the changes to Japan's defense posture were driven explicitly by developments in North Korea.

The most emblematic and controversial change instituted by the prime minister was the reinterpretation of the Japanese Constitution in July 2014. Without sufficient support to amend Article 9 of the Constitution, which prevents Japan from exercising the "right to belligerency," Abe issued via cabinet order a new reading of the article. It expanded the scope of action of the SDF to allow Japan to come to the aid of its allies (i.e. Collective Self-Defense) in cases where they sustain an attack that is deemed to "threaten Japan's survival."[34] The reinterpretation was founded on the aforementioned idea—which permeated the security discourse throughout Abe's tenure—that the Northeast Asian security environment was posing an increasing danger to the national security of Japan.[35]

To be sure, North Korea's behavior was not the sole factor explaining Tokyo's perception of a more challenging geostrategic context. China's growing military capabilities since the 1990s and its turn toward a more assertive defense posture under President Xi Jinping have also raised serious concerns among Japanese strategists. Throughout Abe's nearly eight years in office, however, it was North Korea that most often validated his security-related preoccupations,[36] allowing him to call for beefing up Japanese capabilities without naming China. Abe presented the DPRK as an existential threat requiring the government to take a strong and uncompromising stance. In numerous speeches, both in Japan and abroad, he drew attention to North Korean technological advances and advocated for a stronger national defense. The case was easy to make. As Magcamit explains, "the persistence and direction of North Korean existential threat (provided) Abe and supporters a concretely resonant security frame for demonstrating the urgent need"[37] to take extraordinary measures. With frequent military provocations and bellicose rhetoric directed at Japan, there was a concrete and immediate quality to the North Korean threat, which could not be said of the more diffuse, indirect challenge posed by China.

SANCTIONS, COERCION, AND ALIGNMENT WITH THE UNITED STATES: ABE AND MAXIMUM PRESSURE

The year 2017 brought tensions in Northeast Asia to their apex. The inauguration of U.S. President Donald Trump in January of that year was followed by bursts of strident rhetoric in both Washington and Pyongyang as well as a string of military provocations by Kim Jong-Un. The North Korean leader supervised twenty-one missile tests in 2017, including two that flew over Japan in August and September. On July 4, on the United States' Independence Day—by no means a coincidence—the North successfully conducted its first test of an Intercontinental Ballistic Missile, the Hwasong-14, capable of hitting Alaska. Kim had thus crossed an important technological threshold,[38] bringing North America within reach for the first time. Two months later, he further upped the ante, conducting the country's sixth and most powerful nuclear test to date. In Washington DC, there were increasing talk, fueled by the president himself,[39] of American strikes on North Korea. For the first time since the first nuclear crisis of 1993–1994, there were genuine fears in the region of a second Korean War.

The new American president, trying to distance himself from the Obama administration's "strategic patience" policy on North Korea, adopted an approach that he called "maximum pressure and engagement," with clear early emphasis on the first term. Although the two strategies were in essence less dissimilar than their names suggested, Trump did go further than his predecessor in rallying the international community behind the pressure campaign on the Kim regime. In addition, his administration deployed unprecedented efforts into convincing China to tighten the screws on its recalcitrant neighbor, which Beijing had long avoided doing for fear of provoking instability at its north-eastern border.

Abe, who had deftly cultivated a close personal relationship with Trump from the moment of his surprise election, was all in on the new American approach. On September 17, 2017, in a speech at the United Nations General Assembly, the Japanese prime minister zeroed in on North Korea and made a vigorous call to action. First referring to the decade following the 1994 Agreed Framework signed by the United States and the DPRK, he said:

> What we had to learn is that during the time this dialogue continued, North Korea had no intention whatsoever of abandoning its nuclear or missile development. For North Korea, dialogue was instead the best means of deceiving us and buying time. (. . .) Again and again, attempts to resolve issues through dialogue have all come to naught. In what hope of success are we now repeating the very same failure a third time? We must make North Korea abandon all nuclear and ballistic missile programs in a complete, verifiable, and irreversible manner. What is needed to do that is not dialogue, but pressure. (. . .) What is necessary is action.[40]

On the same day, he published an op-ed in *The New York Times* arguing that the North presented an "unprecedented, grave and imminent threat" requiring "the utmost pressure."⁴¹ Abe's rhetoric maintained the same vigor during the October 2017 election campaign in Japan, when his depictions of Pyongyang's actions as a matter of life and death helped him win reelection.⁴² Abe's strategy was not merely rhetorical. As a non-permanent UNSC member in 2016 and 2017, Japan was at the forefront of international efforts to impose sanctions on the DPRK for its nuclear and missile provocations.⁴³ In addition to imposing new unilateral sanctions on the North and bolstering existing ones, Abe worked behind the scenes at the UN to convince DPRK partners to cut ties with Pyongyang.⁴⁴ From 2018, along with countries like Australia and Canada, Japan significantly expanded its maritime monitoring and surveillance operations against illicit North Korean activities violating UNSC resolutions.⁴⁵

Abe's stance underwent a reversal, albeit tentative at first, after Kim Jong-Un extended his hand to Seoul and Washington in 2018. In his New Year address to the nation, the North Korean leader signaled his willingness to meet with South Korean President Moon Jae-In in order to defuse tensions and discuss the North's potential participation in the Pyeongchang Olympics. On March 8, as tensions were abating in the region, Donald Trump stunned many observers by accepting Kim Jong-Un's invitation to a bilateral summit, to be held in Singapore in June 2018. By summertime, just a few months after the crisis had reached a boiling point, both the South Korean and American presidents had met with Kim Jong-Un in summits heralded as turning points on the peninsula. These unexpected developments made it increasingly difficult for Abe to maintain his hardline. It was revealed in late March 2018, soon after the announcement of the U.S.–DPRK summit, that the Abe administration had sounded out Pyongyang in relation to a potential Abe–Kim meeting.⁴⁶ At the UN General Assembly in September, in stark contrast to his "no dialogue" address a year earlier, Abe declared that he was "ready to break the shell of mutual distrust with North Korea, get off to a new start, and meet face to face with Chairman Kim Jong-Un."⁴⁷

Abe's position continued to soften in 2019. In January, he vowed to improve relations with North Korea, signaling once again his willingness to meet Kim Jong-Un in order to resolve the abduction issue and other matters. Two months later, for the first time since 2007, Japan decided not to back a joint draft resolution with the European Union condemning North Korea's human rights abuses. In May, the Japanese prime minister proposed publicly to meet Kim Jong-Un and for the first time emphasized that he would do so without preconditions. Hopes of a summit remained until the fall, when in October, North Korea tested a series of ballistic missiles, including one that fell into Japan's Exclusive Economic Zone. In response to Abe's criticisms of the tests, Pyongyang closed the door to a summit with Abe with a decidedly undiplomatic statement that called the Japanese prime minister "fool," "idiot," "deformed," and "under-wit," among other invectives.[48]

Abe's attempts at rapprochement with Pyongyang in 2018 and 2019 highlighted the constraints of Japan's North Korea policy. After years spearheading multilateral efforts, along with the United States, to coerce the Kim regime into abandoning its nuclear program, Japan was at risk of being isolated once Trump and other regional powers turned toward full engagement with Kim Jong-Un. While Japan became a more consequential player in regional security under the Abe's leadership, it still lacked the military and diplomatic heft to pursue "maximum pressure" without the United States. At a time when the United States, South Korea, Russia and China were all engaging with Pyongyang, Tokyo was wary of remaining on the sidelines for fear its national interests would be disregarded. These concerns appeared warranted when the American president, eager to engage in denuclearization talks with Kim, was dismissive of repeated North Korean short-range missile tests in the summer of 2019.[49] The prospect of a nuclear deal between Washington and Pyongyang that would satisfy Trump but leave aside Japanese (and South Korean) concerns regarding short- and mid-range ballistic missiles was unpalatable to Tokyo. When Abe left office in September 2020, he remained the only leader in Northeast Asia not to have held a summit with the North.

ABE'S LEGACY AND FUTURE PERSPECTIVES ON JAPAN–DPRK RELATIONS

With almost eight years in office as the head of government, the longest tenure in Japanese constitutional history, Abe's approach to North Korea has the potential to leave a long-lasting impact on bilateral relations. Determined to leave his mark on this most thorny of relationships, from his first stint as prime minister in 2006, he made the North Korea file a central component of his foreign policy. Although his relentless efforts on the abductions issue, which had made his name in the early 2000s, brought him the most acclaim, his legacy will be most keenly felt in the defense and security dimension of Japan–DPRK ties. After returning to the highest office in 2012, he set about accelerating Japan's march toward the normalization of its foreign and defense policies and implemented a series of reforms. In addition to the reinterpretation of the constitution, he reinforced defense cooperation with the United States and other regional partners and expanded the SDF's capabilities. In light of Abe's long-standing views on Japan's defense and foreign policies, the evolution of Japan's stance would have taken place even without a salient North Korean threat. However, Pyongyang's provocations and technological advances added urgency and likely provided further impetus for Abe to implement the reforms. Given the highly securitized nature of Japan–DPRK relations, these changes were bound to impact their interactions and render dialogue difficult. Considering the acute sense of threat already felt in both Tokyo and Pyongyang,[50] reinforcement of either side's capabilities inevitably created a security dilemma that undermined efforts aimed at de-escalating tensions. Apart from the impact of material changes to Japan's defense posture, the increased emphasis on the North Korean threat in the public discourse under Abe often compelled Pyongyang to react strongly—as seen for instance in its November 2019 statement—thus further vitiating the atmosphere.

With the exception of a tentative outreach to Pyongyang in 2018 and 2019, Abe's stance on North Korea was characterized by persistent pressure and the securitization of Pyongyang's military provocations. By consistently framing North Korean actions as an existential danger requiring a commensurate response, the prime minister made it difficult to apprehend the relationship through anything but a security lens. With a harsh security discourse led by the government, mirrored in the national media and supported by the public, it became difficult for Tokyo to envisage a "normal" relationship with Pyongyang, even when it turned—pushed by a change in the regional context—toward a more accommodating posture at the end of Abe's tenure. As illustrated by Kim Jong-Un's repeated rebuffs of Abe at a time of intensifying regional diplomacy, it likely made Pyongyang negatively predisposed toward Tokyo's overtures.

Can the relationship be de-securitized and normalized in the foreseeable future? The ongoing evolution of the Japanese defense posture and the trajectory of the Northeast Asian security environment make it an unlikely prospect. Even if Pyongyang's foreign policy came to conform with international norms, Japan's intensifying strategic competition with China will continue to further drive the strengthening of its capabilities, in turn feeding the North's perception of threat. Moreover, the recent evolution of the Japanese discourse over the SDF's capabilities is pointing toward ever greater securitization of Japan–DPRK relations. As a direct result of the North's continuing advances in missile technology, Abe has pushed for the acquisition of military capabilities that could, according to some interpretations, violate the Japanese constitution. One instance is the debate over strike capabilities. After the plan to install Aegis Ashore, an American ground-based ballistic missile defense system was abandoned in June 2020, discussions[51] over acquiring the capacity the strike enemy bases gained momentum. Such proposals are not new, with Japanese politicians raising the idea as far back as the 1950s, but recent North Korean provocations have explicitly given them further impetus. The LDP agreed in June 2020 to start internal deliberations on the potential acquisition of strike capability.[52] Just before officially stepping down three months later, Prime Minister Abe called on his successor to deepen the party's discussions on the topic. If Abe's hope materializes, it could push Japan away from an "exclusively defense-oriented policy,"[53] the long-standing principle it has maintained under its pacifist constitution. Not only would the decision have a non-negligible effect on its relations with the DPRK, given the country would constitute the most likely target of a hypothetical first strike, but it would also impact relations with China and South Korea, both of whom remain wary of any Japanese move toward normalization. The management of regional concerns over Japan's defense policy will continue to be a challenge[54] and will undoubtedly factor into the final choice. While the adoption of this consequential option is not guaranteed, the Overton window seems to have shifted enough within the ruling party to make discussions on strike capability more frequent, open, and accepted.

Abe Shinzō will be remembered for his obstinate devotion to the abductions issue and his efforts to bolster Japan's readiness against the North Korean nuclear and missile threats. His approach to the reclusive state, however, arguably left bilateral ties in a more precarious position. The enmity is so deep-seated and the mistrust so profound that it will take much more than diffident overtures to unburden the two countries from the weight of decades of antagonism. Unless a substantially different approach is adopted in either capital, the Japan–DPRK relationship will continue to frustrate Japanese policy makers for some time to come.

NOTES

1. Linus Hagström and Marie Söderberg, "Taking Japan–North Korea Relations Seriously: Rationale and Background," *Pacific Affairs* 79-3 (Fall 2006), 373–385.

2. Ra Mason, *Japan's Relations with North Korea and the Recalibration of Risk*, London: Routledge, 2014.

3. John Nilsson-Wright, "Nuclear Crisis on the Korean Peninsula: Strategic Adaptation, the Abe Administration and Extended Deterrence in the Face of Uncertainty," *Japan Forum* 31:1 (2019), 110–131.

4. Korean Central News Agency, "Rodong Sinmum Raps Japan for Tampering with Its Past History," May 22, 2015. http://www.kcna.co.jp/item/2015/201505/news22/20150522-05ee.html.

5. While more crude, North Korea's depictions of Japan are qualitatively similar to the way the Chinese government and media portrayed Japan at the nadir of Sino-Japanese relations from 2012 to 2014. See Benoit Hardy-Chartrand, "Misperceptions, Threat Inflation and Mistrust in China-Japan Relations," *CIGI*. CIGI Paper No. 107 (2016).

6. Chol Hyok Ri, "Japan Should Thoroughly Liquidate Crime-Woven Past," Rodong Sinmun, July 18, 2018. http://www.rodong.rep.kp/en/index.php?strPageID

=SF01_02_01&newsID=2018-07-18-0001; Korean Central News Agency, "Japan's Policy Hostile to DPRK Under Fire," June 19, 2019. http://www.kcna.co.jp/item/2019/201906/news19/20190619-06ee.html.

7. Kawahima Yutaka, *Japanese Foreign Policy at the Crossroads: Challenges and Options for the Twenty-First Century*, Brookings Institution Press, 2003.

8. Martin Fackler, "Japan Now Seems Likely to Rally Behind New Prime Minister's Call for a Stronger Military," *The New York Times*, October 10, 2006.

9. Mason, *Japan's Relations with North Korea and the Recalibration of Risk*.

10. *Ibid.*

11. Funabashi Yōichi, *The Peninsula Question: A Chronicle of the Second Korean Nuclear Crisis*, Brookings Institution Press, 2007.

12. *Ibid.*

13. *Ibid.*

14. Ministry of Foreign Affairs of Japan, "Japan-DPRK Pyongyang Declaration," 2002. https://www.mofa.go.jp/region/asia-paci/n_korea/pmv0209/pyongyang.html.

15. Funabashi, *The Peninsula Question*.

16. The new unit, however, did not meet during his first term and was revived in 2013.

17. Abe Shinzō, "Policy Speech by Prime Minister Shinzo Abe to the 165th Session of the Diet," *Kantei*. https://japan.kantei.go.jp/abespeech/2006/09/29speech_e.html.

18. David E. Sanger, "North Koreans Say They Tested Nuclear Device," *The New York Times*, October 9, 2006. https://www.nytimes.com/2006/10/09/world/asia/09korea.html.

19. Abe Shinzō, "Press Conference by Prime Minister Shinzo Abe Following His Visit to the Republic of Korea," 2006. https://japan.kantei.go.jp/abespeech/2006/10/09koreapress_e.html.

20. Longfan Jiang and Haifan Wang, "North Korea's Peripheral Diplomacy in the 'Post Kim Jong-Il Era' and Its Relationship with Japan," *The Journal of East Asian Affairs* 30-1 (Spring-Summer 2016), 93–119.

21. Key-Young Son, "Constructing Fear: How the Japanese State Mediates Risks from North Korea," *Japan Forum* 22:1–2 (2010), 169–194.

22. Funabashi, *The Peninsula Question*.

23. Anthony DiFilippo, "Cold war Stasis: Past and Continuing Problems in the Normalization of Japan-North Korea Relations," *North Korean Review* 14-2 (Fall 2018), 64–86; Son, "Constructing fear."

24. Stephan Haggard and Marcus Noland, *Hard Targets: Sanctions, Inducements, and the Case of North Korea*, Stanford: Stanford University Press, 2017.

25. *Sankei Shimbun*, "【本社　ＦＮＮ合同世論調査】対北制裁「拉致解決まで続けるべき」８３.９％　内閣支持率４０％台回復、不支持に１ポイント差迫る," June 18, 2018. https://www.sankei.com/politics/news/180618/plt1806180043-n1.html.

26. Obe Mitsuru and Okutsu Akane, "Japan PM Abe announces resignation over worsening health," *Nikkei*. August 28, 2010. https://asia.nikkei.com/Politics/Japan-PM-Abe-announces-resignation-over-worsening-health.

27. North Korea, by most accounts, embarked on its nuclear weapons program in the 1980s, under the leadership of Kim Il-Sung, after dabbling in nuclear technology for two decades.

28. K.M. Sreejith, Ritesh Agrawal, and A.S. Rajawat, "Constraints on the Location, Depth and Yield of the 2017 September 3 North Korean Nuclear Test from InSAR Measurements and Modelling," *Geophysical Journal International*, 220-1 (January 2020), 345–351.

29. Ministry of Defense of Japan, "Defense of Japan 2019," 2019. https://www.mod.go.jp/e/publ/w_paper/wp2019/pdf/DOJ2019_Full.pdf.

30. Under the leadership of Kim Jong-Un, the DPRK has conducted 149 tests as of March 2020. See Nuclear Threat Initiative, "The CNS North Korea Missile Test Database," 2020. https://www.nti.org/analysis/articles/cns-north-korea-missile-test-database/.

31. Ankit Panda, *Kim Jong Un and the Bomb: Survival and Deterrence in North Korea*, Oxford University Press, 2020.

32. Ministry of Foreign Affairs of Japan, "Japan's Security Policy," 2016. https://www.mofa.go.jp/fp/nsp/page1we_000079.html.

33. Government of Japan, *National Security Strategy*, 2013.

34. Ministry of Defense of Japan, "Defense of Japan 2018," 2018. https://www.mod.go.jp/e/publ/w_paper/pdf/2018/DOJ2018_Full_1130.pdf.

35. Adam P. Liff, "Policy by Other Means: Collective Self-Defense and the Politics of Japan's Postwar Constitutional Reinterpretations," *Asia Policy* 24-1 (2017), 139–172.

36. Until 2019, North Korea came before China as top national security concern in Japan's annual Defense White Paper.

37. Michael I. Magcamit, "The Fault in Japan's Stars: Shinzo Abe, North Korea, and the Quest for a New Japanese Constitution," *International Politics* 57 (2020), 606–633.

38. Panda, *Kim Jong Un and the Bomb*.

39. On August 11, 2017, Trump tweeted: "Military solutions are now fully in place, locked and loaded, should North Korea act unwisely. Hopefully Kim Jong Un will find another path!"

40. Ministry of Foreign Affairs of Japan, "Address by Prime Minister Shinzo Abeat the Seventy-Second Session of the United Nations General Assembly," 2017. https://www.mofa.go.jp/fp/unp_a/page4e_000674.html.

41. Abe Shinzō, "Solidarity Against the North Korean Threat," *The New York Times*, September 17, 2017. https://www.nytimes.com/2017/09/17/opinion/north-korea-shinzo-abe-japan.html.

42. Magcamit, "The Fault in Japan's Stars," 606–633.

43. Yasuhiro Izumikawa, "Acting on the North Korea Playbook: Japan's Responses to North Korea's Provocations," *Asia Policy* 23 (January 2017), 90–96.

44. Sakai Kōhei, "首相、イラン訪問に意欲　ロウハニ大統領と会談," Nikkei. September 22, 2016. https://www.nikkei.com/article/DGXLASFS22H0U_S6A920C1PE8000/.

45. Ministry of Foreign Affairs of Japan, "Japan–North Korea relations," 2020. https://www.mofa.go.jp/region/asia-paci/n_korea/index.html.

46. Kikuchi Daisuke, "Pyongyang has discussed the possibility of holding Abe-Kim Jong-Un summit in June: report," *The Japan Times*. March 29, 2018.

47. Ministry of Foreign Affairs of Japan, "Address by Prime Minister Abe at the Seventy-Third Session of the United Nations General Assembly," 2018. https://www.mofa.go.jp/fp/unp_a/page3e_000926.html.

48. Ministry of Foreign Affairs of the People's Democratic People's Republic of Korea, "Japanese PM Condemned for Taking Issue with DPRK's Test-Fire of Super-large Multiple Rocket Launchers," November 7, 2019. www.mfa.gov.kp/en/japanese-pm-condemned-for-taking-issue-with-dprks-test-fire-of-super-large-multiple-rocket-launchers.

49. Jesse Johnson, "Trump plays down third North Korea missile test in eight days as allies' concerns grow," *The Japan Times*. August 2, 2019. https://www.japantimes.co.jp/news/2019/08/02/asia-pacific/north-korea-fires-unidentified-projectiles-sea-japan-third-launch-just-week/.

50. For more on the DPRK's perception of threat, see Benoit Hardy-Chartrand, "Securitization and the construction of external threat in North Korea: effects on Pyongyang's foreign policy," ISA Conference Paper, 2011.

51. For an overview of the debate and the ramifications of a strike capability, see Titli Basu, "Will Japan Pursue a Strike Capability in Lieu of Aegis Ashore?" *The Diplomat*, July 28, 2020. https://thediplomat.com/2020/07/will-japan-pursue-a-strike-capability-in-lieu-of-aegis-ashore/.

52. Tim Kelly, "Pacifist Japan ruling party proposes strike capability to halt missile attacks," *Reuters*, July 31, 2020. https://www.reuters.com/article/us-japan-defence-idUSKCN24W09C.

53. It must be noted that even in the case of the acquisition of a strike capability, barring a constitutional revision, the Japanese government would likely maintain that it continues to adhere to its "exclusively defense-oriented policy." It has already explained that having a strike capability for the purpose of self-defense would not violate the Constitution. See Daisuke Akimoto, "Explaining Japan's policy debate on strike capability," *The Japan Times*, August 13, 2020. https://www.japantimes.co.jp/opinion/2020/08/13/commentary/japan-commentary/explaining-japans-policy-debate-strike-capability/.

54. Basu, "Will Japan Pursue a Strike Capability in Lieu of Aegis Ashore?"

REFERENCES

Abe, Shinzō. "Policy Speech by Prime Minister Shinzo Abe to the 165th Session of the Diet." *Kantei*. 2006. https://japan.kantei.go.jp/abespeech/2006/09/29speech_e.html.

Abe, Shinzō. "Press Conference by Prime Minister Shinzo Abe Following His Visit to the Republic of Korea." 2006. https://japan.kantei.go.jp/abespeech/2006/10/09koreapress_e.html.

Abe, Shinzō. "Solidarity Against the North Korean Threat." *The New York Times*, September 17, 2017. https://www.nytimes.com/2017/09/17/opinion/north-korea-shinzo-abe-japan.html.

Akimoto, Daisuke. "Explaining Japan's policy debate on strike capability." *The Japan Times*, August 13, 2020. https://www.japantimes.co.jp/opinion/2020/08/13/commentary/japan-commentary/explaining-japans-policy-debate-strike-capability/.

Basu, Titli. "Will Japan Pursue a Strike Capability in Lieu of Aegis Ashore?" *The Diplomat*, July 28, 2020. https://thediplomat.com/2020/07/will-japan-pursue-a-strike-capability-in-lieu-of-aegis-ashore/.

DiFilippo, Anthony. "Cold war Stasis: Past and Continuing Problems in the Normalization of Japan-North Korea Relations." *North Korean Review* 14-2 (Fall 2018), 64–86.

Fackler, Martin. "Japan Now Seems Likely to Rally Behind New Prime Minister's Call for a Stronger Military." *The New York Times*, October 10, 2006.

Funabashi, Yōichi. *The Peninsula Question: A Chronicle of the Second Korean Nuclear Crisis*. Brookings Institution Press, 2007.

Ministry of Defense, *National Security Strategy*, Government of Japan, 2013.

Haggard, Stephan and Marcus Noland. *Hard Targets: Sanctions, Inducements, and the Case of North Korea*. Stanford: Stanford University Press, 2017.

Hagström, Linus and Marie Söderberg. "Taking Japan–North Korea Relations Seriously: Rationale and Background." *Pacific Affairs* 79-3 (Fall 2006), 373–385.

Hardy-Chartrand, Benoit. "Misperceptions, Threat Inflation and Mistrust in China–Japan Relations." *CIGI*. CIGI Paper No. 107 (2016).

Hardy-Chartrand, Benoit. "Securitization and the construction of external threat in North Korea: effects on Pyongyang's foreign policy." ISA Conference Paper, 2011.

Izumikawa, Yasuhiro. "Acting on the North Korea Playbook: Japan's Responses to North Korea's Provocations." *Asia Policy* 23 (January 2017), 90–96.

Jiang, Longfan and Haifan Wang. "North Korea's Peripheral Diplomacy in the 'Post Kim Jong-Il Era' and Its Relationship with Japan." *The Journal of East Asian Affairs* 30-1 (Spring-Summer 2016), 93–119.

Johnson, Jesse. "Trump plays down third North Korea missile test in eight days as allies' concerns grow." *The Japan Times*. August 2, 2019. https://www.japantimes.co.jp/news/2019/08/02/asia-pacific/north-korea-fires-unidentified-projectiles-sea-japan-third-launch-just-week/.

Kawashima, Yutaka. *Japanese Foreign Policy at the Crossroads: Challenges and Options for the Twenty-First Century*. Brookings Institution Press, 2003.

Kelly, Tim. "Pacifist Japan ruling party proposes strike capability to halt missile attacks." *Reuters*, July 31, 2020. https://www.reuters.com/article/us-japan-defence-idUSKCN24W09C.

Kikuchi, Daisuke. "Pyongyang has discussed the possibility of holding Abe-Kim Jong-Un summit in June: report." *The Japan Times*. March 29, 2018. www.japantimes.co.jp/news/2018/03/29/national/politics-diplomacy/japan-offers-summit-north-korea-pyongyang-weighing-issue-asahi-reports.

Korean Central News Agency. "Japan's Policy Hostile to DPRK Under Fire." June 19, 2019. http://www.kcna.co.jp/item/2019/201906/news19/20190619-06ee.html.

Korean Central News Agency. "Rodong Sinmum Raps Japan for Tampering with Its Past History." May 22, 2015. http://www.kcna.co.jp/item/2015/201505/news22/20150522-05ee.html.

Liff, Adam P. "Policy by Other Means: Collective Self-Defense and the Politics of Japan's Postwar Constitutional Reinterpretations." *Asia Policy* 24-1 (2017), 139–172.

Magcamit, Michael I. "The Fault in Japan's Stars: Shinzo Abe, North Korea, and the Quest for a New Japanese Constitution." *International Politics* 57 (2020), 606–633.

Mason, Ra. *Japan's Relations with North Korea and the Recalibration of Risk.* London: Routledge, 2014.

Ministry of Defense of Japan. "Defense of Japan 2018." 2018. https://www.mod.go.jp/e/publ/w_paper/pdf/2018/DOJ2018_Full_1130.pdf.

Ministry of Defense of Japan. "Defense of Japan 2019." 2019. https://www.mod.go.jp/e/publ/w_paper/wp2019/pdf/DOJ2019_Full.pdf.

Ministry of Foreign Affairs of Japan. "Address by Prime Minister Shinzo Abe at the Seventy-Second Session of the United Nations General Assembly." 2017. https://www.mofa.go.jp/fp/unp_a/page4e_000674.html.

Ministry of Foreign Affairs of Japan. "Address by Prime Minister Abe at the Seventy-Third Session of the United Nations General Assembly." 2018. https://www.mofa.go.jp/fp/unp_a/page3e_000926.html.

Ministry of Foreign Affairs of Japan. "Japan-DPRK Pyongyang Declaration." 2002. https://www.mofa.go.jp/region/asia-paci/n_korea/pmv0209/pyongyang.html.

Ministry of Foreign Affairs of Japan. "Japan-North Korea relations." 2020. https://www.mofa.go.jp/region/asia-paci/n_korea/index.html.

Ministry of Foreign Affairs of Japan. "Japan's Security Policy." 2016. https://www.mofa.go.jp/fp/nsp/page1we_000079.html.

Ministry of Foreign Affairs of the People's Democratic People's Republic of Korea. "Japanese PM Condemned for Taking Issue with DPRK's Test-Fire of Super-large Multiple Rocket Launchers." November 7, 2019. www.mfa.gov.kp/en/japanese-pm-condemned-for-taking-issue-with-dprks-test-fire-of-super-large-multiple-rocket-launchers.

Nilsson-Wright, John. "Nuclear Crisis on the Korean Peninsula: Strategic Adaptation, the Abe Administration and Extended Deterrence in the Face of Uncertainty." *Japan Forum* 31:1 (2019), 110–131.

Nuclear Threat Initiative. "The CNS North Korea Missile Test Database." 2020. https://www.nti.org/analysis/articles/cns-north-korea-missile-test-database/.

Obe, Mitsuru and Okutsu, Akane. "Japan PM Abe announces resignation over worsening health." *Nikkei.* August 28, 2010. https://asia.nikkei.com/Politics/Japan-PM-Abe-announces-resignation-over-worsening-health.

Panda, Ankit. *Kim Jong Un and the Bomb: Survival and Deterrence in North Korea.* Oxford University Press, 2020.

Ri, Chol Hyok. "Japan Should Thoroughly Liquidate Crime-Woven Past." Rodong Sinmun, July 18, 2018. http://www.rodong.rep.kp/en/index.php?strPageID=SF01_02_01&newsID=2018-07-18-0001.

Sakai, Kohei. "首相、イラン訪問に意欲　ロウハニ大統領と会談." Nikkei. September 22, 2016. https://www.nikkei.com/article/DGXLASFS22H0U_S6A920C1PE8000/.

Sanger, David E. "North Koreans Say They Tested Nuclear Device." *The New York Times*, October 9, 2006. https://www.nytimes.com/2006/10/09/world/asia/09korea.html.

Sankei. "【本社　ＦＮＮ合同世論調査】対北制裁「拉致解決まで続けるべき」８３．９％　内閣支持率４０％台回復、不支持に１ポイント差迫る." June 18, 2018. https://www.sankei.com/politics/news/180618/plt1806180043-n1.html.

Son, Key-Young. "Constructing Fear: How the Japanese State Mediates Risks from North Korea." *Japan Forum* 22:1–2 (2010), 169–194.

Sreejith, K.M., Ritesh Agrawal, and A.S. Rajawat. "Constraints on the Location, Depth and Yield of the 2017 September 3 North Korean Nuclear Test from InSAR Measurements and Modelling," *Geophysical Journal International* 220-1 (January 2020), 345–351.

Chapter 11

Testing a Theory to Destruction
Abe's Legacy and Relations with Russia
James D. J. Brown

There is a case to be made that Prime Minister Abe Shinzō was the most pro-Russian leader in Japanese history. In more than two centuries of modern relations, interactions between Japan and its northern neighbor have frequently been characterized by mistrust and conflict; indeed, even today, the countries lack a formal peace treaty to conclude World War II. Given this context, Abe's energetic engagement with Russia is all the more striking.

At the start of his second term in power, Abe left no doubts as to his ambitions. In fact, on the very day of the election on December 16, 2012, Abe announced:

> I consider relations with Russia to be very important. When I was prime minister, I met President Putin several times. President Putin has been re-elected for a second term and I'll also be prime minister for a second time, and we will improve Japan–Russia relations. Moreover, I wish to resolve the territorial problem and sign a peace treaty.[1]

This initial statement was soon followed by Abe's visit to Moscow in April 2013. This was the first state visit by a Japanese leader to Russia in a decade. The image of Abe planting a cherry tree in the Russian capital was also in stark contrast to the bilateral tensions that had prevailed under the Democratic Party of Japan (DPJ), which held power from September 2009 to December 2012. In particular, DPJ Prime Minister Kan Naoto withdrew Japan's ambassador and accused Russia of committing an "unforgivable outrage" after President Dmitry Medvedev visited Kunashir in November 2010.[2] This island is part of the Russian-held Southern Kurils, which are claimed by Japan as its Northern Territories.

Rather than criticizing Russia, Abe made it a habit of offering praise. He described Putin as "a man who keeps a promise" and someone who is "dear to me as a partner."[3] Abe also visited Russia eleven times between April 2013 and September 2019, including four consecutive trips to the annual Eastern Economic Forum in Vladivostok. It was at this venue in 2019 that Abe oversaw the formal conclusion of the purchase by a Japanese consortium of a 10 percent stake in Russia's Arctic LNG-2 project. Valued at up to $5 billion and 75 percent financed by the Japanese state, this energy investment was the largest deal conducted under Abe's 8-point economic cooperation plan with Russia, which was launched in May 2016.

Of greater concern in Western capitals was that Abe's personal courtship of Putin and promotion of economic relations was accompanied by an unwillingness to confront Russia over instances of foreign-policy aggression. After Russia's annexation of Crimea in March 2014, Japan reluctantly followed the United States in introducing sanctions, yet the measures were carefully designed to be merely "symbolic sanctions to avoid any irritations for Moscow."[4] Even more striking was Japan's refusal to respond to the botched assassination of Sergei Skripal with a nerve agent in the British town of Salisbury in March 2018. Tokyo was the only Group of Seven country not to expel Russian diplomats after the attack, which left one member of the public dead. Indeed, when Foreign Minister Sergei Lavrov met his Japanese counterpart in Tokyo in the days after the attack, he was confronted, not with criticism of Russian belligerence, but with a birthday cake.[5]

Another factor that makes Abe's Russia policy remarkable is that it never had much support with key domestic constituencies. For the duration of the policy, there was grumbling within the Liberal Democratic Party (LDP) about Abe's soft stance on the territorial dispute.[6] The Ministry of Foreign Affairs (MOFA) is also reported to have been frustrated by a policy that strayed from Japan's traditional position and from which Japan's diplomats felt side-lined. Furthermore, because of Russia's weak economy and difficult investment climate, few Japanese businesses have been pressing the government for closer engagement. Indeed, it was the Abe administration that sought to persuade companies to adopt a more favorable attitude, including by creating a cabinet position for economic relations with Russia. Lastly, Russia's image among the Japanese public remains negative, with only 25 percent expressing a favorable opinion and 26 percent telling pollsters that they have confidence in Putin to do the right thing regarding world affairs.[7]

This leaves us with a puzzle. Why did Abe adopt a Russia policy that broke with Japanese precedent, frustrated Western partners, and had little support from within the LDP, the bureaucracy, business, or the public? To answer this question, this chapter is divided into three sections. The first outlines in more detail precisely what Abe changed in Japan's Russia policy and analyzes why he did so. The second addresses how Abe made these changes and, most importantly, how he overcame both domestic and international resistance to the policy. Finally, the third section looks at the question of what legacy will remain after Abe's departure. That is to say, will Japan's Russia policy maintain a pro-Russian course or will it revert to a more traditional line?

WHAT DID ABE CHANGE AND WHY?

Abe's friendly rhetoric and frequent visits to Russia certainly altered the atmosphere in bilateral relations, yet did anything fundamental change in Japan's foreign-policy stance? The Abe government insisted not, stressing that Japan's position on the territorial issue—the most prominent between the countries—remained unaltered, which is that Japan will sign a peace treaty with Russia *after* the resolution of the status of the disputed islands.[8] This contrasts with Russia's willingness to sign a peace treaty without preconditions.[9] As such, under Abe's leadership, just as under previous administrations, the absence of a peace treaty was a consequence of Japan's refusal to conclude an agreement until the territorial question has been settled.

Yet, look a little closer and it is evident that policy really did shift under Abe. Specifically during his time as leader, Abe pursued a strategy to secure the return of only two of the four disputed islands.[10] This was never officially confirmed but it is obvious from several steps taken by the Abe government.

Mostly importantly, in November 2018, Abe agreed with Putin to advance peace treaty talks based on the 1956 Joint Declaration. This historic agreement is the closest thing the sides have to a peace treaty. Although described as a "declaration," the agreement was ratified by the legislature in each country and has the status of an international treaty. As well as ending the state of war and removing Soviet opposition to Japanese membership of the United Nations, the 1956 Joint Declaration includes, as article 9, the following commitment:

> The Union of Soviet Socialist Republics, desiring to meet the wishes of Japan and taking into consideration the interests of the Japanese State, agrees to transfer to Japan the Habomai Islands and the island of Shikotan, the actual transfer of these islands to Japan to take place after the conclusion of a Peace Treaty between the Union of Soviet Socialist Republics and Japan.[11]

Crucially, the 1956 Joint Declaration says nothing about the much larger islands of Iturup and Kunashir. Since accepting the offer presented in Article 9 would mean abandoning a full 93 percent of the disputed landmass, previous Japanese governments have regarded the 1956 Joint Declaration as an insufficient basis on which to conduct talks. These preceding administrations have instead sought to also emphasize the 1993 Tokyo Declaration, which explicitly names all four of the islands. Abe's decision to base talks exclusively on the 1956 Joint Declaration was therefore an historic concession.

Further evidence of the Abe government's newly conciliatory stance was provided by its altered rhetoric. It had previously been customary for Japanese ministers to describe the disputed islands as Japan's "inherent territory" and as being "under illegal occupation." Under Abe, cabinet ministers were instructed to avoid these terms so as not to provoke Russia. This led to awkward moments in parliament as the opposition accused the government of an "obvious retreat" and sought to pressure ministers into using the now proscribed terms.[12] Even more striking was the 2019 edition of Japan's official diplomatic Bluebook. Previous editions had clearly stated that "the Four Northern Islands belong to Japan."[13] This line was removed from the 2019 edition. This contrasted with the treatment of Takeshima (known to South Korea as Dokdo), which continued to be described as "Japan's inherent territory" and subject to "illegal occupation" by South Korea.[14]

Although Abe signaled his acceptance of the loss of the two larger islands, he sought a degree of compensation in the form of joint economic projects. These small-scale activities, which would involve both Japanese and Russian companies, were intended by Tokyo as a way of maintaining access to the disputed islands and re-establishing a long-term Japanese presence. In addition, the projects were viewed as a way of bringing economic benefits to the neighboring community around Nemuro (Hokkaidō), which had been the hub of economic activity on the islands until their occupation by Soviet forces in August and September 1945. It is likely that Abe also calculated that these economic benefits would soften opposition to his territorial compromise among Japanese former islanders, many of whom settled in the Nemuro area after their expulsion from the islands following World War II.

When Abe welcomed Putin to his home prefecture of Yamaguchi in December 2016, the sides agreed to begin talks about these joint economic projects on the disputed islands. The next year, when Abe traveled to Vladivostok in September, they decided to focus on five priority areas: aquaculture, greenhouse agriculture, tourism, wind power, and waste reduction. After that, however, progress was minimal as the sides struggled to agree on the legal jurisdiction under which the projects would be conducted and the rules governing Japanese visits to the islands. By 2020, all that had been achieved was one pilot tourism trip in October 2019 and reciprocal visits by waste management officials.

Overall, Abe's Russia's policy can be characterized as having aimed for "two plus alpha," meaning the return of the two smaller islands plus joint economic projects. However, why did Abe decide to wholeheartedly embrace this agenda during his second stint as prime minister? After all, as well as the policy lacking domestic support, territorial concessions go against the grain for a Japanese leader with a nationalist reputation. Three factors appear to have been particularly influential.

First, it should be noted that "two plus alpha" was not an invention of Abe's. It has existed for over two decades and is particularly associated with Suzuki Muneo, a controversial politician from Hokkaidō. Suzuki was an LDP member of the House of Representatives during the 1990s and was appointed head of the Hokkaidō and Okinawa Development Agencies in 1997. He also became deputy chief cabinet secretary in the government of Obuchi Keizō in 1998. In these positions, Suzuki was a powerful proponent of closer relations with Russia and of joint economic projects on the disputed islands. His influence was curtailed when he was forced to resign from the LDP in 2002 due to corruption allegations, which eventually resulted in his imprisonment in 2010. However, after serving two years, he rebuilt his political career and, in December 2015, was sought out by Abe to serve as an informal adviser on Russia policy, even though Suzuki was still serving a five-year suspension from public office. After that, Suzuki was regularly called to the Kantei (the prime minister's office) to consult with Abe, especially in advance of prime ministerial visits to Russia. Suzuki's remarkable comeback was completed in July 2019 when, following the expiry of his suspension from public office, he secured election to the House of Councilors as a representative of Nippon Ishin no Kai, a right-wing populist party.[15]

Given the regularity of Suzuki's consultations with Abe, it is likely that he exerted some influence over the Japanese government's tactics. However, the importance of Suzuki should not be exaggerated. Rather than Suzuki convincing the prime minister to adopt the "two plus alpha" position, it is more probable that Abe had already convinced himself that this was the most feasible plan for resolving the territorial dispute and therefore sought the guidance of its most prominent advocate. Suzuki's function is therefore most likely to have been in reinforcing Abe's existing beliefs and in offering to use his network of Russian contacts in support of the prime minister's efforts.

A more decisive factor in shaping Abe's thinking was surely national security. There is no doubt that strategists in Tokyo see Japan's security situation as increasingly precarious. This relates to North Korea's nuclear and missile programs, but even more so to China's growing assertiveness in the South and East China Seas, and especially with regard to the Senkaku Islands, which China claims as the Diaoyu Islands. The problem is exacerbated by the relative decline of the United States, as well as by the "America First" foreign policy of President Donald Trump, which placed little value on the U.S.'s alliances. In response, Abe sought to supplement the alliance with the

United States with closer security partnerships with other countries, including Australia and India.

With respect to Russia, the aim was less to develop a true security partnership than to eliminate problems in the relationship. This link between the regional security situation and Japan's desire for closer ties with Russia is made explicit in the National Security Strategy of December 2013, which states, "Under the increasingly severe security environment in East Asia, it is critical for Japan to advance cooperation with Russia in all areas, including security and energy, thereby enhancing bilateral relations as a whole, in order to ensure its security."[16] More specifically, the calculation was that stability in relations on Japan's northern border would enable Tokyo to concentrate on the security threats posed by China and North Korea. In addition, there was the hope that warmer relations would provide Tokyo with opportunities to encourage Moscow to distance itself from Beijing, thereby neutralizing the danger of a genuine alliance between China and Russia.[17]

In light of these security motivations, Abe's desperation to resolve the territorial dispute begins to make more sense. The Southern Kurils/Northern Territories issue is the most obvious obstacle to closer relations between Tokyo and Moscow. Abe's logic appears to have been that accepting a compromise in order to resolve the territorial dispute was a price worth paying for the strategic benefits of a full normalization in relations with Russia.

Although security considerations were seemingly decisive in shaping Abe's Russia policy, personal factors also played a role, including the influence of Abe's father. Abe Shintarō served as Japanese foreign minister from 1982 to 1986, then as general secretary of the LDP from 1987 to 1989. In these roles, and even after he had stepped back from frontline politics, Abe Shintarō remained committed to achieving a breakthrough in relations with the Soviet Union. Ahead of a visit to Moscow in January 1990, he told Ikeda Daisaku, president of Sōka Gakkai: "The Gorbachev era is really a chance for a Japan–Soviet peace treaty. Even if it costs me my life, I want to achieve this."[18] This was not melodramatic language since Abe Shintarō was seriously ill with cancer. Despite fading health, he made one final attempt to achieve a normalization in relations during Soviet President Mikhail Gorbachev's historic visit to Japan in April 1991. As described by Taniguchi Tomohiko, special adviser to Prime Minister Abe, the former foreign minister "put on a padded jacket to conceal his extreme weight loss and rose from his bed to meet the visiting Russian leader. That was Shintaro Abe's last public appearance before his death; his determination to reach an agreement with the Soviets proved fruitless."[19]

This heroic effort had a profound effect on Abe Shinzō. He has spoken of his desire to complete his father's unfulfilled ambitions with regard to Russia, and, during a visit to his father's grave in January 2019, Abe told waiting journalists, "I vowed, no matter what, to move forward with the Northern Territories and peace treaty issues, and to continue to make every effort to put an end to these problems."[20] Abe also credits his father with shaping his thinking about Russia, telling an interviewer in May 2018:

> When I hear the words "Russia" or "Russians", the first thing that comes to mind is the image of a very patient and extremely strong-willed people. My first experience of personal communication with Russians was when I visited your country with my father. . . . On the eve of that trip he told me that Russians value friendship and sincerity, and that they absolutely keep their word.[21]

The parallels between the policies endorsed by Abe Shintarō and Shinzō are also unmistakable. Shintarō promoted an approach described as "creative diplomacy" and prioritized fostering a relationship of trust with Mikhail Gorbachev. Instead of holding back economic cooperation until Moscow offered political concessions, Shintarō encouraged an immediate deepening of economic ties as a means of providing a stronger basis for bilateral relations, which, he hoped, would ultimately lead to resolution of the territorial dispute.[22] All of these are also prominent features of the "new approach" launched by Abe Shinzō in May 2016. What is more, both men were careful to avoid provoking Moscow over the territorial issue. As noted, Abe Shinzō instructed his cabinet in February 2019 to stop using the terms "inherent territory" and "under illegal occupation" to describe the disputed islands. Likewise, Abe Shintarō avoided mentioning "the territorial dispute" when meeting Gorbachev in January 1990, obliquely referring instead to "the difficult issue."[23] Lastly, Abe Shintarō had his own 8-point plan for economic and cultural cooperation with Moscow, with several similarities to the identically numbered plan promoted by his son over two decades later.[24]

A separate point in the category of personal motivations is the issue of legacy. All leaders want to leave their mark, and this desire appears to have been especially strong with Abe Shinzō. He failed to achieve anything of substance during his first disappointing stint as prime minister from September 2006 to September 2007. Having unexpectedly regained the leadership of the LDP in 2012, Abe seems to have been determined that he would not again miss the opportunity to inscribe his name in the history books. This was perhaps amplified by an eagerness to match the achievements of other prominent members of his family. When prime minister from 1957 to 1960, Kishi Nobusuke, Abe's grandfather, succeeded in driving through the controversial revision of the U.S.–Japan Security Treaty, although he was forced to resign shortly afterward. Also, Abe's great uncle, Satō Eisaku, who was prime minister from 1964 to 1972, secured the reversion of Okinawa to Japanese administration after a quarter century under U.S. control. The desire for a comparable legacy can only have intensified as Abe passed all of his predecessors to become the longest-serving prime minister in Japanese history.

Within the realm of foreign policy, Abe frequently emphasized that it was his priority to deliver "a complete settlement of post-war diplomacy and to establish a new era of Japanese diplomacy."[25] From the perspective of the Japanese government, there are two main, unresolved issues affecting post-war relations between Japan and its neighbors. The first is the abduction of Japanese citizens by North Korea during the 1970s and 1980s. In 2002, Pyongyang admitted responsibility for the abductions and permitted five abductees to return to Japan. The Japanese government, however, believes that there are at least another twelve victims and demands that Pyongyang provide a full account of their whereabouts. This issue has contributed to the absence of formal diplomatic relations between Japan and the Democratic People's Republic of North Korea (DPRK). The second major unresolved issue is the territorial dispute with Russia.[26]

When Abe first rose to public attention in the early 2000s—during his time as deputy chief cabinet secretary to Prime Minister Koizumi Jun'ichirō—it was a consequence of his activist stance on the abductees issue. After returning to the prime minister's office in December 2012, Abe resumed efforts to engage with North Korea. This resulted in intergovernmental consultations in Stockholm in May 2014 at which North Korea promised a full-scale investigation into the fate of all relevant Japanese nationals. In response, Japan promised to lift some of its unilateral sanctions. However, following the DPRK's nuclear test in January 2016 and Japan's announcement of further sanctions, Pyongyang declared that it would completely cease all investigations.[27] Although Abe subsequently offered to meet DPRK leader Kim Jong-un "without setting preconditions," the North Korea side did not reciprocate.[28] This absence of progress on the abductees issue after 2014 is another reason why Abe increasingly focused on the territorial dispute with Russia as the most promising area for a legacy-defining breakthrough.

How Did Abe Implement His Russia Policy?

Abe's motivations are important, but just as interesting is how he proceeded with the implementation of the policy. After all, as noted above, Abe's "new approach" to Russia always had many critics both within Japan and among Japan's international partners. To be able to persist with the policy over the course of several years, it was therefore necessary for Abe to shield it from criticism.

Domestically, Abe had the good fortune to be in power at a time of limited political competition. This applies to the parliamentary opposition, which found itself in a protracted period of disarray and fragmentation after its unhappy time in power from 2009 to 2012. It also applies to the LDP itself. In other eras, there have often been several big beasts within the party, all jostling for their turn in the top job. This has contributed to the brief tenure of many Japanese leaders. However, in Abe's case, his second stint as prime minister coincided with a period when several leading figures did not covet his job, either because they had already done it (Asō Tarō) or they were superannuated (Nikai Toshihiro). Furthermore, those who did actively desire to become prime minister—Kishida Fumio and Ishiba Shigeru—were unable to force the issue since neither inspired much enthusiasm within the LDP or wider public. This weakness of inter-party and intra-party competition was convenient for Abe, enabling him to continue with a controversial and under-performing foreign policy, which a prime minister facing more challengers would have been forced to drop.

A second factor that contributed to Abe's unusually free hand was the status of relations between the executive and bureaucracy. Traditionally, Japan's MOFA took a leading role, not only in the implementation of foreign policy but also in its formulation. Indeed, the actions of ministers who sought to change long-held policy positions or shape personnel decisions were viewed as unwarranted inference in Japan's foreign policy by unqualified amateurs. The most famous case of this was the open conflict that broke out between Foreign Minister Tanaka Makiko and senior MOFA diplomats, who regarded her as a foreign policy neophyte and objected to her attempts to return Japan's Russia policy to the position promoted by her father, Tanaka Kakuei, who was prime minister from 1972 to 1974. The tensions became so great that Prime Minister Koizumi was forced to sack Tanaka Makiko in January 2002 and to demote Vice Minister Nogami Yoshiji.[29]

Since those times, control over foreign policy has shifted markedly toward the prime minister's office. This owes much to Koizumi himself, who, by the time he left office in 2006, had pioneered a system of foreign policymaking in which the prime minister's office played a much more active role. This came to be known as "Kantei diplomacy."[30] The power of the prime minister over the bureaucracy was further strengthened by efforts of the DPJ-led government to centralize decision-making power in the hands of elected officials. These reforms were only partially successful but, after returning to power, Abe capitalized on the trend by creating the Cabinet Bureau of Personnel Affairs in 2014. Headed by a prime ministerial appointee, this office is responsible for appointing over 600 key officials, thereby ensuring that the senior bureaucracy is much more tightly controlled by the political leadership than had been the case in the past.[31]

These systemic changes enabled Japan's Russia policy under Abe to be run directly out of the Kantei, and the level of control only increased with time. Harada Chikahito, a former ambassador to Moscow, served as Abe's special representative for relations with Russia and was thereby able to exert some MOFA influence. However, Harada resigned in March 2017, allegedly due to differences over policy direction.[32] This still left Yachi Shotarō, who had been a MOFA administrative vice minister before becoming the first head of Japan's National Security Secretariat (NSS). In this role, Yachi conducted regular talks with Nikolai Patrushev, secretary of the Russian Security Council. Yet, Yachi never appeared at ease with Abe's Russia policy and he had disagreements with Imai Takaya, Abe's executive secretary and a former bureaucrat from the Ministry of Economy, Trade, and Industry (METI).[33] After retiring in September 2019, Yachi appeared to vent his frustration about talks with Russia, telling an interviewer that "There aren't any prospects we can open up. There is nothing else we can do to make progress."[34] Yachi was replaced as NSS chief by Kitamura Shigeru, an Abe loyalist with a background in the National Police Agency and who had served as head of the Cabinet Intelligence and Research Office (CIRO). Kitamura immediately got to work on Russia policy and met with Patrushev within days of his appointment. Aside from Imai and Kitamura, the other prominent figure was Hasegawa Eiichi, another special adviser to Abe and former METI official. Hasegawa was given specific responsibility for realizing joint economic projects on the disputed islands. During the last years of the Abe administration, MOFA was therefore side-lined on Russia policy, bearing the burden of organizing Abe's endless meetings with Putin, yet with no influence over policy direction.

Incidentally, Abe's lack of confidence in MOFA also seems to be a family trait. Before meeting Gorbachev in January 1990, Abe Shintarō stated that "in our relationship with the Soviet Union, I have to show the statesmanship which our Foreign Ministry cannot."[35] It is also no coincidence that Abe Shinzō favors advisers from METI, the ministry in which his revered grandfather, Kishi Nobusuke, served as both vice minister and minister.[36]

Lastly, on the domestic front, it is necessary to consider the Abe administration's management of public opinion. It might be assumed that there would have been a backlash against Abe's pursuit of a two-island deal, which entailed the abandonment of the vast majority of the Northern Territories. However, this problem was avoided through the simple expedient of keeping the public in the dark.

To those who looked closely at Abe's agreement with Putin in November 2018 or who examined the wording of the diplomatic Bluebook, it was obvious that Abe had significantly softened Japan's stance on the territorial dispute. However, the Abe government never admitted to any shift and continued to insist that the official position remained unchanged. What is more, ministers refused to answer questions on Japan's negotiating position. Most blunt in this regard was Kōno Tarō, who served as Abe's foreign minister from 2017 to 2019. At a press conference in December 2018, Kōno repeatedly refused to answer questions about peace treaty talks with Russia, saying "Next question, please" on four successive occasions.[37] He was no more forthcoming in parliament, stating that, "Outside of the negotiations, I will refrain from speaking about the government's policy and way of thinking."[38]

This bald refusal to discuss even the broad outlines of the government's policy is remarkable in a country that is supposed to operate as a liberal democracy. The approach would also have faced difficulties if Abe and Putin had actually signed a peace treaty that prepared the way for the transfer of just two islands. At that stage, an unprepared and unconsulted public would surely have railed against the government's capitulation. However, since an agreement was never reached, the Abe administration's attempt to achieve a two-island deal with Russia was never exposed to extensive public scrutiny.

As well as domestic opposition, the Abe administration had to contend with international criticism. This was a particular risk since Abe's attentive courting of Putin coincided with growing tensions between Moscow and the West, especially over Russia's annexation of Crimea, shooting down of Malaysian Airlines MH-17, cyber-attacks on the German parliament, interference in the 2016 U.S. presidential election, and other similarly controversial actions. In a phone call in February 2016, U.S. President Barack Obama did warn Abe that "now is not the time" to visit Russia. However, with Obama in the twilight of his presidency, the Japanese leader felt he could ignore this advice.[39] In the second half of 2016, Abe went ahead and accelerated his engagement with Russia. This is because the period before the inauguration of the new U.S. president in January 2017 was viewed as a window of opportunity. With Hillary Clinton, a noted Russia hawk, considered the likely election winner, it was thought that the new U.S. administration would pressure Japan to adopt a tougher stance. Instead, Donald Trump's surprise victory gave Abe's Russia policy a new lease of life. Given Trump's complex relationship with Russia and consistent support for closer ties, he was never going to criticize Abe's own efforts at rapprochement.

Safe from criticism from the United States, the Abe administration was able to shrug off expressions of concern from other Western capitals. For example, even though the U.K. foreign secretary and prime minister personally sought to persuade their Japanese counterparts to join the more than twenty countries that expelled Russian diplomats after the Skripal case, Tokyo remained unmoved. Still, Japan did take some steps to placate critics. For instance, prior to his meeting with Putin in Sochi in May 2016, Abe played host to Ukrainian President Petro Poroshenko. Also, just ahead of Putin's arrival in Japan in December 2016, Abe called Poroshenko to reassure the Ukrainian leader about the intended subject of the talks.[40] A similar degree of balance was shown elsewhere. While Japan avoided criticizing Russia directly, Tokyo did agree to sign G-7 joint statements, including those in 2018 that condemned "a pattern of irresponsible and destabilizing Russian behaviour" and that which reprimanded Russia for its forcible seizure of Ukrainian vessels in the Kerch Strait.[41] As with the adoption of symbolic sanctions in 2014, the Abe government's intention was to demonstrate a basic alignment with G-7 foreign policy, yet, at the same time, to avoid antagonizing Moscow.

What is Abe's Legacy When it Comes to Japan's Relations with Russia?

Unlike many of his short-lived predecessors, Prime Minister Abe was able to pursue a consistent foreign policy with Russia and to insulate it from domestic and international criticism. In so doing, Abe was able to accrue a remarkable twenty-seven meetings with President Putin by September 2019. Yet, the success of a foreign policy is not measured in the quantity of encounters. Judged in terms of substantive achievements, Abe's Russia policy must be considered a conspicuous failure.

Abe marked his return to power in 2012 with a commitment to resolving the territorial dispute and signing a peace treaty. However, at the end of his time in office, these goals are as distant as ever. Even the small-scale joint economic projects on the disputed islands, on which talks were initiated in December 2016, proved impossible to implement due to disagreements over legal jurisdiction.

Furthermore, rather than simply being left empty-handed, Abe was humiliated in his dealings with Russia. Despite Abe's shift to a soft stance on the territorial issue, his reluctance to criticize Russian foreign policy, and his attentive courting of Putin, there was no reciprocation. Instead, Moscow's position only hardened, including with the demand that, prior to any agreement, Japan must accept Russia's right to sovereignty over all of the Southern Kurils.[42] Additionally, the Russian leadership took several steps that appeared designed to embarrass the Japanese prime minister. When Abe invited Putin to his home prefecture of Yamaguchi—an honor that was not extended to either President Obama or Trump—the Russian leader arrived three hours late. Moreover, during Abe's visit to the Eastern Economic Forum in Vladivostok in September 2019, Putin took the opportunity to preside (via videolink) over the opening of a fish-processing factory on the Japanese-claimed island of Shikotan. This is despite the fact that, less than a year earlier, Putin had agreed to advance peace treaty talks on the basis of the 1956 Joint Declaration, in which Moscow explicitly promises to transfer Shikotan and Habomai to Japan. Lastly, a further slap in the face was delivered by Russia's revised constitution that was approved by referendum in July 2020.

The purpose of this revision was to reset Putin's term limits so that he can stand again for president in 2024. Yet, the draft also included several further amendments that were designed to rally patriotic support among the public. One of the additions was a clause to ban all territorial concessions. This was a blunt demonstration of how little Abe's claimed "personal trust relationship" with Putin was really worth.[43]

Although Abe's engagement with Russia was a clear failure, it holds lessons for subsequent Japanese prime ministers. Specifically, there has long been the theory that an acceptable territorial deal remained a possibility if only a Japanese leader showed sufficient flexibility and commitment. Advocates of this position, who include Suzuki Muneo and a couple of former MOFA officials, point to Prime Minister Mori Yoshirō's negotiations with Putin at the start of the new millennium and suggest that, had Mori not been replaced by Koizumi Jun'ichirō in April 2001, a deal with Russia could have been achieved. Indeed, Suzuki claims that, before Koizumi reverted to a more conventional four-island approach, "The return of the Northern Territories was before our eyes."[44]

This theory has now been tested to destruction. No Japanese leader could have offered more concessions or have more assiduously cultivated ties with Russia. Yet, rather than achieving the expected breakthrough, Japan's conciliatory stance simply led to heightened Russian demands, including in relation to U.S. forces deployed on Japanese territory.[45] The reality has therefore been demonstrated that Russia has no intention of agreeing to even a two-island deal. Instead, Moscow evidently finds value in the unresolved territorial dispute as a source of leverage over Japanese foreign policy, including as a means of driving a wedge between Tokyo and Washington.[46] So long as an element of hope remains, there may be a temptation for Japanese leaders to offer political and economic engagement with Russia. By contrast, were the dispute to be conclusively resolved, Japan would be free to adopt a more resolute stance vis-à-vis its northern neighbor.

Overall, Prime Minister Abe introduced a notable shift in Japanese foreign policy toward Russia by communicating his willingness to settle for a "two plus alpha" solution to the territorial dispute. Abe also kept tight control over the policy within the Kantei and successfully insulated it from domestic and international criticism. Nonetheless, Abe's efforts ended in disappointment. His legacy in this area is therefore that of a salutary lesson. Future Japanese leaders are still likely to recognize the security rationale for fully normalizing relations with Russia. They are also likely to inherit a foreign-policy decision-making system that is more closely controlled by the prime minister's office than was traditionally the case in Japan. All the same, lacking Abe's personal commitment to this policy area and learning from his visible failure to achieve any progress, subsequent prime ministers are unlikely to pursue engagement with Russia with comparable enthusiasm.

NOTES

1. Vladimir Putin's election victory in March 2012 actually heralded the start of his third term as Russian president. See Ksenia Naka, "Budushchii prem'er Yaponii Abe nameren ukreplyat' otnosheniya s Rossiei" [Future Premier of Japan Abe Intends to Strengthen Relations with Russia], *RIA Novosti*, December 16, 2012. https://ria.ru/20121216/915013917.html.

2. *Asahi Shimbun*, "Hoppōryōdonohi ni Kan shushō 'Roshia daitōryō no Kunashiri hōmon wa bōkyo'" [PM Kan on Day of the Northern Territories: 'Russian president's visit to Kunashiri is an outrage'], February 7, 2011. http://www.asahi.com/special/minshu/TKY201102070453.html.

3. Kirill Agafonov, "Abe schitayet Putina derzhashchim obeshchaniye chelovekom" [Abe considers Putin a person who keeps a promise], *TASS*, February 13. 2017. https://tass.ru/mezhdunarodnaya-panorama/4019491.

4. Maria Shagina, "Japan's dilemma with sanctions policy towards Russia," *Focus Asia*, November 2018. https://isdp.eu/content/uploads/2018/11/Japans-Delicate-Balancing-Act-FA-FINAL.pdf.

5. James D.J. Brown, "Japan and the Skripal poisoning: The U.K.'s fair-weather friend," *Japan Times*, March 27, 2018. https://www.japantimes.co.jp/opinion/2018/03/27/commentary/japan-commentary/japan-skripal-poisoning-u-k-s-fair-weather-friend/.

6. *Hokkaidō Shimbun*, "Gaikō seisho no 'shijima kizoku' sakujo Jimin kara hihan aitsugu" [Deletion of 'ownership of the 4 islands' from the diplomatic Bluebook - A succession of criticism from the LDP], May 11, 2019. https://www.hokkaido-np.co.jp/article/303993.

7. Christine Huang and Jeremiah Cha, "Russia and Putin receive low ratings globally," Pew Research, February 7, 2020. https://www.pewresearch.org/fact-tank/2020/02/07/russia-and-putin-receive-low-ratings-globally/.

8. Gaimushō, "Gaikō Seisho 2020," May 2020, 8. https://www.mofa.go.jp/mofaj/gaiko/bluebook/2020/html/index.html.

9. Denis Pinchuk and Polina Nikolskaya, "Russia's Putin tells Japan's Abe: 'Let's sign peace deal this year'," *Reuters*, September 12, 2018. https://www.reuters.com/article/us-russia-economy-forum-putin-treaty/russias-putin-tells-japans-abe-lets-sign-peace-deal-this-year.

10. The disputed islands consist of Iturup (known as Etorofu in Japanese), Kunashir (known as Kunashiri in Japanese), Shikotan (which has the same name in both languages), and the islets of the Lesser Kuril Chain (which Japan refers to as the Habomai group). For convenience, it is customary to refer to a four-island dispute.

11. Full text of the 1956 Joint Declaration is provided in GRIPS, "The World and Japan Database," https://worldjpn.grips.ac.jp/documents/texts/docs/19561019.D1E.html.

12. *Hokkaidō Shinbun*, "CDP representative Edano: 'Obvious retreat' on Northern Territories issue," June 28, 2019. https://www.hokkaido-np.co.jp/article/319773.

13. Gaimushō, "Gaikō Seisho 2018," May 2018. https://www.mofa.go.jp/mofaj/gaiko/bluebook/2018/html/chapter2_05_01.html#s251.

14. Gaimushō, "Gaikō Seisho 2019," April 2019, 35, 112, https://www.mofa.go.jp/mofaj/gaiko/bluebook/2019/html/index.html.

15. James D.J. Brown, "Japan–Russia Relations and the Miraculous Revival of Suzuki Muneo," *The Asia-Pacific Journal: Japan Focus* 17, issue 18, no. 3 (September 15, 2019). https://apjjf.org/2019/18/Brown.html.

16. Cabinet Secretariat, "National Security Strategy," December 17, 2013, 25. https://www.cas.go.jp/jp/siryou/131217anzenhoshou/nss-e.pdf.

17. James D.J. Brown, "Japan's security cooperation with Russia: neutralizing the threat of a China–Russia united front," *International Affairs* 94, no. 4 (July 2018): 861–882.

18. Asada Masafumi, "Naze Abe shushō ni totte Roshia wa kon'nani 'tokubetsuna sonzai' na no ka" [Why is Russia so 'special' for Prime Minister Abe?], *Gendai Shinsho*, June 14, 2018. https://gendai.ismedia.jp/articles/-/56100?media=gs.

19. Tomohiko Taniguchi and Daniel Bob, "The onsen summit: Why Abe is seeking a settlement with Russia," *The National Interest*, December 14, 2016. https://nationalinterest.org/feature/why-abe-seeking-settlement-russia-18739.

20. Abe Shinzō, *Utsukushii kuni e* [Toward a Beautiful Country], Tokyo: Bungei Shunju, 2006, 34–37; *Sankei Shimbun*, "Abe shinzō shushō, bōfu e nichiro no zenshin chikau" [Prime Minister Abe Shinzō vows to his late father to move forward Japan–Russia relations], January 6, 2019, https://www.sankei.com/politics/news/190106/plt1901060003-n1.html.

21. Sergei Brilev, "Rossiya i Yaponiya delayut upor na meditsinu i 'umnye' tekhnologii" [Russia and Japan focus on medicine and 'smart' technologies], Vesti.ru, May 19, 2018. https://www.vesti.ru/doc.html?id=3019119.

22. Junjiro Isomura, "Shintaro Abe's 'creative diplomacy'," in *'Northern Territories' and Beyond: Russian, Japanese, and American Perspectives*, edited by J.E. Goodby, V.I. Ivanov, and N. Shimotomai. Westport: Praeger, 1995.

23. *Mainichi Shimbun*, "HP wa `Ro ga fuhō senkyo' naikaku-fu, keisai keizoku" [Cabinet Office continues to publish 'illegal occupation by Russia' on its website], February 26, 2019. https://mainichi.jp/articles/20190226/ddm/005/010/033000c.

24. Isomura, "Shintaro Abe's 'creative diplomacy'," 87–89.

25. Shusōkantei, "Dai nihyakuikkai kokkai ni okeru Abe naikakusōri daijin shisei hōshin enzetsu" [Policy Speech by the Prime Minister to the 201st Session of the Diet], January 20, 2020. https://www.kantei.go.jp/jp/98_abe/statement/2020/0120shiseihoushin.html.

26. Japan, of course, also has unsettled post-war issues with South Korea and China. However, according to the official position of the Japanese government, all wartime issues with the Republic of Korea were "settled completely and finally" with the signing of the Treaty on Basic Relations in 1965. Additionally, Japan denies the existence of any dispute with China over the sovereignty of the Senkaku Islands.

27. Ministry of Foreign Affairs of Japan, "Talks between Japan and North Korea on the Abductions Issue," December 28, 2018. https://www.mofa.go.jp/a_o/na/kp/page1we_000069.html.

28. *Reuters*, "Japan's Abe signals shift on North Korea, says will meet Kim without conditions: media," May 3, 2019. https://jp.reuters.com/article/us-northkorea-japan-abe/japans-abe-signals-shift-on-north-korea-says-will-meet-kim-without-conditions-media.

29. Masaru Satō, *Kokka no Wana* [The Trap of the State], Tōkyō: Shinchōsa, 2005, 94–101.

30. Tomohito Shinoda, *Koizumi Diplomacy: Japan's Kantei Approach to Foreign and Defense Affairs*, Seattle: University of Washington Press, 2007.

31. Mayu Terada, "The Changing Nature of Bureaucracy and Governing Structure in Japan," *Washington International Law Journal* 431 (2019).

32. *Mainichi Shinbun*, "Tairo gaikō tantō Harada-shi tainin e getsunai ni mo" [Harada, with responsibility for diplomacy with Russia, to step down within the month], March 22, 2017. https://mainichi.jp/articles/20170322/ddm/005/010/065000c.

33. *Asahi Shimbun*, "Abe names close aides to key security posts, raising concerns," September 24, 2019. http://www.asahi.com/ajw/articles/AJ201909240057.html.

34. *Sankei Shinbun*, "Yachi zen kokka anzen hoshō kyokuchō 'Roshia wa mujōken teiketsu yōkyū' heiwa jōyaku kōshō de" [Yachi, former head of National Security Secretariat: 'Russia demanded uncondition conclusion' in peace treaty talks], January 24, 2020. https://www.sankei.com/politics/news/200124/plt2001240047-n1.html.

35. Isomura, "Shintaro Abe's 'creative diplomacy'," 86.

36. During Kishi's time as minister and vice minister, what later became MITI (then METI) was known as the Ministry of Commerce and Industry (until 1943), then the Ministry of Munitions (1943–1945).

37. Reiji Yoshida, "Foreign Minister Taro Kono repeatedly ignores questions on Russian-held islands ahead of talks on WWII treaty," *The Japan Times*, December 12, 2018. https://www.japantimes.co.jp/news/2018/12/12/national/politics-diplomacy/taro-kono-no-comment-russia-held-islands-ahead-possible-wwii-treaty-talks/.

38. Quoted in *Sankei Shinbun*, "'Shuken o yūsuru shimajima' ha hoppōyontō? Soretomo nitō?" [Are the 'sovereign islands' the 'Four Northern Islands" Or two islands?], June 14, 2020. https://news.yahoo.co.jp/articles/2cb926a3c3ac05bae32874061fbe3f80e0474aeb.

39. Ksenia Naka, "Istochnik: prem'yer Yaponii otkazalsya ot soveta Obamy ne yezdit' v Rossiyu" [Source: Japanese PM rejects Obama's advice not to travel to Russia], *RIA Novosti*, February 23, 2016. https://ria.ru/20160223/1379198257.html.

40. Ivan Zakharchenko, "Abe rasskazal Poroshenko, o chem on budet govorit' s Putinym" [Abe told Poroshenko what he will talk to Putin about], *RIA Novosti*, December 9, 2016. https://ria.ru/20161209/1483237870.html.

41. Ministry of Foreign Affairs of Japan, "G7 Foreign Ministers' joint communiqué," April 2, 2018. https://www.mofa.go.jp/mofaj/files/000357958.pdf.

42. Junnosuke Kobara, "Russia demands that Japan first accept its sovereignty over islands," *Nikkei Asian Review*, January 15, 2019. https://asia.nikkei.com/Politics/International-relations/Russia-demands-Japan-first-accept-its-sovereignty-over-islands.
43. Toko Sekiguchi, "Abe seeks to build trust with Putin in Sochi," *The Wall Street Journal*, February 6, 2014. https://www.wsj.com/articles/abe-eyes-more-trustbuilding-with-putin-in-sochi-1391668569.
44. Muneo Suzuki, *Seiji no Shuraba* [Political Carnage], Tōkyō: Bungei Shunjū, 2012, 197.
45. *Asahi Shimbun*, "Hoppōryōdo ni beigun, pūchin-shi keikai" [Putin warns of the US military on the Northern Territories], November 16, 2018. https://digital.asahi.com/articles/ASLCH4VL1LCHUTFK00T.html.
46. James D.J. Brown, "Putting a spoke in the wheel: Russian efforts to weaken U.S.-led alliance structures in Northeast Asia," *Korea Economic Institute of America*, Academic Paper Series, June 18, 2020.

REFERENCES

Abe, Shinzō. "Sindzo Abe: Prezident Putin mne dorog kak partner, s nim mozhno pogovorit' po dusham" [Abe Shinzō: President Putin is dear to me as a partner, it's possible to speak with him heart-to-heart]. Interview by Mikhail Gusman. *TASS*, November 25, 2018. https://tass.ru/interviews/5826060.

Abe, Shinzō. *Utsukushii kuni e* [Toward a Beautiful Country]. Tokyo: Bungei Shunju, 2006.

Agafonov, Kirill. "Abe schitayet Putina derzhashchim obeshchaniye chelovekom" [Abe considers Putin a person who keeps a promise]. *TASS*, February 13. 2017. https://tass.ru/mezhdunarodnaya-panorama/4019491.

Asahi Shimbun. "Abe names close aides to key security posts, raising concerns." September 24, 2019. http://www.asahi.com/ajw/articles/AJ201909240057.html.

Asahi Shimbun. "Hoppōryōdo ni beigun, pūchin-shi keikai" [Putin warns of the US military on the Northern Territories]. November 16, 2018. https://digital.asahi.com/articles/ASLCH4VL1LCHUTFK00T.html.

Asahi Shimbun. "Hoppōryōdonohi ni Kan shushō 'Roshia daitōryō no Kunashiri hōmon wa bōkyo' [PM Kan on Day of the Northern Territories: 'Russian president's visit to Kunashiri is an outrage']. February 7, 2011. http://www.asahi.com/special/minshu/TKY201102070453.html.

Brilev, Sergei. "Rossiya i Yaponiya delayut upor na meditsinu i 'umnye' tekhnologii" [Russia and Japan focus on medicine and 'smart' technologies]. Vesti.ru, May 19, 2018. https://www.vesti.ru/doc.html?id=3019119.

Brown, James D.J. "Japan and the Skripal poisoning: The U.K.'s fair-weather friend." *Japan Times*, March 27, 2018. https://www.japantimes.co.jp/opinion/2018/03/27/commentary/japan-commentary/japan-skripal-poisoning-u-k-s-fair-weather-friend/.

Brown, James D.J. "Japan-Russia Relations and the Miraculous Revival of Suzuki Muneo." *The Asia-Pacific Journal: Japan Focus* 17, issue 18, no. 3 (September 15, 2019). https://apjjf.org/2019/18/Brown.html.

Brown, James D.J. "Japan's security cooperation with Russia: neutralizing the threat of a China–Russia united front." *International Affairs* 94, no. 4 (July 2018): 861–882.
Brown, James D.J. "Putting a spoke in the wheel: Russian efforts to weaken U.S.-led alliance structures in Northeast Asia." *Korea Economic Institute of America*, Academic Paper Series, June 18, 2020. http://www.keia.org/sites/default/files/publications/kei_aps_2020_brown_200618.pdf.
Cabinet Secretariat. "National Security Strategy." December 17, 2013, 25. https://www.cas.go.jp/jp/siryou/131217anzenhoshou/nss-e.pdf.
Gaimushō, "Gaikō Seisho 2018." May 2018. https://www.mofa.go.jp/mofaj/gaiko/bluebook/2018/html/chapter2_05_01.html#s251.
Gaimushō. "Gaikō Seisho 2019." April 2019, 35, 112, https://www.mofa.go.jp/mofaj/gaiko/bluebook/2019/html/index.html.
Gaimushō. "Gaikō Seisho 2020." May 2020, 8. https://www.mofa.go.jp/mofaj/gaiko/bluebook/2020/html/index.html.
GRIPS. "The World and Japan Database." https://worldjpn.grips.ac.jp/documents/texts/docs/19561019.D1E.html.
Hokkaido Shimbun. "CDP representative Edano: 'Obvious retreat' on Northern Territories issue." June 28, 2019. https://www.hokkaido-np.co.jp/article/319773.
Hokkaidō Shimbun. "Gaikō seisho no 'shijima kizoku' sakujo Jimin kara hihan aitsugu" [Deletion of 'ownership of the 4 islands' from the diplomatic Bluebook - A succession of criticism from the LDP]. May 11, 2019. https://www.hokkaido-np.co.jp/article/303993.
Huang, Christine and Jeremiah Cha. "Russia and Putin receive low ratings globally." Pew Research, February 7, 2020. https://www.pewresearch.org/fact-tank/2020/02/07/russia-and-putin-receive-low-ratings-globally/.
Isomura, Junjiro. "Shintaro Abe's 'creative diplomacy'." In *'Northern Territories' and Beyond: Russian, Japanese, and American Perspectives*, edited by J.E. Goodby, V.I. Ivanov, and N. Shimotomai. Westport: Praeger, 1995.
Kobara, Junnosuke. "Russia demands that Japan first accept its sovereignty over islands." *Nikkei Asian Review*, January 15, 2019. https://asia.nikkei.com/Politics/International-relations/Russia-demands-Japan-first-accept-its-sovereignty-over-islands.
Mainichi Shimbun. "HP wa 'Ro ga fuhō senkyo' naikaku-fu, keisai keizoku" [Cabinet Office continues to publish 'illegal occupation by Russia' on its website]. February 26, 2019. https://mainichi.jp/articles/20190226/ddm/005/010/033000c.
Mainichi Shinbun. "Tairo gaikō tantō Harada-shi tainin e getsunai ni mo" [Harada, with responsibility for diplomacy with Russia, to step down within the month]. March 22, 2017. https://mainichi.jp/articles/20170322/ddm/005/010/065000c.
Masafumi, Asada. "Naze Abe shushō ni totte Roshia wa kon'nani 'tokubetsuna sonzai' na no ka [Why is Russia so 'special' for Prime Minister Abe?]" *Gendai Shinsho*, June 14, 2018. https://gendai.ismedia.jp/articles/-/56100?media=gs.
Ministry of Foreign Affairs of Japan. "G7 Foreign Ministers' joint communiqué." April 2, 2018. https://www.mofa.go.jp/mofaj/files/000357958.pdf.

Ministry of Foreign Affairs of Japan. "Talks between Japan and North Korea on the Abductions Issue." December 28, 2018. https://www.mofa.go.jp/a_o/na/kp/page1we_000069.html.

Naka, Ksenia. "Budushchii prem'er Yaponii Abe nameren ukreplyat' otnosheniya s Rossiei" [Future Premier of Japan Abe Intends to Strengthen Relations with Russia]. *RIA Novosti*, December 16, 2012. https://ria.ru/20121216/915013917.html.

Naka, Ksenia. "Istochnik: prem'yer Yaponii otkazalsya ot soveta Obamy ne yezdit' v Rossiyu" [Source: Japanese PM rejects Obama's advice not to travel to Russia]. *RIA Novosti*, February 23, 2016. https://ria.ru/20160223/1379198257.html.

Pinchuk, Denis and Polina Nikolskaya. "Russia's Putin tells Japan's Abe: 'Let's sign peace deal this year.'" *Reuters*, September 12, 2018. https://www.reuters.com/article/us-russia-economy-forum-putin-treaty/russias-putin-tells-japans-abe-lets-sign-peace-deal-this-year.

Reuters. "Japan's Abe signals shift on North Korea, says will meet Kim without conditions: media." May 3, 2019. https://jp.reuters.com/article/us-northkorea-japan-abe/japans-abe-signals-shift-on-north-korea-says-will-meet-kim-without-conditions-media.

Sankei Shimbun. "Abe shinzō shushō, bōfu e nichiro no zenshin chikau" [Prime Minister Abe Shinzō vows to his late father to move forward Japan-Russia relations]. January 6, 2019, https://www.sankei.com/politics/news/190106/plt1901060003-n1.html.

Sankei Shimbun. "'Shuken o yūsuru shimajima' ha hoppōyontō? Soretomo nitō?" [Are the 'sovereign islands' the 'Four Northern Islands" Or two islands?]. June 14, 2020. https://news.yahoo.co.jp/articles/2cb926a3c3ac05bae32874061fbe3f80e0474aeb.

Sankei Shimbun. "Yachi zen kokka anzen hoshō kyokuchō 'Roshia wa mujōken teiketsu yōkyū' heiwa jōyaku kōshō de" [Yachi, former head of National Security Secretariat: 'Russia demanded uncondition conclusion' in peace treaty talks]. January 24, 2020. https://www.sankei.com/politics/news/200124/plt2001240047-n1.html.

Satō, Masaru. *Kokka no Wana* [The Trap of the State]. Tōkyō: Shinchōsa, 2005, 94–101.

Sekiguchi, Toko. "Abe seeks to build trust with Putin in Sochi." *The Wall Street Journal*, February 6, 2014. https://www.wsj.com/articles/abe-eyes-more-trustbuilding-with-putin-in-sochi-1391668569.

Shagina, Maria. "Japan's dilemma with sanctions policy towards Russia." *Focus Asia*, November 2018. https://isdp.eu/content/uploads/2018/11/Japans-Delicate-Balancing-Act-FA-FINAL.pdf.

Shinoda, Tomohito. *Koizumi Diplomacy: Japan's Kantei Approach to Foreign and Defense Affairs*. Seattle: University of Washington Press, 2007.

Shusōkantei. "Dai nihyakuikkai kokkai ni okeru Abe naikakusōri daijin shisei hōshin enzetsu" [Policy Speech by the Prime Minister to the 201st Session of the Diet]. January 20, 2020. https://www.kantei.go.jp/jp/98_abe/statement/2020/0120shiseihoushin.html.

Suzuki, Muneo. *Seiji no Shuraba* [Political Carnage]. Tōkyō: Bungei Shunjū, 2012, 197.

Taniguchi, Tomohiko and Daniel Bob. "The onsen summit: Why Abe is seeking a settlement with Russia." *The National Interest*, December 14, 2016. https://nationalinterest.org/feature/why-abe-seeking-settlement-russia-18739.

Terada, Mayu. "The Changing Nature of Bureaucracy and Governing Structure in Japan." *Washington International Law Journal*, 431 (2019).

Yoshida, Reiji. "Foreign Minister Taro Kono repeatedly ignores questions on Russian-held islands ahead of talks on WWII treaty." *The Japan Times*, December 12, 2018. https://www.japantimes.co.jp/news/2018/12/12/national/politics-diplomacy/taro-kono-no-comment-russia-held-islands-ahead-possible-wwii-treaty-talks/.

Zakharchenko, Ivan. "Abe rasskazal Poroshenko, o chem on budet govorit' s Putinym" [Abe told Poroshenko what he will talk to Putin about]. *RIA Novosti*, December 9, 2016. https://ria.ru/20161209/1483237870.html.

Chapter 12

Japan's Foreign Policy toward the Middle East and Africa under Abe

Kakizaki Masaki

For decades, Japan had pursued a low-profile, mercantilist, and passive approach to the Middle East and Africa. Its dependence on Middle Eastern oil, constitutional restrictions on the use of hard power, and the U.S.–Japan security alliance are major factors that define and constrain Japan's foreign policy. Though these factors remain unchanged, Prime Minister Abe Shinzo's diplomatic track record during his second term shows that he broadened, diversified, and upgraded Japan's approach to these regions in the last decade.

Abe viewed the Middle East and Africa as geopolitically crucial areas to Japan's national security and as emerging markets for Japanese businesses. In addition, the Middle East and Africa occupy an important place within the context of Japan's Free and Open Indo-Pacific (FOIP) vision that Abe unveiled in 2016 in Nairobi, Kenya. Furthermore, given rising uncertainty in the role of President Donald Trump's America in the regions, Abe carefully and cautiously re-balanced Japan's relationship with the Middle East and Africa by implementing a more independent policy. Staying in power for more than seven years, unprecedented in recent Japanese political history, Abe took advantage of his stable and long tenure to advance Japan's strategic interests in the regions and build stronger bilateral relations with regional powers.

This chapter begins by outlining the basic parameters of Japan's overall foreign policy toward the Middle East and Africa. The subsequent section discusses the political and economic challenges that Prime Minister Abe had to deal with at the start of his second term. The last section considers how and to what extent he changed Japan's policy toward the Middle East and Africa.

PILLARS OF JAPAN'S APPROACH TO THE MIDDLE EAST AND AFRICA

Prime Minister Abe Shinzo inherited five pillars that constitute Japan's overall policy toward the Middle East and Africa. The first pillar is the primacy of energy security. Japan is reliant on the Middle East for almost 90percent of its crude oil, and the Fukushima nuclear disaster in 2011 further increased Japan's vulnerable energy security.[1] In addition, Washington's pressure on its allies, including Japan, significantly reduced oil imports from Iran, forcing Japan to further strengthen its relations with Arab oil-producing countries. Thus, Abe's predecessor, Prime Minister Noda Yoshihiko of the Democratic Party of Japan, dispatched Edano Yukio, then minister of economy, trade, and industry to the United Arab Emirates (UAE) and Saudi Arabia in October 2011 to secure a stable and long-term energy supply.[2] Foreign Minister Gemba Koichiro also visited Saudi Arabia, Qatar, and the UAE in January 2012. These three countries account for 61 percent of Japan's crude oil imports, and Gemba's trip to the region was meant for asking the Gulf oil producers to increase the amount of crude oil shipped to Japan and to seek assurances that oil and gas supplies, as well as their prices, would not be disrupted.[3]

The second pillar is the provision of official development aid (ODA) as the most valuable diplomatic tool for raising Japan's profile. When Abe returned to power in 2012, the largest recipient nation of Japan's ODA in the Middle East was Iraq.[4] Japan agreed to provide new ODA loans through the Japan International Cooperation Agency (JICA) in excess of US$ 3.5 billion to support Iraq's oil sector and strengthen Japan–Iraq relations.[5] Japan also directed its official aid and loans to other Middle Eastern and North African countries, such as Palestine and Sudan, facing a wide range of humanitarian challenges and political conflicts.

The third pillar is related to the Israeli-Palestinian conflict. Japan continues to support a two-state solution and provide financial and political assistance for the capacity and institution building needed to create a functioning Palestinian state. After the 1993 Oslo Accords where Palestine formally recognized the state of Israel, and Israel reciprocated by allowing Palestinians to set up a provisional government, Japan decided to participate in multilateral working groups of the peace process, sponsor confidence-building measures between Israelis and Palestinians, and provide direct bilateral aid to Palestinians in addition to its ongoing contribution to the United Nations Relief and Works Agency for Palestinian Refugees (UNRWA). Japan has also promoted its own flagship project, the Corridor for Peace and Prosperity Initiative, a business and investment model announced by Prime Minister Koizumi Junichiro during his visit to the Middle East in 2006 to aid regional cooperation for peace between Israel, Palestinians, and Jordan using Japan's ODA and other resources.[6] Tokyo believes that it is crucial for Japan's strategic interests in the Middle East for it to help to achieve peace between Israel and the Palestinians because such a deal will remove an obstacle to Japan's simultaneous outreaching to Israel and the Arab world.[7]

The fourth pillar is the previous administrations' expansion of the scope of the Self- Defense Forces' (SDF) involvement in the security of the regions since the 1990s in the name of "international contribution."[8] By relaxing the interpretation of the peace constitution regarding the restrictions on the use of hard power, Japan deepened its commitment to security in the regions while refraining from engaging in combat missions. The maritime and ground SDF forces were assigned to UN-mandated peacekeeping missions in the Middle East, the logistic and refueling operations in the Indian Ocean to assist the U.S.-led war in Afghanistan, humanitarian and reconstruction assistance to Iraq, anti-piracy missions off the coast of Somalia, and the establishment of post–WWII Japan's first overseas military base in Djibouti.

The fifth and final pillar concerns Japan's approach to sub-Saharan Africa, a key diplomatic tool for Tokyo, via the Tokyo International Conference on African Development (TICAD), launched by Japan in 1993. The first three TICAD conferences were held in Japan in 1993, 1998, and 2003 and focused on poverty reduction, improvement of economic and social conditions, and human security in Africa through Japan's ODA. Japan's aid philosophy to low-income African countries emphasizes "self-help" and "partnership" through economic development, offering an alternative development strategy to the so-called Washington consensus that was dominant in Western donors in the 1990s.[9] Another reason Japan launched TICAD was Japan's bid to reform the United Nations Security Council (UNSC) and become a UNSC permanent member-state. African countries constitute a significant portion of UN membership, and Tokyo considered it crucial to win their support through a more assertive aid policy.

Prime Minister Abe's approach to the Middle East and Africa was embedded within the parameters of these pillars that Japan had developed in previous decades. However, the Abe administration adjusted Japan's policy toward the regions to enhance national interests and increase its presence in the politics of the Middle East and Africa under the banner of proactive pacifism.

THE RETURN OF ABE AND CHALLENGES IN THE MIDDLE EAST AND AFRICA

Abe Shinzo returned to power for a second time in December 2012. Abe's second administration started with a series of political and economic challenges to Japan's relations with the Middle East and North Africa which required him to recalibrate Tokyo's foreign policy approach.

The first challenge was Japan's deteriorating energy situation and vulnerable energy security. The 2011 nuclear disaster in Fukushima resulted in the shutdown of nuclear power plants. Nuclear energy provided about 25 percent of the country's electricity before the disaster, but its share in Japan's energy mix plummeted to 1.5 percent in 2012.[10] Although the Japanese government encouraged the use of renewable energy and investment in domestic production of energy resources, the country's energy self-sufficiency ratio dropped from 19.9 percent in 2010 to 6 percent in 2012,[11] the second lowest among OECD countries. Furthermore, growing instability in the Middle East and Africa as a result of the outbreak of popular uprisings like the Arab Spring, the spread of global terrorism, and gradual U.S. withdrawal from the regions made it urgent for Tokyo to strengthen its relations with the capitals of Middle Eastern oil-producing countries and contribute to the regional stability of the regions from which Japan imported more than 80 percent of its oil.

The second challenge was the emergence of Japan's regional competitors, China and South Korea, as influential external actors with vital interests in influencing the geopolitical orientations of the regions and establishing their footholds in emerging markets.[12] For instance, both countries launched their own international fora, like Japan's TICAD, to provide foreign aid to African countries in 2000 and 2006, respectively, and strengthened political and economic relations with the Middle East and Africa. China's One Belt One Road initiative in particular poses a diplomatic challenge for Japan, and the growing presence of China and South Korea in the regions has necessitated Japan's intensification of its diplomatic approach to key regional players, such as Saudi Arabia and the UAE.

WHAT DID PRIME MINISTER ABE CHANGE?

The second Abe administration began under these political and economic challenges to Tokyo's approach to the Middle East and Africa. The question is: what and how did the prime minister change Tokyo's Middle Eastern and African policy? This chapter highlights four issues, including the manner of Japan's political and economic diplomacy in the regions, the expansion of the SDF's role in the security of the regions, Japan's increased political involvement in the region's security, and the redefinition of Japan's aid policy to Africa, as well as the integration of Africa with Japan's geopolitical strategy in the Indo-Pacific region.

Prime Minister-Led Diplomacy in the Middle East and Africa

What characterized Prime Minister Abe Shinzo's approach to the Middle East and Africa was his attempt in taking a lead role in further strengthening Japan's relations with regional powers. Abe was cognizant of the significance of building close and personal relations with political leaders of the Middle East and Africa through high-level political dialogue. Thus, his emphasis on summit meetings with his counterparts in the regions became a cornerstone of Japan's new approach to the Middle East and Africa, contributing to Japan's increased visibility in the regions. In fact, as the longest serving prime minister in Japan, Prime Minister Abe visited the Middle East and Africa more than any other prime minister, resulting in improved relations with regional powers, including Saudi Arabia, the UAE, and Israel.[13]

This prime minister-led diplomacy was, in fact, what Abe had attempted to implement during his first short-lived administration in 2006–2007. In early 2007, after his short trip to the United States for talks with President George W. Bush, he visited five Arab countries—Saudi Arabia, the UAE, Kuwait, Qatar, and Egypt—to discuss cooperation on energy security. Despite Japan's reliance on the Middle East for its energy needs, Abe's predecessors rarely visited the Gulf countries. For instance, Abe's visit to Kuwait was the first by a Japanese leader (TEXT BOX 12.1), and his visits to the UAE and Qatar were the first in twenty-nine years since Prime Minister Fukuda Takeo made a trip to the region during the 1978 second oil crisis.

TEXT BOX 12.1: PRIME MINISTER ABE'S OFFICIAL VISIT TO THE MIDDLE EAST AND AFRICA

April 26 to May 3, 2007:
Saudi Arabia (1st visit in 4 years)
The United Arab Emirates (1st visit in 29 years)
Kuwait (1st visit ever)
Qatar (1st visit in 29 years)
Egypt (1st visit in 4 years)

April 30 to May 3, 2013:
Saudi Arabia (1st visit in 6 years)
The United Arab Emirates (1st visit in 6 years)
Turkey (1st visit in 7 years)

August 24–29, 2013:
Bahrain (1st visit ever)
Kuwait (first visit in 6 years)

Djibouti (1st visit ever)
Qatar (1st visit in 6 years)

October 28–30, 2013:
Turkey (2nd visit during his term of office)

November 13–17, 2013:
Turkey for G20 Summit (3rd visit during his term of office)

January 9–15, 2014:
Oman (1st visit in 24 years)
Côte d'Ivoire (1st visit ever)
Mozambique (1st visit ever)
Ethiopia (1st visit in 8 years)

January 16–21, 2015:
Egypt (1st visit in 8 years)
Jordan (1st visit in 9 years)
Israel (1st visit in 9 years)
Palestine (1st visit in 9 years)

August 25–29, 2016
Kenya for TICAD VI (1st visit in 14 years)

April 29 to May 3, 2018:
The UAE (2nd visit during his term of office)
Jordan (2nd visit during his term of office)
Israel (2nd visit during his term of office)
Palestine (2nd visit during his term of office)

June 12–14, 2019:
Iran (1st visit in 41 years)

January 11–15, 2020:
Saudi Arabia (2nd visit during his term of office)
The UAE (3rd visit during his term of office)
Oman (2nd visit during his term of office)
(Source: Ministry of Foreign Affairs, *Diplomatic Bluebook 2020*, Japanese version, p.14)

Apparently, energy security was the priority of discussions between Abe and his counterparts, but the main goal of his Middle East tour was to bring Japan–Middle East relations to a stage beyond petroleum.[14] Accordingly, Abe was accompanied by a huge delegation of business leaders from all economic sectors in Japan—energy, petrochemicals, finance, and construction—led by Mitarai Fujio, the chairman of Japan's most powerful business lobby group, Keidanren.[15]

Abe's trip to the Middle East in 2007 was significant in the sense that he broke away from the *Seikeibunri* doctrine, a foreign policy principle that separates economic issues from political ones. This doctrine was promoted by Ikeda Hayato, a disciple of Yoshida Shigeru and prime minister between 1960 and 1964, as a strategy to promote commercial relations with the People's Republic of China, which Japan had not yet formally recognized. Ikeda's successors embraced this policy and refrained from deeply interfering with trade and commercial activities conducted by Japanese private firms.

The *Seikeibunri* doctrine influenced not only Japan's policy toward China but also the Middle East.[16] For instance, the Japanese government did not lead a negotiation between a Japanese oil company, INPEX, and Iran's state oil company, National Iranian Oil Co., over a US$ 2 billion project to develop Iran's Azadegan oil field in 2006.[17] Nikai Toshihiro, the then minister of economy, trade, and industry, refrained from clarifying the Japanese government's stance on the negotiation at a press conference, only saying that "we would like to follow developments carefully."[18]

Thus, Prime Minister Abe's initiative to lead economic diplomacy through the Office of Prime Minister (Kantei) and to encourage the government and private business actors to work closer opened a new page in the history of Japan's Middle Eastern policy. Abe maintained and accelerated this diplomatic approach in his second term. Soon after taking office, Prime Minister Abe visited Saudi Arabia, the UAE, and Turkey in 2013 to promote cooperation not only in energy but also in trade, investment, infrastructure development, and security areas. As was the case with his trip to the region in 2007, Abe's 2013 trip to the Middle East was accompanied by a delegation of 383 business executives, including chief officers of Keidanren. Abe also visited Bahrain, Kuwait, and Qatar in August the same year with a delegation of 210 businessmen mainly from firms in energy, petrochemicals, infrastructure, pharmaceuticals, and finance.[19] In these trips, Abe presented himself as the country's top salesperson determined to sell Japan's advanced technology and expertise to the regions. This "top sales" diplomacy was well received by Japanese business firms. Yonekura Hiromasa, the chairman of Keidanren, who accompanied Abe, expressed his gratitude to Abe's leadership and said that "the trip was very productive for the revival and sustainable growth of Japan's economy."[20]

The most important achievement of Abe's tour in 2013 was the nuclear deals that he signed with the UAE and Turkey. The Fukushima nuclear accident raised a series of questions regarding nuclear safety, but Abe pledged to raise nuclear safety standards and share Japan's experience of the nuclear disaster with the international community.[21] The agreement with the UAE, which was the first nuclear deal Tokyo signed after the 2011 nuclear disaster, was to promote cooperation between the countries in the peaceful use of nuclear energy and to enable Japanese firms to sell their nuclear technologies to the UAE. The agreement Abe signed with Turkey during his meeting with Turkish Prime Minister Recep Tayyip Erdoğan allowed the Japan-led consortium of Mitsubishi Heavy Industries and France's Areva (Framatome now) to construct Turkey's second nuclear power plant at an estimated cost of US$ 22 billion. The nuclear power project was, to Abe's dismay, abandoned in early 2020, because the results of a feasibility study conducted by Mitsubishi concluded that safety-related costs would more than double the original estimate.[22]

Abe continued to play the role of the country's salesperson for the next six years in the Middle East and Africa. He took a delegation of Japanese firms and business associations to Oman, Côte d'Ivoire, Mozambique, and Ethiopia in 2014. Abe also strengthened Japan's relations with Israel, which was previously underdeveloped. Israeli Prime Minister Benjamin Netanyahu visited Tokyo in May 2014, and Abe stopped in Tel Aviv during his tour of the Middle East in January 2015. This was the Japanese leader's first ever visit to Israel in 10 years. The improvement of Japan–Israel relations produced a tangible outcome. The Israeli government announced an investment plan to strengthen economic ties and promote cooperation between the two countries in various areas of interest common to both countries, including cyber and information security, space technology, pharmacology, and transportation.[23] Abe Shinzo made an official visit alongside a business delegation, a new standard in Japan's Middle Eastern and African policies.

Abe's New Activist Approach to Security in the Middle East and Africa

The Middle East, and to a lesser extent, Africa, has been the center of SDF overseas activities since the 1990s. Japan sent mine sweeper vessels of the maritime SDF to the Persian Gulf after the 1991 Gulf War ceasefire. The SDF also joined a UN peacekeeping mission—the UN Disengagement Observer Force—to observe the ceasefire between Israel and Syria in the Golan Heights for 17 years (1996–2013), the SDF's longest peacekeeping mission ever.[24] The subsequent years also witnessed the continuous dispatch of the SDF to the Middle East and Africa. In late 2001, maritime SDF vessels were assigned to the Indian Ocean to refuel the warships conducting multinational operations in Afghanistan in the context of the U.S.-led "War on Terrorism." Tokyo sent the SDF troops to assist in the reconstruction of war-torn Iraq in December 2003. In addition to dispatches to the Middle East, Japan established a military base in Djibouti in 2011 to support the Maritime SDF vessels taking part in international anti-piracy operations off Somalia and the Gulf of Aden. Japan also deployed a GSDF engineering unit to South Sudan to help build infrastructure as part of U.N. peacekeeping missions in 2012.

When Prime Minister Abe returned to power in 2012, his main agenda for Japan's security and defense was to advance Japan's role in international security. The Abe cabinet published the National Security Strategy (NSS) of 2013, Japan's first-ever policy document outlining the country's national security doctrine. The NSS declared that Japan "should play an even more proactive role as a major global player in the international community."[25] It also highlighted the importance of "sea lanes of communication, stretching from the Persian Gulf, the Strait of Hormuz, the Red Sea, and the Gulf of Aden to the surrounding waters of Japan, passing through the Indian Ocean, the Straits of Malacca, and the South China Sea" and pledged Japan's greater assistance and cooperation with other countries that share strategic interests with Tokyo.[26]

One of the factors pushing Abe to take a more proactive role in the protection of sea lanes that connect East Africa, the Middle East, and Asia was the rise of China as a geostrategic rival of Tokyo. However, the spread of terrorism in the Middle East and Africa has also played a crucial role in expanding the role of the SDF on foreign soil. In January 2013, only a month after Abe's return to the prime minister's office, an al-Qaeda-affiliated group attacked a gas field in Algeria and took foreign workers hostage. During the crisis, thirty-nine hostages, including ten Japanese nationals, were killed. The prime minister's office considered the possibility of sending GSDF troops, which were deployed in the SDF's base in Djibouti for anti-piracy missions, to Algeria to evacuate those in need of protection, but the Ministry of Defense concluded that the SDF law only allowed the use of airplanes and warships to transfer overseas Japanese and foreign nationals in emergencies. Following this crisis, the Abe cabinet enacted a bill to allow the SDF to use land vehicles for overseas operations in November 2013.[27] The Algerian crisis also prompted Prime Minister Abe to establish a National Security Council (NSC), a new inter-ministry institution to coordinate and implement Japan's national security policies. The Japanese government during the hostage crisis was unable to swiftly collect and analyze information to respond to the situation, and Abe was convinced that it was vital for Japan to create a centralized body to deal with national security issues.[28] The 2015 beheading of two Japanese citizens by militants of the Islamic State in Iraq and Syria (ISIS) also convinced Abe that the SDF should be granted a mandate to conduct a rescue mission to save Japanese nationals abroad, which is not possible under the current SDF law.[29]

Therefore, the second Abe administration sought to strengthen Japan's relations with Middle Eastern countries in the area of defense. Tokyo signed a series of Memoranda of Understanding (MOU) for defense cooperation with Qatar, Saudi Arabia, Jordan, the UAE, and Oman between 2015 and 2019. The institutionalization of security partnerships with the Gulf countries helped Tokyo to increase Japan's presence along the sea lanes between the Persian Gulf and Japan as MSDF vessels began to make goodwill port visits in the region.[30]

In April 2019, Japan dispatched two SDF officers to the Multinational Force and Observers (MFO) in the Sinai Peninsula, a multinational peacekeeping operation to observe the implementation of the 1979 peace treaty between Egypt and Israel. The MFO has been led by the United States outside the framework of the UN, and this was the SDF's first participation in non-UN peacekeeping missions. The dispatch of the SDF to peacekeeping activities outside of the UN command was made legally possible by the national security legislation in 2015, which Abe pushed for, to allow Tokyo to exercise the right to collective defense and expand the role of the SDF in international security.

Greater Political Engagement in the Middle East

In addition to the expanded role of the SDF in the Middle East, the Abe administration also increased Japan's political engagement with the Middle East in line with Abe's proactive pacifism. Japan's attempt to play a greater role in contributing to security and stability in the Middle East was evident in the Middle East peace process and the US–Iran tensions over the latter's nuclear program. Japan's involvement in these two issues demonstrates Prime Minister Abe's attempt to assert Japan's proactive foreign policy.

In February 2013, Japan held the first meeting of the Conference on Cooperation among East Asian Countries for Palestinian Development (CEAPAD) in Tokyo. CEAPAD was established on the initiative of Japan as an international platform to bring together East Asian countries to discuss and coordinate collective assistance for the nation-building efforts of Palestine.[31] This initiative was the outcome of Japan's desire to promote its international status by becoming an indispensable actor in the Middle East peace process, which is of global significance. Although the CEAPAD initiative is a multinational support structure for Palestinians, it has been "exclusively initiated, developed, executed, and coordinated by Japan."[32] Indeed, Prime Minister Abe asserted in his speech on the Middle East peace process during his visit to Egypt in January 2015 that the CEAPAD framework began "under the auspices of Japan" to support Palestine's development by Japan and Southeast Asian countries that had achieved economic progress in the past few decades.[33]

There are two reasons why Japan launched the CEAPAD process, which has held three international meetings so far in 2013, 2014, and 2018. First, Japanese policymakers realized that Japan's previous engagement in the peace process was not recognized internationally. Japan continued to work in various ways to help achieve peace between Israel and the Palestinians as a participating member-state on the multilateral track of negotiations since the Madrid Conference in 1991. However, Japan's declining presence in the peace process became evident a few years later when Japan was opposed by the United States and European countries to participate in the *Quartet on the Middle East*, which was created in Madrid in 2002 as a reinvigorated international framework to bring peace to the Middle East, comprising the United States, the EU, Russia, and the United Nations.[34] As a result, Tokyo concluded that the only way to regain its status in the Middle East peace process was to launch its own initiative.[35]

The second reason is partly due to the rise of China as an external actor in the Middle East. China has become increasingly interested in the Middle East peace process in the last two decades. For instance, Chinese President Xi Jinping announced a proposal for the settlement of the Palestinian question in 2013,[36] the same year when Tokyo launched the CEAPAD initiative. Interestingly enough, China has been excluded from the CEAPAD initiative, although it is one of the most powerful countries in East Asia and both countries want stability in the region. Thus, it is safe to argue that Japan wanted to keep its position as the dominant Asian player in the Middle East by pushing back China's efforts to play a greater role in the peace process.

Under the Trump administration, the gap between Tokyo and Washington regarding their approaches to the Palestine question widened. While Japan's position on the Middle East process did not change under the Abe administration as Tokyo continued to support the two-state solution and opposed Israeli settlements in the West Bank, which is internationally considered illegal,[37] President Trump in 2017 implied the United States' abandonment of the two-state solution and decided to relocate the U.S. Embassy from Tel Aviv to Jerusalem, which Washington formally recognized as the capital of Israel in late 2017. Prime Minister Abe did not agree with Trump's new pro-Israeli policy and Japan voted in favor of a non-binding UN resolution effectively calling on Washington to rescind its recognition of Jerusalem as Israel's capital. Japan's then Foreign Minister Kōno Tarō, who visited Israel and Palestine in December 2017, invited Israeli Prime Minister Benjamin Netanyahu and Palestinian Authority Mahmoud Abbas for a four-party talks in Tokyo that would be also attended by Jared Kushner, who was in charge of President Trump's new Middle East peace plan.[38] Kōno's proposal was an indication of Japan's determination to play a more active role in the Middle East as an "honest broker."

Nevertheless, Japan refrained from directly criticizing Washington's pro-Israeli policy under the Trump administration. Japan's response was only to express deep concerns at the relocation of the U.S. Embassy.[39] Similarly, the Abe administration did not oppose the new Middle East peace plan Trump announced on January 28, 2020. This plan promised the establishment of an independent Palestinian state and the provision of $50 billion for Palestinian development, but it also called on the Palestinians to make substantive concessions regarding territorial integrity and Jerusalem, including Israel's formal annexation of West Bank settlements. During a press conference held immediately after the announcement of Trump's new peace plan, Suga Yoshihide, who was then Japan's Chief Cabinet Secretary, said that "the United States' role in the Middle East peace process plan is quite big, and Japan highly evaluates the strong involvement of President Trump."[40] He added that Japan expects that a "concrete movement will develop to achieve peace soon by this US proposal."[41] Japan's relations with the United States are vital to Japan's security and economy, and the Abe administration, like previous administrations, sought to keep disagreement with Washington on the Middle East peace process less visible so that it would not jeopardize Japan–U.S. relations.

In the case of the Iran–U.S. confrontation over Tehran's nuclear program, Prime Minister Abe sought to reduce tensions between Washington and Tehran. In May 2018, U.S. President Trump withdrew from the Joint Comprehensive Plan of Action (JCPOA), known as the Iran nuclear deal, and decided to reinstate stringent economic sanctions on Iran, escalating tensions between the two countries. The U.S.–Iran relations further deteriorated in 2019 after the Trump administration deployed an aircraft carrier strike group in the Persian Gulf, and Iranian officials said Tehran will not adhere to limits on its heavy water and low-enriched uranium set by the JCPOA.

The standoff between Washington and Tehran became a testing ground for Japan's balancing act. Japan was one of the five countries temporarily exempted from the U.S. sanctions on Iran and was allowed to buy Iranian oil, but President Trump decided not to extend the waiver in May 2019, which forced Japan to halt oil imports.[42] On the other hand, Tehran threatened to close the Strait of Hormuz through which more than 80 percent of Japan's imported oil passes. While Japan needed to maintain its strong relationship with the United States, which urged its allies to take a tougher stance against the Islamic regime, Abe maintained his support for the JCPOA and tried to reduce tensions to ensure the safety of the sea lanes, including the Strait of Hormuz.

In the midst of rising tensions between the United States and Iran, Abe visited Iran in June 2019, becoming the first sitting Japanese prime minister to visit Iran in forty-one years. His mission was to use Japan's cordial relationship with Tehran to ease tensions in the Persian Gulf and to demonstrate Tokyo's diplomatic influence in the region. Before his trip, he spoke by phone with President Trump and the leaders of Saudi Arabia, the UAE, and Israel, the three anti-Iranian regional powers, to explain Japan's policy toward Iran.

In Tehran, Abe met with Iranian President Hassan Rouhani and Supreme Leader Ali Khamenei, urging them to play a "constructive role" in preventing a clash with the United States. However, although Khamenei assured Abe that Iran had no intention to make, hold, or use nuclear weapons, he asserted that Iran will not talk to the United States when Abe hinted that President Trump wanted to negotiate with Iran. After the meeting with Abe, Khamenei released a statement asserting that "I do not consider Trump as a person worth exchanging any message with and I have no answer for him, nor will I respond to him in the future."[43] Abe's visit to Iran did not result in the de-escalation of the tension, and Khamenei's response indicated that Japan was not viewed as a neutral honest broker by the Iranians.

Abe's visit to Iran was further marred by attacks by unknown perpetrators on two tankers, including a Japanese-owned one near the Strait of Hormuz that happened while he was in Tehran. The U.S. government announced that Iran was responsible for the tanker attacks, but the Japanese government neither accepted Washington's claims nor accused Iran of the attacks, because Tokyo did not want to put its relations with Iran at risk, which was a "diplomatic asset" to Japan.[44]

Japan's balancing act between Washington and Iran was best illustrated by the deployment of the Maritime SDF vessels for the Middle East in early 2020 under strong pressure from the United States. Washington urged Tokyo to join the U.S.-led coalition to protect ships from Iranian threats in the Strait of Hormuz, but the Abe administration decided to deploy its MSDF destroyer "independently" to the Gulf of Oman, the Arabian Sea, and the strait of Bab el-Mandeb but not the Strait of Hormuz so that the mission would not antagonize Tehran. After deciding the deployment of the maritime SDF vessel to the Middle East, Abe visited Saudi Arabia, the UAE, and Oman to elicit support and understanding of Japan's decision.[45]

TICAD and FOIP

The Abe administration recalibrated Japan's approach to Africa and redefined the role of TICAD in Japan–Africa relations. Sub-Saharan Africa enjoyed real economic growth, on average, of 4.3 percent from 2000 to 2019. Africa's total population, according to the United Nations, is projected to reach 2.5 billion in 2050. The growing population and relatively high economic growth of resource-rich African nations make sub-Saharan Africa an attractive market for Japan's private sector. The 2013 National Security Strategy defined Africa as a "prospective economic frontier with abundant strategic natural resources and sustained economic growth," suggesting that Tokyo would prioritize the strengthening of economic and trade relations with African countries over the provision of foreign aid.[46] Economic growth in Africa also intensified competition between Japan and its regional rivals, China and South Korea, to expand their influence in the region. Imitating Japan's TICAD process, Beijing and Seoul launched their own multilateral forums, Forum on China–Africa Cooperation and Korea–Africa Forum for Economic Cooperation, respectively, to promote policy dialogue and strengthen trade relations with African countries in the 2000s.

The shift in Japan's African policy from aid to investment under Abe was visible at TICAD V, which was held in Yokohama in July 2013. African representatives urged the Japanese government to increase investment rather than foreign aid, while Japanese companies viewed Africa as an attractive destination for investment. Prime Minister Abe in his keynote speech declared that "what Africa needs now is private-sector investment" and pledged a total of 32 trillion yen to support African growth over the next five years. More than 50 percent of the assistance package was supposed to come from private sector investment.[47] Abe reconfirmed his commitment to support Japanese companies' investments in Africa during TICAD VII held in Yokohama in 2019 as he promised to "do whatever it takes to assist the advancement of Japanese companies in Africa."[48]

Another significant change in Japan's approach to Africa under the Abe administration is related to his Free and Open Indo-Pacific (FOIP) strategy and vision. The FOIP was unveiled by Abe as Japan's foreign and diplomatic policy at the 2016 TICAD VI summit in Nairobi, Kenya. The FOIP aims to preserve and enhance the rule-based maritime order in the Indian and Pacific Oceans that bridge Asia and Africa through the Middle East. Abe in Nairobi said "Japan wants to work with you in Africa in order to make the seas that connect the two continents into peaceful seas that are governed by the rule of law."[49] His emphasis on rule-based, open, and free order in the seas between Asia and Africa was intended to put a brake on China's aggressive moves in the East China and South China Seas, and in so doing protect one of the most important international public good: the free and open Indo-Pacific region.

The FOIP was the first geostrategic policy connecting Asia, the Middle East, and Africa that the Japanese government ever formulated. Africa is not only an economic but also a new strategic partner of Tokyo within the context of the FOIP because policymakers in Tokyo believe it is crucial to work with African governments, particularly East African ones, for anti-piracy and counterterrorism activities to maintain the maritime security of the Red Sea, the Gulf of Aden, and the Arabian Sea that Japan had conducted since 2009.

The FOIP was integrated into Japan's TICAD process at the Yokohama Summit in 2019. As the conference came to an end, the African leaders at the summit stressed "the need to galvanize bilateral, regional, and international stakeholders' collaboration in maritime security including the fight against piracy, illegal, unreported, and unregulated fishing and other maritime crimes, and maintaining a rules-based maritime order in accordance with the principles of international law," and agreed to "take good note" of the Indo-Pacific initiative that Abe had announced in the previous TICAD VI meeting in Nairobi.[50]

CONCLUSION

During his second term, Prime Minister Abe sought to strengthen and diversify Japan's relationships with the Middle East and Africa. Taking advantage of his stable and strong administration, he was able to make Japan–Middle East and Japan–Africa relations more solid and multilayered in the areas of economy, energy, diplomacy, and security. Abe was a unique leader among Washington's allies as the head of government who was able to meet with leaders of disputing Middle Eastern and African countries such as Egypt, Ethiopia, Saudi Arabia, the UAE, Iran, Israel, and Palestine.

Prime Minister Abe sought to raise Japan's profile in the regions through his proactive pacifist foreign policy in the face of China's emergence as a player in the international relations of the regions. He began to lead Japan's economic diplomacy toward the regions by working more openly with Japanese businesses. In line with Japan's overall foreign policy, Abe's Middle Eastern and African approach was intended to revitalize Japan's commitment to security and stability in the regions through active diplomacy and the expansion of the SDF's role. Lastly, Tokyo redefined the TICAD's role and strategically integrated Africa and the Middle East in the security of the Indo-Pacific oceans on which Japan's economy is dependent.

Having said that, however, Abe's foreign policy toward the Middle East and Africa failed to demonstrate political leadership and bring new ideas to resolve regional issues. For instance, Japan's responses to the Arab Spring and its subsequent turmoil, including the rise of the ISIL, were modest at best, contrary to Abe's proactive pacifism. Japan contributed to peacekeeping missions by dispatching the SDF, but it did not take any initiative as a peacebuilder in the post-Arab Spring Middle East. Japan's contribution to the Middle East peace process through the Corridor for Peace and Prosperity and CEAPAD were valuable but short of pushing Israel and the Palestinians to return to a negotiating table. Furthermore, Prime Minister Abe's FOIP vision to enhance the connectivity of Asia, the Middle East, and Africa for regional stability and peace was an ambitious geostrategic policy but unclear on how Africa and the Middle East are strategically related to the security and stability of the Indo-Pacific region.[51]

It is likely that the geopolitical environment of the Middle East and Africa will become more volatile and pose greater threats to Japan's already vulnerable energy security. The United States is expected to reduce its commitment to the Middle East and call on its allies, including Japan, to take a greater role in the maintenance of the sea lanes. At the same time, confrontation between Iran and its adversaries, including Israel, Saudi Arabia, and the UAE, seems unabated for the foreseeable future. China and South Korea are determined to further expand their influence throughout the region. These new geopolitical orientations of the Middle East and Africa suggest that Prime Minister Abe's successors have no choice but to take on stronger roles in protecting its interests and will need to walk a narrow path, balancing the divergent and sometimes competing interests of Tokyo, Washington, and regional powers in the conflict-ridden regions.

NOTES

1. According to Japan's Energy White Paper 2019, created by the Agency for Natural Resources and Energy under the Ministry of Economy, Trade and Industry, 87% of Japan's crude oil imports in 2017 came from the Middle East. Saudi Arabia alone accounted for 39.4% of Japanese imports of crude oil, followed by the United Arab Emirates of 24.8%. See the Agency for Natural Resources and Energy, *Enerugi Hakusho 2019* [*Energy White Paper 2019*], 2019. https://www.enecho.meti.go.jp/about/whitepaper/2019pdf/.

2. Yorihisa Ohta, "UAE, Nihonzei no Yudenken'eki Koushin ni Maemuki, Edano Keisansho" [UAE positive to extend oil concessions, Edano], *Nihonkeizai Shimbun*, October 11, 2011. https://www.nikkei.com/article/DGXNASDF11002_R11C11A0EB1000/.

3. Sami Aboudi, "Japan Asks UAE, S. Arabia for Iran Oil Backup," *Reuters*, January 11, 2012. https://www.reuters.com/article/japan-oil/japan-asks-uae-s-arabia-for-iran-oil-backup-idINDEE8090LY20120110.

4. Ministry of Foreign Affairs, *ODA White Paper 2013* (English Version), 2013, 125.

5. Japan International Cooperation Agency, "Signing of Japanese ODA Loan Agreements with the Republic of Iraq," Press release, October 15, 2012.

6. Nagaoka Kansuke, "Views from the Far East on the Middle East," *Palestine-Israel Journal of Politics, Economics and Culture* 13, no. 4 (2007): 64–68.

7. Ikeda Akifumi, "'Arabu' to 'Beikoku' no Airo de: Nihon no Chuto Wahei Gaiko ha Donoyounishite Seiritsu Shitaka" [Between "Arab" and the "United States": How did Japan's Policy on the Middle East Peace Process Come into Existence?], *Synodos: Academic Journalism*, March 29, 2018. https://synodos.jp/international/21275.

8. Nishida Ippeita, "The SDF Dispatches to the Middle East," *Security Studies* 2, no. 2 (2020): 61–77.

9. Howard P. Lehman, "The Asian Economic Model in Africa: Japanese Development Lessons for Africa," in *Japan and Africa: Globalization and Foreign Aid in the 21st Century*, edited by Howard P. Lehman. London: Routledge, 2010, 25–38.

10. See Agency for Natural Resources and Energy, *Heisei 30 Nendo (2018 Nedo) Niokeru Enerugi Jukyu Jisseki Kakuhou* [Energy Supply and Demand Report 2018], 2018. https://www.enecho.meti.go.jp/statistics/total_energy/pdf/stte_030.pdf.

11. Agency for Natural Resources and Energy, *Energy White Paper 2012* (Japanese edition), 2012, 144.

12. Shiraz Azad, "Seeking a New Role: Japan's Middle East Policy under Shinzo Abe," *East Asia* 34 (2017): 287–305.

13. Christopher Lamont, "Japan's Evolving Ties with the Middle East," *Asia Society Institute*, July 28, 2020. https://asiasociety.org/asias-new-pivot/japan.

14. Ministry of Foreign Affairs, "Press Conference by Prime Minister Shinzo Abe Following His Visits to the United States and Middle Eastern Countries," May 2, 2007. https://www.mofa.go.jp/region/middle_e/pmv0704/press.html.

15. Fujio Mitarai, "Abe Sori no Chuto Rekiho ni Awasete Misshon wo Haken" [Dispatching a delegation along with Prime Minister Abe's visit to the Middle East], *KeizaiTrend* 55, no. 7 (2007): 62.

16. Tominaga Erika, "Japan's Middle East Policy, 1972-74: Resources Diplomacy, Pro-American Policy, and New Left," *Diplomacy & Statecraft* 28, no. 4 (2017): 680.

17. Iwama Koichi, "Abe Shushou Chutou Shigengaikou no Hyoka" [Evaluating Prime Minister Abe's Resource Diplomacy in the Middle East] *Sekiyukaihatsujihou*, 154 (August 2007): 54.

18. *Japan Times*, "Japan, Iran to Continue Talks on Oil Field Project," September 16, 2006. https://www.japantimes.co.jp/news/2006/09/16/business/japan-iran-to-continue-talks-on-oil-field-project/.

19. A delegation of corporate executives to accompany a prime minister's overseas trip was traditionally arranged through Keidanren, but Prime Minister Abe changed the mechanism of selecting firms and organizations to join his trip. According to a local news report, it was Abe's special advisor who prepared a list of participating firms and the Ministry of Economy, Trade, and Industry directly contacted them to ask for their participation. See *Nihonkeizai Shimbun*, "Gaiko, Sabitsuku Kanminrenkei, Zaikai Chikaku Hendo" [Diplomacy, Government-Private Sector Cooperation Getting Rusty], January 29, 2014. https://www.nikkei.com/article/DGXNASFS2203D_T20C14A1SHA000/.

20. *Nihonkeizai Shimbun*, "Keidanren Kaicho: "Hijo ni Minori Ooi" Shusho Doko no Igi Kyocho" [Keidanren Chief 'Very Productive,' Emphasizing the Value of the Prime Minister's Traveling with], May 3, 2013. https://www.nikkei.com/article/DGXNASFS03024_T00C13A5000000/.

21. Prime Minister of Japan and His Cabinet, "Press Conference by Prime Minister Shinzo Abe during His Visit to Turkey," May 3, 2013. https://japan.kantei.go.jp/96_abe/statement/201305/03turkey_naigai_e.html.

22. *Hürriyet Daily News*, "Turkey, Japan Scrap Partnership in Sinop Nuclear Plant in Turkey's North," January 20, 2020. https://www.hurriyetdailynews.com/turkey-japan-scrap-partnership-in-sinop-nuclear-plant-in-turkeys-north-151212.

23. Israel Ministry of Foreign Affairs, "Cabinet Approves Plan to Strengthen Economic Ties with Japan," January 4, 2015. https://mfa.gov.il/MFA/PressRoom/2015/Pages/Cabinet-approves-plan-to-strengthen-economic-ties-with-Japan-4-Jan-2015.aspx.

24. Japan withdew its troops from the Golan Heights in early 2013 due to the escalation of the Syrian civil war that made it hard to ensure the safety of Japanese personnel. See Ministry of Defense, "International Peace Cooperation Assignment Operations in the Golan Heights," *Japan Defense Focus*, no. 37 (February 2013). https://www.mod.go.jp/e/jdf/no37/activities.html.

25. Cabinet Secretariat, "National Security Strategy," December 17, 2013, 1. https://www.cas.go.jp/jp/siryou/131217anzenhoshou/nss-e.pdf.

26. *Ibid.*, 17.

27. *Kyōdō*, "Bill for SDF Rescues Abroad Passed," *Japan Times*, November 1, 2013. https://www.japantimes.co.jp/news/2013/11/01/national/bill-for-sdf-rescues-abroad-passed/.

28. Miyagi Taizo, *Gendai Nihon Gaikoshi* [History of Contemporary Japanese Diplomacy], Tokyo: Chuokoron-shinsha, 2016, 238.

29. Aoki Mizuho, "Abe Wants to Enable SDF to Rescue Citizens Overseas," *Japan Times*, February 2, 2015. https://www.japantimes.co.jp/news/2015/02/02/national/politics-diplomacy/abe-says-working-with-global-community-only-way-to-fight-terrorism/.

30. Nishida, "The SDF Dispatches to the Middle East," 72–73.

31. Ministry of Foreign Affairs, "Conference on Cooperation among East Asian Countries for Palestinian Development (CEAPAD)," February 14, 2013. https://www.mofa.go.jp/region/middle_e/palestine/ceapad_20130214.html.

32. Kai Schulze, "Rivalry in the Middle East? Japan's CEAPAD Initiative and China's Rise," *The Pacific Review* 32, no. 5 (2019): 810.

33. Prime Minister's Office and His Cabinet, "Keynote Speech by Prime Minister Abe at the Joint Meeting of the Japan-Egypt Business Committee," January 17, 2015. https://japan.kantei.go.jp/97_abe/statement/201501/17egypt.html.

34. Raquel Shaoul, "Japan and Israel: An Evaluation of Relationship-building in the Context of Japan's Middle East Policy," *Israel Affairs* 10, no. 1–2 (2004): 290.

35. Schulze, "Rivalry," 816–818.

36. *Xinhua*, "Chinese President Makes Four-Point Proposal for Settlement of Palestinian Question," *Global Times*, May 6, 2013. http://www.globaltimes.cn/content/779577.shtml.

37. Ministry of Foreign Affairs, "Japan's Position on the Peace in the Middle East," January 13, 2015. https://www.mofa.go.jp/region/middle_e/stance.html.

38. Masanori Tobita, "Japan Takes Up Jerusalem Issue, Proposes 4-party Talks," *Nikkei Asian Review*, December 27, 2017. https://asia.nikkei.com/Politics/Japan-takes-up-Jerusalem-issue-proposes-4-party-talks.

39. *Associated Press*, "The Latest: Japan Fears Jerusalem Move Could Stoke Tension," May 14, 2018. https://www.businessinsider.com/ap-the-latest-japan-fears-jerusalem-move-could-stoke-tensions-2018-5.

40. *Arab News*, "Trump's ME Peace Plan Quite Big: Suga," January 30, 2020. https://www.arabnews.jp/en/japan/article_9745/.

41. Ibid.

42. Yuka Obayashi and Florence Tan, "Japanese Refiners Halt Iran Oil Imports as Waiver Expiry Looms," *Reuters*, March 29, 2019. https://www.reuters.com/article/us-iran-sanctions-oil-japan/japanese-refiners-halt-iran-oil-imports-as-waiver-expiry-looms-idUSKCN1RA0BQ.

43. The Office of the Supreme Leader, "Trump Not Worth Sending a Message to, We Won't Talk to U.S.," July 3, 2019. https://www.leader.ir/en/content/23196/Ayatollah-Khamenei's-meeting-with-Japan's-Prime-Minister,-Shinz%C5%8D-Abe.

44. *Jiji*/Reuters, "Japan Distancing Itself from U.S. Claims of Iranian Involvement in Tanker Attacks," *Japan Times*, June 18, 2019. https://www.japantimes.co.jp/news/2019/06/18/national/politics-diplomacy/japan-distancing-u-s-claims-iranian-involvement-tanker-attacks/#.X0jDVsj7Q2w.

45. *Japan Times*, "Saudi Crown Prince 'Fully Supports' Japan MSDF Mission in Middle East," January 13, 2020. https://www.japantimes.co.jp/news/2020/01/13/national/politics-diplomacy/saudi-king-mohammed-bin-salman-shinzo-abe-msdf/.

46. Cabinet Secretariat, "National Security Strategy," 27.

47. Prime Minister's Office and His Cabinet, "The Africa that Joins in Partnership with Japan is Brighter Still," June 1, 2013. https://japan.kantei.go.jp/96_abe/statement/201306/01speech_e.html; See also Mizuho Aoki, "Abe to Africa: Use Aid as You See Fit," *Japan Times*, June 2, 2013. https://www.japantimes.co.jp/news/2013/06/02/national/politics-diplomacy/abe-promises-africa-new-3-2-trillion-in-aid-as-ticad-v-kicks-off/.

48. Ministry of Foreign Affairs, "Keynote Address by Shinzo Abe," August 28, 2019. https://www.mofa.go.jp/af/af1/page4e_001069.html.

49. Ministry of Foreign Affairs, "Address by Prime Minister Shinzo Abe at the Opening Session of the Sixth Tokyo International Conference on African Development (TICAD VI)," August 27, 2016. https://www.mofa.go.jp/afr/af2/page4e_000496.html.

50. Ministry of Foreign Affairs, *Yokohama Declaration 2019*, August 30, 2019. https://www.mofa.go.jp/region/africa/ticad/ticad7/pdf/yokohama_declaration_en.pdf.

51. On the ambiguity of the role of Africa and the Middle East in Japan's FOIP vision, see Amane Kobayashi, "'Indo Pashifikku Koso' to Chuto-Afurika Chiiki" ['Indo-Pacific Vision' and the Middle East/Africa Region], *JIME Chuto Doko Bunseki* [A Monthly Middle Eastern and Energy Bulletin] 18, no. 4 (2019): 1–15.

REFERENCES

Aboudi, Sami. "Japan Asks UAE, S. Arabia for Iran Oil Backup." *Reuters*, January 11, 2012. https://www.reuters.com/article/japan-oil/japan-asks-uae-s-arabia-for-iran-oil-backup-idINDEE8090LY20120110.

Agency for Natural Resources and Energy. *Energy White Paper 2012* (Japanese edition). 2012.
Agency for Natural Resources and Energy. *Enerugi Hakusho 2019* [*Energy White Paper 2019*]. 2019. https://www.enecho.meti.go.jp/about/whitepaper/2019pdf/.
Agency for Natural Resources and Energy. *Heisei 30 Nendo (2018 Nedo) Niokeru Enerugi Jukyu Jisseki Kakuhou* [Energy Supply and Demand Report 2018]. 2018. https://www.enecho.meti.go.jp/statistics/total_energy/pdf/stte_030.pdf.
Aoki, Mizuho. "Abe to Africa: Use Aid as You See Fit." *Japan Times*, June 2, 2013. https://www.japantimes.co.jp/news/2013/06/02/national/politics-diplomacy/abe-promises-africa-new-3-2-trillion-in-aid-as-ticad-v-kicks-off/.
Aoki, Mizuho. "Abe Wants to Enable SDF to Rescue Citizens Overseas." *Japan Times*, February 2, 2015. https://www.japantimes.co.jp/news/2015/02/02/national/politics-diplomacy/abe-says-working-with-global-community-only-way-to-fight-terrorism/.
Arab News. "Trump's ME Peace Plan Quite Big: Suga." January 30, 2020. https://www.arabnews.jp/en/japan/article_9745/.
Associated Press. "The Latest: Japan Fears Jerusalem Move Could Stoke Tension." May 14, 2018. https://www.businessinsider.com/ap-the-latest-japan-fears-jerusalem-move-could-stoke-tensions-2018-5.
Azad, Shiraz. "Seeking a New Role: Japan's Middle East Policy under Shinzo Abe." *East Asia* 34 (2017): 287–305.
Cabinet Secretariat. "National Security Strategy." December 17, 2013. https://www.cas.go.jp/jp/siryou/131217anzenhoshou/nss-e.pdf.
Hürriyet Daily News. "Turkey, Japan Scrap Partnership in Sinop Nuclear Plant in Turkey's North." January 20, 2020. https://www.hurriyetdailynews.com/turkey-japan-scrap-partnership-in-sinop-nuclear-plant-in-turkeys-north-151212.
Ikeda, Akifumi. "'Arabu' to 'Beikoku' no Airo de: Nihon no Chuto Wahei Gaiko ha Donoyounishite Seiritsu Shitaka" [Between "Arab" and the "United States": How did Japan's Policy on the Middle East Peace Process Come into Existence?]. *Synodos: Academic Journalism*, March 29, 2018. https://synodos.jp/international/21275.
Israel Ministry of Foreign Affairs. "Cabinet Approves Plan to Strengthen Economic Ties with Japan." January 4, 2015. https://mfa.gov.il/MFA/PressRoom/2015/Pages/Cabinet-approves-plan-to-strengthen-economic-ties-with-Japan-4-Jan-2015.aspx.
Iwama, Koichi. "Abe Shushou Chutou Shigengaikou no Hyoka" [Evaluating Prime Minister Abe's Resource Diplomacy in the Middle East]. *Sekiyukaihatsujihou*, 154 (August 2007): 52–57.
Japan International Cooperation Agency. "Signing of Japanese ODA Loan Agreements with the Republic of Iraq." Press release, October 15, 2012. https://www.jica.go.jp/english/news/press/2012/121015_03.html.
Japan Times. "Japan, Iran to Continue Talks on Oil Field Project." September 16, 2006. https://www.japantimes.co.jp/news/2006/09/16/business/japan-iran-to-continue-talks-on-oil-field-project/.

Japan Times. "Saudi Crown Prince 'Fully Supports' Japan MSDF Mission in Middle East." January 13, 2020. https://www.japantimes.co.jp/news/2020/01/13/national/politics-diplomacy/saudi-king-mohammed-bin-salman-shinzo-abe-msdf/.

Jiji/Reuters. "Japan Distancing Itself from U.S. Claims of Iranian Involvement in Tanker Attacks." *Japan Times*, June 18, 2019. https://www.japantimes.co.jp/news/2019/06/18/national/politics-diplomacy/japan-distancing-u-s-claims-iranian-involvement-tanker-attacks/#.X0jDVsj7Q2w.

Kobayashi, Amane. "'Indo Pashifikku Koso' to Chuto-Afurika Chiiki" ['Indo-Pacific Vision' and the Middle East/Africa Region]. *JIME Chuto Doko Bunseki* [A Monthly Middle Eastern and Energy Bulletin] 18, no. 4 (2019): 1–15.

Kyodo. "Bill for SDF Rescues Abroad Passed." *Japan Times*, November 1, 2013. https://www.japantimes.co.jp/news/2013/11/01/national/bill-for-sdf-rescues-abroad-passed/.

Lamont, Christopher. "Japan's Evolving Ties with the Middle East." *Asia Society Institute*, July 28, 2020. https://asiasociety.org/asias-new-pivot/japan.

Lehman, Howard P. "The Asian Economic Model in Africa: Japanese Development Lessons for Africa." In *Japan and Africa: Globalization and Foreign Aid in the 21st Century*, edited by Howard P. Lehman. London: Routledge, 2010, 25–38.

Ministry of Defense. "International Peace Cooperation Assignment Operations in the Golan Heights." *Japan Defense Focus*, no. 37 (February 2013). https://www.mod.go.jp/e/jdf/no37/activities.html.

Ministry of Foreign Affairs. "Address by Prime Minister Shinzo Abe at the Opening Session of the Sixth Tokyo International Conference on African Development (TICAD VI)." August 27, 2016. https://www.mofa.go.jp/afr/af2/page4e_000496.html.

Ministry of Foreign Affairs. "Conference on Cooperation among East Asian Countries for Palestinian Development (CEAPAD)." February 14, 2013. https://www.mofa.go.jp/region/middle_e/palestine/ceapad_20130214.html.

Ministry of Foreign Affairs, *Diplomatic Bluebook 2020 (Japanase version)*, 2020."

Ministry of Foreign Affairs, "Japan's Position on the Peace in the Middle East." January 13, 2015. https://www.mofa.go.jp/region/middle_e/stance.html.

Ministry of Foreign Affairs. "Keynote Address by Shinzo Abe." August 28, 2019. https://www.mofa.go.jp/af/af1/page4e_001069.html.

Ministry of Foreign Affairs. *ODA White Paper 2013* (English Version). 2013, 125.

Ministry of Foreign Affairs. "Press Conference by Prime Minister Shinzo Abe Following His Visits to the United States and Middle Eastern Countries." May 2, 2007. https://www.mofa.go.jp/region/middle_e/pmv0704/press.html.

Ministry of Foreign Affairs. *Yokohama Declaration 2019*. August 30, 2019. https://www.mofa.go.jp/region/africa/ticad/ticad7/pdf/yokohama_declaration_en.pdf.

Mitarai, Fujio. "Abe Sori no Chuto Rekiho ni Awasete Misshon wo Haken" [Dispatching a delegation along with Prime Minister Abe's visit to the Middle East]. *KeizaiTrend* 55, no. 7 (2007): 62.

Miyagi, Taizo. *Gendai Nihon Gaikoshi* [History of Contemporary Japanese Diplomacy]. Tokyo: Chuokoron-shinsha, 2016, 238.

Nagaoka, Kansuke. "Views from the Far East on the Middle East." *Palestine-Israel Journal of Politics, Economics and Culture* 13, no. 4 (2007): 64–68.

Nihonkeizai Shimbun. "Gaikō, sabitsuku kanminrenkei, zaikai chikaku hendō" [Diplomacy, Government-Private Sector Cooperation Getting Rusty]. January 29, 2014. https://www.nikkei.com/article/DGXNASFS2203D_T20C14A1SHA000/.

Nihonkeizai Shimbun. "Keidanren kaichō: "Hijo ni minori Ōi" shushō doko no igi kyōchō" Shusho Doko no Igi Kyocho" [Keidanren Chief 'Very Productive,' Emphasizing the Value of the Prime Minister's Traveling with]. May 3, 2013. https://www.nikkei.com/article/DGXNASFS03024_T00C13A5000000/.

Nishida, Ippeita. "The SDF Dispatches to the Middle East." *Security Studies* 2, no. 2 (2020): 61–77.

Obayashi, Yuka and Florence Tan. "Japanese Refiners Halt Iran Oil Imports as Waiver Expiry Looms." *Reuters*, March 29, 2019. https://www.reuters.com/article/us-iran-sanctions-oil-japan/japanese-refiners-halt-iran-oil-imports-as-waiver-expiry-looms-idUSKCN1RA0BQ.

The Office of the Supreme Leader. "Trump Not Worth Sending a Message to, We Won't Talk to U.S." July 3, 2019. https://www.leader.ir/en/content/23196/Ayatollah-Khamenei's-meeting-with-Japan's-Prime-Minister,-Shinz%C5%8D-Abe.

Ōta, Yorihisa. "UAE, Nihonzei no Yudenken'eki Koushin ni Maemuki, Edano Keisansho" [UAE positive to extend oil concessions, Edano]. *Nihonkeizai Shimbun*, October 11, 2011. https://www.nikkei.com/article/DGXNASDF11002_R11C11A0EB1000/.

Prime Minister's Office and His Cabinet. "The Africa that Joins in Partnership with Japan is Brighter Still." June 1, 2013. https://japan.kantei.go.jp/96_abe/statement/201306/01speech_e.html.

Prime Minister's Office and His Cabinet. "Keynote Speech by Prime Minister Abe at the Joint Meeting of the Japan-Egypt Business Committee." January 17, 2015. https://japan.kantei.go.jp/97_abe/statement/201501/17egypt.html.

Prime Minister of Japan and His Cabinet. "Press Conference by Prime Minister Shinzo Abe during His Visit to Turkey." May 3, 2013. https://japan.kantei.go.jp/96_abe/statement/201305/03turkey_naigai_e.html.

Schulze, Kai. "Rivalry in the Middle East? Japan's CEAPAD Initiative and China's Rise." *The Pacific Review* 32, no. 5 (2019): 809–830.

Shaoul, Raquel. "Japan and Israel: An Evaluation of Relationship-building in the Context of Japan's Middle East Policy." *Israel Affairs* 10, no. 1–2 (2004): 273–297.

Tobita, Masanori. "Japan Takes Up Jerusalem Issue, Proposes 4-party Talks." *Nikkei Asian Review*, December 27, 2017. https://asia.nikkei.com/Politics/Japan-takes-up-Jerusalem-issue-proposes-4-party-talks.

Tominaga, Erika. "Japan's Middle East Policy, 1972-74: Resources Diplomacy, Pro-American Policy, and New Left." *Diplomacy & Statecraft* 28, no. 4 (2017): 674–701.

Xinhua. "Chinese President Makes Four-Point Proposal for Settlement of Palestinian Question." *Global Times*, May 6, 2013. http://www.globaltimes.cn/content/779577.shtml.

Chapter 13

Japan's Global Image

Nancy Snow

Japan's global image has been dominated by the man at the top, Abe Shinzo, the longest serving prime minister who announced his resignation from office in August 2020 due to declining health. Abe's tenure in office contributed to a rise in Japan's stature in the world, but his revisionist and right-wing policies bolstered rancor in the region and did not resolve the country's persistent problems, including but not limited to the growing gap in gender equality and access, as well as Japan's weak global communication. However, Abe succeeded in making global societies and their governments care more about his "beautiful country" Japan. As the world moves into its third decade of the twenty-first century, the Japanese people will need to think beyond Abe, his vision, and his policies in order to broaden the landscape of what the world imagines when they think "Japan."

In order to understand Japan's global image in the context of the Abe years, one cannot begin by projecting the future of the nation-state on business-as-usual terms. In 2020, Abe's final year as prime minister, everything the world once knew and took for granted about globalization unraveled—travel and tourism, international educational exchanges, global business trips, and face-to-face encounters evaporated almost overnight. The world went from fresh air *Under the Tuscan Sun*[1] Italian bliss to suffocating *Outbreak*.[2]

The Japanese government's wish to become one of the countries on every global citizen's travel bucket list took a disastrous turn when international borders and major cities were sealed in a panic, as if the new coronavirus needed official permission to enter. Japan's global image took a dive due to major missteps early on, including its disastrous public relations handling of the outbreak aboard the Diamond Princess cruise ship docked in Yokohama in February[3] and the agonizing postponement of the Tokyo Olympics decision in late March.[4] It took outside pressure from *gaijin* (the Japanese word for foreigner) media and the would-be athletes to get the government to act.[5] Indecision in the face of urgency puzzled onlookers who expected more, given Japan's reputation for handling disasters.

To be fair to Japan, global communication misfires were happening to varying degrees in nation-states across the globe, but in one twenty-three-nation survey conducted by Singapore's BlackBox Research and France's Toluna, Japan's Abe administration managed to hit rock bottom in the government's handling of the virus outbreak as judged by its own citizens,[6] where responses by the Chinese and Vietnamese governments ranked highest.[7] What could Japan have possibly done so wrong when its confirmed infections and mortality rate were so low (and have remained so) in comparison to the rest of the world?[8] For a country that was expecting to welcome the best athletes and the world's media in a matter of months, it wasn't the internal coronavirus numbers that negatively impacted its global image. At the time Abe Shinzo announced he would be retiring for health on August 29, 2020, Japan had recorded 1,255 deaths (about 8.3 per million residents), one of the lowest fatality rates globally though relatively high for Asia.[9] Japan's struggle under Abe was—as it has so often been—in its strategic communications.[10] There seemed to be no one at the top who could explain Japan's response to those living through the pandemic reality occurring outside. Abe's governmental response was to seal out the world for nearly six months, making it difficult if not impossible for its own foreign workers and resident aliens to return had they gotten stuck overseas, whereas in other developed countries resident aliens, especially those with spouses and/or children who were nationals, were not treated differently from citizens. This put the *Kasumigaseki* (Japanese word for government bureaucracy) in an awkward impasse with its most important bilateral relation, the United States, as well as its pro-Japanese government entities like the American Chamber of Commerce in Japan (ACCJ) and the U.S. Embassy in Tokyo. The normally politically agnostic ACCJ went public with a campaign to end the travel ban for non-Japanese residents as a matter of business principle, as did the European Business Council.[11]

PERSONALIZING JAPAN'S GLOBAL IMAGE

National image and impression management operates in stages, from imagination, to mediated reality, and, if one is fortunate enough, personal experience. In comparison to the rest of the world, Japan's global image is viewed as a unique case, to borrow the favorite bromide of the *Nihonjinron* (a school of thought in Japan which, along orientalist lines, views Japan as unique and impossible to understand by outsiders) literature that has been observed from the Tokugawa to the modern era.[12]

At the pseudo-environment level, my own picture of Japan consisted primarily of war-driven images of either attack (Pearl Harbor) or suffering (Hiroshima, Nagasaki) that permeated my mind growing up in America. Japan was a former enemy, defeated imperial power, and now a friend to the United States, a place that had experienced the full spectrum of American hard power in the 1940s but had grown into an economic and soft power superpower with seemingly no hard feelings about the past. It was more Sony than *kamikaze*.

In his book, *The Image*, Daniel J. Boorstin writes, "The tourist looks for caricature; travel agents at home and national tourist bureaus abroad are quick to oblige."[13] But so are government ministries eager to draw distinct lines between what's to be expected inside by those visiting from outside. Moments after I first stepped foot in Japan at Narita International Airport in the summer of 1993, Japan's unique ways were shared in the form of a 10-page handout distributed to all of us neophytes participating in a cabinet-level international youth exchange dubbed "International Youth Village."[14] The handout's title, "Some Japanese Cultural Characteristics,"[15] was authored by Osamu Muro, who twenty-five years earlier had published a book title *Introduction to Japan*.[16] The handout contained some gems. I learned that men "drink heavily and it is fairly common for men to become drunk. The amount of alcohol a man can drink is seen as a sign of his strength and manliness." Women were likely to put their hands in front of their mouth when laughing, while "it is common to see men spit on the street or train platforms in full view of others." The Japanese people were presented as "wet" or sentimental, and in communication, "do not highly value eloquence and oratory." People from outside Japan are called *gaijin* (aliens—literally meaning "person from outside"), and no matter how fluent an alien's Japanese might be, he or she remains *gaijin* and would not be accepted as a Japanese by a Japanese. Finally, I was visiting a nation of pragmatists: "The enemy of yesterday can easily be the friend of today." This pragmatism was a relief in light of the twentieth-century relations between the United States and Japan.

My observation over the three weeks that followed was that Japan was run by men. Men —sober or not—were the standout fixtures in business and politics. They were front office while women were back office or highly proficient coffee and tea cart support staff with graduate degrees. Women were as highly educated as their male counterparts, but their perceived productive value dropped off precipitously at the office or ministry door. I could only conclude that women ruled the home, because they had to have some power somewhere! Once back in the United States, I arranged an interview with the wife of the Japanese ambassador, who asked me if I were married and then shared the Christmas cake parable about the ideal age of a Japanese woman (25) for marriage.

OLD HABITS AND OLD IMAGES DIE HARD

Fast forward to 2013, and BBC correspondent Anita Rani, like many other reporters on first-time assignment to Japan, shared with her global viewers as she walked the Shibuya crossing that "Japan is so different to any other country in the world."[17] The program special from the most respected international broadcaster in the world was called "No Sex Please, We're Japanese," and it set tongues wagging about national stereotypes. Japan's low fertility rate was not the worst in the world, but compared to other countries like Italy, Germany, and Singapore, it seemed to be correlated with the least amount of sex. In its place, Rani discovered with fascination, was the virtual girlfriend or pop idol. Rani interviewed a few men in their 30s, one of whom said, "I think twice about going out with a 3D woman."[18] The same year sexless Japan entered the media spotlight, Prime Minister Abe Shinzo began his first year of his return to office. Abe secured the Summer Olympics for 2020, and Japan was off to the races. By 2020, seemingly everything good would happen to Japan. Women would be occupying 30 percent of the corporate suites and boards of directors, upward of 300,000 international students would be at Japanese universities, and over 30 million tourists would be dropping by Japan per annum. The first goal was unrealized, but the latter two were reached by 2019.[19]

It seemed there was no place on the planet at the time like Japan and its top-ranked capital Tokyo,[20] both of which were riding the highest wave of global anticipation for success in the third decade of the twenty-first century. Las Vegas sure bets could be placed that an economic and cultural tsunami would emerge from the global spotlight. Not only that, the expected good times for Japan and its relationship with the world would transcend the ups and downs of the Abe administration decade that preceded Japan's golden moment. His legacy would fade the more that Japan's image rose.

Japan was set to take the world by storm in the areas where it most prominently stands out—off-beat entertainment, high culture, a mix of the modern and the traditional, and inimitable hospitality.[21] David Haigh, CEO of Brand Finance, echoed the widely held sentiment in the first year of Reiwa that the best was yet to come: "Japan is increasingly becoming a tourism hotspot, with millions visiting every year hoping to soak up the culture and explore all the country has to offer. With the nation currently hosting the 2019 Rugby World Cup and next summer's Tokyo 2020 Olympics just around the corner, there is no doubt we will see an even greater uplift in Japan's brand strength in the future."[22] *Conde Nast,* too, named Japan the best big city to visit in 2019. The same year, Japan overtook the United Kingdom for fourth place in a ranking of the world's top nation brands after the United States, China, and Germany.[23] The London-based cultural affairs and global lifestyle magazine

Monocle devoted its December 2019/January 2020 issue predominantly to Japan, which its international team of panelists also named #1 overall in 2019 in its Global Soft Power ranking. "From the G20 and Rugby World Cup in 2019 to hosting the Summer Olympics in 2020, Japanese hospitality is in the limelight."[24] Contributing writer Ben Davis praised the country for its "impeccable service, responsible citizenship and warm hospitality" as just some of the practices that it can teach the world, along with the country's earned "culture of making" with "Made in Japan" indicating high quality as well as the legendary reputation for preparing, even over-preparing, for disasters.[25]

The unforeseen circumstances of the global pandemic wiped away the anticipated premium return on investment to Japan's nation brand related to hosting the Summer Olympics on schedule. For a country well known for being prepared for and handling natural disasters, including the 3/11 triple disaster (earthquake, tsunami, nuclear meltdown), nothing could have prepared Japan for such a precipitous drop in global recognition.

THE MEN IN THE MIRROR

Through this Japan watcher's eyes, it is imperative that we look back in the rearview mirror to the policies and personality of the nation's chief politician, Abe Shinzo, who oversaw Japan's global image reconstruction since 2012. His major presence on the international stage coincided with my research into Japan's public diplomacy after 3/11,[26] and no matter how hard one attempts to assess the country's assets separate from its politics, Abe cannot be delinked from Japan's reputation and image. It would be like evaluating the United States separate from the influence and perplexing presence of Donald Trump. It's an impossible task when these men take up most of the media mind space about their respective countries.

Unlike Trump, who casts aspersions over a country divided by two main political parties, Abe is the executive head of Japan's only large national party that has ruled the country almost uninterrupted since the 1950s. No other parties have exerted much influence on the nation's brand overseas, especially considering that global publics do not follow Japanese politics with the same attention they might American politics. Abe's style of leadership is centralized and top-down, driven by the *Kasumigaseki* district of Tokyo, where the government ministries are located.

Throughout his second-term tenure, Prime Minister Abe has faced little political opposition and survived a number of cronyism corruption charges that functioned as little more than speed bumps for slowing the Abe agenda. In terms of sheer global recognition, Shinzo Abe has been able to step onto the stage at a level not seen since the administration of Yasuhiro Nakasone (1982–1987). Nakasone, who died in 2019 at age 101, had his own personal brand style with his counterpart in the United States, Ronald Reagan, and the "Ron–Yasu" relationship preceded by decades the "Shinzo–Donald" connection, though with more success for the former dyad. Unlike Abe, who was unable to simultaneously maintain close ties with China, South Korea, and the United States, Nakasone has been credited with promoting closer ties from Japan to both China and South Korea.[27] He maintained his popularity overseas and with the Japanese people, though less so with his fellow LDP parliamentarians.[28] Abe, on the other hand, has maintained steadier control of the LDP while seeing his popularity diminish over time with the Japanese people.[29]

Abe's prominence and the global reach of his administration coincided with the government's public participation in social media outreach, especially via Facebook and Twitter, where the prime minister has been mocked and criticized by overseas publics and increasingly by the Japanese public. The "Abe lounging at home" video from April 2020, intended to calm the Japanese people during the pandemic, backfired nationally and went viral globally, becoming like a joke meme. Within days, it had been viewed over 18 million times.[30] It exhibited a lack of sensitivity to the rise in human suffering and uncertainty, as it showed the prime minister petting his dog, relaxing to music, watching TV, and drinking tea. At worst, it raised questions about how out of touch the head of state had become with the daily goings on of his people, who were forced to adjust to an abrupt and unforeseen change in normalcy and high degrees of uncertainty about the future.[31] Immediate parallels could be made between Abe's tone deaf posturing and his close ties to a very unpopular American president. Like with Abe's socially distant nonchalance displayed in the video, Trump is often accused of standing on his own agenda and personal legacy above all, seen clearly in his repeated downplaying of the severity of COVID-19, his stance being that if you don't look for the virus, the cases go away.[32]

These aspects of the Abe and Trump style of leadership in the handling of the coronavirus, which project a lack of empathy and understanding toward others, has not won much domestic or global approval.[33] By August 2020, both Abe and Trump's favorability had declined to some of the lowest numbers in their tenure, with Abe and his cabinet's favorability plummeting to an ignoble range of 29 percent at the initial management of the pandemic, to 35 percent when Japan recorded a presumed second wave uptick in coronavirus infections right before the Obon holiday season in August.[34] Trump's favorability slid to 41 percent public approval three months before the November 2020 election, with projections that he had less than a third of a chance to be reelected. If Abe were hoping to catch on with a rising star in his liaisons with the Trump administration, his hopes were dashed.

BRAND ABE'S EFFECTS ON JAPAN'S GLOBAL IMAGE

Standing front and center with Brand Japan is Brand Abe, and Brand Abe has had mixed results with its goal of advancing Japan's image in the world. Working in Abe's favor is the fact that Japan is very much back on the global map: people talk about Japan more, and want to know what Tokyo is thinking on matters of state beyond just economic and fiscal policies, which so dominated the rise of Japan before China took to the stage. Outside the corridors of government bureaucracy, Japan and Tokyo are seen among global publics as the world's most creative places.[35] Japan's appeal to the rest of the world, particularly its soft power,[36] has never been higher,[37] but at what political cost? An obvious tension exists in having a divisive head of government obsessed with righting and repairing past wrongs to represent the image of the place and its public moreso than the place itself can represent on its own.

We need to look back to what gave rise to the desires and motivations of this man, whose political dynasty makes him anxious for Japanese image redemption and repair. Abe's actions directly impact Japan's global image, most notably perhaps his hawkish views on over seventy years of Japan's pacifist branding that followed its defeat in World War II. Instead of pursuing a mediation role in the Northeast Asian region, Japan under Abe has sought to give verbal muscle to the country's foreign and military policies by openly sparring with both China and South Korea in third rail political battles. These include challenging the so-called "Comfort Women" sexual slavery legacy,[38] censoring middle-school textbooks from teaching what Mr. Abe called their "self-torturing views of history,"[39] or playing to ultranationalist constituencies through a visit to Yasukuni shrine early in his second term, a tradition which he rightly ended after the inevitable backlash.[40] Richard Cohen, fifty-year political columnist at *The Washington Post,* indicted both Brand Japan and Brand Abe at the end of 2014, suggesting that the country was losing its good image appeal:

> Japan is working hard at forgetting. Its prime minister, Abe Shinzo, suggests in code-talk that Japan was the victim of World War II—no war criminals at all, thank you—and its influential conservative press, with a wink from the government, is determined to whitewash the country's use of sex slaves during the war. This sort of thing can be catching. Maybe others will forget why they consider Japan a friend.[41]

The famous domestic fixer-upper Marie Kondo, whose skill set is a personification of Japan's neat and trim image in the world, is matched by the strivings of the political fixer-upper Shinzo Abe. Born nine years after the end of World War II, he is driven not by sparking joy like Kondo,[42] but by a need to declutter and simplify the past. This may spark joy for the Japanese prime minister, but it sparks more contempt and criticism from close neighbors, whose reactions serve as drivers of Japan's extended image in the world.[43] This adversarial environment of competing narratives about the past is the promotional linchpin in Japan's global image production.

To the west of the Japanese archipelago, Abe looks at past embittered relations with the competing great power of Asia, China, and to a young buck nation like South Korea, a bitter pill ex-colony that does not know the meaning of respecting an older brother. To the east, Abe considers the postwar relations between the victorious United States and defeated and depleted Japan. He cannot help but imagine a nation impacted by these shadow countries that flank its own self image. It is not only the past that defines the man—one specific family member drives Abe's need to keep looking behind: he's seeking redemption first for his grandfather, Nobusuke Kishi, and second for his nation.

THIS IS PERSONAL

Global image, to the extent that it matters to any country leader, as it invariably does,[44] is important to Abe if it enhances Japan's soft power perception, not reality, and if it enhances his and his grandfather's legacy. Abe is cleaning up the chaos that was left behind when his grandfather was ignobly detained as a war criminal without trial for three years after the end of World War II before regaining his freedom. His grandfather kept the family tradition of politics going with his appointment as prime minister, but it's the humiliations that Abe responds and reacts to the most. His grandfather Kishi, carefully groomed into becoming a "friend of the United States,"[45] left his ambivalent Americanophile predilections with his grandson who, in his second term, became the closest allied head of state with his conservative counterpart in the White House, Donald J. Trump.

I have been a Japan observer, in general, and Abe watcher, specifically, since Abe Shinzo reemerged on the global stage in his second term in December 2012 after his initial short and uneventful one-year stint from 2006 to 2007, at which time Abe was reported to have stepped down due to a chronic health condition. My own understanding of Japan's global image is deeply tied to my image of Japan's longest-serving prime minister. Abe's second term was timed ideally; I was first an overseas armchair observer, and then became an in-country field researcher. I held an Abe Fellowship in Japan months after he took office in December 2012, which allowed me trips back and forth between the United States and Japan. The Abe Fellowships themselves are tied deeply to Japan's global image in the late twentieth century—they emerged in the immediate aftermath of Japan's stinging checkbook diplomacy label, applied to its perceived financial participation without risk involvement in the 1980s that ultimately culminated in the first Gulf War (1990–1991).[46]

After the Gulf War it was clear, Courtney Purrington writes, "Japan can no longer be an economic giant and political pygmy in international affairs."[47] The Abe Fellowships remains one of the highest profile academic means to elevate Japan's image on the global stage. They have become prized fellowships for Japanese and American scholars from elite institutions to conduct independent research on pressing issues affecting the U.S.–Japan relationship. The Japan Foundation's Center for Global Partnership (CGP)[48] was established in April 1991 to set up the Abe Fellowships to not only reignite Japan–U.S. commitments but also to honor the memory of Abe Shintaro, who had actively served in high-profile diplomatic negotiations as Prime Minister Yasuhiro Nakasone's foreign minister.

Abe's father was once heir apparent to become prime minister were it not for his death in May 1991 at the relatively young age (by Japanese standards) of 67, as well as the taint of the Recruit scandal. Ronald Yates of the *Chicago Tribune* observed that "Mr. Abe not only set a record as Japan's longest reigning postwar foreign minister, from 1982 to 1986, but was instrumental in pushing Japan onto center stage of global politics. During the Iran–Iraq war, for example, he succeeded in establishing diplomatic dialogues with both Baghdad and Tehran in an effort to find a peaceful solution to the bloody conflict. Japan was the only industrialized nation to manage that. He was active in talks with Gorbachev after stepping down as foreign minister, and Mr. Abe's reputation as one of Japan's top statesmen was assured."[49] My research focused on Japan's nation brand activities and public diplomacy policies after 3/11. I soon realized that Japan's global image was inextricably tied to Abe's fortunes and vice versa, which worked well for other heads of state like that of the Obama administration. But Brand Abe could no more rescue Brand Japan than Brand Obama could rescue Brand America.[50]

Brand Abe represents the most public relations and image-focused prime minister in Japanese history, helped along by the tools of modern communication that allow for more global and domestic public outreach and public opinion feedback. To his credit, Abe Shinzo has placed Japan on the world stage to a greater degree because of the global communications focus of his administration. Abe's success in shaping Japan's global image was based on good timing and global curiosity about the enigmatic economic and cultural giant that was shrinking in relevance to a rising Chinese economy and a rising South Korean cultural rival. The decision was made in his second term to link Brand Japan directly to Brand Abe, lending to Abe's team constructing media-friendly slogans, such as Abenomics and Womenomics, both of which played a large part in making Japan more relevant to the world, grabbing headlines and magazine covers across the globe.

In May 2013, just five months after Abe took office again, *The Economist* magazine placed a triumphant Superman-like image of a smiling Abe on its cover, flying high as a leader over not only Japan but also the world.[51] The graphic showed Abe wearing a suit jacket over his superhero garb with the yen symbol on his chest. Flanked on either side were two Japan Air Self-Defense Force fighter jets. The accompanying article observed that "the man in Japan with a plan" Abe "has sketched out a programme of geopolitical rebranding and constitutional change that is meant to return Japan to what Mr. Abe thinks is its rightful place as a world power."[52] These words and the accompanying image show a leader whose commitment to Japan's global image mirrors that of the United States during the Obama era, when Brand Obama defined so much of the rehabilitated reputation and image of the United States after the George W. Bush administration. Obama's elevation of America's core moral values and respectability after eight years of an unpopular "war on terror" and two equally unpopular active interventions in Iraq and Afghanistan were undoubtedly contributing factors for how Abe Shinzo set out to elevate Japan's significance in the world.

Japan under Abe 2.0 (2012–present) became a place subject to worldwide envy. In spring 2013, the famed Nobel Laureate economist Joseph Stiglitz declared that he was bullish on Abenomics: "There is every reason to believe that Japan's strategy for rejuvenating its economy will succeed: the country benefits from strong institutions, has a well-educated labor force with superb technical skills and design sensibilities, and is located in the world's most (only?) dynamic region."[53]

A major impetus for the rejuvenation of Japan's economy was the shot in the arm known as Tokyo 2020. The Summer Games were to be the most heavily sponsored international sporting event in history, with an expected return in the hundreds of billions by 2030.[54] They were awarded based on what the press described as the prime minister's charismatic and direct plea to reassure the International Olympic Committee that any nuclear contamination from Fukushima would be well under control and need not be of concern.[55] Abe left the G20 meeting in Russia early to make a personal pledge to the IOC. Regarding the radiation, he promised: "It has never done and will never do any damage to Tokyo. There are no health-related problems until now, and nor will there be in the future. I make the statement to you in the most emphatic and unequivocal way."[56] In response, IOC president Jacques Rogge referred to the final decision of Tokyo over Madrid and Istanbul as a choice based on the city brand's image and reputation as "a safe pair of hands."

Japan's global image at the time of the Olympics bid was that of the highest quality in service and safety. No doubt Japan's steady and calm response to 3/11 and the global outpouring of support that followed represented a story line for the Olympic spirit in 2020 that was hard to dismiss. If Japan's global image were measured by a gestation period of Abe's first nine months in office (December 2012–September 2013), this baby would be healthy and happy. The combined dreams of post-3/11 recovery, resilience, and redemption that characterized Abenomics and the Olympics put Japan on the global map like nothing in recent memory. However, just three months later, Abe, perhaps emboldened by his success streak, severely damaged his and the nation's brand by appearing in person at Yasukuni Shrine to make a ceremonial donation to the war dead, including war criminals, which produced immediate blowback both regionally and internationally.

JAPAN'S WELCOME MAT TO THE WORLD

Throughout Abe's tenure, Japan's global image has been helped along by an unprecedented door-opening to the world, most clearly seen in the hosting of two specific demographics: tourists and international students. The Japan Student Services Organization (JASSO) maintains statistical data on incoming international students and the most recent pre-coronavirus figures from May 2019 (published in April 2020) showed that Japan was host to 312, 214 overseas students across language schools and higher education, with 228,403 at higher education institutions and 83,811 in short-term Japanese language training. Nearly 40 percent (39.9%) were from the People's Republic of China (124, 436), followed by another 23.5percent students from Vietnam (73,389). In 2011, Japan had hosted only 138,075 students in higher education institutions and another 25,622 for language training. This record uptick characterized by the globalization of Japan's society and educational sector was spurred forth in part by rising competition in the region. In 2015, international ranking measures like the annual *Times Higher Education World University Rankings* showed Chinese universities overtaking Japan for the first time, just five years after China passed Japan as the world's second-largest economy.

Japan's global image under Abe has staked the second decade of the twenty-first century after the triple disaster of 3/11 on economic and cultural globalization, a major part of which has been to internationalize Japanese university campuses by hiring more foreign faculty and offering four-year English-language university degrees. However, these goals have been insufficient because far fewer Japanese students participate in international classroom settings like those found on American campuses. In the last five academic years of the 1990s (AY 1994/95–AY 1998/99, the Institute of International Education *Open Doors* reports that "Japan was the leading sender of students to the U.S., but has since fallen to eighth due to surges in students from India, China, South Korea, and Saudi Arabia, the effects of a rapidly aging Japanese population, and other factors including the global economy and the recruiting cycle of Japanese companies."[57] Twenty years ago, the United States alone hosted nearly 48,000 Japanese students on U.S. campuses. That number has now been cut to more than half to under 20,000 students, according to *Open Doors 2019*,[58] China sends ten times the number of students to the United States than Japan does, leaving Japan to make up only about 3 percent of the total international student population in the United States, while India and China combined total 40 percent.

Despite the record numbers of tourists who visited Japan and the foreign students who increasingly chose Japan for study abroad or language training in the pre-COVID-19 era, these policies have not dramatically altered Japan's intellectual importance in international relations. Japan's image abroad remains pop culture-centric and not foreign policy prominent, despite its win record in Nobel prizes and Tokyo's Michelin stars that outshine all others.[59] This is the fallout of the Cool Japan craze that followed Douglas McCray's 2002 article in *Foreign Policy* magazine, the concept of which carries weight to this day, seen as recently as a May 2020 article by fashion writer Marc Bain about Japan's global image titled "Gross National Cool: How Japan's global image morphed from military empire to eccentric pop-culture superpower."[60] As is the norm for many pop culture pieces on Japan's influence in the world, Bain's article contained references to every stereotypical touch point, including the rise of anime and manga, Hokusai's *The Great Wave*, *Godzilla*, and Hayao Miyazaki's 2003 Oscar winner *Spirited Away*. His point was that Japan's soft power superpower status in global popular culture has transformed in two decades from "fierce to loveable."

Japan Studies is growing in food and culture areas worldwide,[61] but not so much in the social sciences nor policy, if one can measure its value through an informal search in various scholarly websites like Academia and ResearchGate. Japanese faculty lag behind its counterparts in China or South Korea, who publish more in English-language journals, and are at times rewarded with reduced teaching loads or awards for publishing in higher index journals. According to the *2019 Global Go To Think Tank Index Report*, Japan ranks nine out of the top ten of countries by number of think tanks with 128.[62] The numbers are there, but many are not globally influential. As Warren Stanislaus observed in his study of Japan's think tanks, "The policy-making process has traditionally been viewed as a concern only for the government and there is scarce room for access from potential external actors. *Kasumigaseki* (an area in Tokyo where most government ministry offices are located) has effectively operated as the nation's think tank."[63] One of Japan's most influential think tanks, itself an arm of the Ministry of Foreign Affairs, is the Japan Institute of International Affairs (JIIA). In its 60th anniversary year, the JIIA held its first Tokyo Global Dialogue conference in December 2019. This was the first time that such a global dialogue conference was held in English and welcomed more international speakers,[64] though perhaps predictably, given the government and policy focus, 90 percent of the speakers were old men.

For their part, international women did participate in the Abe-sanctioned World Assembly of Women (WAW) meetings in Tokyo but gender equality numbers have failed to keep pace. By most recent measures, gender equality in Japan has fallen to its lowest ranking (121st among 153 countries).[65] The hoped-for gains by 2020, with up to 30 percent women in management, did not materialize, mainly because the goal was not incentivized. Prime Minister Abe's presiding over several high-profile international gatherings of the world's top market economies, including the G7 Ise-Shima Summit in 2016 and the 2019 G20 Osaka Summit, raised the profile of Japan as a host country, but not as a country with much independent agency in foreign affairs. At each venue, Abe Shinzo was overshadowed by the presence of Barack Obama in 2016 (especially his Hiroshima speech that became an immediate popular read in its Japanese version) and by Donald J. Trump in 2019. Abe's pledge to the IOC that Fukushima would be "under control" and therefore Japan was ready to host the Olympics in 2020 mattered little when the novel coronavirus came into play in early 2020. In a year that was to be the country's big reveal to the world after the triple disaster of 3/11, weak strategic communications, characterized by lax and lagging government response to COVID-19, led to heavy criticism at home and abroad.

CONCLUSION

Japan's primary focus on the central government's global communication capacity and the personal diplomatic brand of the Abe administration, complete with its soft power consequences on image and reputation worldwide have brought much-needed attention to a Japan that was mired in a decades-long continuum between loss and passing. First, the economy tumbled amidst rapid globalization-induced changes, and then Japan's reputation for economic wizardry and technological prowess took a hit. By the time Abe triumphantly returned to office in late 2012, too much of the media's sharp focus was placed on Abe's image and his personal relations with other political leaders, culminating in his ill-fated comradery with Donald Trump. The "man at the top" approach overshadowed persistent systemic problems in Japan, including negative demographic indicators and the continued underusage of Japan's most valuable natural resource: the contributions of women in society. When people talk about Japan around the world, they do not pay close attention to Japan's politics and policies. Instead, the cultural power of Cool Japan is what continues to drive the Japanese-related narratives around most of the world. Japan remains weak in its global communications and must strive to improve through decentralizing its official storytelling away from Tokyo to a more grassroots, innovative human-interest level.

NOTES

1. Frances Mayes, *Under the Tuscan Sun: At Home in Italy*, San Francisco: Chronicle Books, 1996.
2. Wolfgang Petersen, *Outbreak*, United States: Warner Bros, 1995.
3. Nancy Snow, "Japan's government has failed coronavirus communications test," *Nikkei Asian Review*, February 21, 2020. https://asia.nikkei.com/Opinion/Japan-s-government-has-failed-coronavirus-communications-test.
4. Nancy Snow, "Swift Olympic cancellation will boost Japan's soft power," *Nikkei Asian Review*, March 20, 2020. https://asia.nikkei.com/Opinion/Swift-Olympic-cancellation-will-boost-Japan-s-soft-power.
5. Stacy St. Clair, "Postponing the 2020 Olympics may be 'inevitable'," *Chicago Tribune*, March 23, 2020.
6. Jiji/Kyodo News Service, "Abe administration bombs in global survey on coronavirus response," *The Japan Times*, May 9, 2020.
7. Karen Gilchrist, "China gets top score as citizens rank their governments' response to the coronavirus outbreak," CNBC, May 6, 2020. https://www.cnbc.com/2020/05/07/coronavirus-china-vietnam-uae-top-list-as-citizens-rank-government-response.html.
8. Michael Penn, "How Some Asian Countries Beat Back COVID-19," Duke Global Health Institute, August 12, 2020. https://globalhealth.duke.edu/news/how-some-asian-countries-beat-back-covid-19.
9. International SOS, COVID-19 in Japan Report, August 3, 2020. https://pandemic.internationalsos.com/reports/covid-19-in-japan-august-aug-03-2020.
10. For background, see Nancy Snow, "Under the Security Umbrella: Japan's Weak Storytelling to the World," *Defence Strategic Communications* 8 (Autumn 2020): 173–188.
11. Magdalena Osumi, "ACCJ calls for equal treatment of non-Japanese residents hit by travel ban," *The Japan Times*, July 17, 2020.
12. Harumi Befu, *Hegemonity of Homogeneity: An Anthropological Analysis of Nihonjinron*, Melbourne: Trans Pacific Press, 4.
13. Daniel J. Boorstin, *The Image*, New York: Harper & Row, 1964, 106.
14. Cabinet Office, History: International Youth Exchange Programs, https://www8.cao.go.jp/youth/kouryu/en/history.html.
15. Osamu Muro, "Some Japanese Cultural Characteristics," Handout. International Youth Village, July–August 1993.

16. Osamu Muro, *Introduction to Japan*, Tokyo, Japan: Asian Economic Press, 1968.

17. Anita Rani, "No Sex Please, We're Japanese," BBC2 *This World*, December 2013. https://www.bbc.co.uk/programmes/b03fh0bg.

18. Ibid.

19. See Tetsushi Kajimoto, "Women in management at Japan firms still a rarity: Reuters poll," Reuters, September 13, 2018; MOFA, Student Exchange Programs, https://www.mofa.go.jp/policy/culture/people/student/index.html; and JTB Tourism Research & Consulting Co., Japan-bound tourism statistics chart, https://www.tourism.jp/en/tourism-database/stats/inbound/.

20. See Samantha Grindell, "Tokyo Japan was named the best city to visit in 2019," Business Insider, October 27, 2019. The result is based on a *Conde Nast Traveler* Readers' Choice survey that ranked Tokyo number one "Best Big City" in the world based on a poll of its 600,000 readers.

21. For a discussion of how Japanese hospitality helped to win the Summer Olympics bid, see Elisa Ivana Pellicano, "Representing Japanese Hospitality: Takigawa Christel's Speech for the 2020 Tokyo Olympics," *Journal of International and Advanced Japanese Studies* 11 (February 2019): 89–98.

22. Brand Finance, *"Nation Brands 2019,"* October 2019, 11.

23. Jun Tanaka, " Japan Overtakes UK in Nation Brands Ranking," Press Release, Brand Finance Japan. https://brandfinance.com/press-releases/japan-overtakes-uk-in-nation-brands-ranking/.

24. "Soft Power Ranking/Global." *Monocle,* no. 129, December 2019/January 2020, 50.

25. Ibid.; Ben Davis, "Japanese lessons: 10 things that Japan can teach the world," *Monocle,* no. 129 (December 2019/January 2020): 72–73.

26. See Nancy Snow, *Japan's Information War,* CreateSpace Independent Publishing Platform, first edition, July 17, 2016. https://www.ssrc.org/publications/view/japan-s-information-war/. This publication is based on a SSRC Abe Fellowship, "From Operation Tomodachi to No Nukes: Rethinking the Public in Japanese Diplomacy Since 3/11," A revised Japanese language version is forthcoming from Bunshindo Shoten Co Ltd, Tokyo, Japan.

27. *Nikkei Asia,* "Former Japanese Prime Minister Nakasone dies at 101," November 29, 2019. https://asia.nikkei.com/Life-Arts/Obituaries/Former-Japanese-Prime-Minister-Nakasone-dies-at-101.

28. See Karel van Wolferen, *The Enigma of Japanese Power,* New York: Vintage Books, 1990, 150–152; and *Japan Times,* "Nakasone's great achievements as a pragmatist," Staff editorial, December 2, 2019.

29. Satohiro Akimoto, "Testing the resiliency of the Abe administration," Japan Political Pulse, Sasakawa Peace Foundation USA, July 28, 2020. https://spfusa.org/category/japan-political-pulse/.

30. Nancy Snow, "Abe's cheesy video highlights Japan's coronavirus PR failure," *Nikkei Asian Review*, April 25, 2020.

31. Reuters, "Japan PM Abe criticised as tone deaf after lounge-at-home Twitter video. 'Who do you think you are?' became a top trend on Twitter," April 12, 2020.

32. Calvin Woodward and Hope Yen, "AP FACT CHECK: Trump's see-no-evil posture on coronavirus," Associated Press, June 27, 2020.

33. William Pesek, "Japan could be on the brink of a second wave. Will Shinzo Abe act?" *The Washington Post*, Opinion, August 10, 2020.

34. See *Asahi Shimbun*, "Cabinet support rate falls to 29% over response to virus, Kurokawa," May 25, 2020. http://www.asahi.com/ajw/articles/13401687; and Yifan Feng, "Abe's sinking support seen spurring more Japan economic stimulus," *Bloomberg*, August 6, 2020. https://www.bloomberg.com/news/articles/2020-08-06/abe-s-sinking-support-seen-spurring-more-japan-economic-stimulus.

35. Adobe, "Globally Japan and Tokyo are rated as most creative places," from *State of Create: 2016*. https://www.slideshare.net/adobe/full-study-adobe-state-of-create-2016.

36. The London-based Portland Communications and the USC Center on Public Diplomacy coordinate the publication of "The Soft Power 30," which defines soft power as "the use of positive attraction and persuasion to achieve foreign policy objectives. Soft power shuns the traditional foreign policy tools of carrot and stick, seeking instead to achieve influence by building networks, communicating compelling narratives, establishing international rules, and drawing on the resources that make a country naturally attractive to the world."

37. In back-to-back annual reports since 2015, Japan ranks in the Top 10 of soft power.

38. S. Nathan Park, "Shinzo Abe's Legacy is a Wrecked Relationship with South Korea," *Foreign Policy*, September 4, 2020. https://foreignpolicy.com/2020/09/04/shinzo-abe-japan-south-korea-war-nationalism/.

39. Yuka Hayashi, "Japan's Textbook Changes Get Failing Grade From Neighbors," *Wall Street Journal*, April 7, 2015. https://www.wsj.com/articles/japanese-middle-school-textbook-changes-raise-irk-china-south-korea-1428402976.

40. Rupert Wingfield-Hayes, "Why Japan's Shinzo Abe went to Yasukuni shrine," BBC News, December 26, 2013. https://www.bbc.com/news/world-asia-25518137.

41. Richard Cohen, "Will Japan's habit of rewriting history affect its future," *The Washington Post*, December 8, 2014. https://www.washingtonpost.com/opinions/richard-cohen-how-will-japans-habit-of-rewriting-its-history-affect-its-future/2014/12/08/54093bcc-7f0d-11e4-8882-03cf08410beb_story.html.

42. Marie Kondo, *The Life-Changing Magic of Tidying Up: The Japanese Art of Decluttering and Organizing*, Berkeley, CA: Ten Speed Press, 2014, 41.

43. Arirang News, "[Global Insight] Why Japan should acknowledge its wartime sex slavery program as a human rights issue: Int'l Memorial Day for Comfort Women," Arirang TV Global Insight, August 14, 2020. https://www.youtube.com/watch?v=pJmZA0XszsQ.

44. Kenneth Boulding, *The Image*, Ann Arbor, MI: University of Michigan, 1961, 2.

45. van Wolferen, *The Enigma of Japanese Power,* 149.

46. Courtney Purrington, "Tokyo's Policy Responses During the Gulf War and the Impact of the 'Iraqi Shock' on Japan," *Pacific Affairs* 65, no. 2 (Summer, 1992): 161–181.

47. Ibid., 170.

48. Center for Global Partnership, "About Us," https://www.cgp.org/about_us.

49. Ronald E. Yates, "Shintaro Abe, 67, Guided Japan in Global Politics," *Chicago Tribune*, May 15, 1991.

50. John A. Quelch and Katherine E. Jocz, "Can Brand Obama Rescue Brand America?" *Brown Journal of World Affairs* XVI, no. 1 (Fall/Winter 2009): 163–178.

51. See *The Economist*, May 18, 2013 edition.

52. Ibid.,"Japan – Abe's master plan."

53. Joseph Stiglitz, "The Promise of Abenomics," World Economic Forum, in collaboration with Project Syndicate, April 8, 2013.

54. Leo Lewis and Murad Ahmed, "Japan: how coronavirus crushed Abe's Olympics dream," *Financial Times*, March 30, 2020.

55. Ossian Shine,"Tokyo gets 2020 Games with help from prime minister," Reuters, September 7, 2013.

56. Ibid.

57. Institute of International Education, OPEN DOORS FACT SHEET: JAPAN, Educational Exchange Data, Open Doors, 2015.

58. Open Doors, https://opendoorsdata.org/.

59. Monica Burton, "Michelin announces 2020 Stars for Tokyo: The city still has more stars than any other," *Eater*, November 26, 2019. https://www.eater.com/2019/11/26/20983620/michelin-stars-2020-tokyo-japan.

60. Marc Bain, "GROSS NATIONAL COOL: How Japan's global image morphed from military empire to eccentric pop-culture superpower," *Quartz*, May 21, 2020. https://qz.com/1806376/japans-image-has-changed-from-fierce-to-lovable-over-the-decades/.

61. Jake Adelstein, "The Japanese Food Boom Shows No Sign of Slowing Down," *Forbes*, October 2, 2017.

62. James G. McGann, "2019 Global Go To Think Tank Index Report," *TTCSP Global Go To Think Tank Index Reports*. The Wharton School of Business Think Tanks and Civil Societies Program. Philadelphia, PA: University of Pennsylvania, 2020, 42. https://repository.upenn.edu/think_tanks/17.

63. Warren A. Stanislaus, "Seeking an Independent Voice: Japanese Think Tanks," *Global Asia* 10, no. 1 (2015): 1. https://www.globalasia.org/v10no1/focus/seeking-an-independent-voice-japanese-think-tanks_warren-a-stanislaus.

64. MOFA, "The 1st Tokyo Global Dialogue and Reception Hosted by Foreign Minister Motegi," December 1–2, 2019. https://www.mofa.go.jp/fp/pp/page4e_001164.html.

65. Yu Yoshitake, Junichi Bekku, Okabayashi, and Erina Ito, "Japan ranks 121st in gender equality among 153 countries," *The Asahi Shimbun*, December 18, 2019.

REFERENCES

Adelstein, Jake. "The Japanese Food Boom Shows No Sign of Slowing Down." *Forbes*, October 2, 2017.

Adobe. "Globally Japan and Tokyo are rated as most creative places," from *State of Create: 2016*. https://www.slideshare.net/adobe/full-study-adobe-state-of-create-2016.

Akimoto, Satohiro. "Testing the resiliency of the Abe administration." *Japan Political Pulse*, Sasakawa Peace Foundation USA, July 28, 2020. https://spfusa.org/category/japan-political-pulse/.

Arirang News. "[Global Insight] Why Japan should acknowledge its wartime sex slavery program as a human rights issue: Int'l Memorial Day for Comfort Women." Arirang TV Global Insight, August 14, 2020. https://www.youtube.com/watch?v=pJmZA0XszsQ.

Asahi Shimbun. "Cabinet support rate falls to 29% over response to virus, Kurokawa." May 25, 2020. http://www.asahi.com/ajw/articles/13401687.

Bain, Marc. "GROSS NATIONAL COOL: How Japan's global image morphed from military empire to eccentric pop-culture superpower." *Quartz*, May 21, 2020. https://qz.com/1806376/japans-image-has-changed-from-fierce-to-lovable-over-the-decades/.

Befu, Harumi. *Hegemonity of Homogeneity: An Anthropological Analysis of Nihonjinron*. Melbourne: Trans Pacific Press, 2001.

Boorstin, Daniel J. *The Image*. New York: Harper & Row, 1964.

Boulding, Kenneth. *The Image*. Ann Arbor, MI: University of Michigan, 1961.

Brand Finance. *"Nation Brands 2019."* October.

Burton, Monica. "Michelin announces 2020 Stars for Tokyo: The city still has more stars than any other." *Eater*, November 26, 2019. https://www.eater.com/2019/11/26/20983620/michelin-stars-2020-tokyo-japan.

Cabinet Office. History: International Youth Exchange Programs. https://www8.cao.go.jp/youth/kouryu/en/history.html.

Center for Global Partnership. "About Us." https://www.cgp.org/about_us.

Cohen, Richard. "Will Japan's habit of rewriting history affect its future." *The Washington Post*, December 8, 2014. https://www.washingtonpost.com/opinions/richard-cohen-how-will-japans-habit-of-rewriting-its-history-affect-its-future/2014/12/08/54093bcc-7f0d-11e4-8882-03cf08410beb_story.html.

Davis, Ben. "Japanese lessons: 10 things that Japan can teach the world." *Monocle*, no. 129, December 2019/January 2020.

The Economist, "Japan – Abe's master plan." May 18, 2013.

Feng, Yifan. "Abe's sinking support seen spurring more Japan economic stimulus." *Bloomberg*, August 6, 2020. https://www.bloomberg.com/news/articles/2020-08-06/abe-s-sinking-support-seen-spurring-more-japan-economic-stimulus.

Gilchrist, Karen. "China gets top score as citizens rank their governments' response to the coronavirus outbreak." CNBC, May 6, 2020. https://www.cnbc.com/2020/05/07/coronavirus-china-vietnam-uae-top-list-as-citizens-rank-government-response.html.

Grindell, Samantha. "Tokyo Japan was named the best city to visit in 2019." Business Insider, October 27, 2019.

Hayashi, Yuka. "Japan's Textbook Changes Get Failing Grade From Neighbors." *Wall Street Journal*, April 7, 2015. https://www.wsj.com/articles/japanese-middle-school-textbook-changes-raise-irk-china-south-korea-1428402976.

International SOS. COVID-19 in Japan Report, August 3, 2020. https://pandemic.internationalsos.com/reports/covid-19-in-japan-august-aug-03-2020.

Institute of International Education. OPEN DOORS FACT SHEET: JAPAN, Educational Exchange Data. Open Doors, 2015.
Japan Times. "Nakasone's great achievements as a pragmatist." Staff editorial, December 2, 2019.
Jiji/Kyodo News Service. "Abe administration bombs in global survey on coronavirus response." *The Japan Times*, May 9, 2020.
JTB Tourism Research & Consulting Co., Japan-bound tourism statistics chart. https ://www.tourism.jp/en/tourism-database/stats/inbound/.
Kajimoto, Tetsushi. "Women in management at Japan firms still a rarity: Reuters poll." Reuters, September 13, 2018.
Kondo, Marie. *The Life-Changing Magic of Tidying Up: The Japanese Art of Decluttering and Organizing*. Berkeley, CA: Ten Speed Press, 2014.
Lewis, Leo and Murad Ahmed. "Japan: how coronavirus crushed Abe's Olympics dream." *Financial Times*, March 30, 2020.
Mayes, Frances. *Under the Tuscan Sun: At Home in Italy*. San Francisco: Chronicle Books, 1996.
McGann, James G. "2019 Global Go To Think Tank Index Report." *TTCSP Global Go To Think Tank Index Reports*. The Wharton School of Business Think Tanks and Civil Societies Program. Philadelphia, PA: University of Pennsylvania, 2020. https://repository.upenn.edu/think_tanks/17.
MOFA. Student Exchange Programs, https://www.mofa.go.jp/policy/culture/people/student/index.html.
MOFA. "The 1st Tokyo Global Dialogue and Reception Hosted by Foreign Minister Motegi." December 1–2, 2019. https://www.mofa.go.jp/fp/pp/page4e_001164.html.
Muro, Osamu. *Introduction to Japan*. Tokyo, Japan: Asian Economic Press, 1968.
Muro, Osamu. "Some Japanese Cultural Characteristics." Handout. International Youth Village, July-August 1993.
Nikkei Asia. "Former Japanese Prime Minister Nakasone dies at 101." November 29, 2019. https://asia.nikkei.com/Life-Arts/Obituaries/Former-Japanese-Prime-Minister-Nakasone-dies-at-101.
Open Doors. https://opendoorsdata.org/.
Osumi, Magdalena. "ACCJ calls for equal treatment of non-Japanese residents hit by travel ban." *The Japan Times*, July 17, 2020.
Park, S. Nathan. "Shinzo Abe's Legacy is a Wrecked Relationship with South Korea." *Foreign Policy*, September 4, 2020. https://foreignpolicy.com/2020/09/04/shinzo-abe-japan-south-korea-war-nationalism/.
Pellicano, Elisa Ivana. "Representing Japanese Hospitality: Takigawa Christel's Speech for the 2020 Tokyo Olympics." *Journal of International and Advanced Japanese Studies* 11 (February 2019): 89–98.
Penn, Michael. "How Some Asian Countries Beat Back COVID-19." Duke Global Health Institute, August 12, 2020. https://globalhealth.duke.edu/news/how-some-asian-countries-beat-back-covid-19.
Pesek, William. "Japan could be on the brink of a second wave. Will Shinzo Abe act?" *The Washington Post*, Opinion, August 10, 2020.

Petersen, Wolfgang. *Outbreak*. United States: Warner Bros, 1995.
Purrington, Courtney. "Tokyo's Policy Responses During the Gulf War and the Impact of the 'Iraqi Shock' on Japan." *Pacific Affairs* 65, no. 2 (Summer, 1992): 161–181.
Quelch, John A. and Katherine E. Jocz. "Can Brand Obama Rescue Brand America?" *Brown Journal of World Affairs* XVI, no. 1 (Fall/Winter 2009): 163–178.
Rani, Anita. "No Sex Please, We're Japanese." BBC2 *This World*, December 2013. https://www.bbc.co.uk/programmes/b03fh0bg.
Reuters. "Japan PM Abe criticised as tone deaf after lounge-at-home Twitter video. 'Who do you think you are?' became a top trend on Twitter." April 12, 2020.
Shine, Ossian. "Tokyo gets 2020 Games with help from prime minister." Reuters, September 7, 2013.
Snow, Nancy. "Japan's government has failed coronavirus communications test." *Nikkei Asian Review*, February 21, 2020. https://asia.nikkei.com/Opinion/Japan-s-government-has-failed-coronavirus-communications-test.
Snow, Nancy. "Abe's cheesy video highlights Japan's coronavirus PR failure." *Nikkei Asian Review*, April 25, 2020.
Snow, Nancy. *Japan's Information War*. CreateSpace Independent Publishing Platform, first edition, July 17, 2016. https://www.ssrc.org/publications/view/japan-s-information-war/.
Snow, Nancy. "Swift Olympic cancellation will boost Japan's soft power." *Nikkei Asian Review*, March 20, 2020. https://asia.nikkei.com/Opinion/Swift-Olympic-cancellation-will-boost-Japan-s-soft-power.
Snow, Nancy. "Under the Security Umbrella: Japan's Weak Storytelling to the World." *Defence Strategic Communications* 8 (Autumn 2020): 173–188.
"Soft Power Ranking/Global." *Monocle*, no. 129, December 2019/January 2020.
Soft Power 30. https://softpower30.com/.
Stanislaus, Warren A. "Seeking an Independent Voice: Japanese Think Tanks." *Global Asia* 10, no. 1 (2015): 1. https://www.globalasia.org/v10no1/focus/seeking-an-independent-voice-japanese-think-tanks_warren-a-stanislaus.
Stiglitz, Joseph. "The Promise of Abenomics," World Economic Forum, in collaboration with Project Syndicate, April 8, 2013.
St. Clair, Stacy. "Postponing the 2020 Olympics may be 'inevitable.'" *Chicago Tribune*, March 23, 2020.
Tanaka, Jun. "Japan Overtakes UK in Nation Brands Ranking." Press Release, Brand Finance Japan. https://brandfinance.com/press-releases/japan-overtakes-uk-in-nation-brands-ranking/.
van Wolferen, Karel. *The Enigma of Japanese Power*. New York: Vintage Books, 1990.
Woodward, Calvin and Hope Yen, "AP FACT CHECK: Trump's see-no-evil posture on coronavirus." Associated Press, June 27, 2020.
Wingfield-Hayes, Rupert. "Why Japan's Shinzo Abe went to Yasukuni shrine." BBC News, December 26, 2013. https://www.bbc.com/news/world-asia-25518137.
Yates, Ronald E. "Shintaro Abe, 67, Guided Japan in Global Politics." *Chicago Tribune*, May 15, 1991.
Yoshitake, Yu, Junichi Bekku, Sawa Okabayashi, and Erina Ito. "Japan ranks 121st in gender equality among 153 countries." *The Asahi Shimbun*, December 18, 2019.

Chapter 14

Japan and the World under Abe Shinzō's Premiership

Trying to Become a Rules Maker

Robert Dujarric

For over two centuries, from the 1630s to 1850s, Japan decoupled itself from the world. During this Era of Seclusion (in Japanese *Sakoku Jidai*/鎖国時代, a term actually coined much later), the archipelago was not entirely "closed," but the Shogunal administration strictly regulated minimal intercourse with the outside world. In the 1850s, Americans, Russians, and western Europeans broke in through the front door. They forced Edo, at gunpoint, to agree to their demands to "open" up Japan. (Edo, the seat of the Shogun's government, was renamed Tokyo in 1868 when the Emperor relocated from Kyoto to the city.)

Neither the Europeans nor the Americans colonized the country. But, for several decades after the unsolicited appearance on Japanese shores of diplomats, merchants, and missionaries backed up by warships, Japan was at their mercy. They shrunk its sovereignty, bestowing upon themselves extraterritoriality and the right to set Japan's customs rates. Under the shadow of the naval and military supremacy of the West, Japan's ability to take action overseas was constrained by Western officials. For all practical purposes, Japan was a rules taker, not a rules giver.

As it grew stronger after 1868, Japan reduced and then ended the formal encroachments on its sovereignty. It morphed from prey to predator, attacking China (1894–1895) and thus securing dominion over Taiwan (1895). Nevertheless, the Triple Intervention by Russia, France, and Germany in 1895 nullified some of the gains Japan had obtained from a defeated Qing dynasty. This episode—seared into the minds of Japanese policymakers—demonstrated that Tokyo's freedom of maneuver ended where the red lines of the Western nations started. It could make rules, but only if the Western capitals agreed with them.

A few years later, Japan, with the strength of its expanding military and benefiting from Anglo-Russian competition, successfully promoted itself to the level of rules maker. The Anglo-Japanese Alliance of 1902 made it a partner of the United Kingdom—at the time, Britain was in relative decline, but it still ruled the waves and the greatest empire the world had ever seen. This treaty, followed by the victorious Russo-Japanese War of 1904–1905, marked Japan's entry into the ranks of the Great Powers. It invaded Korea, formally annexing it in 1910, and built an informal empire in China.[1]

For the following decades, Japan was a key actor in Northeast Asia. It had to accept some rules while shaping others, but this was the case too for even the strongest of nations. Had Japan been situated in western Europe, its economy, being lesser than Italy's and not even a third of Germany's or the United Kingdom's, would have looked small.[2] Its army and navy, industrial technology, agriculture, scientific research, and universities would have been conspicuously inferior to Europe's big powers.

However, Japan was 8,000 kilometers from the heartlands of Europe and the United States (whose economy was seven times larger)[3]. It held a regional monopoly on modern administrative, technological, and military skills, as well as hardware over its near and distant neighbors, China and the few remaining feeble states of Southeast Asia. Despite Russia, a fairly backward European monarchy, bordering Japan's Korean colony, the bulk of its population and modest industry were over 6,000 kilometers away in Europe. Distance from the West afforded Japan a buffer, and notably the Europeans were more preoccupied by their fellow European foes than by Japan. American power in the Pacific was on the rise, but the United States also had interests to defend in the western hemisphere and Europe.

World War I found Japan on the winning side. It acquired German Micronesia north of the equator as a League of Nations mandate, but did not gain as much as it wanted after 1918. It failed to obtain a "racial equality clause," which would have ended racist restrictions on Japanese immigration, due to opposition from Australia and the United States.[4] When confronted by the desires of the most powerful Western states, Japan was still a rules taker.

Nevertheless, the weakening of the European colonial powers after World War I, the dislocation brought to Russia by defeat and revolution, and American isolationism provided an opportunity for Japan to extend its power in Asia. In 1931, it conquered Manchuria, and in 1937 invaded other regions of China. Then came the takeover of American, European, and Australian holdings in Southeast Asia and the Pacific starting in 1941. For a brief period, Japan was the sole rules maker in an enormous zone ranging from Burma to

Kiska in the Alaskan Aleutian chain, Inner Mongolia to Wake Island, and even northeastern New Guinea.

Japan's experience as a Great Power was short. Just over forty years after it sank the Russian Baltic Fleet at the Battle of Tsushima (also called the Battle of the Sea of Japan, *Nihonkai kaisen*/日本海海戦), the empire was in the last stages of collapse. The Allied Occupation (in practice a solely American affair) deprived it of its sovereignty, returning it to the category of rules taker. The victors stripped it of its colonial holdings, as well as of islands Japanese considered part of their homeland (the Southern Kuriles/Northern Territories, *Hoppōryōdō*/北方領土). The Occupation ended in 1952 with Tokyo remaining very much a rules taker. It relied entirely on the United States for its security against hostile continental communism in Asia. American intervention in its internal affairs was considerable.

It is important to realize that Japan remained poor, making it less able to shape its environment. West Germany and Japan are thought of as parallel cases of defeated nations that recovered quickly, but their economic trajectories were vastly different. Pre-war Japan was a dual economy, with a modern sector cohabitating with a vast primitive agrarian one, well behind Germany in industry, science, and technology. The task for Japan after 1945 was not just recovery but also catch-up (much like Italy). While Japan of the early 1960s was rich by Asian standards, by West German and even more so American ones, it was poor. To conserve foreign exchange, Japanese were not allowed to travel overseas for tourism until 1964.[5] By contrast, in 1962, 5 million West Germans were already holidaying abroad.[6] In 1965, there were close to 8 million cars registered in West Germany,[7] compared to just over 2 million in Japan,[8] though Japan's population was around 165 percent of West Germany's.

Where its geographical isolation from the developed world once lent to its regional power, post–World War II, this isolation became detrimental. Japan's neighborhood consisted of hostile communist regimes and economically insignificant countries until South Korea, Taiwan, and parts of Southeast Asia took off in the late 1960s.

In the security realm, being in a bilateral pact with the United States as opposed to a multilateral one like NATO found Japan caught in a particularly unbalanced partnership. This situation was reinforced by its much smaller investment in national defense than that of the western European countries during the Cold War (about 1% without conscription compared to 3% or more in most cases in western Europe along with the draft).[9]

Tokyo focused on containing the demands made by the United States for Japan to contribute more to the common defense. It avoided participation in American operations in Asia, never committing personnel overseas to support American deterrence in Korea or wars in Southeast Asia. Its most critical contribution was limited to providing U.S. forces with bases in Japan and maintaining Self-Defense Forces to protect Japan and its immediate approaches. Outside of the protective bubble, Japan built to manage its ties with the United States, it was a rules taker. Tokyo lacked the military resources to deter its foes on its own and had absolutely no coercive power. Even more than NATO states, it delegated its security to Washington in an arrangement that benefited both sides. Beyond this, Japan was not particularly active in international political–military affairs. It disbursed official development assistance (ODA) to Asian states, partly for diplomatic reasons but also, like other nations, to help its domestic industry. In international affairs more generally though, it opted to maintain a low profile.

Turning to economic policy: from the start, Tokyo established a protectionist mercantilist moat, which the United States accepted early on given the small size of the Japanese economy. Over time, Americans tried to foster a more liberal economic regime in Japan, but with limited success. Japan was much more of a rules maker in this sphere than in the diplomatic-military realm. As Japan's national income rose spectacularly, its weight in economic rules making increased. It became a more important participant in international negotiations on trade, investments, and currency issues, but it focused more narrowly on defending its own interests rather than seeking to define the international economic and financial system.

The very limited role of foreign enterprises in Japan (FDI in Japan amounts to 4 percent of GDP compared to 36 percent in the United States and 26 percent in Germany in 2018)[10] partially due to a dislike on the part of the government for outside investments, further disconnected Japan from the world and continues to do so in 2020. To this day, few Japanese work in the various organizations that play a role in global economic rules making (such as the International Monetary Fund, World Bank, Organization for Economic Cooperation and Development, Bank for International Settlements, or World Trade Organization). Almost no Japanese economists influence policymaking. This has reduced Japan's ability to influence the agenda that plays a definitive role in determining international rules in trade, investments, and monetary affairs.[11]

JAPAN AFTER THE END OF THE COLD WAR

With the end of the Cold War, Japan engaged slowly in more visible diplomatic and security activities. Starting with twenty-seven electoral observers sent to Namibia in 1989, Japan has taken part in several UN peacekeeping operations.[12] These deployments have always been to areas where the risk of casualties was very low. Troops left when the location's situation took a turn for the worse (as with Golan Heights and South Sudan).

Outside of the UN peacekeeping framework, in the aftermath of the U.S.-led Operation Desert Storm to expel the Iraqi army from Kuwait to return the emirate to its monarch, the Japanese government dispatched minesweepers in 1991 to remove mines after Iraqi defeat.[13] In December 2001, Japanese vessels deployed to the Arabian Sea to assist United States and other coalition navies taking part in operations against the Taliban regime in Afghanistan following 9/11. Their tasks were limited to refueling. Later, Self-Defense Forces personnel moved to Iraq in 2004 to help with water purification. Japan supplied naval and air assets to anti-piracy missions of the coast of East Africa and the Arabian Sea. In the process, in 2011, the Self-Defense Forces established a small base outside in Djibouti (chapters 6 and 7 go into further details).

Except for some joint exercises with the U.S. military, the SDF has historically been insular. However, the Japanese armed forces gradually moved to engaging other militaries. They took part in exercises and engaged in staff talks and in "2+2" meetings with defense and foreign ministers. By international standards, these activities are fairly small, but they reflect a change in Japanese behavior from earlier decades (See chapter 7). In the area of development aid, Japan also began to engage African countries in 1993 with the Tokyo International Conference on African Development.[14]

ABE SHINZŌ RETURNS TO POWER IN 2012

By the early 2010s, when Abe returned to power, Japan had gone a long way from being only a rules taker. It carried some weight in global policy-making councils that defined international economic norms and was sufficiently strong to ignore or bend these norms when it didn't like them. In the security field, it had carved a "safe space" to define its contribution to the alliance with the United States, but it could not be called a rules maker. The various overseas missions and deployments of the SDF gave it some influence, but on a limited scale. Its diplomatic clout was also not on par with its economy's size.

Japanese premiers have rarely focused mainly on international security and diplomatic affairs as opposed to trade. Abe belongs to a small group of post-war leaders whose primary interests have been foreign and security policy. Yoshida Shigeru (PM 1946–1947, 1948–1954) was the most consequential, but his was an exceptional situation as "foreign" affairs until April 1952 meant dealing with the American General Headquarters in downtown Tokyo to whom, as prime minister of a defeated country, he reported. Kishi Nobusuke (1957–1960), who led the revision of the Security Treaty was another "national security premier." Nakasone Yasuhiro (PM 1982–1987) was partially in the same category, but much of his energy was spent on economic matters, namely the explosive trade relations with the United States, the Plaza Accord of 1985 (to let the yen appreciate), as well as on domestic reforms (notably the Japan National Railways privatization).

Abe, like several Japanese prime ministers from the 1990s onward, is the scion of a prominent lineage. His pedigree is not as aristocratic as that of Prime Minister Hosokawa (1993–94), who was the grandson of wartime premier Konoe, distant relative of the Emperor, descendant of the *daimyo* (大名/ lord) of Kumamoto and of the Fujiwaras, second only to the Imperial Family in prestige. Nor were Abe's forebears as deeply rooted in post-1868 politics as Prime Minister Hatoyama (2009–2010), whose family, including a former prime minister (grandfather) and two cabinet members (father and brother), has sat in the Diet since 1892, only two years after the Japanese parliament first opened.

Abe Shinzo's father was foreign minister. His grandfather was Kishi Nobusuke, who served as premier from 1957 to 1960, a minister during World War II, was arrested as a suspected "Class A" war criminal by the U.S. Occupation and then released, going on to become one of the leaders of the U.S.-backed and financed Liberal Democratic Party. Kishi's brother, Satō Eisaku, also served as premier from 1964 to 1972. Abe's ancestry is relevant, in that he has talked of his father's interest in settling the territorial dispute as an inspiration for his Russia policy (see chapter 12). He often invokes the memory of his controversial grandfather, known both for his role in Imperial Japan's wars and his strong-arm tactics to obtain the ratification of the Security Treaty revision in 1960. Kishi's aims throughout his life were clearly to make Japan more of a rules maker. Looking back on the near decade Abe spent in the *Kantei* (官邸, the Prime Minister's Office), how has he changed Japan's place in the world and its ability to shape its environment?

Abe's tenure as premier has coincided with a fair amount of stability in the region. For any leader, each day brings its lot of crises. A broader historical perspective, however, reveals that since Abe has been prime minister, there have been no radical changes in international affairs comparable to the demise of the Soviet empire. The "rise of China" was old news in 2012. North Korea conducted nuclear and missile tests before Abe came back to the *Kantei*. Taiwan remained a potential hotspot, but not more than usual. The 2008 global financial meltdown was history, though its effects were still felt. Farther from Japan, there were no armed conflicts on the same scale as the first years of the Afghan post-9/11 conflict and the U.S. invasion of Iraq. Even with the protectionist demands of the Trump administration, Abe has also served at a time where, unlike the decades from the 1960s to the 1990s, the prime minister was not fighting one trade or currency war after another.

Additionally, Abe benefited domestically from the long-term decline of factions within the ruling party. In the heyday of LDP hegemony, faction heads were the barons of a collegial arrangement. The premier was, at most, *primus inter pares*—he was unable to act without the approval of other faction chiefs, whom in some cases wielded more power behind the scenes than the man sitting in the prime ministerial chair.[15] Over the past decades, the factions have withered, giving the LDP president—who doubles as prime minister when the party is in power—more leeway to impose his views. Furthermore, under Abe, the opposition has been particularly impotent, removing another impediment to the premier exercising power.

Only two real shocks occurred during Abe's tenure up to now. One was Donald Trump's election. However, this was less cataclysmic for Japan than for America's western European allies. Trump's racialized xenophobia and disregard for human rights as an international issue is a challenge to the ideological foundations of the moderate politicians who govern most of western Europe, but is of little importance to Japanese officials. Trump's vociferous hostility toward the EU and NATO as institutions had no counterpart in Japan. For Abe, Trump's election raised serious questions, but not on the same scale as it did in Brussels and Berlin. Moreover, Trump's confrontational attitude toward China was welcomed by the Japanese government.

COVID-19 has been the second storm to hit the Japanese ship of state. As the pandemic is not yet over, it is too early to pass judgment on its impact. For a variety of reasons, Japan was relatively lightly hit by European and American standards (fifty times fewer deaths relative to its population than the United States in July 2020), though Taiwan and South Korea had even fewer fatalities per capita.[16] Thus, as of July 2020, it has not had the same impact on Japanese politics as in many other nations, though its economic impact has forced the government to focus most of its energy on the virus since the spring of 2020.

Throughout his time as prime minister, Abe hid neither his admiration for his grandfather nor his devotion to the Yasukuni Shrine, where he worshipped in person in 2013 and to which he sends regular offerings. Yasukuni Shrine, where Japan's fallen soldiers and sailors—including war criminals—are honored, also includes a museum denying the Nanjing Massacre. Japanese leaders' visits to its grounds have been a bone of contention with South Korea and China, and sometimes with the United States. His goal for constitutional revision and laws to provide for a more robust national defense worthy of a proud nation was known to all. He was often portrayed by his opponents as an unrelenting nationalist plotting with bellicose hawks in the Pentagon. To many of his supporters in both Japan and the United States, he was the man who could rectify the mistakes of Article 9 (the "war renouncing" clause of the U.S.-drafted constitution), foster a stronger and military to allow Japan to take a more robust role as a partner of the United States in Asia.

The reality of Abe's premiership was more prosaic. If anything characterized Abe, it was a strong sense of realism. Not only realism as used in international relations theory but realism in the sense that he was aware of the desires of Japanese citizens. The Democratic Party's perceived incompetence cost its coalition power in 2012, paving the way for Abe's second term as premier. The message from voters was a cry for a return to the more stable LDP cabinets with a focus on the economy, not a call for a dramatically new course. Notably, there was no "demand" on the part of the voters for new or more ambitious action in the fields of diplomacy, trade, or defense. Therefore, Abe made it clear to the electorate that he cared about the economy and the standard of living. Opinions diverge on his achievements in this area (see chapter 3), but we can say that his stewardship of the economy was neither exceptionally successful nor was it catastrophic.

His longevity in the *Kantei* indicated that he could read the electorate as well as the constraints imposed by Japan's geostrategic reality. Chapter 2 notes that under Abe, the prime minister as an individual and the *Kantei* as an institution were more powerful than in the past, but the Japanese premier still does not exercise the same dominion over policy as a strong British chief executive and No. 10 Downing Street might. No post-occupation Japanese premier, Abe included, came close to equaling Margaret Thatcher or Tony Blair in domination of the scene, imposing their will over other politicians, the bureaucracy, and if needed public opinion, over a long period in office.

Several chapters have looked at specific bilateral relationships (the United States, China, Russia, North Korea, South Korea, the Middle East, and Africa), and others have focused on its military diplomacy, its security policy, and its image abroad. But how can we look at the ways Abe affected Japan's relationship with the world as a whole?

Abe came from a strain of Japanese conservatism that accepts the United States as the cornerstone of Japan's security. It takes it for granted that Japan cannot fully secure its independence on its own, but at the same time feels resentment over the actions of the post-war American occupation, such as the demotion of the Imperial Institution, the International Military Tribunal for the Far East (IMTFE, also known as the Tokyo Trial or the Tokyo War Crimes Tribunal), which sentenced some Japanese leaders to death, and a constitution deemed too liberal. There is also a strong desire on their part for Japan to have more autonomy and be less of a rules taker and more of a rules giver.

The most logical method to achieve these goals would be for Japan to have a much larger military. There are many ways for states to exert influence in the world, but generally armed forces play a pivotal role in the equation. Japan could easily afford to devote two or three times more than it does today to the Self-Defense Forces, and there has indeed been some increase in the strength of the SDF, with the government having passed new laws that make it easier to resort to force. As chapter 7 explains, Japan is now more wont to use the Self-Defense Forces for diplomatic purposes through joint exercises with other militaries, visits by Japanese warships, and technical assistance to some countries. Chapter 6 notes that Japan takes part in some naval patrolling and anti-piracy operations in Southwest Asia and Africa, but these remain small for a country with a $5 trillion gross domestic product. These have, to some extent, brought about stronger security ties with other nations, but their import must be relativized. For Tokyo's new partners, Japan will remain a secondary or lesser element in their security policy, for the simple reason that Japan's power projection abilities are small and its prudence well known.

Abe saw that anything more than marginal additions to Japan's military and the associated expenses were not compatible with winning elections. Any attempt to drastically inflate the proportion of the national budget devoted to national security affairs was doomed to failure. Consequently, he did not go beyond what the traffic could bear, which meant relatively modest increases when national income grew.

There is no evidence that relative to its potential enemies (China, North Korea) and its ally (US) the SDF are more potent than eight years ago— Relative Japanese military strength in 2020 is likely not greater than eight years ago. If one believes the more alarmist views of China's People's Liberation Army's growth, Japan could even be weaker relative to its principal adversary than a decade ago.

The use of military force, or the credible threat of doing so, is one way to exert influence on events, but under Abe, Japan remained extremely cautious of such actions. Even compared to Germany, another nation with a reluctance to resort to military means, Japan stands out. Whatever his personal predilections might be, Abe was very much a risk-averse realist when it came to deploying Japanese service members overseas. Abe invested significant political capital in security legislation to make it less difficult for Japan to resort to force (chapter 6), but these arcane discussions, often disconnected from the reality of combat operations, revealed that the threshold for Japan to use deadly force against its foes is extremely high. Some commentators also focus on Article 9 itself, but even if it did not exist, it would change very little. Japan's disposition when it comes to the military is the product of public opinion, post-1945 political culture, and domestic and foreign factors unrelated to the constitution. Thus, when it comes to "rules making," Japan continues to renounce the threat of force as a tool to make rules when dealing with the world, except in cases of a direct and obvious imminent threat to its narrowly defined security.

Another way to help shape rules and wield influence is through international organizations, and for this purpose, governments maneuver to position their nationals in leadership roles in international organizations. Yet by 2020, there was not a single Japanese person leading any of the 15 UN-affiliated organizations[17] despite Japan being a major contributor to the UN system.[18] It is worried about China's reach in international organizations (for example the WHO during the COVID-19 pandemic), yet Tokyo has not managed to get Japanese nationals into many positions of power, whether to run major UN agencies or to work as professionals (where Japanese are dramatically underrepresented). Though there have been Japanese who ran some UN agencies in the past, there were never many, and under Abe the numbers reached zero. Some of the reasons for this failure are deep-seated, such as the paucity of competitive candidates, but a lack of political and financial investment can also be blamed.

In terms of government action with tangible and visible consequences, the most notable successful effort by Abe Shinzo to establish Japan as a rules maker was in the realm of trade. Following Donald Trump's decision to leave the not-yet ratified Trans-Pacific Partnership (TPP), Japan found itself confronting the possible collapse of the entire TPP project. Besides its perceived economic benefits, TPP was for Tokyo and its American supporters part of a process to bind the United States more closely to its Asian allies and bring other Asia-Pacific nations into the orbit of the U.S.–Japan alliance to deal with China from a position of greater strength. Besides lowering barriers to trade and investment flows, the strategic objective of the TPP for Tokyo was to create a Japanese–U.S. counterweight to China in the Asia-Pacific region.

Japan, under Abe's leadership, rescued the program by creating a Comprehensive and Progressive Agreement for Trans-Pacific Partnership (CPTPP) with the original TPP parties minus the United States. Tokyo then negotiated a bilateral trade agreement with America that contained many of the TPP provisions. This was one of the rare occurrences in the post–World War II era of Tokyo successfully taking the lead in an important agreement with security as well as commercial implications. Tokyo also reached an agreement with the EU on an Economic Partnership Agreement. If the CPTPP lives to its promises, and if at one point the United States chooses to join it, it will be the most important legacy left by Abe in regards to Japan's relationship with the world. This was a case where Abe personally invested himself and deserves credit for the outcome.

Japan also holds the presidency of the Manila-based Asian Development Bank and is one of the most important members of the World Trade Organization (WTO), though under Abe there has been no clear increase in either the visibility of the ADB or Japan's role in the WTO.

One other addition to Japan's engagement with the world has been a new focus on "globalized human capital/human resources" (グローバル人財/人材, *guroubaru jinzai*)[19]. This led the Abe cabinet to liberalize the issuance of visas for foreign professionals and later for unskilled workers. At the lower end of the labor market, these policies arose as a result of Japan's below replacement fertility rate, pushing businesses to seek government support for importing foreign labor. At the upper end, for foreigners with university degrees, it comes from the belief that Japanese businesses must bring in highly skilled non-Japanese to improve their ability to compete globally by internationalizing their managerial labor force and bringing in foreigners with skills that are rare in Japan (cultural and linguistic cosmopolitanism and IT developers being two examples).

These policies predate Abe Shinzo's premiership, but they gained traction under him, especially with a liberalization of employment visas for unskilled laborers and a liberalization of the regime for professionals. These changes illustrate Abe's pragmatism—he is neither cosmopolitan nor committed to multiculturalism and immigration, but prioritized economic logic over ethnonationalism. From 2012 to 2019, the number of foreign permanent residents rose from around 625,000 to 739,000 and non-permanent residents with work permits from 224,000 to 272,000, to which must be added an increase from 151,00 to 411,000 "technical trainees" (mostly young unskilled workers).[20]

If continued, these actions could add another dimension to Japan's place in the world. Attracting foreigners, besides the benefits to Japan's economy, would significantly strengthen Japan's connections with the outside world. Very few Japanese possess the cultural and linguistic skills to interact with foreigners. Residents from overseas working in Japan can help bridge that gap, strengthening Japan's ability to understand and influence developments abroad. Their presence, and later their Japan-born children, can also assist Japan in growing future generations that will be more globalized and capable of playing a role in the world beyond the shores of the archipelago.

Along the same line, more foreigners have entered Japanese universities, with numbers increasing from around 138,000 in 2012 to 228,000 in 2019.[21] This trend, which started well before Abe's arrival, is combined with the development of more degree programs taught entirely or partially in English. They aim at attracting foreign students and offering Japanese the possibility of studying in English with non-Japanese professors and classmates while remaining in their country.[22]

If these trends, along with more foreigners in the labor force, could provide the means for Japan to move from the periphery to the center. At the same time, Japan-educated foreigners could give Japan a cadre of non-Japanese who are familiar with the country and strengthen its ties with the outside world. A good precursor has been the Japan Exchange and Teaching Program, initiated in 1987 to bring young foreign college graduates to Japan to teach English.[23] Expanded over the years to include other languages, it has engendered a community of foreigners with ties to Japan, many of whom went on to work in Japan or in Japan-related activities in their home countries.

The impact of labor market and educational transformations will take a long time to be seen, and at this stage, the numbers remain very small. Around 4 percent of Tokyo's residents are foreigners, a very low percentage for the biggest metropolis of a large developed world economy. These processes, both in immigration and the entry of international students, are societal developments that in the long-term can give Japan greater rules making capability. Prime Minister Abe's cabinet has played a role in this, but the genesis of these programs predates him. If they are to reshape Japan, numerous future premiers will have to continue to support and enhance these policies.

HAS ABE BEEN TRANSFORMATIONAL?

None of the decisions and actions taken by Abe when it comes to Japan's relationship with the world have been revolutionary. Japan's security and military policy in 2020 has remained similar to that of the LDP administrations of the first decade of the twenty-first century. In some ways, he has been more cautious than Prime Minister Koizumi Junichiro (2001–2006), who decided to send soldiers to Iraq (albeit for a non-combat mission), disregarding the Japanese public's opposition to the American invasion.[24]

Although concluding the CPTPP was an impressive success, economic policy remains defined by a strong dose of protectionism, exemplified by the obstacles foreign investors, even those from America, face in the Japanese capital markets. Furthermore, the opening of the labor market to foreigners remains limited. Japan is not a top-choice destination for global talent, though often for reasons that are not the consequences of policy. Many positions require fluency in a language that is not widely known outside the country and a mastery of Japanese societal norms which few outsiders understand. The slow seniority-based promotions which still define most of corporate Japan have their advantages, but don't appeal to mobile international professionals.[25] It will certainly take a long time for Tokyo to have the pulling power of cities, such as Berlin (a good comparison since Germany, like Japan, is neither a New World country nor one with a vast former overseas empire). If the United States continues to reject immigration, Canada, Australia, New Zealand, and Europe are more likely to benefit than Japan.

The educational "opening" of Japan also has to be seen in perspective. Japan is far from becoming an educational middle power, let alone a superpower. Many of its English-taught programs are little more than English language instruction classes for Japanese and other Asian students. Some foreign students attend schools with minimal requirements and devote most of their time to working in low-paid jobs, transforming their student visas into de facto work permits. At the earliest, it will take another decade to see if Japan can put itself on the international education map. The author, based at Temple University, Japan Campus, will also note the refusal of the Japanese authorities, both prior and during Abe's tenure, to grant the school, the only full-scale foreign university in Japan, the same tax-exempt status which private Japanese universities enjoy. This is despite Temple being from the United States, which Tokyo considers its most important partner by far.

As noted, these demographic and educational changes take time to have an impact. Eight years is, by definition, too short for such a transformation to be felt. In fact, the response to the COVID-19 crisis under Prime Minister Abe illustrated the appeal of seclusion (鎖国/Sakoku, the "closed country") to the government. Japan, like most countries, imposed restrictions on entry into the country in the wake of the pandemic, but whereas Japanese citizens were allowed as long as they followed certain quarantine procedures to travel in and out of Japan, foreign residents working and paying taxes in Japan, and in some cases the parents of Japanese children, were denied such rights for numerous months. This is at odds with most other countries who put their permanent residents in the same category as their nationals.

This was not solely the product of xenophobia. There were rational epidemiological reasons to restrict the movements of a class of residents (foreigners) which has a far higher propensity to cross borders than Japanese nationals, but it also reflected the fact that, in 2020, the Japanese state took it for granted that all Japanese residents were Japanese citizens and overlooked the reality that foreigners were now embedded productively in its society. Either the prime minister shared this view or was unable to affect the decisions of the bureaucracy.

COVID-19 was also a failed opportunity for Japan to display its leadership, much as it was for the EU. Under previous Republican or Democratic presidents, the United States would have taken command of an American-led international effort to deal with the pandemic, ranging from treatments and vaccines to defining the actions that needed to be coordinated across the planet. The lack of interest on the part of Washington during the Trump presidency for this global task offered an opportunity for others to fill the vacuum. The Abe cabinet ignored this vacuum and focused solely and effectively on managing the Japanese aspects of the crisis where a more ambitious Japan would have risen to the occasion to show that it could be a global problem-solver. It could have mobilized like-minded partners to step into the void left by America's retrenchment, demonstrating to the world that Tokyo was a more reliable and effective partner than Beijing, which had failed to ring the appropriate alarm bells at the start of the epidemic in Wuhan.

COVID-19 also highlighted the consequences of dependence on China for critical supply chains. Without getting into the pros and cons of decoupling from China, this was another opportunity for Japan to show leadership. With the most sophisticated economy in Asia, an alliance with the United States, and an interest in enlarging partnerships with the EU, Canada, and Australia, Japan could have led a broad supply-chain adjustment coalition to sideline China. As far as is known, it took no such action, either out of a lack of imagination or due to a desire to avoid furthering tensions with Beijing.

The last area where a more dynamic premier might have acted is in the realm of gender. As chapter 5 demonstrates, Japan's record in the past eight years on gender has not been much better than in past administrations. Related to this, Japan is now one of the few liberal democratic countries, along with Italy, South Korea, and former communist states of Central Europe that bans same-sex marriages. Besides being good for Japan itself, a more aggressive and effective program to boost gender and sexual equality in Japan would have been one way to put Japan on the map as a forward-looking society.

CONCLUSION

In conclusion, Abe did take steps to make Japan more of a rules maker than it was prior to his assuming office, but like other premiers since Japan recovered its formal sovereignty in 1952, he did not radically alter the course of the country in order to do so. This is the result of the internal dynamics of Japanese politics, its geopolitical environment, and, through an accident of history, the absence of any politician combining the will to change course with the skills to transform objectives into achievements.

Additionally, Japan's population is declining. From January 2013 to December 2020, Japan registered an estimate of 7,838,000 births compared to 9,829,000 deaths. Though immigration cut the population loss to "only 1.75m,"[26] Japan is rapidly aging, making for fewer and fewer Japanese entering the labor force. This demographic abyss makes it harder to grow the economy to make Japan count more in the world. Japanese public opinion, as noted, is relatively satisfied with Japan's international status. There is no groundswell of support for a more muscular foreign policy. A risk-averse position seems to satisfy the bulk of Japanese voters, including those of the LDP. Had an enormous crisis hit Japan in recent years—such as a Sino-American war or a North Korean nuclear strike—the Japanese people might have entertained taking the country on a new path. But, in the absence of such dramatic developments, voters value continuity.

Looking at the premier as an individual, Abe was figuratively and literally a child of the LDP. The LDP nearly holds the world record for uninterrupted power. Unlike communist parties, it achieved such longevity in a liberal democracy by generally avoiding head-on clashes with important segments of the electorate, especially after the first, more confrontational, decades of its rule. Abe graduated from a second-tier university unlike most men in prominent positions in Japan, and owed his position in society to his grandfather, his grand-uncle, his father, and the party they and their associates built since the 1950s. His resume was not that of an outsider and combative reformer à la Margaret Thatcher, nor was it that of a gambler—one illustration of this was the war against the Islamic State (ISIS or Daesh). Unlike the invasion of Iraq, this operation had near unanimous support, ranging from all NATO states to Turkey, Iran, Saudi Arabia, and beyond. A more forceful Japanese premier might have committed the SDF, perhaps not for front-line duty, but at least to "show the flag." Nothing of the sort happened. This attitude, perhaps justified due to the nature of Japanese opinion, gave the impression that Japan is eager to seek new partners to support it in East Asia, but unwilling to show much reciprocity.

The consequences of Abe's moderation are that almost eight years later, he leaves office with Japan's place in the world still where it was when he returned to the prime ministership in 2012. There have been only marginal changes here and there. Visitors returning to Earth after a decade in another galaxy would find some unbelievable changes on our planet, starting with the United States, but they would easily recognize Japan and where it stands in relations with other countries. For some, it will mean that Abe was not sufficiently transformational and failed to prepare the country for the challenges ahead; for others, it will be a sign that he was a successful premier who kept Japan on a track that has served it well since the 1950s.

Very few men or women are transformational, especially outside of periods of great upheavals. Abe's term in office, when looking at his impact on his country's place in the world, put the Japanese premier in the majority of heads of governments whose impact has ranged from minimal to marginal. He also, to his credit, belongs to the category of leaders who have not taken catastrophic decisions that left their nations in ruin, as was the case for the men, including his cherished grandfather, who ruled Japan during the 1931–1945 wars.

NOTES

1. See Peter Duus, Ramon H. Myers, and Mark R. Peattie, eds., *The Japanese Informal Empire in China, 1895–1937*, Princeton: Princeton University Press, 1989.

2. OECD, *The World Economy*, Volume 1: A Millennial Perspective and Volume 2: Historical Statistics Appendix A: World Population, GDP and GDP Per Capita,

Benchmark Years, 1820–1998, July 4, 2020, 184 and 206. https://read.oecd-ilibrary.org/development/the-world-economy/appendix-a_9789264022621-6-en#page40.

3. Ibid.

4. See Thomas W. Burkman, *Japan and the League of Nation: Empire and World Order, 1914-1938*, Honolulu: University of Hawaii Press, 2008.

5. James Mak, Lonny Carlile, and Sally Dai, "Impact of Population Aging on Japanese International Travel to 2025," East West Center, Economic Series No. 73 (October 2004): 2.

6. Christopher M. Kopper, "The Breakthrough of the Package Tour in Germany after 1945," *Journal of Tourism History* 1, no. 1 (2009), Table 1.

7. See Statista, "Number of registered cars in Germany from 1960 to 2020," https://www.statista.com/statistics/587764/number-of-registered-cars-germany/ showing July 4, 2020 having 9.267 cars; and Steven Tolliday, "Enterprise and State in the West German Wirtschaftswunder: Volkswagen and the Automobile Industry, 1939-1962," *The Business History Review* 69, no. 3 (Autumn 1995): 239. Table 2 shows a 1964 car ownership rate implying around 8.6m cars in West Germany.

8. See Susan C. Townsend, "The 'miracle' of car ownership in Japan's 'Era of High Growth', 1955 – 73," *Business History* 55, no. 3 (2013): 503. Figure 1 shows 2.181m cars in 1965.

9. See various issues of Institute for International Strategic Studies, *Military Balance*.

10. See OECD, "FDI positions, main aggregates BMD4," 2018. https://stats.oecd.org/Index.aspx?QueryId=64238. Measurements of FDI are far from precise, but the gap gives an idea of the difference between Japan and two other large mature liberal economies.

11. See Robert Dujarric and Ayumi Takenaka, "Parochialism Japan's failure to internationalize," in *Critical Issues in Contemporary Japan* by Jeffrey Kingston. London: Routledge, 2019.

12. MOFA, "Japan's Contribution to UN Peacekeeping Operations," January 31, 2005. https://www.mofa.go.jp/policy/un/pko/pamph2005.html.

13. Reiji Yoshida, "Anticipating more muscular missions, MSDF launches new minesweeper," *Japan Times*, October 27, 2016. https://www.japantimes.co.jp/news/2015/10/27/national/anticipating-muscular-missions-msdf-launches-new-minesweeper/.

14. MOFA, "The First Tokyo International Conference on African Development (TICAD 1)," 1993. https://www.mofa.go.jp/region/africa/ticad/ticad1.html.

15. See Jacob M. Schlesinger, *Shadow Shoguns: The Rise and Fall of Japan's Postwar Political Machine*, Simon & Schuster, 1997.

16. Johns Hopkins University, Coronavirus Research Center. "Mortality Analyses: Cases and mortality by country," https://coronavirus.jhu.edu/data/mortality.

17. Jiji Press, "Japan worried about falling leadership presence at international bodies," *Japan Times*, June 28, 2020. https://www.japantimes.co.jp/news/2020/06/28/national/politics-diplomacy/japan-leadership-international-china/.

18. See John McArthur and Krista Rasmussen, "Who actually funds the UN and other multilaterals?" Brookings, January 9, 2018. https://www.brookings.edu/blog/order-from-chaos/2018/01/09/who-actually-funds-the-un-and-other-multilaterals/.

UN budgets are highly complex, but Japan is clearly an important contributor (per author's discussion with UN official on July 5, 2020).

19. Both words are pronounced the same way as *jinzai*, but 人財 is human capital whereas 人材 is human resources.

20. Per Japanese Ministry of Justice, Immigration Services Agency, 2019 Data, http://www.moj.go.jp/nyuukokukanri/kouhou/nyuukokukanri04_00003.html and Japanese Ministry of Justice, 2012 Data on Foreign Residents, http://www.moj.go.jp/content/001234011.pdf.

21. See Japan Student Services Organization, Statistics, https://www.jasso.go.jp/en/about/statistics/intl_student/data2019.html and https://www.jasso.go.jp/en/about/statistics/intl_student_e/2012/index.html.

22. See Annette Bradford and H. Brown, eds., *English-Medium Instruction in Japanese Higher Education: Policy, challenges and outcomes*, Bristol: Multilingual Matters, 2017.

23. See JET Programme, "Introduction," http://jetprogramme.org/en/about-jet/.

24. Paul Midford, *Japanese Public Opinion and the War on Terrorism: Implications for Japan's Security Strategy*, edited by Muthiah Alagappa. East-West Center, 2006. www.jstor.org/stable/resrep06515.

25. See Garcia Liu-Farrer, *Immigrant Japan: Mobility and Belonging in an Ethnonationalist Society*, Ithaca, NY: Cornell University Press, 2020.

26. See US Census International Database, https://www.census.gov/data-tools/demo/idb/region.php?T=13&RT=0&A=both&Y=2017&C=JA&R=.

REFERENCES

Bradford, Annette and H. Brown, eds. *English-Medium Instruction in Japanese Higher Education: Policy, Challenges and Outcomes*. Bristol: Multilingual Matters, 2017.

Burkman, Thomas W. *Japan and the League of Nation: Empire and World Order, 1914-1938*. Honolulu: University of Hawaii Press, 2008.

Dujarric, Robert and Ayumi Takenaka, "Parochialism Japan's Failure to Internationalize." In *Critical Issues in Contemporary Japan* by Jeffrey Kingston. London: Routledge, 2019.

Duus, Peter, Ramon H. Myers, and Mark R. Peattie, eds. *The Japanese Informal Empire in China, 1895-1937*. Princeton: Princeton University Press, 1989.

Japanese Ministry of Justice, Immigration Services Agency. 2019 Data. http://www.moj.go.jp/nyuukokukanri/kouhou/nyuukokukanri04_00003.html.

Japanese Ministry of Justice. 2012 Data on Foreign Residents. http://www.moj.go.jp/content/001234011.pdf. Accessed 20 July 2020.

Japan Student Services Organization. Statistics. https://www.jasso.go.jp/en/about/statistics/intl_student/data2019.html and https://www.jasso.go.jp/en/about/statistics/intl_student_e/2012/index.html. Accessed 20 July 2020.

JET Programme. "Introduction." http://jetprogramme.org/en/about-jet/. Accessed June 28, 2020.

Jiji Press. "Japan worried about falling leadership presence at international bodies." *Japan Times*, June 28, 2020. https://www.japantimes.co.jp/news/2020/06/28/national/politics-diplomacy/japan-leadership-international-china/. Accessed July 5, 2020.

Johns Hopkins University, Coronavirus Research Center. "Mortality Analyses: Cases and mortality by country." https://coronavirus.jhu.edu/data/mortality. Accessed July 5, 2020.

Kopper, Christopher M. "The Breakthrough of the Package Tour in Germany after 1945." *Journal of Tourism History* 1, no. 1 (2009).

Liu-Farrer, Garcia. *Immigrant Japan: Mobility and Belonging in an Ethno-nationalist Society*. Ithaca, NY: Cornell University Press, 2020.

Mak, James, Lonny Carlile, and Sally Dai. "Impact of Population Aging on Japanese International Travel to 2025," East West Center, Economic Series No. 73 (October 2004): 2.

McArthur, John and Krista Rasmussen. "Who actually funds the UN and other multilaterals?" Brookings, January 9, 2018. https://www.brookings.edu/blog/order-from-chaos/2018/01/09/who-actually-funds-the-un-and-other-multilaterals/.

Midford, Paul. *Japanese Public Opinion and the War on Terrorism: Implications for Japan's Security Strategy*, edited by Muthiah Alagappa. East-West Center, 2006. www.jstor.org/stable/resrep06515. Accessed July 5, 2020.

MOFA. "Japan's Contribution to UN Peacekeeping Operations." January 31, 2005. https://www.mofa.go.jp/policy/un/pko/pamph2005.html. Accessed July 4, 2020.

MOFA. "The First Tokyo International Conference on African Development (TICAD 1)." 1993. https://www.mofa.go.jp/region/africa/ticad/ticad1.html. Accessed June 25, 2020.

OECD. "FDI positions, main aggregates BMD4." 2018. https://stats.oecd.org/Index.aspx?QueryId=64238. Accessed July 4, 2020.

OECD. *The World Economy*, Volume 1: A Millennial Perspective, and Volume 2: Historical Statistics, Appendix A: World Population, GDP and GDP Per Capita, Benchmark Years, 1820–1998. July 4, 2020. https://read.oecd-ilibrary.org/development/the-world-economy/appendix-a_9789264022621-6-en#page40.

Schlesinger, Jacob M. *Shadow Shoguns: The Rise and Fall of Japan's Postwar Political Machine*. Simon & Schuster, 1997.

Statista, "Number of registered cars in Germany from 1960 to 2020." https://www.statista.com/statistics/587764/number-of-registered-cars-germany/.

Tolliday, Steven. "Enterprise and State in the West German Wirtschaftswunder: Volkswagen and the Automobile Industry, 1939-1962." *The Business History Review* 69, no. 3 (Autumn 1995): 329.

Townsend, Susan C. "The 'Miracle' of Car Ownership in Japan's 'Era of High Growth', 1955 – 73." *Business History* 55, no. 3 (2013): 503.

US Census International Database. https://www.census.gov/data-tools/demo/idb/region.php?T=13&RT=0&A=both&Y=2017&C=JA&R=. Accessed July 20, 2020.

Yoshida, Reiji. "Anticipating more muscular missions, MSDF launches new minesweeper." *Japan Times*, October 27, 2016. https://www.japantimes.co.jp/news/2015/10/27/national/anticipating-muscular-missions-msdf-launches-new-minesweeper/. Accessed July 4, 2020.

Index

Abbas, Mahmoud, 239
Abe Shintaro, 19, 214–15, 218, 259
Abe Shinzō: "*Abenomasku*", 45;
  Abenomics, 2–3, 26, 45, 51–52,
  129, 259–61; Abe Statement, 70th
  anniversary, 154–55; first resignation
  from office, 23, 152, 194; first term
  (2006-2007), 19, 127, 179, 191, 193,
  215, 233, 258; second resignation
  from office, viii, 36, 41, 50, 149,
  169–70, 195, 200, 251–52; second
  term (2012-2020), 34, 127, 152, 164,
  171, 179, 260
Acquisition, Technology, and Logistics
  Agency, 95
Act for Promotion of Women's
  Participation and Advancement in
  the Workplace, 67
Act on the Protection of Specially
  Designated Secrets, 1, 33, 36, 95,
  130
administrative track (for women), 65
"Aegis Ashore" program, 94, 135, 201
AI monitoring, 50
Air Defense Identification Zone, 88
Algerian crisis, 237
Allied Occupation. *See* United States
  (U.S.), occupation (of Japan)
Al-Qaeda, 237

American Chamber of Commerce in
  Japan (ACCJ), 252
anemic demand, 28, 30, 36
Anglo-Japanese Alliance (1902), 272
Anti-Piracy Act (2010), 97
Anti-Prostitution Law, 74
APEC Summit, 153–54, 160
Arab Spring, 232, 243
Article 9 (of the constitution), 23, 90–
  93, 135, 140–41, 150, 155–57, 179,
  197, 277, 279
Article 24 (of the constitution), 64
Article 53 (of the constitution), 7
Article 76 (of the SDF Law), 157
Asia Infrastructure Investment Bank
  (AIIB), 133, 160–61
Asian Development Bank (ADB), 101,
  280
"Asian pivot", 98–99, 132
"Asian Tiger" status, 176
"Asia-Pacific Democratic G3 plus the
  United States", 152
Asō Tarō, 41
Association of Southeast Asian Nations
  (ASEAN), 101, 114, 117–18,
  161–64

Bank of Japan (BOJ): Governor Kuroda,
  3, 32

Basic Law for Society with Declining Number of Children, 65
Basic Plan on Space Policy, 94
Basic Policy for National Defense, 91
Battle of Tsushima, 273
Biden, Joseph, 139
Blair, Tony, 110
"bubble economy", 20, 36

Cabinet Bureau of Personnel Affairs, 217
Cabinet Intelligence and Research Office, 218
Cabinet Legislation Bureau, 5
Candlelight Revolution, 172, 180, 183
capacity building, 101, 111, 113–14, 118, 161
career track (for women), 65, 67
chief cabinet secretary (CCS), 6
China, 2, 21, 23, 28, 99, 161–64, 176, 191–92, 201–2, 235, 254, 256, 258, 271–72, 277; Belt and Road Initiative (BRI), 111, 130, 160, 232; China-Japan relations, 149, 151, 153, 156–57; counterbalance to, 99, 149, 156, 160, 280; and COVID-19, 101, 139; economic interdependence with (Japan), 36, 103, 136, 140, 150–52, 284 ; economic modernization, 160; expansion, 98, 164, 213–14, 242; investments, 90, 101; and the Middle East, 239, 243–44; military presence, 149; and North Korea, 195, 197–200; overseas students, 261–62; People's Liberation Army (PLA), 155, 158, 279; policy, 149, 151–52, 156, 163–64; prime ministerial visit to, 87, 137, 149, 160; reactions to Abe's Yasukuni visit, 130, 134, 153–55, 171, 179, 182; "Regarding Discussions toward Improving Japan-China Relations" (document), 153; rise of, 128, 133, 197, 237, 239, 257, 276; territorial issues, 50, 88, 100, 151, 164; Tiananmen Square Massacre, 151; trade war with the U.S., 99
Civil Code, 73–75, 80
Code for Unintended Encounters at Sea (CUES), 118
Cold War, 90, 92, 273–74
collective self-defense, ix, 5, 93, 95–96, 102, 132, 141, 156–59, 197
colonization of Korea (by Japan), 177, 183, 192
"comfort women", 49, 89, 95, 100, 169, 172–78, 181–82, 257; "comfort stations", 171, 173–75; Ministry of Foreign Affairs agreement (2015), 89, 169–70, 176–80
"commitment strategy", 113
"comprehensive security", 92
Conference on Cooperation among East Asian Countries for Palestinian Development (CEAPAD), 238–39, 243
constitutional revision, 41, 49–50, 87, 92, 102, 156–57, 277
consumption tax, 31, 33–35, 131, 141
Convention for Eliminating Discrimination Against Women (CEDAW), 73, 75–76, 80
"Cool Japan", 262, 264
coronavirus. *See* COVID-19
Corridor for Peace and Prosperity Initiative, 230
Council on Economic and Fiscal Policy, 4
Council on Security and Defense Capabilities, 110
COVID-19, 31, 35–36, 41–52, 79–81, 101, 127, 139, 164, 251, 255–56, 263, 277, 280, 283–84; controversies, 45; countermeasures, 46, 51; Diamond Princess cruise ship, 42, 251; testing, 43–45; transmission, 41, 44, 48; travel ban, 45, 252
cronyism, 46, 255

declining birth rate, 63
defense budget, 137

defense engagement, 107–14, 117–20
Democratic Party of Japan (DPJ), 24, 30, 128; bilateral tensions with Russia, 209
Diet (Parliament), 7, 9–13, 20, 30, 33, 93, 96–98, 276; and Abe Shinzo, 6–8, 14–15, 52, 156, 177, 179, 194; control of, 24, 129; dissolution of, 8, 13–14; and the *Nippon Kaigi*, 173; opposition within, 7, 10–11, 13; special session of, 7
diplomatic Bluebook, 212, 218
disaster relief, 100, 112, 161
displacement centers, 47
domestic opposition, 219
domestic violence (DV), 74, 78

Eastern Economic Forum, 210, 220
emperor, 63–64, 75–76, 174, 271; emperor system, 173
energy security, 230, 232–34
equal employment law, 63
Equal Opportunity Act for political candidates, 69
European Business Council, 252
European Union (EU), 199; and COVID-19, 283–84; Economic Partnership Agreement, 280; and the Middle East, 239; Strategic Partnership Agreement, 99–101; and Trump, 277
Exclusive Economic Zone (EEZ), 199
Experts Group, 46

"family system", 64, 73, 75
female heir (to the Imperial throne), 63, 75
fertility rate, 63, 77, 80, 254, 280
"Five Eyes" intelligence group, 130
Foreign Direct Investment (FDI), 151, 274
France, 67, 99–100, 271; Areva, 236
"Free and Open Indo-Pacific" (FOIP), 99, 101, 108, 111–20, 150, 160–63, 229, 242–43

Free Trade Agreement (FTA), 129, 136
Fukuda Takeo, 233
Fukuda Yasuo, 153, 182
Fukushima nuclear disaster, 42, 230, 232, 235. *See also* 2011 triple disaster
Fundamental Law on Space, 94

G7 Summit, 133, 141
"Galapagos phenomenon", 27
gender equality, 63–65, 67, 79–81, 251, 263, 284
Gender Equal Opportunity Law for Recruitment, 65
geopolitical anxiety, 111
Germany, 21, 28, 100, 141, 254, 271–72, 274, 279, 282; and COVID-19, 42, 47; West Germany, 273
global climate issues, 140
global gender equality index, 63
Global Gender Gap Index (GGGI), 67
global image, 251–52, 255, 257–59, 261
global supply chains, 27
Golan Heights, 236, 274
"goodwill exercises", 119
Gorbachev, Mikhail, 214, 218
"Go To" Travel, 49
"Greater East Asia Co-prosperity Sphere", 173
Great Powers, 272–73
grey-zone, 94, 98
Guidelines for Japan-U.S. Defense Cooperation, 132
Gulf of Aden, 89, 98, 115, 119, 236–37, 242
"gunboat diplomacy", 110

Harada Chikahito, 218
Hasegawa Eiichi, 218
Hatoyama Yukio, 161, 276
Health and Welfare Ministry, 23
Hiroshima, 50, 101, 133–34, 196, 263
history problem, 150
Hong Kong, 87, 101, 164
Hosokawa Morihiro, 276

hostages, 93, 95, 237
Host Nation Support (HNS), 139
human rights, 140, 152, 277; Human Rights Convention, 79; violations, 176, 199
"human security", 92–93, 231

Iijima Isao, 25
Ikeda Hayato, 235
immigrants, 68, 79; technical trainees, 23, 36, 281; workforce, 23, 252
Imperial family, 63, 75, 276
Imperial House Act. *See* Imperial Household Law
Imperial Household Law, 74, 76
Imperial Japan, 170, 173, 276
Indian Ocean, 90, 99, 108–9, 111–13, 115, 119–20, 155, 231
Indo-Pacific, 107, 112–14, 118–20, 142, 161–64, 232, 242–43
Intercontinental Ballistic Missile, 198
Intergovernmental Consultations on Abductions, 194
international law, 118, 157, 162; regarding maritime order, 98, 112, 243
International Peace Support Act, 132
international students, 254, 261, 282
International Whaling Commission (IWC), 137
Iraq, 21, 90, 92
Islamic State in Iraq and Syria (ISIS), 237, 285
Israeli-Palestinian conflict, 230–31; two-state solution, 230, 239; West Bank, 240

Japan-Africa relations, 241, 243
Japan-Australia-India Trilateral Dialogue, 162
Japan Civil Liberties Union (JCLU), 76
Japanese companies, 26–27, 33; reform of, 27
Japanese elite, 25–26, 30, 34

Japanese military, 95, 107–8, 112–13, 118–19
"Japanese miracle", 28
Japan Exchange and Teaching Program (JET), 281
Japan Foundation, 259
Japan-India Asia-Africa Growth Corridor, 101
Japan Institute of International Affairs (JIIA), 262; Tokyo Global Dialogue, 263
Japan International Cooperation Agency (JICA), 230
Japan-Iraq relations, 230
Japan-Israel relations, 236
Japan Medical Association (JMA), 43–44
Japan-Middle East relations, 234, 243
"Japan Model" (for coronavirus response), 43–44
Japan Post Office, 22; privatization of, 22
"Japan Revival Strategy", 129
Japan-ROK relations, 169–70, 172, 179, 181, 185; Basic Treaty on the Relations between Japan and The Republic of Korea (1965), 175–77; removal from trade "white list" (ROK), 172, 181; territorial disputes, 50, 212; 2018 ROK Supreme Court rulings, 171, 176, 178, 181
Japan Socialist Party, 20
JAXA, 94
Joint Comprehensive Plan of Action (JCPOA), 240
joint exercises, 111, 275

Kan Naoto, 42, 51, 177, 183, 209
Kantei, 2, 6, 12–13, 15n4, 213, 217, 221, 235, 276, 278; "Kantei diplomacy", 217
Kasumigaseki, 20, 252, 255, 262
Keidanren, 73, 234–35
Kerch Strait, 220
Khamenei, Ali, 241

Kim Jong-Il, 193
Kim Jong-un, 88, 135–36, 180
Kishi Nobusuke, 20, 50, 142, 215, 218, 258, 275–76
Kitamura Shigeru, 218
Koike Yuriko, 35, 48, 173
Koizumi Junichiro, 12, 19–22, 65, 77, 100, 109, 127, 151–53, 179, 193, 216–17, 221, 230, 282
Kōmeitō, 133, 135
Kondo, Marie, 257
Kono statement, 171, 174–75, 177, 182
Kōno Tarō, 219, 239
Koo, Richard, 32, 37n2
Korean liberation (1945), 170
koseki, 74
Kushner, Jared, 239

labor shortage, 67–68, 79
language schools, 261
Lavrov, Sergei, 210
"Law Concerning Measures relating to Actions by the Militaries of the United States and Other Countries", 159
"Law Concerning Measures to Ensure the Peace and Security of Japan in Situations in Areas Surrounding Japan", 158
League of Nations, The, 272; "racial equality clause", 272
Lee Myung-bak, 89
Lehmann shock, 24
Liberal Democratic Party (LDP), 2, 20, 49, 63–64, 73, 128, 131, 138, 183, 194, 210, 217, 256, 276, 278, 282, 284

Madrid Conference (1991), 239
Malabar exercise, 119
Manchuria, 272
maritime cooperation, 119, 162
maritime security, 100, 111, 113, 118–19
Matsui, Kathy, 72

Medvedev, Dmitry, 209
Meiji: era, 80; period, 25, 31; Restoration, 156
Memoranda of Understanding (MOU), 237
Merkel, Angela, 141
Middle East and Africa: five pillars, 230; instability, 232; policy, 232, 235–36
military diplomacy, 107–11, 113–14, 117–20, 278
Ministry of Defense (MOD), 93, 108, 111, 113, 237
Ministry of Economy, Trade, and Industry (METI), 164, 218
Ministry of Finance (MOF), 30, 32–33, 46
Ministry of Foreign Affairs (MOFA), 50, 93, 111, 114, 161, 178, 210, 217–18
Ministry of Justice, 73
Moon Jae-in, 52, 89, 100–101, 169, 175, 178, 180
Moritomo Gakuen, 36, 46
Multinational Force and Observers, 238
Murayama statement, 154, 175, 177, 183
Muro, Osamu, 253

Nakasone Yasuhiro, 127, 142, 256, 259, 275
Nanjing Massacre, denial of, 277
national defense, 93–95
National Defense Program Guidelines (NDPG), 94
national emergency, 43, 47
National Institute for Defense Studies (NIDS), 109–10
National Institute for Infectious Diseases (NIID), 44
National Police Agency, 93
national referendum, 133, 156
National Security Council (NSC), 4, 93, 130, 237
National Security Secretariat (NSS), 108, 120, 153, 218

National Security Strategy, 93, 96, 98, 110–11, 113, 130, 214, 237, 241
naval diplomacy, 108, 113
Netanyahu, Benjamin, 236, 239
NHK, 33, 45
Nihonjinron, 252
Nikai Toshihiro, 235
"1955 regime", 4–5, 8–11, 14
1956 Joint Declaration, 211, 220
"1972 regime", 151
1993 Tokyo Declaration, 212
Nippon Ishin no Kai, 213
Nippon Kaigi, 169–70, 173–75, 177, 179, 182–83
Nobukatsu Fujioka, 173
Noda Yoshihiko, 230
North Atlantic Treaty Organization (NATO), 99–100, 273–74, 277, 285
Northeast Asian security environment, 197, 201
North Korea: abduction of Japanese citizens, 2, 21, 141, 191, 193–95, 199–200, 202, 216; denuclearization, 169, 195; human rights abuses, 199; Kim regime, 196, 200; Koizumi 2002 summit, 193; missile tests, 132, 135, 191, 195–96, 198–200, 213, 276; 1994 Agreed Framework, 198; North Korean threat, 130, 136–37, 193, 196–97, 201–2, 214; nuclear program, 192, 194–96, 213, 276; policy, 191–92, 200; reconciliation (ROK), 172; ROK-DPRK summits, 180
nuclear deals (with the UAE and Turkey), 235
nuclear energy, 232, 235

Obama, Barack, 128–29, 134, 219, 259, 263
Official Development Assistance (ODA), 90, 230–31, 274
Official Secrets Act. *See* Act on the Protection of Specially Designated Secrets

Okinawa, 45, 131, 215; Henoko, 131, 140
One Belt, One Road Initiative. *See* China, Belt and Road Initiative (BRI)
Osaka G20 Summit, 90, 138, 262–64
Oslo Accords (1993), 230
Ozawa Ichiro, 24

pacifism, 102, 131
Panmunjom, 138
Park Chung-hee, 175, 178
Park Geun-hye, 89, 169–70, 175–76, 178, 180; impeachment, 172, 180
Partnership on Sustainable Connectivity and Quality Infrastructure, 101
"patriotic education", 23, 79, 174
Patrushev, Nikolai, 218
PCR tests, 44
Peace and Security Law, 1
Peace and Security Maintenance Act, 132
peace-keeping operations (PKO), 97, 134, 274
peacetime military activities, 109, 114
Pearl Harbor, 101, 134
Pence, Mike, 136
personal protective equipment (PPE), 46–47
Plaza Accord (1985), 30, 276
"politics of apology", 150–51; "apology fatigue", 177
pop culture, 262
Poroshenko, Petro, 219
port calls, 111, 113–17, 119, 238
post-war: business success. *See* "Japanese miracle"; constitution (Japan), 150, 155–56; diplomacy, 150; economic policy, 274; era/period, 29, 141, 152, 164; Japanese history, 127, 132, 138; Japanese political order, 20, 22, 24. *See also* "1955 regime"; Japanese security policy, 120, 132; relations, 216
privatization: of Japan National Railways, 276; of Japan Post Office, 22

"proactive pacifism", 96, 130, 231, 238, 243
public health, 42, 46, 48, 51
public opposition, 30, 52
Purrington, Courtney, 259
Putin, Vladimir, 103, 209–12, 218–22
Pyeongchang Olympics, 88, 180
Pyongyang Declaration, 193
Pyongyang Summit (2002), 194

Quad, 119, 152, 160–64; Quad Ministerial, 163
Quartet on the Middle East, 239

Rani, Anita, 254
Reiwa (era), 138
"Rising Sun" flag, 180–81
rogue state, 192
Roh Moo-Hyun, 194
Rouhani, Hassan, 241
Rugby World Cup (2019), 254–55
Russia: annexation of Crimea, 210, 219; Arctic LNG–2 project, 210; disputed islands, 211–12, 214–15, 218, 220–21; 8-point economic cooperation plan, 210, 215; negotiations with, 2, 211, 214, 219, 221–22; "Northern Territories" (Southern Kuriles), 88, 141, 209, 212, 214–15, 218, 220–21, 273; and North Korea, 195, 200; peace treaty, 211, 215, 219–20; policy, 210–14, 217, 219–20, 276; prime ministerial visit to, 209–10, 213; revised constitution, 220; Russo-Japanese War (1904-1905), 272; "symbolic sanctions", 210; territorial dispute, ix, 50, 88, 101, 141, 209, 212, 216

Sakoku (seclusion), 271, 283
same-sex marriage, 3, 80, 284
Satō Eisaku, 20, 50, 127, 215
sea-lanes, 111, 113, 237, 244
Sea of Japan, 273

Securing Education Opportunity Law, 79
"security diamond", 99, 155, 160, 163
security policy, 91, 108, 113, 120, 130, 132–33, 135, 140, 155–56, 158, 164
Seikeibunri doctrine, 235
Self Defense Forces (SDF), 87, 89–103, 120, 132, 134–35, 155, 158–59, 197, 231, 236–38, 243, 274–75, 278–79; Japan Maritime Self Defense Forces (JMSDF), 108, 114–15, 180, 236, 241; minesweepers, 275
Senkaku (Diaoyu), 101, 132, 151, 153, 159, 164, 213
separate surnames, 3, 64, 75
Sewol ferry incident, 180
Shangri-La Dialogue, 112
"Ship Rider" initiative, 114, 117–18
single member districts, 2, 12
single mothers, 63, 77–78
six-party talks, 195
Skripal, Sergei, 210
snap elections, 135
social distancing, 41, 48
Somalia, 231, 236
South China Sea, 118, 140, 151, 155, 158, 164, 237, 242
Southeast Asia, 100, 272–73; Japanese activities in, 107–8, 113, 115, 118; strengthening of states, 111
South Korea, 2, 28, 88, 100, 150, 170, 172, 178–79, 182–83, 192, 202, 256–58, 262, 273, 284; and COVID-19, 43, 47, 52, 101, 277; freezing of Japanese assets, 89; General Security of Military Information Agreement (GSOMIA), 89, 95, 138, 172, 181–82; and the Middle East, 232, 242, 244; naval vessel "lock-on", 181; and North Korea, 195–96, 200; reactions to Abe's Yasukuni visit, 130, 153
South Sudan, 97, 134, 236, 274
state of emergency. See national emergency
"State Shinto", 174

statesmanship, 142, 169, 218
Status of Forces Agreement (1960), 99
Stiglitz, Joseph, 260
Strait of Hormuz, 240–41
strategic communications, 252, 263
"strategic tolerance", 140
Suga Yoshihide, 4, 52, 80, 120, 164, 170, 217
Supreme Court, 73, 75
Suzuki Muneo, 213, 221
Syngman Rhee, 175

Taiwan, 88, 151, 158, 164, 271, 273, 276; and COVID-19, 45–47, 52, 277
Takenaka Heizo, 22
Takeshima (Dokdo), 89, 101, 171, 181, 212
Tanaka Kakuei, 22, 24, 217; *Tanaka gundan*, 22, 24
Tanaka Makiko, 217
Tehran nuclear program, 240
territorial disputes, 50, 171
Territorial Law (China), 151
"three arrows." *See* Abenomics
three pillars (defense), 94, 112, 120
Tokyo International Conference on African Development (TICAD), 99, 101, 112, 160, 231, 241–43, 275
Tokyo Olympics (2020), 34–35, 43, 50, 138, 251, 254–55, 260–61, 263
Tokyo War Crimes Tribunal, 173, 177, 278
Tomohisa Takei, 113
Tomomi Inada, 117
tourism, 35
Trans-Pacific Partnership (TPP), 98, 129, 141, 280; Comprehensive and Progressive Trans-Pacific Partnership (TPP11), 98, 136, 280, 282
Triple Intervention (1895), 271
Trump, Donald, 88, 103, 128, 131, 134–38, 142, 180, 195, 197–98, 213, 219, 229, 240–41, 255, 258, 263; election, 133, 277, 280, 283; Nobel Peace Prize, 138; Trump administration, 98, 135, 137, 239–40, 256, 276
Tsai Ing-wen, 52
"two plus alpha", 212–13, 221
"2+2" dialogues, 99, 275
2011 triple disaster, 33, 42, 128, 255, 261
2015 Security Legislation, 157–58

unemployment, 26, 35
unilateral sanctions, 194–95, 199, 216
Unit 731, 180
United Kingdom (U.K.), 99–101, 115, 219, 254, 272; and COVID-19, 42; defense engagement, 107, 109, 111
United States (U.S.), 90–91, 98–101, 129, 152, 192, 213–14, 219, 253–56, 258, 260, 272, 274, 280, 282, 285; and China, 133, 140, 149, 163; cooperation with, Japanese, 114, 200; and COVID-19, 35, 42, 45, 47, 277, 284; dependency on, Japanese, 134, 140, 273, 278; and gender equality, 67, 78; intelligence exchanges with, Japanese, 95, 100; international students, 262; and Japanese military, 90, 95–96, 119, 137, 158–59, 238; and the Middle East, 90, 233, 239–41, 244, 275; and North Korea, 135–36, 196, 198, 200; occupation (of Japan), 19, 155, 192, 273, 276, 278; and the QUAD, 160–62; reactions to Abe's Yasukuni visit, 131, 277; and Russia, 210; security ties (with Japan), 35, 99–100, 108, 118, 131, 135, 139–40, 150, 155, 158; and South Korea, 175, 181; trade, 21, 28, 137, 139, 274, 276; trade war (with China), 88. *See also* China, trade war with the U.S.; "war on terror", 115, 236, 260; withdrawal from the TPP, 98, 136, 141. *See also* Trans-Pacific Partnership (TPP)

UN Relief and Works Agency for Palestinian Refugees (UNRWA), 230
UN Security Council (UNSC), 93, 97, 194, 199, 231
U.S.-Japan: agreements, 91; alliance, 93–94, 132, 135, 140–42, 150, 159, 229, 275; relations, 128, 133–35, 139–40, 142, 240, 253, 259; Security Treaty, viii, 20, 90–91, 96, 102, 142, 159, 215; Security Treaty (1960 revision), 20, 90, 275–76; trade agreement, 136; trade friction, 28
U.S. military: Afghanistan, war in, 231, 276; infections among, 44; invasion of Iraq, 285; Operation Desert Storm, 275; presence in Okinawa, 45, 149

"Vientiane Vision", 117

weak leadership, 41

women's employment, 43, 72
"womenomics", 43, 50, 72, 259
Worker Dispatching Law, 67
World Assembly of Women (WAW), 263
World Health Organization (WHO), 139, 280
World Trade Organization (WTO), 274, 280
World War I, 272

xenophobia, 277, 283
Xi Jinping, 88, 103, 149, 153–54, 156, 160, 197, 239; summit with, 43

Yachi Shotarō, 218
Yasukuni Shrine, 20, 87, 130–31, 151–54, 171, 179, 182, 257, 261, 277
Yoshida Doctrine, 101–2, 141–42
Yoshida Shigeru, 1, 127, 275

About the Contributors

Laney Bahan is a research assistant and freelance editor with first-hand exposure to critical issues pertaining to Korea. Her current research focuses on transitional justice, and her interests extend to youth political engagement in democratization processes and peace studies.

James D. J. Brown is associate professor of political science at Temple University, Japan Campus, where he is also coordinator of the international affairs major. He holds an undergraduate degree from the University of York and postgraduate degrees from the universities of Edinburgh, Glasgow, and Aberdeen. His main area of research is Japan–Russia relations. Dr. Brown's work has been published in several academic journals, including *International Affairs, Asia Policy, International Politics, Post-Soviet Affairs, Europe-Asia Studies, Problems of Post-Communism,* and *The Asia-Pacific Journal: Japan Focus*. His two most recent books are *Japan, Russia and their Territorial Dispute: The Northern Delusion* (2017) and *Japan's Foreign Relations in Asia*, edited with Jeff Kingston (2018). He regularly writes op-eds, including for *Nikkei Asia, The Japan Times,* and *The Diplomat*, as well as in Russian for the *Carnegie Moscow Center* and in Japanese for *Nikkei Business*.

Guibourg Delamotte (PhD), a French and Australian dual citizen, is senior lecturer (MCF, habilitated to supervise research) of political science at the Japanese studies department of the French Institute of Oriental Studies (Inalco). She lectured at Sciences Po Paris for seven years. She teaches international relations, Japanese politics, and classes on contemporary Japan. She is a research fellow at the French Research Institute on East Asia (IFRAE, CNRS). She is currently also a distinguished research fellow at the Japan Forum on International Relations and an adjunct fellow at the Institute for

Contemporary Asian Studies (Temple University Japan, Tokyo). She has been invited as invited fellow by the University of Tokyo's Research Center for Advanced Science and Technology (2022) and the National Institute of Defense Studies attached to the Japanese Ministry of Defense (2010). She defended her "Habilitation to supervise research" (HDR) at Sciences Po Paris (2016). Her PhD dissertation (Ecole des Hautes études en sciences sociales) received the Shibusawa-Claudel Award (2008). She graduated from the University of Oxford (M. Jur), Paris 2-Panthéon-Assas (M. Law), Inalco (Japanese), and Sciences Po Paris (BA, Masters in IR). As a PhD candidate, she was international research student on a Lavoisier scholarship (French MoFA) at the University of Tokyo's School of Law and Politics (2003–2004). She recently published *Géopolitique et géoéconomie. Puissance et conflits* (coed.) and *Géopolitique du Japon* (La découverte, 2021), *Le Monde vu du Japon* (ed.) (2019) and *Japan's World Power: Assessment, Vision and Outlook* (2017). Her academic theses include "La Démocratie japonaise, singulière et universelle" (2022) and "La Politique de défense du Japon" (2010).

Robert Dujarric has been co-director, Institute of Contemporary Asian Studies, Temple University Japan, since 2007. After several years in finance at First Boston and Goldman Sachs, he moved to a Washington think-tank, focusing on security issues. He is a former council on foreign relations (Hitachi) international affairs fellow in Japan. He is the author of several books and articles, including *America's Inadvertent Empire with William E. Odom* (Yale, 2004). Raised in Paris and New York, he is a graduate of Harvard College and holds an MBA from Yale University.

Benoît Hardy-Chartand is an adjunct professor in the Department of Political Science and International Affairs at Temple University Japan, in Tokyo, where he teaches courses on international affairs and security. He is also a fellow at the Raoul-Dandurand Chair of Strategic and Diplomatic Studies in Montreal. Previously, Hardy-Chartand was a senior research associate at the Centre for International Governance Innovation (CIGI), a Canadian think-tank, and taught at University of Montreal.

Kakizaki Masaki is an associate professor of political science at Temple University, Japan Campus (TUJ), and adjunct lecturer at Showa Women's University. He also serves as a collaborative researcher at the JIME Center, Institute of Energy Economics, Japan (IEEJ). Previously, he taught at the University of Utah, Westminster College, Kanda University of International Studies, and Sophia University. His key areas of expertise are Turkish politics and foreign policy. He has published research on party politics, social movements, political confidence, and multiculturalism in contemporary Turkey.

Jeff Kingston is director of Asian Studies and professor of history at Temple University Japan. Most recently, he wrote *The Politics of Religion, Nationalism and Identity* (2019) and *Japan* (2019), edited *Critical Issues in Contemporary Japan* (2019 and *Press Freedom in Contemporary Japan* (2017)) and co-edited *Press Freedom in Contemporary Asia* (2019) and *Japan's Foreign Relations with Asia* (2018). He also wrote *Nationalism in Asia: A History Since 1945* (2016) and edited *Nationalisms in Asia Reconsidered* (2015). He edited a special issue for the *Asia Pacific Journal: Japan Focus* on the Tokyo 2020 Olympics and Pandemic Asia. His current research focuses on transitional justice and the politics of memory.

Tosh Minohara is professor of U.S.–Japan Relations at the Graduate School of Law and Politics, Kobe University, where he holds a joint appointment with the Graduate School of International Cooperation Studies. He received his B.A. in international relations from University of California, Davis, and his M.A. and PhD in political science and diplomatic history from Kobe University. He has published many monographs of which his first was, *The Japanese Exclusion Act and US-Japan Relations* [in Japanese] (2002). He is also the co-editor of *Tumultuous Decade: Empire, Society, and Diplomacy in 1930s Japan* (2013), *Decade of the Great War: Japan and the Wider World during the 1910s* (2014), *The History of U.S.–Japan Relations: From Perry to Present* (2017), and most recently *Beyond Versailles: Reverberations of the "1919 Moment" in Asia* (2020). He is the recipient of the Shimizu Hiroshi Prize and the Japan Research Prize.

Murakami Hiromi is an adjunct professor at Temple University Japan and a visiting scholar at Global Health Innovation Policy Center at National Graduate Institute for Policy Studies (GRIPS). Previously, she's involved in various policy projects in U.S./Japanese institutions, including Center for Strategic and International Studies (CSIS), the Health and Global Policy Institute, Economic Strategy Institute, and GRIPS. Her expertise includes state–industrial relations, public policy, and global health policies. Murakami is also a senior fellow at Economic Strategy Institute and an adjunct fellow at Global Health Policy Center at CSIS. She holds an MBA in international business, and a PhD in international relations from the School of Advanced International Studies at the Johns Hopkins University. She writes op-eds including *Japan Times, CSIS*, and *East Asia Forum*, and has jointly authored "*Japan Restored*" (2015) with Clyde V. Prestowitz and translated it into Japanese.

R. Taggart Murphy is professor emeritus of international political economy at the University of Tsukuba. He was one of the founding members of the university's MBA program in international business in 2005 and served as program chair from 2011 to 2014. A former investment banker with 12-year experience in the Japanese financial markets, he began his academic career in 1998 at the university, teaching courses in the Political Science Department, the College of International Studies, and the Graduate Program in International Political Economy. He has also been non-resident senior fellow at the Brookings Institution and an adjunct professor in the Political Science Department at Temple University's Tokyo campus.

He is the author of the *Japan and the Shackles of the Past* (2014), *The Weight of the Yen* (1996) and, with Akio Mikuni, *Japan's Policy Trap* (2002), winner of the 2002 Association of American Publishers Professional and Scholarly Award for Economics. He is a frequent contributor to *The New Left Review* and his articles have also appeared in the *London Review of Books*, *Fortune*, *The National Interest*, *The Harvard Business Review*, and *The Asia-Pacific Journal: Japan Focus* among others.

Nonaka Naoto has been professor of political science at Gakushuin University since 1996. A PhD student at the University of Tokyo, his PhD dissertation was an empirical comparative study of the major political parties in Japan and France. He then concentrated on the comparative study of central ministries and agencies in Japan and France, especially in terms of the career paths of so-called highflyer bureaucrats. In recent years, he has been working on comparative parliamentary study with a particular focus on France, Japan, and the United Kingdom. As part of this effort, he has been building a database of speech texts and conducting research by using new analysis methods developed in the field of natural language processing.

His published studies in English include "From Weak Prime Minister to Proactive Prime Minister: Domestic Political Conditions and their Transformations" (ed.), *Japan's World Power. Assessment, Vision and Outlook*, 2019, p. "The Origins and Consequences of Diet Rationalization in Postwar Japan," (ed.), "*Comparative Study on Parliamentary Cabinet System*, 2019, p. 157–176, 229–259." "Was postwar Japanese politics majoritarian?" (The Society for Comparative Politics, 2016, "*Comparative Study on Core Executives*, p. 39–73)." "LDP System' and Japan's Post War Politics: Has the Post War Japan had a Parliamentary Cabinet Government?" Paper presented at the annual conference of the Political Studies Association (Manchester, April 14–16, 2015), "Time Resources and Deliberative Patterns in the Japanese Diet," *Studies in Oriental Culture* 17 (2015), p. 426–466.

Alessio Patalano, PhD, is a reader in East Asian Warfare and Security at the Department of War Studies (DWS), King's College London (KCL). He specializes in maritime strategy and doctrine, Japanese military history and strategy, East Asian Security, and Italian defence policy. Dr. Patalano is currently visiting professor at the *Japan Maritime Command and Staff College* (JMCSC). His monograph *Post-war Japan as a Seapower: Imperial Legacy, Wartime Experience, and the Making of a Navy* (2015) received international recognition, is currently used for teaching purposes at the Japanese staff college, and is being translated into Mandarin. Dr. Patalano's current research focuses on the impact of strategic geography on Indo-Pacific security dynamics and is writing a new study of the Japanese post-war submarine rearmament.

David H. Satterwhite earned his PhD in Comparative & Korean Politics from the University of Washington (1994), benefitting from a Fulbright award for dissertation research at Korea University (1986–1987), followed by a post-doctoral award at UC-Berkeley (1995–1996). His career has included a decade in support of the democratization effort in the ROK (1974–1983), teaching NE Asian & Korean Politics (including at TUJ), administrative positions (Exec Director, Fulbright Japan, 204–13, coterminous as Board of Overseers, TUJ), & study-abroad positions, including his present Directorship, CIEE Kyoto Center, Japan.

Nancy Snow (PhD, international relations) is professor emeritus of communications at California State University, Fullerton and Pax Mundi Professor of public diplomacy, Kyoto University of Foreign Studies. In 2020, she was Walt Disney Chair in Global Media and Communications, Schwarzman College, Tsinghua University, where she taught a course in "Public Diplomacy and Pandemic." Snow was an Abe fellow and visiting research professor at Keio University where she researched Japan's public diplomacy after 3/11 and published *Japan's Information War* (English and Japanese versions). She was a Fulbright student in Germany (Bayreuth, Regensburg) and a Fulbright professor at Sophia University in Japan. Snow is the author/editor/co-editor of thirteen books, including the *Routledge Handbook of Public Diplomacy* 2nd edition (with Nicholas J. Cull); *The SAGE Handbook of Propaganda* (with Paul Baines and Nicholas O'Shaughnessy); *Information War*; *Propaganda, Inc.*; and *Propaganda and American Democracy*.

Soeya Yoshihide retired from Keio University in March 2020, and is now professor emeritus. His areas of interest are politics and security in East Asia/the Asia-Pacific/the Indo-Pacific, and Japanese diplomacy and its external relations. Having obtained PhD majoring in world politics at the Rackham School of Graduate Studies of the University of Michigan in 1987, Dr. Soeya joined Department of Political Science at Faculty of Law of Keio University as assistant professor in April 1988, and was promoted to associate professor in April 1991, then to professor in April 1995. During the 32 years at Keio University, he served as the director of its Institute of East Asian Studies for six years until September 2013, and as the director of its Center for Contemporary Korean Studies for five years until March 2016. He has published extensively in Japanese and in English. Among others, he wrote or co-authored the following books in English: *Japan's Economic Diplomacy with China, 1945–1978* (1998); with Kokubun Ryōsei, Takahara Akio, and Kawashima Shin, *Japan–China Relations in the Modern Era* (2017) [Translated by Keith Krulak]; with L. Williams Heinrich and Jr., Akiho Shibata, *United Nations Peace-Keeping Operations: A Guide to Japanese Policies* (1999). He coedited with Tadokoro Masayuki and David A. Welch, *Japan as a 'Normal Country' ?: A Country in Search of its Place in the World* (2011).

www.ingramcontent.com/pod-product-compliance
Lightning Source LLC
Chambersburg PA
CBHW021346300426
44114CB00012B/1096